D0498533

Latinos in the United States

LATINO PERSPECTIVES

Gilberto Cárdenas, series editor

INSTITUTE *for*

Latino Studies

UNIVERSITY OF NOTRE DAME

The Institute for Latino Studies, in keeping with the distinctive mission, values, and traditions of the University of Notre Dame, promotes understanding and appreciation of the social, cultural, and religious life of U.S. Latinos through advancing research, expanding knowledge, and strengthening community.

305.86
Ab16a

Latinos in the United States

The Sacred and the Political

WITHDRAWN

Second Edition

DAVID T. ABALOS

University of Notre Dame Press

Notre Dame, Indiana

LIBRARY ST. MARY'S COLLEGE

Copyright © 2007 by University of Notre Dame
Notre Dame, Indiana 46556
www.undpress.nd.edu
All Rights Reserved

Manufactured in the United States of America

Reprinted in 2008

Library of Congress Cataloging-in-Publication Data

Abalos, David T.
Latinos in the United States : the sacred and the political /
David T. Abalos. — 2nd ed.
    p.   cm.
Includes bibliographical references and index.
ISBN-13: 978-0-268-02025-5 (pbk. : alk. paper)
ISBN-10: 0-268-02025-6 (pbk. : alk. paper)
1. Hispanic Americans—Ethnic identity. 2. Hispanic Americans—
Cultural assimilation. I. Title.
E184.S75A63   2007
305.8968'073—dc22
                                        2006039805

∞ *The paper in this book meets the guidelines for permanence
and durability of the Committee on Production Guidelines for Book
Longevity of the Council on Library Resources.*

To Our First Grandchildren,

Matthew and Jazmin Abalos and Nicholas Abalos Place

The Third Generation of Our Family Born in This Country

Contents

Preface to the Second Edition

I wrote the first edition of *Latinos in the United States: The Sacred and the Political* primarily because my Chicana/Chicano students at Princeton urged me to write a book in which I could share with a broader audience what we had learned together in a new course, Politics 342, Latino Politics in the United States. I was blessed to teach the first departmental course that was dedicated to exploring the politics, history, and culture of Latina women and Latino men in the United States as part of the permanent course offerings in the Politics Department at Princeton University. The Latino Politics course came into being in 1981 as the result of a political coalition between the members of the Chicano Caucus and the African-American and white students to achieve the approval of the course.

Even then the Chicana/Chicano students had a wonderful political sense about them. They were offered the opportunity to name the course "Chicano Politics in the United States" but chose to draw upon a broader understanding of themselves as Latina women and Latino men as members of *La Raza*, a term that means the community that embraces all members with a Latin American heritage. They made a political decision to go beyond a nationalistic perspective to create the foundations for a new kind of comunidad Latina in this country. This was a prophetic move on their part. In the past twenty-five years almost everything has changed. The demographics are very clear: by 2050 Latinos will comprise an astounding 25 percent of the population of the United States which will put tremendous political and economic power in the hands of the Latino community. The growth of the undocumented community is an unparalleled historical event; undocumented workers and their families, although many may try to deny it, have become an integral part of the U.S. economy. This phenomenon tests the capacity of the country to respond with wisdom and compassion to what is really a worldwide revolution, millions of workers on the move outside the borders of their nations looking for work and a better life. Latinos who are U.S. citizens are faced with the challenge of responding to the plight of our compatriots as fellow human beings and of letting our creative imagination fire our hearts as we look for ways to protect their humanity and ours. This is one of the biggest challenges facing our Latino community at the present time.

Education is the key to the future well-being of the Latino community. In the 1960s during the Civil Rights struggles when Chicano/Latino students looked around there were almost no teachers, faculty, or administrators who came from their background, almost no courses addressed their concerns as Latinas and Latinos in this country. At the heart of the schools, the curriculum, they were rendered invisible and expected to join the powerful in order to gain recognition through assimilation. They refused. Because they could not recognize themselves as valuable members of their schools, Latina women and Latino men enacted a political course of action that enabled them to celebrate and critique their heritage as an essential part of their education. Through this exercise of ethnic/racial politics, they made history; they succeeded in transforming the curriculum and bringing about changes that impacted their schools for the better. This kind of personal, political, and historical creativity was brought about by students with a burning passion for justice. We need this kind of commitment to justice and compassion once again.

In the spring semester of 2001 when I taught Latino Politics once again at Princeton so much had changed. I dedicated the course in love and friendship to my colleague, Manfred Halpern, who immensely enriched my life by introducing me to the theory of transformation, the theoretical fiber by which I wove the story of Latina/ Latino politics. Professor Halpern died on January 14, 2001 just before the beginning of the semester. Prior to his death he asked me to finish his book, *Transforming the Personal, Political, Historical, and Sacred Faces of Our Being in Theory and Practice*. It is a truly brilliant work and much of what I learned on the development of the theory of transformation and how to relate it to practice is reflected in the new material included in this second edition. Professor Halpern guided me through the writing of the first edition of this book and he continues to be my guide. It was he who led me into the realm of underlying forming sacred sources that is the radical grounding for all that I teach, write, and live.

In my first lecture of the spring semester of 2001 at Princeton, I commented to my students that I never thought that twenty years after first teaching the course on Latino Politics in the United States that I could say, "Never again will anybody be elected President of the United States without the Latina/Latino vote." I remember that day and the sense of pride I felt. But I did not want the students, the majority of whom were non-Latino, to think that this was a display of arrogance. I wanted to highlight the sacrifice and the love that was given to us by those who came before us, like my mother and father, so that we could arrive at this point where as a community we could experience such hope and promise.

But as the book makes clear a generation later we still have much to do and far to go to realize the fullness of our humanity. This book continues to be concerned, but now with a greater sense of urgency, with the politics of transformation, the creation of the fundamentally more loving and just in all aspects of our lives. As I wrote in the Introduction to the first edition, my hope is that the feelings, intuitions, ideas, and vision that I articulate in this book will put into words what so many Latinas and Latinos have long known but were unsure how to express. There is no greater compliment and blessing for a teacher/scholar than for students or readers to tell you that you spoke and wrote what they were feeling.

It is a profound blessing to be able after twenty years to revisit my first book that changed my life. As a Chicano/Latino scholar and teacher I am deeply grateful to the women and men at the University of Notre Dame Press, especially Julian Samora, John Ehmann, and Ann Bromley who together with their colleagues made a political decision some thirty years ago to give a voice in the world of book publishing to Latinas/Latinos. Prior to this few books were published by mainline university presses or commercial publishing houses that were concerned with la comunidad Latina and, just as important, written by members of the community. Besides opening the door to tenure and promotion, the publication of our books gave us as members of the community confidence that we had something to say to our colleagues, our students, our community, and to people from all backgrounds. Opening the door to the presence of our personal gifts by a politics of inclusion in the world of publishing changed the way we as Americans view our history; this actually was the making of a new story, a new history that told the fuller story of America. This was accomplished by a Catholic university press that considered the telling of our story a part of their sacred and political mission.

Foreword

This book brings us a radically new understanding of the political choices facing Latino men and women living in the United States. Politics here means all that we can and need to do together. Understanding the threats and opportunities that face Latinos is here grounded upon a theory of transformation.

Why a theory and therefore also a practice of transformation? The idea of theory first came into being in Greece to describe the compassionate act of meditating upon the dying and rebirth of a god, and therefore of all human beings for whom this god constituted their force of life. Each year Greek cities sent a representative to an enactment of this drama of dying and being reborn. Each representative upon his return had to report in public on his experience of this transformation.

Theory first arose, and always arises, out of the same beginning as transformation. Both begin with a great dying—with the death of what was once held to be sacred, empowering, and secure. Both renew our questioning and our compassion. Both demand our participation, personally and politically, in a drama of rebirth. Theory constitutes our shared understanding of how the cosmos of human relationships can be nourished, destroyed, and re-created with love and justice. But such a shared theory of practice is transforming only if it liberates each individual to make his and her own creative contribution, which is always—as a proof of freedom—unique in its actual, concrete practice, even while it expresses underlying patterns that (theory shows) we share by virtue of our species-being.

The theory of transformation which David Abalos here pioneers in applying it to Latino communities in the United States is both a critical and a creative theory. It is concerned with our participation in changing both underlying forces and their concrete manifestations in human relationships when they have become unbearable or fruitless as well as in nourishing them knowledgeably and lovingly as we help to make them just.

The chief difficulty in understanding this theory of transformation stems from the fact that it deals not only with the concrete and the particular. It takes the sensuously concrete with utmost seriousness: everyone needs their daily bread and each particular child needs our daily care. But this theory also sees every concreteness as the manifestation of underlying patterns that it recognizes and analyzes as living forces with real powers of their own. None of the concepts of this theory are to be understood as mere abstractions. Instead they point to real underlying, patterning forces in our life. The wondrous, confusing, miserable, boring, exciting, inspiring immediacy and specificity of our life is one real face of our being. It also symbolizes and (if we are theoretically informed) reveals the other real face of our being: its transpersonal depths.

Let us take a roundabout road in discovering the nature of this theory. If we take what looks like the straightest and quickest road, we are likely to mislead ourselves. Rushing into the first chapter or browsing in the middle of this work, we might suppose that the theory of transformation offers us a catalogue of nine relationships and four paradigms, or ways of life, as a system of classification that one or two social scientists thought instrumentally useful for a particular purpose at hand. This supposition would be entirely mistaken. It is true that this theory offers about a dozen new concepts. That is the least of it. What is being offered here is an entirely new way of seeing and living.

The nine archetypal relations and four archetypal paradigms or ways of life which David Abalos puts to use for re-visioning Latino life are discoveries about the range of fundamental choices open to any and all of us. This theory of transformation is different from most theories in the modern social sciences, philosophy, and psychology in that it is empirical and normative at the same time. It helps us analyze what practical choices we have and also whether they are just or unjust. We are not accustomed to such theories. Most of us suppose that the analysis of what is and the evaluation of whether it is just is the business of two distinct, indeed separated, realms of life. Especially since the seventeenth century we have come to accept a gap between what we call the "is" and the "ought," politics and religion, practical life and philosophy, the objective and the subjective. This theory of transformation rejects and overcomes such distinctions, not by returning to old dogmas or offering new ones. It is founded instead on the discovery of archetypal patterns of human relationships and ways of life which any human being can examine and validate in her and his own life. Why are we to bother with archetypes and thus with our participation in the patterning forces of the transpersonal or sacred realm of being?

I never planned to go in that unfamiliar and strange direction. After I had published *The Politics of Social Change in the Middle East and North Africa* (Princeton, 1963) analyzing the revolutions in progress from Morocco to Pakistan—the forces, groups, ideas, and institutions dissolving or emerging—a fundamental question still baffled me. Muslim society had persisted for nearly fourteen hundred years (more than twice as long as the Roman Empire), able to cope with conflicts and changes, assuring collaboration over a large area while giving rise to two radically different experiences of justice, one orthodox, one transforming. Muslims during that long period contributed greatly to world civilization.[1] Why is it that Muslim societies today whether rich or poor, parliamentary or authoritarian, traditionalist or socialist, tribal or nationalist cannot deal with continuity or change, collaboration or conflict, or the achieving of justice?

I returned to the Middle East and North Africa with what seemed to me in the 1960s a straightforward social-science type of question: Suppose one wishes to experience (or observe) all five of the following issues *simultaneously* at stake in any human relationship: continuity as well as change, collaboration as well as conflict, and also the achieving of justice. How many qualitatively different ways of enacting these five faces of relationship are there? I discovered that human beings have altogether nine different ways of structuring such relationships. David Abalos' first chapter will spell out these nine ways, which are the same in underlying structure whether I relate to myself, to other persons or groups, or to ideas or values or problems. I thought then that these nine forms of relationships were the most useful abstractions possible for inquiring why relationships were dissolving among Muslims (and all other peoples around the world) and also why relationships were breaking between individuals and groups and their inherited concepts and norms.

Then it dawned on me that I had missed an essential dimension in the inquiry into a great dying. The despair, demoralization, and confusion of Muslims was a response not only to the breaking of the concrete, inherited manifestations of their repertory of relationships or to the crippling effect of trying to maintain old relationships in the face of new challenges. An entire way of life was disintegrating. To Muslims it felt as if a sacred force that had for long infused all aspects of being was being shattered. How can we grasp a way of life!

To discover our way of life we need to ask, "Why, ultimately, am I enacting this (or any other) relationship? Why, ultimately, am I

doing what I am doing?" It turns out that to this "Why?" there are
only four answers, that is, only four underlying patterns or paradigms for organizing life. One can answer that I ultimately do what
I do because a mysterious and overwhelming source ordained how
life hangs together and what we must do to keep it that way. Orthodox Muslims, Catholics, Jews, and most peoples in the past answered thus, whatever their concrete manifestation of the paradigm
of emanation. Or, as more and more people reply today, we say that
there is no answer to such an ultimate why: no way of discovering
it; no way of proving it; no way of getting people to agree on it. Thus
we live in a paradigm of incoherence. Individuals in this paradigm,
therefore, know no ultimate limits to the pursuit of self-interests.
Or as the way of life of emanation continues to unravel and the way
of life of incoherence with its promise of power proves to be unavail-
able to many or the many are seen as a threat to the powerful, we
can choose violence as the way to preserve the past or protect privilege. This leads to the creation of the fundamentally new but worse
in the paradigm of deformation. And there is a fourth answer: to discover the ultimate structures and choices of the cosmos of human
relationships and lovingly choose what is most just. This means living in the service of the paradigm of transformation. These brief
hints concerning paradigms or ways of life David Abalos will elaborate upon in chapter one and throughout his work as constituting
the most basic choices open to us.

At this point of the inquiry I came to recognize that I was not
developing intellectually convenient abstractions but discovering
underlying archetypes, transpersonal forces that pattern all concrete
manifestations of our lives. That there are nine archetypal relationships (when those five issues cited earlier are simultaneously at
stake) and four archetypal paradigms (or ways of life) is a discovery
about the reality of human nature both in its concreteness and its ultimate depths. It is an empirical discovery: anyone can test or report
on the quality of each and the number of all in his and her own life.
And it is an empirical discovery as well about the justice that is intrinsic to each relationship and each way of life as we enact it. No
external judgment is imposed afterward from a subjective, ideal,
pragmatic, or dogmatic position. David Abalos' elaboration and
analysis will make this clear.

Within any archetypal way of life the pattern necessarily hangs
together the way it does. Within any archetype (and we always live
within an archetypal way of life) its living forces will move all the

concrete manifestations of our life according to its underlying pattern. But we can free ourselves to choose among archetypal ways of life and to participate as well in creatively giving shape to their particular expressions. That freedom is fully ours, however, only within the way of life of transformation.

To explain this last statement further requires one more turn into the depths of our being. Since we mean by transformation the persistent creation of fundamentally new and better relationships, the question we must now ask is, "Where is such a new relationship to come from?" When I suddenly say, "I never thought of that before!" where was that thought before?

To the question regarding the source of the fundamentally new and better, philosophers throughout the ages have produced four possible answers. One answer is that there is in fact nothing ever fundamentally new under the sun. What we call new is the old rearranged. Such modifications are certainly possible, but Christ did not merely rearrange Judaism; Buddha did not merely rearrange Hinduism; Picasso did not merely rearrange representational art. A second answer is that the new comes into being by random movements. No doubt accidents happen, some for the better, some for the worse; but we cannot spend our lives waiting only for a lucky accident. A third answer is: do not ask this question. This answer has two different forms. One is the response of orthodox religion, reflecting the paradigm of emanation: only god in his own infinite wisdom brings forth the new and better; it is not for us to ask how or why. The other is the response of conventional science, reflecting the paradigm of incoherence: scientists have not yet discovered how the fundamentally new comes into being, and they will never be able, as scientists, to answer any question regarding what is ethically better. That, in our dire personal and political need, leaves us with the fourth answer.

The fourth answer begins by pointing to the right direction, into mysterious depths. What is now newly differentiated and conscious for us, a new thought or feeling or image, was a moment ago undifferentiated and unconscious. "Un" in both words states a truth to be taken seriously: initially we do not know. Philosophers such as Plato (d. 347 B.C.) started millennia ago to inquire into this mysterious source of the new. They recognized that most of their neighbors living in the way of life of emanation regarded this source not only as mysterious but also as overwhelming. However, the philosophers of the counter-tradition of transformation such as Avicenna

(d. 1037), Meister Eckhardt (d. 1327), Moses Maimonides (d. 1204), Giordano Bruno (d. 1600), and Hegel (d. 1831) saw that we can also experience this source as one of continual creation in our life, and they asked how we might lovingly and justly participate in continual creation. Lovingly and justly: they (and we) know from our daily experience that the underlying sources of our life can also spring forth destructively. Our task is never a merely simple obedience to the transpersonal depths, never a merely shrewd, conscious translation of whatever pours forth into practice, but rather a conscientious, creative collaboration with the depths and with our neighbors.

In their investigations the philosophers of the counter-tradition of transformation realized long ago that this transpersonal source of our being gives form to the particular through underlying patterns, that is, through archetypes. In our own time Carl Gustave Jung explored the sacred realm of archetypes. The work of identifying archetypal patterns is far from complete. This present theory of transformation is only the most recent contribution to this inquiry. But we are building upon one of the oldest insights when we say that it is the archetypal paradigm of transformation that gives us the deepest understanding of the process of creating fundamentally new and better relationships and the greatest freedom to share in such work.

However much we suffer, however much we desire to return to an old security or move on to a new salvation, nothing will change if we merely believe in this transpersonal source of creation, worshipping it obediently as a god of a fixed and final revelation. However much we fight for change, nothing will come of it if we, because we are secular revolutionaries, reject all knowledge and experience of the transpersonal because others have for so long worshipped it as god. I arrived at the realization that we must become conscious of our link to the transpersonal depths, not because I had been a believer in god (I was not), but because there are no other good answers to the question that arises out of a great need around the world: Where are fundamentally new and better relationships to come from?

This answer is also a radically democratic answer. We can all free ourselves to participate with the transpersonal depths in the work of creation. We share these transpersonal depths by virtue of being human. They are transpersonal in the sense that they move through each person. We face fundamental choices. We can, as in the paradigm of emanation, become uncritical embodiments of these sources in the depths, that is, of the archetypes, as well as of the source of all sources, whom we have usually called god. We can, as in the paradigm of incoherence, fantasize that there are no such sources and turn the inspirations that nonetheless well up within us into merely subjective drives for pursuing our self-interest. Or we can, as in the paradigm of transformation, recognize that this transpersonal realm of living sources and underlying patterning forces is the realm of the truly sacred. It follows that each of us, as a concrete manifestation of that realm, is also sacred. Each of us is for that reason precious, and each of us, as an image of these creative sources, is also free to help ourselves and each other to be transforming beings with understanding and love and justice.

David Abalos' work is devoted above all to this transformation. My own manuscript on this subject, *Transforming the Personal, Political, Historical, and Sacred Faces of Our Being in Theory and Practice,* will still need a couple of years to be completed. But it is entirely right that David Abalos should pioneer even now in applying this theory to the destiny of what is soon to be or may already be the largest minority in the United States. Because he was for many years a student for the priesthood but did not join it, he knows the established past and its emanational inheritance, yet is free to evaluate its present meaning. Because he grew up of Mexican parentage in Detroit but has returned on frequent study trips to Mexico, he knows Latino culture in its origins and its migrations. Because he has taught students in both Catholic and Ivy League universities, and also educated workers, nurses, and priests, he has a wide and deep comparative grasp of the problems of transformation.

David Abalos became a student of mine more than fifteen years ago, just as the theory of transformation was beginning to take shape. As a colleague he has ever since been one of the most concerned and fruitful contributors, critics, teachers, and practitioners in the development of this theory.

In November 1970 he wrote to me that the majority of Catholics who are not yet breaking with their traditional roots are like India's Untouchables. They *are* India. Ghandi needed to embrace his past if he were to participate lovingly in changing the past. David Abalos then added: "A similar awareness came to me. Unless I could transform my own prejudices, destructiveness and hatred towards my own past, I would not be able to help others to change their consciousness. Thus I am once again redefining my life and searching my past for continuities and yet recognizing that the discontinuities were necessary for me even to have asked the questions that changed my consciousness."

David Abalos has not ceased to ask ever anew what the past of his religion and culture symbolizes in terms of deep insights and of turning points arrested and not yet taken into transformation. His present work opens doors not opened before.

Manfred Halpern
Professor of Politics
Princeton University

September 20, 1985

NOTE TO THE FOREWORD

1. To speak of Muslim society is to speak of a culture which deeply and directly influenced Spanish culture for about six hundred years. The orthodox experience of Islam may well have helped to develop or reinforce Spanish devotion to masculine heroism, patriarchalism, patron-client dependencies, and the repression of the feminine. The transforming forces in Muslim society—for transformation is not a modern discovery, but rather has become now a more desperate and widespread need in the face of growing incoherence—also bore early and splendid fruit in Spain. As almost nowhere else, Christians, Jews, and Muslims in Spain collaborated from the tenth to the twelfth century in developing the theory, art, and practice of transformation—material which has much influenced this present work. To destroy this transforming movement was the principal task which the Inquisition set for itself.

To apply the theory of transformation to Muslims or to people of Spanish or any other origins is simply to exemplify the application of a theory that applies as well to you and me and her and him, without exception.

Acknowledgments

It was first of all my wife Celia who brought the first edition of this book to fruition with her loving encouragement and expertise. Celia transformed the scrawl of my poor penmanship into a beautiful new reality by her prowess on the word processor. She brought to life my ideas on the monitor screen and in print. With this current edition of the book Celia was equally involved but in a new way; since the first book she guided me to become independent by learning how to do my own typing, cutting, and pasting in preparing a manuscript for publication.

My children, David Jerome, Veronica, and Matthew, have become my friends and mutual guides on our journey of transformation. When Veronica was five years old she wrote us a note asking: "Why did you born me?" I have never ceased to tell her and her brothers "Because I love you."

My friend and colleague Manfred Halpern, as one of my first teachers at Princeton and later as the director of my dissertation, became a guide to me as I began my vocation as a teacher and scholar. His generosity was outstanding; he helped me to write my book while he had not yet finished his own book on transformation. His teaching and writing live on through me and generations of other Princeton students whom he blessed with the personal, political, historical, and sacred faces of his being.

My Mexican parents, Luís and Luz Ávalos, Luís and Celia Dorantes, and my grandparents on Celia's side, José and María Hernández, taught me the importance of the journey of transformation by taking the risk of leaving their loved ones in Mexico to create new generations of Mejicanas/Mejicanos in a new land. I owe much to my brothers and sisters, Angie and Jim, Vicki and Leroy and Bill, Louis and June, Louie and Deanna, Miguel and Denise, Sylvia and Tom, Dolores and Adam, Chuck and Diane, Alice and all their children as well as my sister Marge and my brother Sal who died recently.

A special recognition is owed to my Chicana/Chicano students: Myrna Santiago, Luz Calvo, Susana Villalón, Roberto Barragán, Mike Montoya, and Michael López who made Latino Politics in the United States a reality at Princeton. In 1985 five of my students, Joél Barrera, Martín Gutiérrez, René Flores, Saúl Romo, and Charles Fontana wrote a truly remarkable document, *A Report to President Bowen: The Status of Latino Students at Princeton.* In this report in addition to asking for more Latina/Latino faculty and administrators and courses on Latinos in the United States, they saw themselves as members of the university community who had not only received the benefits of a good education but also as representatives of the Latino community who reciprocated by contributing the gift of their presence and culture to the university. Many other students over the years blessed my life at Princeton, Yale, and Seton Hall, especially Juan Salvador López, Juan José González, Valentín Tinajero, Aaron Bianco, Daniel González, Karen Barajas, Juan Carlos Aguirre, Kelly Sanabria, Sylvia Rodríguez, Trish García, Amparo González, Marina Cervantes, Victoria Celia Laws, Troy Bilbao-Bastida, Monica Bravo, Rob Santoro, Carlos Avila, Johanna López, Jackie Rangel, Nicole Haston, Blake Lyon, Michael Long, Brendan Carroll, Bettina Miguez, Cynthia Loomis, Sandra Bruno, Barbara Soliz, José Escobar, Marilyn Waite, Jennifer Scott, Stephanie Steel, Miriam López, Jacqueline Rodríguez, Michael Dickinson, Lou Ferrara, Jomayra Méndez, Bethzaída Cordero, Adolph Falcón, José Adámes, Omayra Arocho, María Montañez, Kathy Rosado, Coryn Snyder, Tracey Garripoli, Seojatan Omadai, Annick Routhier-Labadie, Maeve Lopreiato, Tom Holowka, Matthew Demian, Jenna Vogel, Nick Manzella, and Mary Jennings. A special thanks to Carlos Avila who after reading the first edition of the book sent it to Chris Zepeda who contacted me without our having met and told me how much the book had meant to him and after reading part of the revised manuscript encouraged me to complete it. Gracias; un fuerte abrazo.

My colleagues at Seton Hall have inspired me to discover ever anew that to serve our students is the greatest vocation. Among those who have graced my life are: Gisela Webb, Peter Ahr, Bernhard Scholz, Carlos Rodríguez Matos, Chuck Carter, Janet Easterling, Kathy Rennie, Phil Kayal, Joe Palenski, Pat Kuchon, Amar D Amar, Phyllis Russo, Robin Cunningham, Walter DeBold, Charles Yin, Larry Greene, Al Hakim, Linda Ulak, Gail Iglesias, Bernadette Wilkowski, Marty Kropp, Anthony Lee, and Dick Liddy.

Over the years I have received the blessings of hospitality as a visitor in the Politics Department at Princeton from colleagues who welcomed me as a member of the university community: Paul Sigmund, Jim Doig, and Fred Greenstein, with a special thanks to Nancy Bermeo, Chris Mackie, Gayle Brodsky, Lisa Baratta, Dorothy Dey, and Chris Achen. Donna Willitts of Princeton University library was a great source of help to me and my students.

In my work with elementary and secondary teachers there are several persons who stand out: John Ward, the former principal of Hightstown High School; Ms. Zaida Padilla, the ombudsperson of the Paterson School District; and Hector Bonilla, the former principal of Barringer High School in Newark. Each of them had the courage to use the authority of their office to protect children from the hurts of discrimination. Each stepped forward urgently to create a more loving alternative educational environment. They, together with their wonderful faculty and staff, nurtured and enhanced the personal, political, historical, and sacred faces of their students with a truly wonderful attitude of caring and compassion.

In my home town of East Windsor in Mercer County, New Jersey, as a community we are facing what countless towns and small municipalities across the nation are experiencing, the daily arrival of new immigrants looking for a better life. In the struggle to respond with love and justice to the *recien llegados*, the new arrivals, it is a blessing to work with some deeply caring people: Bob Patten, the mayor of Hightstown and his wife Kathy; Luz Horta; Betty Witherspoon; Lydia Santoni-Lawrence; and the truly dedicated professional staff from the Princeton Health Care System who have provided excellent health care services to our Latino community, especially Robbi Alexander, Yahiza Castillo, and Patti Giro. I want to give special recognition to Chief William Spain and Lt. James Brady who are, together with the women and men of the East Windsor Police Department, outstanding public servants. Over the last few years I have come to know them as deeply caring professionals who have done so much to protect the rights of some of the most vulnerable people in our community, the undocumented. My conversations with Dick Scaine helped me to see that my work with the undocumented community requires us to transcend our narrow nationalism in favor of a planetary vision that sees each person as equal and sacred. Finally, I am deeply grateful to the following members of our new community who gave me the gift of trust: William Castro, Manuel Arpe, Luz Saquipay, Antonieta Montero, Miriam Astudillo, Carlos Celleri, Wilson and Cumandá Hernández and their children Amy and Marco.

My extended family shares a common soul, a spirit of concern and compassion for one another and for others that draws us together: Profs. Alberto Pulido, University of San Diego, Davíd Carrasco, Harvard University, and Silvia Villa, Northeastern Illinois

University, Chicago Teachers' Center, from whom I have learned much; Vivian and Frank Morales; Casto and Miriam Maldonado; Dick and Mary Scaine; Jim Palladino; Marge and Nick Martucci; Carol and Bill Petscavage and Maggie Biunno; Josephine and Joe Carpenter; Dick and Sandy Adinaro; Father Miguel Valle, one of the finest priests whom I have met; Frank and Jayne Lenzo and their children, Angela, Jessica, Courtney, and Joey; Jim and Jane Brady together with their children, Caitlin, James Patrick, Danny, and Emily.

Finally, I am grateful to the people at the University of Notre Dame Press, my editors, Lowell Francis, Rebecca DeBoer, and Carole Roos, as well as to Margaret Gloster, Kathryn Pitts, and Katie Lehman, all of whom together made this a better book. A special thanks also to Ms. Ann Bromley for her help in bringing this book to fruition.

Introduction

I hate objectivity. I am convinced it's a Western, white, male plot to rob the rest of us of our experience by negating our point of view and thus invalidating our being.
—*Myrna Santiago*

This comment on the poverty of objectivity that excludes the subject, the person, was written by a young Chicana/Latina complaining about how all of us have been wounded by our socialization in this culture. In a similar vein Elizabeth Dreyer, a Jungian analyst, reminds us to resist "the allure of the abstract at the cost of the concrete." Evelyn Waugh's character Sebastian in *Brideshead Revisited* is scolded by his cousin for not upholding the family honor and the tradition of scholarship at Oxford. Sebastian comments that his cousin unfortunately will never know what he has learned this semester: "That to know and love another human being is the beginning of wisdom."

I want to offer a different kind of book, a book that addresses the contemporary issues that we are facing with the close-up lens of the self, myself. In the midst of such general/abstract concerns as undocumented workers, the growing political power of Latinos as the largest community of color in the nation, the debate over bilingual education, the rise of an upwardly mobile Latino middle class, the war against terrorism that has led once again to ignoring our common concerns with Mexico and the other Latin American nations, and a United States foreign policy in Latin America which for decades was obsessed with the specter of communism but is now facing a rising tide of democratic populism, I want to begin with the personal, the autobiographical, the subject, the self—the self as the center of all revolution whether it be in the social, political, or religious realm. Furthermore, I believe that what I am experiencing as an individual Chicano/Latino male is being experienced by a growing number of Latino men and Latina women: Puerto Ricans, Cubans, Ecuadorians, Colombians, Dominicans, and other communities from Latin America. But when we look around for direction, myself

1

included, we find little to assist us. Thus I write this book as a source of guidance for myself and other Latinas and Latinos. By relating and reflecting upon our personal lives and searching for a meaningful theoretical framework we can better explain what is happening to us. Too often our own best scholars are seduced by their academic training. To be accepted into the circles of university life they end up doing statistical studies and other detached, allegedly neutral scholarship. They thus turn themselves and us, their fellow Latinos, into abstractions. To be objective such a method abstracts from the concrete and then relates the conceptual abstractions to other concepts abstractly until we have "pure," distilled objective truth. In this context the personal becomes the residual category. Descartes in his famous treatise, *On Method*, spoke of liberating students from all cultural baggage in order to purify them so that they could bring to their studies an objective self. And this point of view is precisely the issue: the emphasis on abstraction, objectivity, methods, and techniques moves us away from the concrete, the subject, the personal, the touchstone of reality. Anything that cannot be quantified, such as love, truth, beauty, and justice, is regarded as a purely subjective category that blurs the objective search for truth. Each person's views are just as good as another, that is, almost worthless. This attitude severs our soul and fragments us into the empirical versus the normative, the abstract concept versus feelings, and object versus subject.

My friend and colleague Manfred Halpern guided me through an extraordinary theory of transformation, which he discovered, re-created, and then reinterpreted as a guide for our time. He taught and wrote about the theory for over thirty years in the Politics Department at Princeton University. By means of the theory and his friendship he helped me to find myself and in so doing brought me into a new world that I had glimpsed but not really entered. Like Ken Kesey's friend, Vik Lovell, he guided me to a lair of dragons, where I needed to face the dragons within myself.

He taught me that at every moment of our lives we are somewhere on the journey through the core drama of life and that underlying all of reality are four fundamental choices, four archetypal ways of life: emanation, incoherence, deformation, and transformation. Three of these ways of life arrest our lives and render us partial selves because we have not reached the goal of the journey, the self. Manfred in his work made an invaluable contribution to a 2,000-year-old tradition that has been witnessed to by members of the counter-tradition of transformation in every universal religion: life is an unfinished struggle between the self, the world, others, and our sacred sources. When human beings first became conscious, evolution was immeasurably affected and accelerated because the undifferentiated mystery of the source of all sources was now given conscious direction by human creation and participation. Our vocation as human beings is to respond to the sacred impulse within and participate in a bi-unity with the deepest sacred in finishing creation. All is unfinished. What a marvelous task! All of us are made whole when we build a new and more loving world by enacting our being together with the deepest sacred.

The view of life underlying this theory is available to each of us by the very nature of our being human. Each of us can discover in our own lives the journey of transformation as the core drama of life. The theory is intended to provide concepts, ideas, and words that point us to underlying sources that determine the deeper value, structure, and meaning of our lives. The theory provides us with the language to express the reality that has always been in us that we may have intuited but were at a loss to express. Thus each of us can participate in the theory of transformation. To live this theory is to participate in the drama of the life and death of sacred sources. Manfred Halpern has served me essentially as a guide, a rare guide, who invited me, via the teaching of this theory in a contemporary context, on a journey that he himself was still traveling. But this is also the journey of our parents and countless other pilgrims from many cultures and ages. In this sense we are no longer talking only about Latino patterns, culture, and symbols of transformation but about a universal human task that all are called upon to undertake. My hope is that as Latinas and Latinos we are still sufficiently unspoiled by assimilation into power or not yet so numbed by the experience of rejection that we can serve as witnesses to others of what authentic transformation is all about. The theory of transformation will serve as our guide to help give us direction and continuity through the journey of our personal, political, historical, and sacred lives.

An explanation of the theory in its main components is found in the first chapter. I will then apply the theory to practice to demonstrate its capacity to explain our daily lives. We will see how the theory can be employed to organize and give meaning and direction to specific problems by offering new and better alternative stories and relationships. Issues such as the family, politics in the community, education, male-female relations, and racism will be explored from the perspective of the theory of transformation. I shall do this by using examples taken from our everyday encounters as Latinas and Latinos.

The second chapter is dedicated to going home as the search for the deeper self. The authentic self is the key to any transformation whether in the personal, political, historical, or sacred realm. If we do not know who we are, we will merely accept the definitions of those around us who seek to turn us into happy consumers.

In chapter 3, the family as relationships-in-motion is explored as well as the stories of matriarchy and patriarchy in male-female relationships and the impact of transforming the family on the raising of children. Among Latinos, the family, as in all cultures, is of fundamental importance for nourishing and forming the next generation. The stories and relationships in the service of underlying ways of life that are practiced by parents in relating to each other and to their children shape children's future connections to authority in the public realm. If we learn in the family how to love and dissent, obey and disagree, struggle and cooperate simultaneously, then we will be prepared to participate in shaping a public environment that is conducive to caring deeply about the individual sacredness of each person.

To be political, to participate in shaping new and better institutions on a basis of equality with others and to be able to bring about justice and compassion in this situation here and now, is the focus of chapter 4. We need concrete and specific examples of how Latinas and Latinos can create new kinds of institutions that are responsive to the needs of people. Alternative patterns of relating, such as new forms of autonomy or institutionalized power in the service of transformation, are necessary because they allow large numbers of individuals and groups to collaborate on a sustained basis in connected roles. This is a personal and political relationship which makes organizing unions, food co-ops, medical clinics, and other forms of collective action possible. U.S. institutions are largely organized around bureaucracy for the sake of preserving power and preventing change, and so in order to bring about changes we need to create new concrete manifestations of organizations in order to use these new boundaries as liberated zones that encourage innovation and experimentation to protect and enhance the abilities of all members of the community.

In chapter 5 we will consider the role of the sacred as the ground of our being in renewing the personal, political, and historical faces of our being. We shall consider four sacred sources between which our community has often not distinguished. Three of the sacred sources, the lords of emanation, incoherence, and deformation, split off from the deepest sacred source of transformation and arrest life in a fragment of the core drama of life. Each source is the ultimate grounding for the archetypal ways of life of emanation, incoherence, deformation, and transformation. For Latinos the lord of emanation is the one usually referred to when we say *Ay bendito!* O my God! or *Queriendo Dios,* God Willing, often manifesting a passive stance in the presence of an all-powerful absolute lord, the lord of sin, shame, and guilt. The second, the lord of incoherence, is the lord of *la maquina,* the machine, or the brutal relentless system of competition and power that takes on a life of its own. This is the lord of assimilation that says that we have to brutalize each other in order to survive. This is the capitalistic lord to whom we pray to send us a few more stocks and bonds and to increase our competitive edge over others. Our third sacred source is the lord of nothing, of deformation, who inspires us through violence, revenge, and anger to make life fundamentally worse as we hurt ourselves with drugs or turn against others due to fantasies of superiority based on race, class, gender, religion, or sexual orientation. Our fourth choice is the god of transformation who invites us to journey again and again through the core drama of life and by so doing gain the creative imagination by which to renew history, our self, and our neighbor.

In chapter 6 the question of how we are to relate to the greater society is pursued: liberation or assimilation. Once we begin to gain success in the greater society, will we struggle to assimilate or choose the liberation of transforming our lives? Assimilation, in the final analysis, is a form of self-hatred and the deprecation of our ethnic and racial heritage. This is so because assimilation strips us of our selfhood for it signifies that an authentic self is not necessary and, as a matter of fact, is a handicap if people are to join the powerful and dominate others. Stripped of the deepest sacred source and our own identity the personal, political, historical, and sacred faces of our being are wounded and our Latino heritage is rendered meaningless and a burden because it is stigmatized. The politics of liberation demands that we be a self fully present with our particular cultural enrichment.

Chapter 7 asks the question: "What is the task for our educated and professional Latinas and Latinos in shaping our communities?" We shall, in this context, redefine the meaning of what it means to be a middle-class professional and demonstrate that those of us who have professional skills do not have to accept the therapy of individual success. The system based on power knows how to co-opt us by embracing those of us who have "made it." We have choices other than following or becoming *caciques*, the new rulers, or *vendidos*, those who sell themselves to the highest bidder. Latina/Latino professionals can be part of a transforming middle class who aggressively step forward with skills to build a more compassionate and just community.

Chapter 8 addresses the question: "Where do we go from here?" I shall explore four models or choices available to la comunidad Latina by which to shape the relationships, the archetypal stories, and the personal, political, historical, and sacred faces of our being. The four choices include, first, the traditional model characterized by uncritically perpetuating the inherited stories and relationships within which we were raised. Second is the assimilationist model that leads Latinas and Latinos to reject their inherited relationships and culture only to assimilate into the power relationships of U.S. society. The third model is a search for total power and security wherein Latinas and Latinos experience a self-wounding, wounding others, or the wounding by others in the name of leaders and movements who promise to lead us to a golden past but actually lead us into death. Finally, we shall look at the transforming model, the only choice within which we can be fully Latino and American but in a fundamentally new way. This is the strategy of reacquiring ourselves. Through this return to our own deepest sources we can re-vision and transform what it means to be a Latina woman and Latino man still growing her or his own identity. This process of excavation and discovery will simultaneously empower us to contribute to the formation of America as it continues the great experiment of creating a new kind of society and thus re-discover its soul.

Education as the most important civil rights issue facing our community in the twenty-first century is our concern in chapter 9. We all know that the credentialing that comes with education, especially higher education, is the road to acquire the necessary access to make it in this country. Latinas/Latinos are the youngest and the fastest growing group in the nation. Our children are also the most likely to drop out of school. All of the battles that we fought over affirmative action and bilingual education in the late 1960s and the 1970s are déjà vu all over again. Latina and Latino children are now arriving in the schools of small towns all over the country. School districts are in shock and many times respond with hostility when they are really at a loss as to what to do with the latest wave of immigrants, most of them Latinas/Latinos. Strategies of transformation to respond to this challenge will be discussed.

In writing this book, I have been moved by a strong impulse to explain myself to myself, to clarify meanings through writing and to share with Latinas and Latinos what I have come to know in my depths. There have been many times when I have been disappointed reading the scholarly books, anthologies, and commentaries regarding our community. What is available is usually not very helpful to many of us and in many cases I consider the material to be misleading and even damaging. Lately I have been developing new courses for Latina and Latino students. To this day there are too few courses or serious academic studies that are devoted to the various Latino groups in our midst. American universities are still hung up on the Black-White paradigm that is evident when there are discussions on race, diversity, and affirmative action. This is in spite of the amazing demographic changes of the last ten years and the fact that we are now the largest community of color in the nation. Latin American Studies programs only address our problems in Latin America and often consider Latina/Latino Studies lacking in scholarship and academic legitimacy. We are too often viewed as a monolithic abstraction as "Hispanics" in survey courses on race and ethnicity or urban studies or in courses on deviance and crime. This is one way by which we are turned into invisible people. Many Chicano and Puerto Rican Studies programs with their corresponding readings are often narrow in scope and at times suffer from a nationalistic exclusiveness. Many books and articles tell us what is but not what can or ought to be. Most of the academic literature has the underlying assumption that in time Latinas and Latinos will simply assimilate and their complaints will go away. This is not the way for me.

I believe that the greatest contribution of this book is that it not only critiques what is but offers alternatives that are fundamentally more loving and just. I hope Latinas and Latinos will see themselves in these pages and that they will be able to derive an understanding of and a strategy for their lives. Finally, my further hope is that other communities of color along with European-American ethnic groups will also be able to see themselves as a result of reading this book. If so, we might come to discover that we all need each other in order to be fully human.

1. A Theory of Transformation

In all my borned days I never seed
Nothing unto like this here a-fore!
'Course I ain't really been lookin'
For nothin' like this either.
—*Pogo*, 1955

It is the theory that allows us to see.—Albert Einstein

A theory of transformation shall serve as our guide to give us a new perspective by which to view the archetypal dramas, relationships, and ways of life being enacted by Latina women and Latino men by asking the question, "In the service of what way of life are you living your life?" This theory of transformation reminds us that all of us are on a journey through the core drama of life together with our neighbor and the deepest source of transformation. The fulfillment of the journey requires us to bring forth in their wholeness the personal, political, historical, and sacred faces of our being in all aspects of our lives.

One of the central motifs I will use in examining the personal, political, historical, and sacred faces of our being is that of the journey of transformation as the core drama of life. The archetype of the journey is central in the lives of all Latinas and Latinos. Our forebearers came to this country seeking a new life, a better life, at the cost of great personal suffering and risk. They left behind loved ones, a familiar land and culture, to journey into the desert of an unknown land with a strange language and customs. But they came and they endured. So our foremothers and forefathers enacted in their lives one of the oldest archetypal stories of humanity, uprooting their lives, traveling in the desert of the unknown, and creating a life in a new land. The Aztecs were told by means of a vision to travel south into the Valley of Mexico and when they saw an eagle perched on a cactus eating a serpent to consider that place holy ground. They were to stay and settle the land. This is the sacred story underlying the founding of Tenochtitlán, or Mexico City. But the symbolism of the journey of transformation as the core drama of life not only points us to a spatiotemporal reality, it is also a sacred story, an archetypal drama that points us inward, home, within our selves into the deeper depths. It is an invitation to travel within the valleys and mountains of the inner world in order to discover a new landscape of the deepest sacred and of the self. This internal voyage is the journey that we are all called upon to travel so as to create a new connection between the external concrete reality of our lives and the realm of underlying sacred forming sources. This is the road to wisdom that affirms the meaning and value of the concrete precisely by guiding us into the underlying archetypal realm that gives to all of concrete reality its deeper meaning and value.

A New Theoretical Perspective

We need guidance; we need the discipline of a theory that allows us to participate in analyzing and understanding what is being revealed. Einstein put it best when he said that it is the theory that allows us to see, to see a new world, to ask new questions. Sheldon Wolin has used the method of Michael Polanyi to remind us of the element of surprise and playfulness in the tacit dimension.[1] Theory is not a lock-step method by which we capture reality. Theory and its choice is a conversion, a turning around of our being by which we receive a fuller view of the world, self, other, and the deepest sacred source. Method is not a well-beaten track but a process of taking the next step in our daily task of creating, nourishing, breaking, and re-creating the institutions and structures of our personal and political lives.

The word "theory" can be traced to its Greek roots as participation in the life and death of a sacred source. To theorize regarding ourselves-in-process is to struggle with the sacred sources in our depths. In short, we need a theory that will allow us to see, to link together the personal, political, historical, and sacred faces of our being. Our current education and socialization provide us only with fragments.

Traditional social scientists always ask us to rearrange what is already present as the only reality. But the fundamentally new arises out of the underlying sacred forming sources. If the realm of the archetypal remains unexplored and unconscious, it will become demonic and possess us. Our theory, if it is to be a viable alternative to theories that only name the superficial aspects of our life, needs to address this underlying archetypal dimension. Thus, a theoretical analysis that enriches our lives is really an attempt to respond in an archetypal or symbolic manner to the fundamentally new that is available to us through our experience of the sacred. But more importantly, our participation in helping to shape and direct the fundamentally new by giving it a concrete face is essential. We together with the sacred continuously shape life dialectically; change emerges out of struggle between complementary forces such as the masculine-feminine and the human-divine that brings about a new reality or transformation. There is no final resting place in a continuous process of transformation. All of us, then, are experiments of the depths, we are in reality temples, crucibles, and vessels, carriers of the sacred.

The theory of transformation that we shall use in this book was developed by Manfred Halpern.[2] It is an extraordinary theory in its ability to recognize the relationships that link us to ourselves, to others, to common problems, and to our sacred sources, that is, the personal, political, historical, and sacred faces of our being. The theory allows us to understand the connection between individual human behavior and what goes on in politics and society. To know archetypal stories, relationships, the four faces of our being, and archetypal ways of life that we enact on our journey is to know something crucial of how the whole of life hangs together. The theory being presented here provides us with an interrelated set of testable generalizations that allows us to deal with problems which are central to all human relations, formulated in terms of concepts that are not culture bound and that allow us to use the same concepts and interrelated hypotheses for intrapersonal, interpersonal, and intergroup relations.

The theory in relation to the practices in our daily lives is an invitation to understand and participate in a sacred story at the heart of our existence. My exploration with you of how we can re-discover the deeper reality of our lives as Latinas and Latinos is based on the realization that there is a fundamental structure to life that is given to us by the core drama of life, a drama with three acts. We either arrest ourselves in fragments of this journey—the partial ways of life of emanation, incoherence, and deformation—or we move toward fulfillment by journeying through all three acts of the drama until we reach transformation.

Facts about Latina women and Latino men—their socioeconomic status, their levels of employment, their income, their
level of participation in the workforce, how many years they have of
schooling—tell us little about our lives. To know this data might be
helpful to analyze voting behavior or for advertising groups but it
leaves us with a description of fragments. We need to know on a
deeper level what is happening in our lives.[3] Our theory will allow
us to go beyond mere descriptions of what is. It is not enough to describe reality, we need to transform it. We can only know what our
lives are like and to change them for the better if we ask different
questions through a new lens, the theory of transformation.

Talk of structures and functions, equilibrium, and the priority
of systems are of little use in helping us to build new and more fruitful and nourishing lives. None of us has ever seen a system sit down
and have a hamburger or walk across a busy street. But we have all
seen ourselves or others enact concrete relationships that became
systemic or routinized ways of doing things, that is, we all act out
set roles, or as most often happens, roles enact us. We become part
of an impersonal system by allowing ourselves to be made into
bloodless extensions who carry out expected behavior.

To take ourselves back is to become conscious of what is being
done to us, and to begin to realize the cost of the stories and the relationships that we practice in the service of truncated ways of life
that arrest us as partial selves. What do these relationships or institutions do to us as human beings and, perhaps more importantly, of
what human capacity do we deprive ourselves as a result of this way
of being, living, and acting? We are more than external, social beings. Our sacred face connects us to and is grounded in and nourished by those underlying realities known as sacred sources, or archetypal depths that we all share by virtue of our humanity. It is
what D. H. Lawrence described as that space of timelessness and un-
knowing beyond the morning star to which the old tired gods return
and from whence the new gods are born.[4]

LIVING IN A TIME OF INCOHERENCE

A time of crisis, separation, or breakdown is accompanied by
confusion and pain. The means by which we ordered our experience,
our relations to others and the world, begin to deteriorate. Life becomes unbearable, untenable, and unfruitful. The breakdown of au-

thority throughout our society is symptomatic of a cultural revolution that is taking place. All institutions and authorities, systems of thought and relationships are in crisis. What the Latino community is experiencing is symptomatic and analogous of what the whole of our society is confronting. To break from a society that subjects and excludes us is the same archetypal process as a Latino separating himself from a view of life dominated by a patriarchal father or a Latina rejecting the culturally established definitions of motherhood and housewife. This is a universal crisis that threatens all established authority. Everywhere there is doubt, searching, and breaking away.

Modern social science has reduced its pursuit of the understanding of the Latino community to statistics, variables, and the use of questionnaires. Social scientists want to quantify the facts of our lives in an attempt to create a mathematical certainty they hope will capture the meaning of our culture and people. None of their methodologies or instruments has proven capable of telling us what is really happening on the deeper levels in our lives. Sociologists and political scientists study the institutionalized power of the current ruling class based on white, male privilege without knowing about the realm of the archetypal, the underlying sacred forming sources, nor the difference between these sacred sources. As a result they can only describe the outward manifestations of our lives and the stories that we live by counting, looking for variables, and interviewing. But they cannot help us to free ourselves from powerful inherited stories such as capitalism, racism, patriarchy, and uncritical loyalty that are manifestations of deeper sacred forces that possess us, especially because we remain unconscious of them. Nor can they tell us how we can participate in the process of transformation that enables us to know and reject the stories that render us partial selves so we can create fundamentally more loving and just alternatives.

Because we continue to rely on traditional social science, we know very little about who we are, why our lives are breaking, and where we are going. In fact, postmodernists or poststructuralists have left us completely bereft. Practitioners of these theories are opposed to the theory being applied here because it points us to living, underlying patterning forces, archetypes. They consider this kind of theory to be essentialist, universal, and structured, which takes away our freedom. But the theory of transformation being employed here has no intention of upholding any kind of established order—the order which benefits those in power—nor does it seek to replace the old theories with a new power theory. Most of all, this is not an attempt to set up a new dogma as theory. Yes, it was necessary, as many social scientists and feminists have argued, to demolish the structures and functions of the then-prevailing dominant theory that upheld the power of the old guard in the academy and in policy making. But once this was accomplished, we were left with no theory by which to re-construct our lives. Any theory which seeks to make sense of our lives on a deeper level and that hangs together so that we are able to see a structure in our lives is quickly dismissed.[5] So what I ask is that you the reader remain skeptical and yet open as you are invited to personally participate by testing this theory with your own experiences and to evaluate whether or not the theory here applied in fact allows us to see, understand, and participate in creating alternatives that are new and more just. Do I ask that you make a leap of faith? No, if this means blind acceptance as belief. Yes, if faith means taking a risk by being open to a new experience. Although this theory is indebted to Jung and his understanding of archetypes, it fundamentally disagrees with him. Jung had almost nothing to say about the process of transformation. He was silent on the political and historical aspects of our being and wrote nothing at all about archetypal ways of life in which we enact the relationships and stories of our lives and from which we draw the deeper meaning and value of what we enact.[6]

We can only know what our lives are like if we ask different questions: "What are the stories that we are now practicing? Where are Latinas and Latinos in the core drama of life? What do the four faces of their being look like as they struggle for wholeness?" And the most important question: "In the service of what way of life are they enacting the stories and relationships of their daily living?" In the midst of the changes swirling around us, we as Latina women and Latino men share much. All of us have in common many of the same underlying archetypal stories and relationships, even though those stories and relationships may be practiced in the service of radically different ways of life. I want to tell this deeper story. I want to reveal our struggle to be a woman, a man, a person, a self, what we share as a people by looking at our lives through a new lens, the theory of transformation.

The theory of transformation can tell us whether the stories and relationships connecting Latina women and Latino men are used creatively or destructively. The theory also makes a fundamental value judgment: the only viable alternative to the way of life of emanation that is now dying, and to a way of life of incoherence committed to grasping power after power, and to the way of life of deformation that promises total security in the embrace of a conquering hero who leads us to the abyss through violence and death is to a way of life committed to the creation of fundamentally new and better relationships.

What is the empirical test for the existence of any particular archetypal drama? We can see and experience its enactment always through the four concrete faces of our being. And our description and analysis of its underlying structure, dynamics, values, and purpose in the service of one of the four overarching archetypal ways of life always hold true and are never otherwise and certain actions can never take place within that particular archetypal drama.[7] For example, in the archetypal drama of transforming love there can never be any domination or possession of one person by the other. In this story we are both free to enact the fullest possible repertory of relationships in order to respond to new kinds of problems and to be wholly present to each other with the personal, political, historical, and sacred faces of our being. By contrast the story of romantic love leads to the possession of one's lover, limits the relationships available to her or him, dramatically impacts on the four faces of our being for the worse, and deprives us of the freedom to respond to new problems especially if those problems cause us to ask new kinds of questions. The underlying patterning forces of these two stories wherever we encounter them, be it in Mexico or France or the United States, as long as they historically endure, remain the same even though their particular manifestations will differ from moment to moment. A single case to the contrary of these theoretical statements puts any hypothesis regarding any archetype into doubt.[8]

> We cannot discover and make the basic choices we have in our life unless we learn how to inquire into the nature and values of these living, underlying, sacred patterning forces. We call these forces of our being archetypal dramas as we analyze their underlying structure, dynamics, values, meaning, and purpose. Thus the word "drama" is used not as a metaphor but as a description of how these forces are really structured and really work. We also speak of archetypal dramas as sacred sources— sacred sources that in the ways of life of emanation, fragments, and deformation possess and command us, but in the experience of transformation, as we shall see, the deepest source opens up its and our participatory capacity.[9]

In contrast to Plato, archetypes as forms are not eternal and good. One of the four archetypal ways of life that we shall be exploring, deformation, is destructive. Archetypal dramas are born and also die. Emanation as a way of life is dying. The archetypal drama of the state was born about 5,000 years ago; the archetypal drama of the nation-state was born only about two hundred years ago. Archetypes come into being, persist, and die with our help.[10]

We live somewhere in the core drama at every moment of our life, in arrest or in movement. This is a highly unfamiliar statement, but this book is filled with such statements, all of which are empirically testable.

> Let me now take you through these three Acts of the core drama of life, to show that we have a choice between only four fundamentally different ways of life, ways of life that establish the ultimate meaning, purpose and value of everything we enact in their service. By "ultimate" I do not mean on Judgment Day, but the different deepest grounds we can discover now within any of the four ways of life. And this exploration of the four ways of life also demonstrates that we can discover and experience the deepest and widest compassionate justice and love—only in one of them. In regards to this last claim, at no time do I offer anything to believe in. But in contrast to any dogmatic belief, I shall be asking you to risk faith in this empirical theory—that is, to risk trust in actually participating in the journey it describes to the fundamentally new and better in order to discover whether in fact this theory is true.[11]

The Core Drama of Life and the Origin of the Four Ways of Life

The source of transformation, the deepest source of our being, created the most important story: the core drama of life. Only this story fulfills the need for persistent transformation. The core drama of life is a three-act drama that must be enacted again and again. Why? The deepest source is still creating the universe.[12] From the beginning, creation was intended to bring forth the fundamentally new and better. The core drama of life requires participation in all of its three acts by the deepest source and human beings. Our deepest source is not perfect nor finished; the deepest source continues to create. Neither are we perfect. We together with the deepest source need to continually choose to respond to new problems by journeying through the core drama of life. Only humans, drawing upon the deepest sacred source, can participate in transformation without a preprogrammed outcome.

But there are three other sacred sources. Unfortunately, they have the power to arrest us in fragments of the core drama of life and thus to frustrate the work of transformation. Why are lesser sacred forces or lords able to arrest our lives in different acts and scenes of our journey? This is not a puppet play. The story of transformation has to offer us and the lords of emanation, incoherence, and deformation the capacity and freedom to say no and yes to this story that constitutes the heart of creation. These partial lords try to prevent us from hearing the voice of the deepest source who reaches out to us in order to further transformation.[13] To reach the goal of the core drama of life in Act III, Scenes 1 and 2, wherein we practice transformation, we must continuously say no to the archetypal lords who enchant us. We need to free ourselves from these lesser sacred sources and the ways of life that they inspire and to be filled anew by the deepest source of transformation. To choose to make life fundamentally more loving and compassionate is to participate with each other and the source of transformation as the deepest ground of our being.[14]

> Telling the story of this drama tells us something we are rarely told: How in actual practice can we transform ourselves? How can we actually find a fundamentally better way and test it by translating it into practice together with our neighbors?[15]

There are no deeper acts of life than the three acts of the journey through the core drama of life.[16] When we as Latina women and Latino men arrest life, and therefore our self in one of these acts before we reach the third act, we stunt our growth in a fragment of the core drama. And because it is only a fragment, it leaves us partial selves, fragile, wounded, and angry, no matter how much power we may accumulate within it. Each time we enact this drama in its fullness as the archetypal journey of transformation, we together with the deepest sacred source are mutual participants in the process of continuous creation. In this drama all human beings can by the very nature of our humanity consciously, critically, creatively, and caringly participate in fulfilling the core drama of life. But this cocreation can only take place if we realize our own story by overcoming the arrested and fragmented aspects of a partial self.[17]

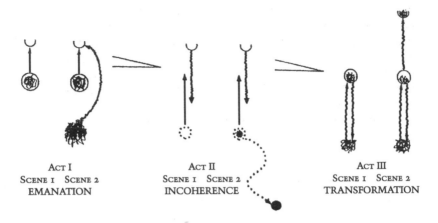

ACT I
SCENE 1   SCENE 2
EMANATION

ACT II
SCENE 1   SCENE 2
INCOHERENCE

ACT III
SCENE 1   SCENE 2
TRANSFORMATION

Figure 1.   The Core Drama of Life Symbolized

It is the core drama of life also because of the fact that three of our choices constitute either fragments of this core drama (we arrest ourselves in Act I or in Act II) or a fragmenting movement into its exit, but it also offers us a fourth choice. The choice of transformation as a way of life means a readiness to journey together with the deepest sacred source of our being again and again through the entire core drama of life every time an unresolved problem of understanding confronts us. When we acquire new insight as to how to confront any new problem, a new understanding or wisdom has been discovered, a wisdom that is fulfilled by our creation of fundamentally new and more loving forms of justice and compassion.[18]

Act I, Scene 1: The Way of Life of Emanation

We always begin in emanation in Act I, Scene 1, at the very least in the relationship of emanation as extensions of powerful others such as our mother or father who provide us with security, love, and nurturance. We need emanation as a relationship to survive. But what should be a temporary and loving initiation into the journey of life is too often frozen and dogmatized into a permanent relationship and the end of our journey. For most of recorded history, emanation became not a step forward in a quest but a whole way of life. We were caught in the overwhelming embrace of mysterious others. We were raised to be uncritically loyal to an established lord that legitimized the power of our mothers and fathers and the stories of patriarchy, uncritical loyalty, and machismo. We were bound within these archetypal dramas that seemed to give us the justice of deep security and which we could not dare to criticize.

Because we were told to believe that the final truth had been given to us, our lives were arrested here so that Act I, Scene 1, was turned into an entire way of life in the service of emanation.[19] In this overarching way of life we are forbidden to ask new questions about our life and culture because these realities had been determined as true for all time. To doubt their eternal truth is to be threatened with sin, shame, and guilt. Archetypal stories such as patriarchy, matriarchy, uncritical loyalty, and romantic love were given their ultimate legitimacy by the lord of emanation. Under the influence of this lord, men and women lived the stories and relationships available to them as the will of this lord. This partial lord, who split off from the source of transformation, is traditionally worshipped as a masculine lord in the three world religions of Christianity, Judaism, and Islam. He in-spires (literally, breathes within) his followers to repress any idea that would go against the truth revealed once for all. The lord of emanation is the sacred origin of the domination of the archetype of the masculine over the feminine. One of the most important stories enacted in the service of emanation in the Latino community that maintains the supremacy of men is the story of patriarchy.

Patriarchy simply defined means the systematic domination of women by men. It is important for us to know how this story is practiced in our daily lives and that it has devastated our community for generations:

- Women are seen primarily as producers of children.
- They carry the honor of the family in their sexuality.
- Their main task in life is to be housewives.
- Women are expected to be sensitive, emotional, soft, and gentle.
- Women are never allowed to be economically autonomous.
- They are subjected to a double moral standard.
- Women are forced to become manipulative in order to survive; for the lifelong repression they have endured they gain their part of the bargain by driving their men to provide for them.

- This story is always in the service of emanation, incoherence, or deformation.
- The four faces of both women and men are undermined by repression.
- This story wounds the next generation.
- The sacred source of emanation blesses this story as the fate of both men and women.
- This story cripples both men and women because neither can become a full person.

As Latinas and Latinos many of us continue to practice the inherited story of patriarchy that determines male-female relationships as final and ultimate because they are the revelation of a mysterious lord.[20] This is how the status quo comes to be final: we are forbidden by the stories we live to create conflict or change in favor of continuity and collaboration; our sense of justice is perverted to be the security that comes with the enforcement of revealed dogma. The cost we pay is the repression of the fullness of the personal, political, historical, and sacred faces of our being.

Since we are radically wounded, cut off from our deepest source, arrested in the possessive embrace of this lord that we referred to as "God," we Latina women and Latino men cannot develop a new consciousness. Our creativity is taken away from us. We are forbidden new relationships to others outside our family and community, and we cannot pursue shared goals with others. We diminish our own humanity and that of others in order to protect and maintain the tradition of male superiority.

Act I, Scene 2: A New Inspiration

In our cosmos of continuous creation, the second scene of Act I opens a chasm of doubt again and again. We hear from the realm of the underlying sacred sources even in the midst of our repression. The way of life of emanation is fragile precisely because we have an inner need to continuously experience the fundamentally new and more loving in order to turn the fundamentally new toward the fundamentally better. For this reason there are two scenes in Act I. In Scene 2, we are filled with new ideas and intuitions that have their origin beyond the official voice of conscience formed by our culture and society. This inner voice, rooted in underlying sacred sources, undermines our repression. But we cannot assume that these new voices are to the good. We need to test them to discern whether or not they are fundamentally new and better or if they are destructive. We have hope and risk faith that the new inspiration comes from the deepest source of transformation.

> A new inspiration in Scene 2 can come from any of the four sacred sources. Initially, while we still remain in Act I, that new inspiration will also remain mysteriously powerful to us. In fear of opening new doors, we can repress this new inspiration with the help of our already established archetypal Lord and his concrete emanational embodiments in our life, but we do this at the price of understanding ourselves less and diminishing our freedom and capacity to respond to new problems.[21]

Act II, Scene 1: The Way of Life of Incoherence

If we respond to these new feelings and give up trying to repress them, we leave Act I, Scene 1. We rebel and break with significant others who have held us in the embrace of emanation. By rejecting our former source of mystery we champion this new inspiration and become its prophet because in its new light we find our earlier story unbearable, untenable, or unfruitful. But that decision compels us to leave the security of the arrested—and arresting—truth of the emanational container of Act I and enter into Act II—the Act of incoherence.

The way of life of emanation is everywhere dying. People like you and me are no longer willing to deny our own fundamentally new experiences, ideas, and hopes. When Latina women begin to move toward rebellion by acting out their own desires, too often Latino men respond by attempting to restore their inherited privilege. Many resort to violence when women and children dare to raise questions. Many Latino men cannot accept the challenge because the story of patriarchy and machismo together with the story of uncritical loyalty make it very difficult for us to see any other possibilities.

Initially Act II, Scene 1, moves us into rebellion in which we break with those who tried to hold us as possessions. But we need to keep going on the journey to free ourselves not only from our actual fathers but on the deeper level from the story of patriarchy that gave our fathers and patriarchal authorities their mysterious power over us. Many of us were seduced by the allure of the wider society that told us that true freedom is to be found in the pursuit of self-interest and power as the American dream. So rather than continue on the journey through the core drama of life and its fulfillment in transformation we arrested our lives. What began as a form of liberation from the repression of emanation as a way of life is now arrested in a whole new way of life, incoherence.

By assimilation into the way of life of incoherence Latinos are inspired to create themselves into upwardly mobile, aggressive individuals. Assimilated Latinos think like those in the dominant society who live in this fragmented way of life and become cut off from their own selfhood, neighbors, and the deepest sacred source as partial selves. Why partial selves? Because in this way of life enacting the stories of competence and capitalism we do not have a clue as to who we are and do not ask questions as to the meaning of our lives. We are not fully present to respond to new kinds of problems since our consciousness is controlled by the pursuit of self-interest. We are caught in an emanational relationship to incoherence as a way of life that we cannot analyze. "To make it" is the new heaven, the goal of this kind of change. Assimilated Latinos are taken over by a fragment of life, a profession, endowed with a source of mystery that will give them identity. Rejecting the lord of emanation some believe that they have now become "secularized" and are free from the old moral bonds. But without knowing it we are actually possessed by a new sacred source, the lord of incoherence. The system based on power is grounded in this lord and it possesses us just as powerfully as did the lord of emanation, but now without the same sense of security; the only certainty is knowing that nothing is secure or lasting. Since there is no ultimate meaning or value or love, we have to get what we can while the going is good. This anxiety feeds our constant need to compete without ever being able to get out of the game unless we pay a price, face incoherence, and transform it.

Latino parents lose much of their authority in this conflict between ways of life. Many parents, to cover their own sense of loss in the greater world, demanded a total loyalty at home. Resistance by a daughter or son was met by subjection or the violence of total exclusion. But unlike the traditional world of emanation there is another world beyond the door of the home that provides a repertory of other relationships that threatens the concrete inherited forms of relationships that kept us dependent. The Anglo world offers forbidden relationships: a personal and social autonomy by gaining the relationships of autonomy, the right to be left alone in isolation, increased bargaining power through education, new buffers such as teachers and counselors, boyfriends, a new identity as an American along with symbols of success portrayed daily in the media. With these options available it becomes increasingly difficult to re-create the vigor of the original security. Rebellion was a strategy to gain a better leverage within the family and therefore restored and strengthened the traditional repertory of relationships; rebellion now is far more serious, because the threat to punish the child who does not obey or the independent daughter or the angry wife might end with them never returning. So instead of changes *within* the available repertory of relationships, there is now the threat of change *of* the repertory, of creating previously forbidden relationships and entering *into* a new way of living and relating that our parents, husband, or lover cannot dominate. This results in incoherence and the possibility of deformation or transformation.

Having taken our new ideas and intuitions seriously in Act I, Scene 2, we entered into Act II, Scene 1, wherein we succeeded in breaking with our parents and other authority figures and embarked upon a path of open rebellion. But in the first scene of Act II, we were free to arrest the journey and institutionalize rebellion. As a community Latino men and Latina women are currently facing perhaps our greatest challenge: how to create a new and more compassionate culture as we find ourselves living in the midst of the story of capitalism. Because we live in a hostile world, rather than continue our journey, some of us create fortresses to escape a world we do not understand.[22]

We pay a heavy price for assimilating into the story of capitalism. The lord of incoherence inspires us to practice all of our personal gifts in the pursuit of power and self-interest. This way of life takes us over and our relationship to this overarching drama is one we cannot understand. We get trapped in stories of a perpetual competition that turns our relationships into contests of mutual suspicion and fear. Assimilation is deadly for la comunidad Latina. When we join the powerful we, too, become possessed by the story of capitalism. In addition we are filled with the self-hatred that comes from believing we are inferior until we become successful, as defined by white European Americans. The failure to compete, to achieve power and status, often leads Latino men to forms of domination in the home, the last resort of wounded masculine pride.[23]

Let us consider what practicing the story of capitalism does to our humanity as Latino men and Latina women and the price paid for assimilating into this story. The following are the characteristics lived and practiced within this drama.[24]

- In order to survive we are tempted to become immoral and insincere.
- We cannot afford to be intimate.
- We are always looking over our shoulder lest we be overtaken.
- We wear masks.
- All of our relationships are in danger of being corrupted by the competition for power.
- We belong to an impersonal system that turns us into a fragment.
- Nobody knows me in my wholeness.
- The bureaucracy of the system renders a person into an anonymous abstraction.
- This story is always in the service of incoherence and/or deformation.
- We cannot practice the four faces of our being in their fullness.

In the story of capitalism, we agree on procedures that keep us from physically assaulting or killing each other as we struggle with one another in the name of self-interest. To overcome our vulnerability we seek power that, of course, increases our anxiety. There is no security. We turn this attempt to organize insecurity, without being able to name it, into a whole way of life, a way of life I call incoherence. We are all had by this story. The powerful, the less powerful, and the powerless are all wounded but still collude with each other to believe that this is the only way to live.

Capitalism is the official story of U.S. society that arrests our lives in Act II, Scene 1, in the service of incoherence.[25] Incoherence as a way of life is often in collusion with deformation. In order to practice the story of capitalism we have to be prepared to hurt those who threaten us. When European Americans become annoyed that I do not want members of la comunidad Latina to assimilate, I explain that I do not want them to accept and practice the story of capitalism. I explain the deeper meaning of this story, how it wounds our humanity. Capitalism is not America at its best; America fulfills its promise when we practice the story of participatory democracy.[26]

As Latinas and Latinos we wake up day after day not really knowing what this way of life is doing to us and to our community. We get angry and we sit with one another and talk about how the Anglos are using us. Again and again we rebel against them in our conversations and, at times, through our actions. But since we are only breaking with our actual antagonists in Act II, Scene 1, we remain caught by the lord of incoherence, by the archetypal story of capitalism. We merely rebel against Anglo power and bosses. At times we succeed in replacing Anglo male domination with Latino male domination, but nothing has really changed. The color of the people seeking power might change but, on the deeper level, people are still being held and possessed by the same story of capitalism. Since we are arrested in the first scene of Act II, we cannot in fact know ourselves nor our own best self-interest. We know ourselves only as fragments, unable to realize our deeper humanity.

> But now as we participate in the journey of transformation, we need to move through both Scenes of Act II and not arrest ourselves in its first Scene as a permanent rebel. Yes, in the first Scene of Act II, we rejoice as a new rebel prophet—and also experience the often painful opposition of others. But prophets, as al-Farabi told us in 10th century Damascus, are compelled by their sacred source to speak, but they do not yet know what they are talking about. We need next to move on into the second Scene of Act II in order to discover and to understand three levels of reality that had once both enchanted and enchained us in order to empty ourselves of them in this second Scene.[27]

It is not enough to break with European-American domination; we need to experience a deeper breaking. We need to empty our soul of the archetypal story of capitalism in the service of incoherence that inspires and gives mysterious power to our white or brown bosses. We need to focus our anger by becoming radical, going to the roots of the problem. Otherwise we will become just like the bosses. They are not the enemy; they are also victims of a story that destroys our humanity when we become obsessed with greed and power. The real enemy is the story of capitalism and because we do not understand the power of these sacred stories we repeat history, that is, live the same stories. Because most of us remain unaware of the world of archetypal sacred forces that possess us, we wake up one day and realize that only the outer appearances have changed. The story remains as powerful as before.

Act II, Scene 2: The Way of Life of Deformation

Deformation is the exit from the core drama; deformation diminishes our humanity and places us in the service of destructive death.[28] At the second scene of Act II we have a choice: either we

empty ourselves of the stories and partial ways of life that have possessed us or we turn to violence in order to hang on to the old stories, and thereby hurt ourselves and others. In the modern age, deformation is becoming more prevalent. Because of the inherent fragility
of emanation and of incoherence as ways of life, people whose security is threatened often turn toward violence to preserve their way of
life, and thus exit the core drama of life in the service of deformation. Violence always fails to make things better or even to return
them to the way things were. Because many of us are excluded from
the realms of power, we feel increasingly powerless. At home the
way of life of emanation continues to break into fragments. What
deformation promises is not just power, but absolute power. If Latina women and Latino men join a gang, deal drugs, or give in to fantasies of superiority over other ethnic groups, they feel they have the
power of life and death over others. Or if they turn to violence against
themselves because they accept the view of inferiority held by others, this can lead to forms of self-wounding. Power now becomes
total power. What people who seek power are really after is total security even as the ground shifts and opens beneath their feet.

Latino men are caught in two crumbling ways of life: in the
dying way of life of emanation they are trying to uphold the legiti-
mation of masculine authority that worked for them before and in
the way of life of incoherence they are failing to make it. Thus many
Latino men are driven to violence against themselves and others at
home and in the wider society. Some Latina women who see what
this society is doing to their men also try to make the old stories
functional again. But what begins as an attempt to restore the story
of patriarchy in the service of emanation in order to compensate for
powerlessness in the Anglo world now becomes patriarchy in the
service of deformation, destructive death at the exit from the core
drama of life for both men and women. This explanation exposes the
lie that the return to family values and the old respect are ideals
worthy of keeping. Many Latina women and Latino men are angry
with their lives because they are losing contact with their own roots
and, even though they are trying to assimilate, they are not getting
ahead. Too many of us vent our rage on others whom we want to
keep below us in the hierarchy of power.

Violence has always been a part of the strategy to preserve the
way of life of emanation. Deformation has always been available
as an ally of men who kept guard over the container of emanation.
Wives for generations have been beaten as a matter of right by Latino men. And many children were beaten by their mothers who

also sought to uphold the traditional values based on authority and respect. It was not necessary for a woman or a child to be in open rebellion to be assaulted. The greatest and ever growing danger in current circumstances is that the hidden resentment of the husband will erupt at any time in an irrational manner in the form of violence. The Latino culture gave men permission to abuse their wives both psychologically and physically, just to let them know who is boss. It was the Latina woman's duty to accept this violence. It was the wife's duty to keep the children in line. Both men and women in the Latino community have colluded in practicing the relationship of deformation as victim and victimizer for generations. But practicing deformation as a way of life differs from deformation as a relationship. Violence becomes systematic and threatens to destroy our families, both physically and psychically. Latina mothers and spouses were raised to believe that they must have done something to cause an eruption of anger so they are always prepared to blame themselves and to forgive. Latina women enter into a conspiracy with Latino men that guarantees the violence will go on in the service of deformation.

Our self-identity as Latina women and Latino men is badly bruised by an inability to make it in this society. Our self-image is distorted by the view that the dominant culture has of us. We are unhappy but we do not know what to do except to try to compensate for our sense of powerlessness by exercising total power in the home. When we fail to get the respect from our children if we are a working single mother or a Latino male trying to support the family we either turn to violence against ourselves or others or we give up. In this situation people live on the edge of the abyss. Why is this so? We continue to repress, deny, and destroy new ideas, feelings, intuitions, and stories that question our tradition and who we are. We are prepared to hurt ourselves and others in order to keep our family and world intact. The inability to acknowledge crucial aspects of our lives is what constitutes the danger of being a partial self. In order to preserve a stunted identity in a truncated world, the road to violence opens up again and again.

The present expressions of the archetypes of masculinity and femininity in the Latino community are but a few of the possibilities we might create. Our current models and expressions of being a woman or a man are profoundly flawed because men have historically practiced maleness as a way of being superior to women. This view was affirmed by the most recent meeting of the Baptists in Salt Lake City who declared that it is God's will that women should submit, albeit graciously, to their husbands.[29] The Catholic Church and some other Christian denominations as well as conservative Islam and Judaism encourage the same submission of women to men. In this kind of atmosphere the essence of femininity becomes the negation of the feminine self for the sake of enhancing the masculine. To ask women to efface themselves for the sake of men who have no idea who they are is to move more deeply into ignorance.

> But machismo still reigns. Sexual and physical abuse is common among all social classes in Latin America. It is less and less acceptable to say so publicly, but many people, including many women, still view women as a man's property. They see sexual violence as besmirching the honor of a woman and, if she is married, the honor of the husband to whom she belongs. This view is still found in the law. In at least 10 countries, a rapist can escape punishment by marrying his victim. Her family often pressures her into agreeing, to restore her honor and assure a husband for a woman considered tainted.[30]

Killing a woman to recover one's honor is still practiced in Muslim countries. This practice is justified on the premise that a woman's body is not her own but the property of the men in the family. Sexual relations outside of marriage are totally unacceptable. The honor of a man is physically located in the vagina of the woman. Any alleged unclean act dishonors and humiliates the men in her family.[31]

> *Our Second Choice in Act II, Scene 2: Emptying Ourselves of Partial Ways of Life and the Stories Enacted in Their Service*

> At the end of Act II there exists the only exit from the core drama of life. But, this time, we do not throw ourselves into this exit, possessed by the archetypal way of life of deformation. Participating instead in transformation, we use that exit to empty ourselves of, not repress, the old Lords' archetypal patterning force that give structure and value to the dramas and ways of life that are in their service because we now understand why all three partial Lords have become alien to our being.[32]

If the new inspiration in the second scene of the first act had come from the deepest sacred source of our being, it will by now have opened our insight, courage, and capacity to free ourselves from the concrete relationship to people, ideas, and values that had once contained us but that we can no longer bear.[33] That is the first level of understanding and action. But to say no in Act II, Scene 1, to rebel only against particular concrete manifestations of the archetypal drama of which we, too, had been an emanational embodiment is at most to bring about incremental and superficial changes within the same archetypal drama. For example, we may overthrow the Tsar of Russia but Stalin in fact becomes another concrete manifestation of the same archetypal story of total rule as Tsar Ivan the Terrible. Or we may break with our mother but then our lover becomes another concrete expression of the same story of possessive love. We need to go beyond this concrete breaking.

In Act II, Scene 2, having broken with our actual father we now empty ourselves of the story of patriarchy in the service of emanation in the depths that gave our fathers their mysterious hold over us. This is the second and third level of understanding and action we can reach in the second scene of Act II of incoherence: to participate in a deeper breaking with living, underlying patterning forces—to free ourselves both of the archetypal dramas and relationships and also of the archetypal way of life that had hitherto commanded our life and kept us limited in wisdom and its fruits in love and justice. Centuries ago, theorists of transformation said: "To know yourself is to know your Lord." In Act II, Scene 2, we can come to know which partial sacred source—partial once again meaning "biased and incomplete"—had till now possessed us and to know the deepest sacred source now helping to free us.[34]

Unless we come to understand archetypal dramas and ways of life, we cannot get out of them, or if they break because of the actions of others, the breakage leaves us stranded. We become philosophers in the second scene of Act II by learning to unlearn and by learning how to open ourselves to a previously unfamiliar understanding.

We do not have the power to destroy any living, underlying patterning force, but without the participation of our concrete personal face, and hence also without our diminished political, historical, and sacred participation, the drama loses its strength. We in a very real sense starve the story to death by refusing to feed it with our concrete lives. If enough people reject it, it may die, for no sacred source can persist without its concrete faces.

We need as a community to recognize the stories and ways of life that strangle us and to void ourselves of the archetypal dramas of patriarchy, uncritical loyalty, matriarchy, machismo, the disappointed male, homophobia, tribalism, capitalism, and the wounded self. It is these underlying ways of life and stories that are the enemy. We have a right to be angry because of what was done to us as Latina women and Latino men, but there can be no revenge in the story of transformation. We need only the courage released by our anger to first engage our oppressor. Then we need to go beyond them because they are also victims. It is the deeper causes, the stories and the partial ways of life that are wounding all of our lives. Once we have emptied ourselves in Act II, Scene 2, of these destructive stories we send them, not ourselves or others, into the abyss at the exit from the core drama. We now free ourselves in Act III, Scene 1, to hear anew from the deepest source of our being and in the second scene of Act III we try out in practice with our neighbors our new vision.

Act III, Scenes 1 and 2: The Way of Life of Transformation

When we have thus emptied ourselves, we can count on being filled anew. This is indeed a cosmos of continuous creation. In the first scene of Act III, we hear again from our deeper sources, but this time in contrast to our experiences of this inspiration in the second scene of Act I, we now understand what is inspiring us. We now risk faith in this new experience. We are indeed participating in continuous creation—but now of the fundamentally new that is also fundamentally better—with the creator of the core drama of life who also created us in that image, namely as creators.

But it is not enough to be inspired and to understand our transforming task. We need now to enter the second scene of Act III to test this new inspiration. We not only feel deeply moved but we understand consciously, critically, creatively, and caringly what it is that we can and need to do together with the deepest source of our being and with our neighbors in order to bring about a society based on justice and compassion. In this kind of participatory politics we discover in actual practice whether our new wisdom is in fact fundamentally better in resolving our present problems that have been obstacles to justice and compassion or nourishing anew the roots of such already discovered fruitful outcomes.[35]

Transformation never turns us into the great one, the all-wise one, who can solve all problems for everyone. Act III is never "the" final act of wisdom and salvation. No transformational outcome is perfect or absolutely better, but it is fundamentally better than what existed before in understanding, compassionate love and justice as demonstrated by actual testing with our neighbors. It cannot be imposed on others through revolutionary violence. No one can be coerced into transformation. . . .

What we need now in order to complete our present journey in Act III, Scene 2 are not leaders and followers, not gurus and disciples but guides. Our best beginning now is to be a living example of the experience of the journey of transformation, not simply of its conclusion at this moment but to personally and politically enact our new wisdom by implementing a passion for justice. We are now capacitated to guide others through this same journey and help them to realize when their vision and practice leaves them partial and wounded human beings. We cannot understand how to love our neighbor with a new and better kind of justice until we have come to understand and love ourselves.[36]

For example, a surgeon participating in transformation who has thus learned how to love himself or herself, in addition to operating on our body to overcome our pain, will also ask and seek help to answer: Why did this pain arise? Did someone beat or infect you? What can we do to prevent this from happening again? Will you neglect yourself or be neglected by others when you get home? Do you have enough income to pay me and to nourish yourself? What can we do about these vital matters with the patient and with others competent in their specialties but also in collaborating to deal with the whole problem in order to restore wholeness of being? We need competent surgeons—yes, but also wise and compassionate doctors who love himself or herself and thus also their neighbors— enacting justice based on compassionate love through all four faces of their being.[37]

The fundamentally new and better cannot come from our current cultural stories or religious institutions if they inspire us only to a life in which we fantasize about eternal truth given once for all or about power to control others or absolute power over the life and death of those others, the outsiders. We need to turn to the deepest sacred source in order to shape a more compassionate and inclusive world. Our participation as sons and daughters of the deepest sacred is necessary to transform the personal, political, historical, and sacred faces of our lives.

To journey through the story of transformation is the vocation to which all of us are called. The way of life of transformation provides the only context within which Latinas and Latinos can express the wholeness of our being. But the deepest source is free to continuously re-create the world only when people like you and me are prepared to personally decide to be political in order to create a new and more open and just history and when the sacred face of our being incarnates the sacred source of transformation that inspires us. Participation in persistent transformation belongs to each of us by the very nature of our humanity.

We have it in our hands as a community to create a new and transforming cultura Latina in this country as political innovators, faithful partners, guides, and nurturing parents who are grounded in transformation. People like you and me give a new expression to what it means to be human by coming to know, critiquing, emptying ourselves of destructive stories and ways of life, and creating new and more compassionate stories in the service of transformation. Latinos and Latinas, people of color, women, men, and individuals from all backgrounds are manifesting the four faces of our being by making a personal decision to create new and more compassionate stories and thus reject the stories that diminish our humanity. Through our political face we can give shape to an environment in which we are free to enact what is necessary to bring about justice. Together we can create a new turning point for our nation, a new history, a new aspect of the story of democracy, multicultural diversity that is an affirmation that each of us has a sacred face. Most of us were never told that each of us by the very nature of our humanity has a personal, political, historical, and sacred face by which we shape daily life. Furthermore we were not taught to question our culture so that by critique and dialogue we could constantly renew and transform our heritage through our conscious participation. We became a part of the culture and most often lost our ability to empty ourselves of the destructive stories and partial ways of life by allowing ourselves to be made into uncritical participants who carried out pre-programmed behavior. In this way our cultura Latina took on a life of its own and we became the mere recipients of the past, rather than the persistent creators of our culture.

Now let us go on to see how in the context of daily life Latino men and Latina women connect themselves to one another and to the world around them and when and how these relationships fail to allow them to respond to new kinds of problems.

THE NINE ARCHETYPAL RELATIONSHIPS ENACTED WITHIN THE SERVICE OF FOUR DIFFERENT ARCHETYPAL WAYS OF LIFE

What constitutes our first world-wide revolution consists precisely in the breaking of the concrete, inherited manifestations of archetypal relationships and the dying of the way of life of emanation. Everywhere in the world societies and cultures founded on an ultimate truth and ways of doing things as the will of an ultimate source are being undermined and subverted. This collapse of meaning and purpose gives rise to a profound anxiety that opens up both fearful and creative possibilities.[38]

In all of our encounters between self and other in recorded history and in all societies, there are, according to the theory of transformation, only nine forms of relationship that give people like you and me the capacity to deal simultaneously with continuity and change, collaboration and conflict, and the achieving of justice. In addition each of us has of the very nature of our being human a fivefold capacity: our unconscious, our consciousness, our creativity, our linking with others, and our use of just means. These five aspects of our capacity are enacted through the nine archetypal relationships that apply to all intrapersonal, interpersonal, and intergroup relations. These nine relationships apply to all groups, from our family or affinity groups to political parties to nations or to the human species. We also connect ourselves to those forces that have been called the sacred, the unconscious, or god. We can know how others in our past have related to one another because there are only nine relationships in recorded history and in human society. You and I can test the claim that this hypothesis applies to all human experience by examining our own experiences.[39]

The theory of transformation points us to the realization that our task is to deal with constant change. Our lives are always in the process of creation, nourishment, preservation, death, and re-creation. This perpetual process of change is given shape by nine specific archetypal relationships, and they in turn are given their deeper meaning by the four archetypal ways of life in whose service we enact relationships. Practiced in the service of a particular way of life, each of our nine archetypal relationships has its own capacity to relate ourselves to self, our neighbor, problems, and the sacred.

Let us now proceed to an explanation of the nine forms of encounter enacted in the service of the four radically different ways of

life: emanation, incoherence, deformation, and transformation. To
be able to tell which relationships are allowed by a particular society
tells us what any person or group is free to express and what they are
forced to repress. No current society encourages the use of all nine
relationships and some expressly forbid the free use of all nine relationships in the service of transformation. All current human societies discourage our full human capacity.

Figure 2 is a drawing that provides us with a symbolic repre-
sentation of the nine archetypal relationships by which we shape
daily life and the four ways of life in the service of which we enact
these relationships. It is a mandala symbolizing the nine archetypal
relationships: emanation, subjection, isolation, buffering, direct bargaining, autonomy, incoherence, deformation, and transformation.
These are the patterns by which we shape daily life and act out the
stories of our lives. We encounter problems in our lives when the
concrete, inherited forms of these underlying patterns of relationship no longer give us the ability to deal with the five issues of daily,
human performance: continuity and change, collaboration and conflict, and justice. In regard to the five aspects of capacity each relationship differs in its ability to connect us to new consciousness,
creativity, linkages to others, the experience of shared justice with
others, and the ability to reach the deepest source of our being. Each
concrete form of an archetypal relationship gives us a different
ability to cope with these five issues of performance and the five aspects of capacity.

These relationships will be fully explained with examples in
this chapter and throughout the book. Our goal is to understand how
to take the concrete, inherited manifestations of these nine archetypal patterns into our own hands so that when they break we can
create new concrete combinations of these archetypal patterns that
will restore to us the capacity to respond to new problems with love
and justice.

THE TRADITIONALLY ACCEPTABLE REPERTORY OF RELATIONSHIPS AND WAY OF LIFE

Emanation

In the relationship of emanation you or I treat another person,
such as our son or wife, as an extension of our selves. If wives accept
the denial of their own separate identity because of the mysterious

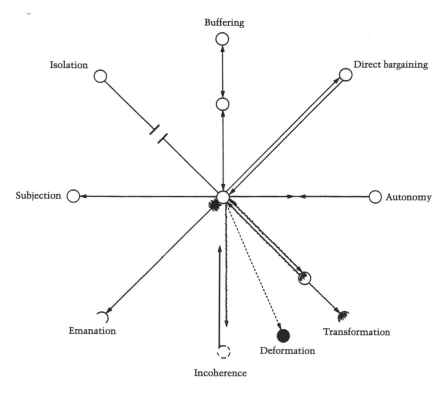

Figure 2.　Nine Archetypal Relationships Symbolized

and overwhelming power of the source of this emanation, husbands have a mysterious power over them. If women dutifully obey men in the relationship of emanation, they are rewarded with security. All of us began life as children vulnerable to the powerful others in our home. We had no choice but to yield our identity to the mysterious and overwhelming power of our mother until we felt strong enough to risk our security by freeing ourselves. However, some of our fathers or mothers want to keep us in the container of emanation, seeing their children as carbon copies of themselves, that is, as emanations of themselves. In the Latino culture when a woman marries she often transfers the relationship of emanation with her father to her husband. It could be said that she never left home. Others treat their property or their employees in this way. Many individuals remain eager to surrender themselves as loyal extensions of a political movement, a dogma, or a lover.[40]

The relationship of emanation is the most prevalent and, perhaps, the most powerful relationship in the Latino community to
this day. It points out an unexamined, unconscious, uncritical relationship to a mysterious and overwhelming source that contains us
and within which we live inherited stories. Indeed we are not even
conscious of archetypal stories. We see the relationship of emanation practiced by many Latino men who see women and their children as a mere extension of themselves. Moreover, they see themselves as the expression of their father's personality. Most Latino
men and Latina women were raised in inherited stories, especially
patriarchy and matriarchy, and believe that their lives are determined by their fathers or mothers. What was good enough for our
mothers and fathers is good enough for us. Given this perspective,
change cannot possibly arise.

Many Latina women and Latino men agree to be passive to repress conflict. No other relationship among the nine offers us as
much security as emanation. Many are tempted to remain in its embrace in order to avoid participating freely in conflict and change.
Thus we submerge our lives and live as an extension or shadow of an
other: father, uncle, mother, husband, or brother. But the relationship of emanation is not in itself destructive. The relationship of
emanation can be enacted in profoundly different ways that are determined by which of four different ways of life it serves. For example, in the service of transformation, emanation can be used temporarily to nurture the young; in this way the flow of emanation can
be redirected to allow for emergence rather than containment. This
is why it is necessary for us always to ask the question: "In the service of what way of life am I practicing the stories, four faces of my
being, and relationships of my life?"

Subjection

In the relationship of subjection both parties such as myself
and my father are fully present, but in reality both of us are denied a
full presence and an identity of our own. The relationship is still unequal; it still rests upon the experience of overwhelming power. But
this power, which was mysterious in emanation, becomes naked in
subjection. I now clearly see that my father makes the decisions
about my life and he also recognizes this fact. We both realize how
the denial of access to money controls my life in his efforts to keep
me under control.[41] We see subjection being enacted when Latino
men, husbands, fathers, and sons command women as their birth-

right. It is a father or husband controlling the spending of the family's finances. Subjection exists whenever I control others as a means to my end. In subjection, conflict is no longer repressed but suppressed. In the wider society Latinas and Latinos are in turn subjected by the powerful. They often cannot be themselves by speaking their mother tongue and telling the stories of their heritage. Rules defined by the dominant culture tell us how to behave. The powerful everywhere often combine emanation and subjection when relating to the less powerful. Newly arrived Latinas and Latinos are prepared to show authority figures in this country a traditional respect and they retain their fear of being hurt by the powerful. The dominant group controls the society by determining continuity and change in accordance with what is necessary to preserve their power. Latinas and Latinos are aware of having little or no power to step forward and initiate change. Getting along in the society at large is based on the rules of the game defined solely by the powerful. Justice in the relationship of subjection consists of a harsh message: even now in order to survive the majority of Latinas and Latinos need to accept the supremacy of power of the white male. This lack of power in the wider society is what often leads to a more desperate use of the relationship of subjection at home on the part of Latino men who are compensating for their humiliation at the hands of other, more powerful males.

Buffering

This is a relationship in which conflict and change are managed by mediators. Buffering is carried out by a mediator, broker, or by a concept.[42] Buffering is very important in la comunidad Latina. *Madrinas*, godmothers, and *padrinos*, godfathers, are very important mediators for young people as they seek to break away from the oppressive hold of their parents. As in all patriarchal societies, Latinos and Latinas use buffering to create conflict and change in a culturally acceptable manner by having others, who are seen as the peers of their parents, intervene on their behalf. In this way directly questioning or contradicting of our parents is avoided. To directly challenge a parent is considered a sin. Justice in buffering allows us to obtain a better outcome through the intervention of an aunt or grandmother. Thus godparents, a teacher, or a member of the clergy are able to win considerable exceptions for children from the strict rules of the family. When Latinas and Latinos take their place as adults in the community they become sources of emanational authority and thereby participate themselves as buffers on behalf of others. In this way the next generation is lamed by the relationship of buffering in the service of emanation, a relationship that is intended to perpetuate the dependency of the young and the power of authority, especially male authority. For generations the freedom of Latina women and children relied on the ability and skill of the mediator. Buffering became a central relationship to maintain male dominance. As a result men and women were and continue to be deprived of the ability to confront problems face to face.

Isolation

Isolation is a relationship that Latina women who live in emanational relationships to Latino men were forbidden to practice. In this relationship, two people or groups agree to leave each other alone. Both sides agree to avoid any conflict that would lead to change between them. In this case justice means a degree of freedom, the right to be left alone. But both parties need to agree not to bring about any change in the other. Isolation cannot be achieved alone. The other must agree to cooperate.[43] If a Latina woman or Latino man says, "You leave me alone," she or he is attempting to practice the relationship of isolation in order to avoid conflict and change. But if one or the other does not agree and comes knocking on your door demanding that you come out and speak, then this is not isolation but rather incoherence, two people who cannot agree on how to relate. Instead of isolation, there is a consciousness of broken connections. Patriarchal fathers and matriarchal mothers who possess their children in the relationship of emanation assume that their children will always want to be near them since they are the source of power who give children love and security. Parents feel a need to control their every move and refuse to allow them isolation. Latina women who are especially denied the practice of physical isolation, use emotional detachment by which they retreat into themselves as a substitute for not being able to physically withdraw. Fathers and husbands are quick to challenge a moody withdrawal and see it as a threat to their sense of control.

Direct Bargaining

In the relationship of direct bargaining, a daughter and mother agree to allow conflict in order to bring about change with each other directly. Justice consists in the better bargain that one side or the other may achieve, but both agree with the result of the bargain. This relationship allows a Latino male, in relationship to his father, or a Latina woman, resisting her husband or father, the right to advance their self-determination by struggling with one another to gain a more advantageous bargain and thereby change the balance of power between that person and themselves.[44]

By means of gifts or favors, the less powerful party looks to change the balance of power by gaining bargaining leverage. In fact the one who provides a favor is implying that: "You owe me something in exchange for my gifts or good behavior." From time immemorial Latina women knew that the way to get a better deal from men was through the leverage of sex and food. In exchange for these services, their husbands often relented and allowed them favors. The use of direct bargaining in the service of emanation is one of the most effective ways to head off real transformation. When strict parents see that they are losing their control over a rebellious son or daughter, they offer a better deal within the story of patriarchy. They allow them to go to a dance but they must be home early or take a younger brother or sister as a chaperone. The strategy here is to stretch the traditional container, to provide it with elasticity so that it gives without breaking. The intent is to keep children loyal and respectful. In this way the story of patriarchal dominance is reformed, that is, we made the story bearable but without allowing the story of patriarchy to be challenged. Time and again in traditional societies anger is reduced to catharsis, emotional outbreaks that are intended to send people back to an enchanted but enchained container.

Whether the demand is for submission to the will of a father, lover, or god, each Latina and Latino in the way of life of emanation had five choices. They could entirely immerse their self and yield to becoming an extension of the other; or they could accept their subjection in response to the domination and power of the other; or they could bargain directly with the lord of emanation, or mother, wife, husband, or father, saying in each case: "In return for being loyal to you as the source of my mystery and accepting my submission, I expect something for my good behavior or I will not end my rebellion." Or if they lacked the power to bargain or refused to submit or to give in totally, they could resort to buffering, asking the mother-in-law to mediate with her son or saying the rosary to intercede with La Virgen, or using rose water with sugar to expel evil spirits or amulets to filter out el mal ojo, the evil eye. Or they could attempt one of the forbidden relationships such as isolation that was considered a form of rebellion that the powerful refused to allow as a pattern of encounter. And when we rebel against authority legitimized by "god," the lord of emanation, we are vulnerable to experiencing the relationship of deformation, violence that is intended to restore us to being obedient and respectful. This then was and still is for many Latina women and Latino men the repertory of relationships available to respond to the daily tensions of life. What held the whole world together was the overarching sacred canopy of the way of life of emanation that embraced two hierarchical cosmologies, the indigenous and Catholic-Christian. In both worlds there is a clear chain of emanation that links participants to one common source, the sacred from on high. From the lord of emanation flows the authority that legitimizes the link between ruled and ruler, husband and wife, child and parent.

THE FORBIDDEN REPERTORY OF RELATIONSHIPS AND WAY OF LIFE

All societies or the body politic shape our ego. Through socialization the community introduces us to the *acceptable* repertory of concrete forms of the nine archetypal relationships. That is to say that not all nine forms of our archetypal relationships are everywhere seen as positive options. Consequently, people are forbidden to exercise certain patterns of relating; often we are not even aware of the existence of alternatives. The traditional way of life of emanation excluded relationships of autonomy or boundary management, isolation, incoherence, and transformation.

Autonomy

Autonomy is a relationship in which both a Latina woman and a Latino man are entitled to claim certain boundaries or autonomous zones of jurisdiction within which each of them exercises power based on education or competence. Both of them agree that justice in the relationship of autonomy is the right of each to sustain or enlarge their area of power and autonomy.[45] This relationship profoundly threatens male domination because it questions the relationships of dependency. A Latina young woman can now go to university and become a doctor or lawyer so she can achieve economic autonomy. Latino men want this relationship for themselves and for their wives when two bread winners are needed to support the family. But in our domestic relations we have often tried to deny autonomy to Latina women. In addition, to keep women dependent, when they worked outside the home, a Latina woman was required to hand over her check. In the wider U.S. society the relationship of autonomy, together with direct bargaining, is the most powerful relationship. Both patterns are necessary to survive in this country. Autonomy and direct bargaining signify the attainment of power. But this relationship can be subverted and used in the service of transformation. A competent Latina doctor can choose to use her skills and the autonomy granted to her as a physician to protect the rights of her patients rather than to enhance her own personal power. The relationship of autonomy in the service of transformation is the relationship enacted when Latinos and Latinas assert their right to organize and participate in the building of a union, a union that truly represents the rights of working women and men.

Unions in the history of Latinas and Latinos have been one of the most important means to end the relationships of subjection and isolation that hurt us in the wider society. To form a union people bargain with one another to create a relationship of autonomy leading to collective power. A union such as the United Farm Workers or the United Auto Workers gives them the capacity for the first time to participate politically in a large-scale, sustained, autonomous, and coordinated public institution. To create a union that works on explicit legal principles allows its members to protect themselves against those boundary managements or the autonomous zones of power of the large corporations that took advantage of unorganized workers and oppressed them.

Labor unions can and have been corrupted from within by bosses who betray the original democratic nature of the union and run it on relationships of emanation as a personal fiefdom through the use of the relationship of subjection. But unions do carry the potential to be used positively as organizations to achieve equal participation in the fruits of one's labor. Our lack of the relationship of autonomy helps to explain why for so long Latinas and Latinos were cheated when it came to contracts; they were paid low wages, often one half to one third of the pay given to Anglo workers. At times they accepted the word of a boss because they were living the repertory of relationships, especially emanation, wherein honor and one's good word connected persons in a common task. But we cannot count on the good intentions of the boss, seller, or landlord.

Those who control the institutions of power monopolize the relationship of autonomy to prevent others from becoming potential competitors. We need to remember that this is taking place within the story of capitalism in the service of incoherence where all that matters is power. Power is power because it is not shared and because the powerful make it a scarce commodity for those on the bottom. In this way of life characterized by constant rebellion by those below against those who are above them, there can be no room for justice and compassion. This is why we need the relationship of buffering practiced by the federal government using its great power within its use of the relationship of autonomy to create change on behalf of those who cannot protect themselves. The fight over Affirmative Action is all about redrawing the boundaries that the powerful want to preserve for their own kind.

Why Organizers Fail is a study of a rent strike and analysis of its failure.[46] The Chicana women and Chicano men involved found it difficult to confront Anglos who were relating from a position of power based on explicit principles set down in contracts that were weighted in favor of those who drew up the contract. They also failed to organize different groups in the community for united action. The African Americans did not trust the Chicanos because they thought that they were too weak, or, in our terms, did not have a sense of individual or group autonomy with which to confront Anglo bureaucrats. It is one thing to ask people to organize around common problems, but it is still another to ask them to let go of relationships enacted within a way of life that still holds them and to enact relationships that are foreign to them.

Incoherence

In the relationship of incoherence a Latina woman and a Latino man face each other in the same place and at the same time but are unable to agree on how to relate. Incoherence is the painful recognition that the relationships that had previously connected them— emanation, subjection, buffering, and direct bargaining—are now broken. It is the experience of discontinuity rather than continuity, of change that is unintended and uncontrolled. It is conflict because they cannot agree on any form of cooperation, leading to injustice for both self and other.[47] All of the inherited relationships which had previously connected them to each other are broken: she refuses to continue to relate to him as if he is the source of her mystery in emanation; she will no longer obey him as he commands her in subjection to stop her rebellion; she defiantly rejects the relationship of buffering that allows him to use his mother-in-law to persuade her to come home or to rationalize that "All Latino men are like me" as he attempts to disarm her anger; she no longer is willing to bargain with him by allowing him to give her gifts or to make promises of a better life; and she also refuses to consider his betrayal as the basis for getting concessions because of any guilt that he feels. Both stand in the presence of each other and cannot agree on how to relate, hence the relationship of incoherence.

What deepens the incoherence are acts of freedom: going to school, getting a job, going out alone without his consent. When they realize that they are losing, some Latino men accept the fact that a Latina woman can use the relationship of autonomy in the wider society but, when it comes to their home life, they are usually against sharing the decision making. Also it makes it more acceptable because they are giving their wives permission to work or go to school as an attempt to subvert their freedom. When confrontations take place Latina women are entering into the process of transformation: they listen to their own inner voice in Act I, Scene 2; then enter into rebellion in Act II, Scene 1 in which they break with those who are trying to keep them in Act I, Scene 1; they are now moving toward transformation. But if they are to free themselves not only from this marriage but from the underlying story of patriarchy and the way of life of emanation that gave husbands their mysterious power over them, then they need to break on a deeper level in Act II, Scene 2, by emptying themselves of the stories, relationships, and the ways of life that held them as possessed women.

Once they have emptied themselves of the stories of patriarchy and uncritical loyalty and the way of life of emanation they are now free to create new and better stories and relationships in the service of transformation. In Act III, Scene 1, they have created the story of the transforming self. For the first time they know who they are as they come forth as a person. And now with the political and historical faces of their being they can reach out to others like their children and friends to become a guide in Act III, Scene 2, as they assist others. Latina women who choose transformation dramatically change the four faces of their being. Their personal face emerges in wholeness. They experience themselves for the first time as a person who can live without being dependent and helpless; their political face practices a politics of compassion, inclusion, and justice as they work to help young women and men experience the fullness of their lives; they create a different and open history by putting in place a new and better story. With their sacred face they become co-creators with the sacred source of transformation to bring about the more loving and just in all aspects of life.

Deformation

Deformation is the relationship that is enacted when a person makes a decision to use violence that diminishes the humanity of himself or others. Societies still bound by tradition legitimize violence in order to maintain order. The officially sanctioned use of violence by a whole culture preserves the status quo. The dominant see their life and everything they stand for disintegrating; they want to punish the rebels. Men and women lamed by the inability to see life anew are unable to respond to new demands on the part of their citizens, workers, daughters, sons, or neighbors. But we have a choice. We are pulled in two fundamentally opposed directions; on the one hand, we can choose to create new and better relationships or we can try to crush those who challenge our privileged status. The latter choice brings us to use the relationship of deformation, for example, people who resort to violence because they do not know what to do in a world where their authority is questioned. But from the very moment they turn to violence, the relationship of deformation puts them on the road to destructive death in the way of life of deformation. Emanation as a way of life colludes with deformation as a way of life through its readiness to turn to violence whenever anybody questions its ultimate truth. Because deformation attempts to restore the past, it is often confused with emanation. Deformation carries an overwhelming and mysterious power. It is pseudo-emanational, a fake emanation, in the guise of emanation that can possess us. The relationship of deformation connects us to a demonic sacred source and moves us toward destructive death in key aspects of our life.[48] This relationship is often used when the relationships of emanation, subjection, buffering, and direct bargaining no longer work to uphold traditional authority. It is the use of violence as an attempt to force people back to the old relationships.

Fortunately, we can be inspired to break with archetypal relationships, empty ourselves of destructive archetypal stories, and the partial ways of life of emanation, incoherence, and deformation. But that requires our connecting to a more powerful sacred source, the deepest source of transformation. Only this sacred source is powerful enough to help us to empty ourselves of both the concrete and the archetypal bonds that are now enchaining us.

Transformation

The relationship of transformation connects us to the drama of transformation and to our deepest source. We no longer need external sources of emanation like our father or mother as our ultimate source of truth. We do not reject our loved ones but rediscover them in a new way. People like you and me are now conscious of those sources in the depths that constitute the archetypal ways of life and the stories of our lives. To enact this relationship is to participate in creating fundamentally new and better dramas and relationships. We can create, nourish, and end relationships that no longer help us to achieve justice; we can recreate new forms of relationships to deal with new problems; we can woo new combinations into being.[49] In Act III, Scene 1, Latina women and Latino men, connected to their deepest source are inspired by a new vision of how to shape life by enacting the story of the transforming self. In the second scene of Act III, they reach out to assist others as guides. And this newfound wholeness enables us to enact not only all nine relationships but an infinite number of concrete manifestations of each relationship. We create, nourish, and destroy in order to create and transform time and again.

ARCHETYPAL RELATIONSHIPS IN THE SERVICE
OF FOUR WAYS OF LIFE

As was stated earlier, the nine archetypal relationships do not stand alone. Each of the nine archetypal relationships in their concrete manifestations derive their deeper meaning and value from a wider context, a whole way of life, either that of emanation, incoherence, deformation, or transformation. The four ways of life determine the quality of our stories and relationships; consequently, archetypal relationships are neither negative nor creative in themselves. But the relationship of transformation can never be used in the service of emanation, incoherence, or deformation; it is always to the good. Can the relationship of deformation ever be enacted in the service of transformation or is it always destructive? No, the relationship of deformation can be used in the service of transformation but only when we do not initiate the violence against others. We may hurt others in as limited a form as possible solely in order to protect our lives and that of others. We need to look for ways to disarm the aggressor, capture him or her, and resort to deadly force only if other measures have failed. The use of the relationship of deformation in the service of emanation, incoherence, and deformation is always negative because violence is intended in emanation to preserve the only truth against non-believers—the infidels both within and without—to protect our power in incoherence, and to maintain ultimate power over the life and death of others in the way of deformation.

Thus the quality, the ultimate meaning, of the archetypal relationships is given to them by the way of life in which we choose to enact them. We need to ask the question: "In the service of what way of life am I practicing the relationships and stories of my life?" For example, we usually assume the relationship of subjection is negative. But subjection in the service of transformation is necessary when we forbid a child to light matches because the intent is to protect their life and the lives of others. Subjection in the service of emanation is the use of the relationship to force somebody to remain in the container as an extension of somebody else. In the service of incoherence, subjection is used to dominate others as a means to our own end. Subjection in the service of deformation is enacted to put a person in fear for their lives because he or she is considered a threat to the powerful. In the chapters that follow I shall give many examples of the use of the nine archetypal relationships and how they are enacted in the service of different ways of life. Emanation, incoherence, deformation, and transformation as archetypal relationships differ from emanation, incoherence, deformation, and transformation as whole ways of life. We shall always specify which we mean, the relationship or the entire way of life.

Practicing the Four Faces of Our Being in the Service of Transformation

Each of us has a personal, political, historical, and sacred face, but only in the service of transformation can we fully experience and express the four faces of our being. The process of transformation takes place first of all in our individual depths, our personal face. Only a person can choose to be political. Our personal face is necessary as we choose to be political to bring about a new turning point in the creation of a new history; the deepest source of our being connects to the sacred face of our being and inspires us to bring about new forms of justice and compassion. The four faces of our being are always present and we ignore any one of them at our

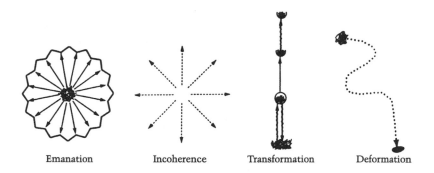

| Emanation | Incoherence | Transformation | Deformation |

Figure 3.   Four Archetypal Ways of Life Symbolized

peril. We need to reach beyond our personal lives to the political and historical networks that severely limit our capacity.

> From the perspective of transformation as a way of life, our personal face is not simply subjective or just our own self. It is the face of our being that is in each human being truly unique. It is also the face that has the capacity to free us to participate with the deepest sacred source of our being—a reality we shall be exploring throughout this book. And that being, like ours, needs to augment and fulfill itself by engaging also in critical, creative, compassionate and just participation politically and historically.[50]

To resist the racism that erases the humanity of our personal face requires us to struggle against structural deformation in the society that continues to cripple us and others. We need to enact the political face of our being by asking always what we can and need to do together with our neighbors in order to liberate ourselves from the dramas practiced by our culture and the wider society that wound us.

> Our political face is expressed by what we can and need to do together with each other in creating a more just history, all of us together with the sacred. The "political" therefore does not, as we commonly believe, refer only to official competition for public power and for the advantages of power. It includes loving, playing, meditating, learning, teaching, producing, consuming,

risking trust in testing new inspirations in actual practice, and connecting with others in order to bring fundamentally new and better kinds of friendship, joy, beauty, compassionate love, wisdom, and justice into being. Thus every relationship and every drama in which we participate is political. The theory and practice of transformation thus puts into question the roots and branches of politics now and also its scarce and diminished fruits and its possessive and exclusionary harvests.[51]

We make history by enacting the historical face of our being and creating a new turning point by struggling with both the immediate concrete tyranny and its underlying forming source.

Our historical face is constituted by the living inheritance of dramas and ways of life that arose in the past and that continue to move us through the present into the future. If our past no longer nourishes us and confines our vision and our capacity, we can also create turning points into a different future—historical turning points therefore also in the personal, political, and sacred face of our being.[52]

To cast out demons in our personal lives and society by political action means that we have freed our sacred face from the lesser lords and connected to the deepest sacred source of transformation.

Our sacred face? We all experience and express the sacred face of our being whether we are believers, agnostics, atheists, or those participating in transforming their lives, whether we are conscious of it or not. We experience it most strongly and particularly as the process of creativity, as courage, as deep attraction and caring, as commitment to justice even in the face of threats from others, as various forms of hate or love. All these are experiences that cannot be fully put into words. Our sacred face in different ways of life may be expressed in the words or fervor of dogma or of deep skepticism or of exclusive commitment to rationality or outward formulas, which by themselves alone cannot fully explain such a commitment to either dogma or rationality. Our sacred face is also the channel at every moment from and to the living underlying patterning forces of our life.[53]

ARCHETYPAL ANALYSIS: IN THE SERVICE OF WHAT
WAY OF LIFE AM I DOING WHAT I AM DOING

The description of the theory of transformation provided above gives us the tools to participate in archetypal analysis. At every moment of our lives we are somewhere in the core drama of life, in one of its acts and scenes, living stories, enacting the nine relationships, and practicing the four faces of our being in the service of one of the four ways of life. When we do archetypal analysis we realize that the concrete stories and relationships and the four faces of our being are manifestations of deeper, underlying sacred forming sources that we call archetypes. We know only the surface, the concreteness of life, when we describe the external reality of our daily life. To get to the deeper underlying meaning we ask the question: "In the service of what way of life am I practicing the stories and relationships and the four faces of my being?" The answer to this question tells us where we are in the core drama of life. We learn what stories and relationships we are practicing and whether we are enacting stories, relationships, and the four faces of our being in their fullness or arresting our lives in fragments of the core drama as a partial self.

Our task as Latinas and Latinos is to learn through archetypal analysis how to actually live and practice transformation by choosing to live stories, relationships, and the four faces of our being as loving manifestations of our deepest source. Our participation in the life and death of the stories and ways of life that possessed us and the resurrection of fundamentally more loving and just sacred stories that we never practiced before is the meaning of justice relevant for our times. The old stories and ways of life needed our involvement to remain alive and active. By withdrawing from them, we deny them life. By personally and politically allying ourselves to the deepest source of transformation we can participate in making transformation concretely alive and present in all aspects of our lives. This is our new won freedom in Act III, Scenes 1 and 2, not only to choose among existing archetypal dramas but also to create new ones that will do justice to ourselves, to others, and to the deepest source. For example, by creating neighborhood centers that serve the young, the sick, the unemployed, and the elderly and by changing the parameters of what we can and need to do together, we have shaped a new historical path. Breaking inherited patterns that condemned people to docility and silence and replacing them with new and better ways of relating to each other enables the community to participate in the decisions that affect their lives.

Strategies of transformation emphasize creating new and better relationships and stories we can share in all aspects of life. What would the fundamentally new and better be like? Imagine a situation in which we would not see the poor and discriminated against as potential threats to our political and economic position or future but as opportunities if our tax money and our joint political action enlarged their opportunities in life. What would the new and fundamentally better be like? Now we cannot even imagine such a society. Why? Because we feel that our present being, our own position, however better than theirs, is only a fragile fragment of life. We are made anxious by the thought of still more competition by people unlike us. We need first of all to free ourselves to see ourselves and others as fellow human beings and to care for ourselves and others as fellow human beings. To express our fundamentally new understanding and courage to engage in the experience of transformation, we hope to inspire others by our example and our helping hand to share the fullness of life with us and to remove the barriers that stand in the way.

Only in the service of transformation is our capacity—our unconscious, consciousness, creativity, linking with others, and our use of just means—kept in lively tension with the changing realities of life, for in the way of life of transformation, the concrete realization of transformation is never experienced as a final solution. To enter into the relationship of transformation becomes the final moment of a particular turn in the process of transformation. Nourishing this new experience of transformation will inevitably reveal new suffering and threats and new joys and opportunities. To live in the service of transformation is therefore persistently to experience an archetypal process of breaking relationships, moving into incoherence, and entering anew into the relationship of transformation.[54]

Let us proceed now to apply theory to practice as we respond to the following questions: "Where did Latina women and Latino men get caught? How and why did they lose their way? What are the strategies that will be necessary for us to practice so that we can rediscover the deeper capacity of who we are and change our lives for the better?" This theory can help us understand how the four faces of our being, the relationships, and the stories being lived by us as Latina women and Latino men are being used creatively or destructively. What is so compelling and truthful regarding this theory is that people like you and me can live it and test it with our own experiences. The theory of transformation helps us to make sense of our lives, and to see how the whole of our experiences hang together.

2. The Search for Latina/Latino Identity

> To keep people out of trouble, keep them out of themselves.
> —*J. J. Rousseau*

To be a self, and to have an identity rooted in one's selfhood beyond the socialized self in the best of situations, is never a given but a problem and a struggle to be resolved. A Latina/ Latino identity is presently being created out of the elements of our past with our present conditions serving as the catalyst. To choose to be a self and a Latina/Latino is a twofold political act; both are acts of resistance against a system based on the anti-self and against a dominant society and culture that wants us all to be "white" or devoid of our color and consciousness. We need to grow our own racial and ethnic identity, our own Latina and Latinohood.

Going Home

One of my earliest memories of being a Mexican, a Chicano, a Latino, was a profoundly sad and terrifying experience. Across the street and down the block a fight between a Mexican man and a white patron in a bar had spilled out into the street. The Mexican man was bleeding; he staggered to the front of the tavern and began to shout: "¡Viva México!" The only thread of hope that he could grasp was his native home, his fatherland and motherland, the focal point of his identity at the moment his personhood was being assaulted. Equally impressive was the fear that it created in me. I could not have been more than five years old, and yet I distinctly remember the paranoia I felt that others would identify me with him. I wanted him to stop shouting "¡Viva México!" The whole scene is indelibly marked in my memory, especially when the siren of the

51

police car at last broke the murmur of the crowd and increased the man's appeals to Mexico. When they took him away I was relieved.

I knew instinctively even then that Mexicans were supposed to disappear into the anonymity of the city. Anything that made us stand out in bold relief, such as a Mexican man shouting with grief and pain, made us all uneasy. Nobody had given me, as a preschool child, talks about American society, the melting pot, or Anglo-Saxon values. They did not have to. My self and others like me received the message in a thousand nonverbal ways: differences in food, clothing, language, and a sense of fear that we did not belong. I wanted to be like them and was amazed by their cars, large beautiful homes, expensive clothes, and orderly lives.

Many years later in Mexico I learned that although I had become a university professor, I was still considered a *pocho*, an Americanized Mexican born in the United States, a displaced person with no real culture or homeland. This experience is similar to that of Puerto Ricans from the mainland who are called *Nuyorican* by their relatives on the island. There is a critical struggle going on over the identity of the Mexican and other Latino communities that is rooted in ambivalence. In small museums in the states of Puebla and Querétaro in Mexico there is evidence of a deep anti-European, anti-Catholic sentiment. Local artists depict the Aztec and Mayan warriors as the romantic heroes of a pre-Columbian past. The Indian, in plumed headdress, conquers the blue-eyed, blonde, bearded Spaniard, knocking him from his horse. In Mexico the year 1973 was officially designated as "El Año de Juarez." Juarez was of Indian descent: dark skin, dark eyes, black hair, and stocky. In Peru and Bolivia, as well as in Mexico and Puerto Rico, local *curanderos*, healers, still resist the Catholic faith by performing their sacred rituals after five hundred years of Catholic, European hegemony. And yet the social, economic, and political reality of Mexico, as of all other Latin American nations, is just the opposite. It is the Europeanized, Catholic, white groups that dominate economically, politically, and socially. Throughout Latin America the advertisers use *rubios* and *rubias*, blonde men and women, for their models. The middle class refers to the peasants as *inditos*, primitive and backward children. In Argentina, Uruguay, and Paraguay the descendants of British, Italian, and German settlers do not identify themselves with the Spanish-speaking indigenos or mestizos. In Brazil there are reports that the government, through its Bureau of Indian Affairs, followed a policy of genocide against the Indians in the Amazon region. Rigoberta Menchú Túm, the heroine of the Quiché Maya Indians of Guatemala who won the Nobel Peace Prize in 1992 has been an outspoken opponent of the government of Guatemala over its treatment of its indigenous people. In Mexico, the Zapatistas rose up against the government in 1994 and asked for land and justice and captured the imagination of the nation by highlighting the age-old racism practiced against the indigenous people of Mexico.

In Venezuela there has been a serious split in the country between the business class and the followers of President Hugo Chávez who is an avowed socialist. An oil strike that lasted for months and wrecked the economy was led by the opposition that took power by means of a coup that lasted only a few days. The majority of the people rallied to support Chávez. The country has been on the verge of civil war and there have been a series of proposals made to avert a conflict, notably one set forth by former president Jimmy Carter. On August 15, 2004, a record number of voters turned out to defeat a recall election to remove Chávez, who confidently prepared to run again in 2006. It is important to note that there is not only a class issue here but also one of race. The professional and business middle class is known as *mantuanos*, whites, and the peasant and working class are primarily *pardos*, Indians. Despite the five hundred years since the Conquest one of the most important stories remains the drama of tribalism within which the European element of the country continues to consider itself superior to the indigenous people and the mestizos, or those of mixed blood.[1] "An Indian is coming into the Palace" was the warning call from guards whenever an Aymara-Quechua indigenous person was seen approaching the palace in La Paz, Bolivia. There is now a rebellion against light-skinned elites who are more connected to their European roots. From Argentina to Venezuela there is an awakening taking place by the dark-skinned mulattos, *pardos*, *caboclas*, or Indians. An amazing emergence of indigenous power is taking place in the Bolivian Congress that is now almost 50 percent indigenous.[2]

The examples given above are classic examples of how the story of capitalism in the service of incoherence colludes with the story of racism in the service of deformation. The business and upper classes of Latin America have an intense dislike and contempt for the indigenous people in their countries. The Conquest and its attitudes are very much alive. It is their economic interests coupled with racism that have led the middle class to disassociate themselves from their own people. Rigoberta Menchú said it best in her acceptance speech for the Nobel Prize when she spoke of the rights and concern for "the future of more than 60 million Indians that live in our Americas, and their outcry because of the 500 years of oppression that they have endured. For the genocide beyond comparison that they have had to suffer throughout this epoch, and from which other countries and the elites of the Americas have profited and taken advantage."[3] The economic penetration of all Latin America that began in earnest in the second half of the nineteenth century perpetuated to this day a class structure that has caused a great gap between European and Mestizo/Indian or Amerindian, rich and poor. The wealthy have no desire to be identified with an indigenous culture, so they create a culture based on consumption.

There has been a virulent racism in Latin America from its inception as the insistence on *limpieza de sangre*, purity of blood, by the Inquisition shows. Although this policy was aimed at Jews and Moriscos (Spanish Muslims), it inevitably was extended to the indigenous population of Latin America and still later to African slaves.[4] In some instances, as in Puerto Rico, the Indian Taíno Arawak population was completely decimated by a combination of disease, warfare, hunger, and slavery. The intermarriage that followed the conquest of Latin America was an unavoidable necessity. The Church insisted on blessing these unions, but it proved to be more of a forced wedding than a blending of cultures, religions, and peoples.

The "converted" Jews and Moriscos that found their way to the New World in spite of the Inquisition became an integral part of Latin American society. Some Jewish converts took the Christian name of "de la Cruz" (of the Cross) to emphasize the extent of their loyalty to the new faith. To this day, in places such as Santiago, Chile, important families with the name "de la Cruz" are the descendants of these converts. All Latina women and Latino men in the U.S. are a combination of various indigenous groups, with Spanish, Portuguese, African, Muslim, and Jewish blood in their veins.[5] With all of these elements of blood and spirit combined in the crucible of his or her life, the Latina and the Latino remain in search of an identity.[6]

The Spain of *Los Reyes Católicos* (the Catholic rulers, Ferdinand and Isabella) was a nation unified by blood and the cross. The Basques and Catalans still revive ancient nationalistic feuds. In their campaign against the Jews and Moriscos, especially in Andalucía, Isabella and Ferdinand destroyed one of the oldest centers of cultural creativity. This was the land of the Kabbalistic Jews and of Sufi poets and philosophers such as I'bn Arabi. Some of these displaced peoples came to the New World to build new lives. They were among the soldiers, adventurers, and settlers who brought down the Inca, Mayan, and Aztec empires. African people were brought as slaves to the Caribbean and the eastern areas of South and Central America. They also intermarried and brought their religion and beliefs to the New World. All of these diverse elements were held together, at least on the surface, by European military might. The emergence of the coalition among peasants, intellectuals, and liberals during the wars of national liberation in the early part of the nineteenth century broke the European political tyranny. Unfortunately, it was quickly followed by European and American economic and cultural dominance. The old patterns of cultural behavior based on Mediterranean and Indian values of honor, respect, and deference to authority were devastating to a population faced with aggressive individualists committed to rationally organized economies and the logic of free enterprise. The native middle class became middle class precisely because it assimilated into the European prototype of the self-made man. The business class learned how to enact the relationships of autonomy and direct bargaining that were necessary to survive in the market economy of capitalism. It became the privileged buffer between their people and the international market economy. The industrialization that began in Latin America at the end of the nineteenth century further displaced indigenous cultural values. The behavioral patterns of the rural areas, especially the traditional relationships of emanation and subjection, were seen as signs of weakness. To survive one had to learn how to be aggressively independent, forthright, *listo*, an individual without the fetters of personal shame.

There is a sense of solitude at the core of our selfhood. As Octavio Paz has written, "We get drunk to confess what lurks in our depths, the white society drinks to forget itself."[7] No one should be fooled by the polite deference manifested in smiles, "Sí, Señor," and the stereotype of the Josés and Marías; these are but ritualized avoidances that hide unresolved feelings of anger and rage. A cultural habit of avoiding direct confrontation by practicing the relationship of buffering has led us to repress our angry feelings, chew them, swallow them, but they remain eating away at our insides.

As we look around we have to wonder how many of us are part of the problem. Have not all of us to some extent been taken over and become supporters of a system of human relations based on power that ultimately divides us and absorbs us? Hobbes told us over three hundred years ago that our identities were being shaped, not by our value as a person, but by our class standing, power, prestige, and possessions. We all live in the belly of the whale and we

need to learn how to be in the story of capitalism in the service of incoherence and not be devoured by it. This strategy of being simultaneously an insider and an outsider, being in the system but not of it,
will be taken up in chapter 7.

Latinas and Latinos have partially maintained their language,
religion, and culture, although we are constantly reminded of how
much we have lost. We are in a diaspora: we belong nowhere. Many
of us after several generations in this country do not want to go
home to our native land but we are not content here, so we try to belong by joining the powerful through assimilating. And we see the
real sin of racism: white people who forgot who they were forced
others to forget who they are. We were made dull, we were not born
dull. But we assist the process by playing the role, *jugando el papel
que el otro requiere de nosotros,* that another assigns to us.

We need to break out of the stories, the ways of life, and the relationships that bind us in a system that impoverishes all of us. The
real hope is an imaginative politics based on a people connected to
their deepest source. Otherwise we are doomed to perpetuate a system that is a permanent state of rebellion against others who have
more than we have and that we want to take from them. The alternative is a process of transformation that points us homeward, that
is, inward to our sources, *el tesoro de nuestra riqueza,* the treasure
chest of our riches. Latinas and Latinos are becoming aware of a profound sense of alienation from others and our selves. The possibility
of our creating a new future is problematic. I have no doubt that we
have the capacity to create ourselves anew but I am not sure if we
will take the risk. What then is the basis for concern? In the past
we blamed the Spanish conquerors, or the new intruders, the Yan-
quis, and more recently the racism and discrimination for our problems. No doubt there is some justice in this. But there is something
else in us that immobilizes us, that isolates us from others and ourselves, so that the creation of a new people is aborted by individuals
incapable of rising above their desire to be invisible and alone. The
reason for this is both cultural and historical. We know that the Indians of our heritage charted time backward and not forward. The
Mayas, for example, calculated 300,000 years into the past but calculated no further into the future than twenty years. Every two decades the world was doomed to end. Time was cyclical, and each
person was connected to the cycles of death and rebirth. The arrival
of the Spaniards and the Conquest destroyed this cyclical understanding of time by imposing upon it linear time. There followed a
series of political, economic, and social upheavals that postponed a

radical analysis and response to the Conquest. There was evangelization, urbanization, the beginnings of industrialization, wars of national liberation, and the arrival of the international political economy, especially in the form of the American businessman. All of these events prevented us from resolving the issues of our own identity until recent years.

We have survived in this country and in our own homelands. Yet this survival has often been at great cost and some have gone underground to work within the system to wait for a better day. There are times when we are aware that our isolation really masks a gnawing fear that we are powerless. I have heard countless times an analysis of what is going on with a scathing rhetoric. But when there is no action to follow it up, cynicism or fatalism sets in: "Well, what are you going to do? That's the way life is; the rich always get what they want and we will always be on the bottom." These rationalizations are a form of buffering that attempts to deflect our overt acts of docility. This type of rebellion actually means that the system has won. While we outsmart the dominant in our minds, the real masters are reinforced in their belief about our inferiority because of our alleged docility. True, the master needs the slave for his services, but subtly the slave needs the master for his own identity. When we get angry, we engage in periodic paroxysms of rebellion. The system responds to these outbreaks in a classic manner: it enacts the relationship of subjection and then when we are subdued, the powerful practice the relationship of direct bargaining by buying us off with consumer goods that send us back to our solitude. By allowing ourselves to be bought off, we respond to the logic of the system and become mere rebels, since our response is dictated by the consciousness of the system. The powerful will give us all the catharsis we want, that is, allowing us to purge our emotions, blow off steam, get it all out as long as we do not work for real change in our own lives and in the society around us. This kind of emoting usually ends with strengthening the system, that is, the perpetuation of the stories and ways of life that hold us as partial selves. The dominant fear is that people of color will form liberated zones of autonomy, new forms of boundary management in the service of transformation that link people of color and people of good will in a common cause by which to bring about systemic and structural change that betters their lives.

In *One Hundred Years of Solitude* Gabriel García Márquez writes an epic story of Latin America seen through the life of a family, the Buendías. There is plenty of action: thirty-two revolutions, lovemaking, death, mass murder, birth, all of the elements of the drama of life and history. Yet nothing really changes for the characters; at the heart of the issue is a deadly solitude that permanently lames the individuals. All of the main characters die alone, incapable ultimately of sharing their life with others. The novel ends with the final obliteration of Macondo, the fictional city founded in the heart of the jungle. Just before Macondo is blown off the face of the earth by a biblical hurricane, the last survivor of the Buendía family is reading the Sanskrit manuscripts that contain the key to the future of the family. As he reads the parchment he is blown away and with him the memory of Macondo and all its inhabitants, all condemned to death because they never lived. The author concludes with this powerful statement: "Races condemned to one hundred years of solitude did not have a second opportunity on earth."[8] This is not simply death, but total and absolute annihilation with no possibility of new life to redeem it.

Creating the alternative is the most difficult task of our unfinished story. It is not enough to analyze what does not work and to participate in deconstructing; we need to offer alternatives that are new and better. In this task I would like to return to some of our most intuitive people: our intellectuals, artists, poets, and playwrights. This is a crucial strategy because so many of our social scientists, theologians, and philosophers who have suffered from an inferiority complex bred by years of being *nadie*, nobody, have too often turned elsewhere for their theories and insights. The majority of Latina and Latino scholars spend too much time studying the works of Western European and North American social scientists. Seldom do we rely on our own insights and experiences. We are always concerned about how mainstream intellectuals will evaluate our work. We need to free ourselves to refer to the contribution of the indigenous pre-Columbian stories of our people that tell us of universal symbols of nourishment, destruction, and creation by which we can build a new and more just culture.

What we continue to search for is a universalism that exists in the indigenous vision. We look again for the beginning of a new age that the Caribs, Mayas, Aztecs, and Incas initially saw in the landing of Columbus. Our indigenous forebearers shared with the rest of humanity a belief that the whole of creation participated in a cosmic process of creation, nourishment, and destruction so that the next generation might renew our lives and the earth. There lives in the consciousness of the Latina and the Latino the impending sense of the new world that was promised by the gods. The new world arrived but brought with it a system of oppression for the people.

Under the surface of disappointment is a response that threatens to arrest our journey of transformation by an escape into solitude and invisibility that exacerbates our incoherence. But side by side with this fatalism there is emerging a new hope, choosing to create our destiny that will end not in violence but in the creation of a new humanity: "It is as though the guilt of the victor stands on the threshold of a creative breakthrough in the darkening consciousness of the victim as prelude to the birth pangs of a new cosmos."[9] Fate dealt us a bad hand but because we are free to enact the historical face of our being we are not bound to be the captives of the past; our destiny consists in our capacity and freedom to empty ourselves of the old stories and to create fundamentally more loving and just alternatives.

The purpose of our writers, playwrights, theologians, philosophers, and professors must not be to "civilize" us or assimilate us into the present stories and ways of life that preserve a system of power but to enlighten us through a process of *conscientización*, an awakening that brings to fruition the personal, political, historical, and sacred faces of our being.[10] Two Latin American novelists, Alejo Carpentier in *The Lost Steps* and Luis Asturias in *The Green Pope*, lead us in their works through the archetypal journey of transformation taking place in our inner depths that they see as the beginning of our search for reunification and spiritual renewal. Their concerns with the past "demand a kind of cyclic computation where one is aware of moving into the future as much as one is aware of recreating the past." They urge us not to repeat the past or to fall under the spell of its romance, but to *re-create* it by choosing and discerning those elements that will lead us now and in the future out of a dead end. For these writers the peasants are not only natives but are the roots of our past, of our cultural continuity. The culture is in our bones. By acknowledging it we cause the darkness of the apocalypse to recede, and García Márquez's novel of destruction takes on new meaning. The author is reminding us of the indigenous stories, and in these archetypal stories we find a fuller expression of universal archetypes: the re-creation of the individual person and of the world that follows destruction. The appeal to these stories has both a psychological base and a value as a social and political protest.

Asturias is therefore taking up the stream of writing that had been established by the Indians centuries before him. Always it expresses the need to transcend the condition of entrapment by use of the universal myth. Therefore, in Asturias's portrait

of the President as the archetype of the Terrible Mother in *El
Señor Presidente,* there is at once social protest in its own right
against the dictatorship of Estrada Cabrera, and also the continuity of the Indian literature of myth. The novel on these
levels, describes a condition of social and psychological entrapment which is also universally applicable to all races and cultures of the world that have developed an indigenous myth of
suffering.[11]

By wrestling with our heritage we can go beyond the despair of
fatalistic entrapment that ends in personal, political, historical, and
sacred passivity by falling into apathy characterized by solitude, invisibility, and docility. It is important to know that our ancestors
knew about and *participated* in a universal drama of creation, nourishment, and uprooting in order to plant the fundamentally new and
better. In their own way they understood and participated in *gnosis,*
that is, knowledge of the process of transformation. This is the process that we choose to reenact with the necessary adaptation to our
own historical period. The process of continuous creation is a spiral
that moves beyond the cyclic repetition of the past in order to re-
create the past toward an open future. Systems, that is, stories and
ways of life, possess us and take on a life of their own only when we
remain unconscious of them.

We need to persistently remind ourselves that the world and
the networks of stories and ways of life that shape it constitute a
persistent co-creation of persons together with the deepest underlying sacred source of transformation that needs us to be concrete in
the world. Thus no system can or has the right to become an object
over and against us without our participation. We have a responsibility to question, to rebel against an objectivity that is considered
perfect or finished, to empty our souls of destructive stories and
ways of life, and to open ourselves to being filled anew with fundamentally new and more loving alternatives. This process affirms
that we as co-creators are not finished. We are always more than our
creations.

I return to where I began: it is precisely because we cannot be
who we are in our deepest selves that we have to reject this current
system. We can only be strong enough to confront the system when
we know who we are, having journeyed through the core drama to
Act III, Scenes 1 and 2, when we are fully present as whole persons
capable of responding to new problems. Do we need jobs, housing,
and employment? Yes. Yet we want more than that; we want the

right to all of these human necessities *and* the right to be ourselves. This means confronting stories and relationships enacted in the service of partial ways of life that prevent us from creating more loving and just alternatives. In this struggle we will not reject persons of other cultures and races. Far from it. We owe it to them and to ourselves not to continue to give the impression that making it in this system dominated by the stories of tribalism in collusion with capitalism in the service of a way of life of fragments is what life is all about. Because we love our selves, our deepest sacred source, and our fellow human beings, we need to create conflict and change. The conflict is capable of breaking the spell of the deep sleep into which we have been cast through being led to believe that we live in the best of all possible worlds.

Let us consider why we are not at home in our present system by examining attempts to lull us back to sleep. Education for Latinas and Latinos can be used as a subtle form of co-option and assimilation. It can be used to give people new opportunities. But too often the ultimate goal is assimilation, taking the best of our young people and allowing them to join the powerful. There is fear of competition by the powerful; they do not fund the schools of the poor who are usually synonymous with people of color at the same level as suburban predominately white schools. But for la comunidad Latina there is also the question of political and cultural resistance. For example, language has much to do with culture, but many of the advantages of being bilingual are being reduced to the economic: bilingual secretaries, businessmen, lawyers, and so forth have greater opportunities. This reduction of our native language to status pursuits divorces it from its cultural matrix. To emphasize the bicultural means that there is a struggle going on within us; the bicultural never allows us to be truly at home here. We live in an economic system that wants us all to be "nonbody" producers working to have a better future. Once again it is our artists and writers, Miguel Ángel Asturias and Octavio Paz, Alberto Sandoval-Sánchez, Sandra Cisneros and René Marqués, Demetria Martínez, Leslie Marmon Silko, and Martha Rosa Villareal who remind us that we are a people of festival, of the celebration of the body, and of the eternal return contained in the present, who are not at home until we discover that we need to go within ourselves to discover our inner realities as our home. The cultural implications of this must not be lost. The Anglo-Saxon part of our culture in this country castigates us for an attitude of *mañana, tomorrow,* because it is nonproductive. The English ancestors of this nation look for purity from the world and the body through hard work. As Max Weber and R. H. Tawney[12] have taught us, it was this kind of religious ideology based on purification that contributed so much to the rise of the capitalist economy. But the religious views that helped make the Anglo Saxon superior in banking and industry make them uncomprehending of those who are not Calvinists or Horatio Algers. The indigenous people were considered to be listless and lazy heathens who were predestined to failure not only in this world but in the next.

As Octavio Paz has written, because the United States rejected the Native Americans it has no Indian past, no dialectical opposite, no shadow, no specifically American roots that can fulfill, balance, complete, or transform the European ones. The United States did not merge with the Native American Indians but extinguished them. This cruelty had another result: the stories of domination and segregation, capitalism and racism/tribalism, in the culture-exalted behavioral patterns traditionally called virile: aggressiveness, individualism, and competitiveness.[13]

In comparison, the Spaniards, who were also cruel at first, denied but then grudgingly conceded the humanity of the Indian; they finally granted him a soul. Therefore, the approach in Latin America, because of people like Bartolomé de las Casas, the first bishop of Mexico who was vilified and denounced for his efforts to assimilate and convert the Indian, eventually resulted in the mestizo reality of Latin America.[14] Initially the Indians were shocked by these strangers and often resisted too late. What remained after the Conquest was a people of superimposed pasts that every Latina and Latino carries in his or her bones: the continuity of several thousand years of the Indian past beating in their blood and the imposed European culture. This facing between two pasts, between two civilizations, provides every Latina woman and Latino man with an internal dialectical force that lies fallow. Octavio Paz powerfully demonstrates the emergence and confluence of the Indian and the Spanish traditions in the frenzy of the festival.[15] Paz states that festival is what makes the Latino *political.* It is a sign and time of resistance. Earlier Paz had written that the time of promoting and honoring the warrior mentality was anachronistic:

> . . . modern time, linear time, the homologue of the idea of progress and history, ever propelled into the future, the time of the sign non-body, of the fierce will to dominate nature and tame instincts, the time of publication, aggression and self-mutilation—is coming to an end.[16]

The myth of the eternal return frees us to participate in the journey of transformation; it is the return of the revolution as festival. Festival celebrates community; *la fiesta* is Dionysiac, frenzy, voluptuousness, and color. It is a communion that is participation, not separation, joining not breaking away, a great coming together, a bathing in the waters of the eternal return, in the primordial waters of beginning. It is baptism, renewal, transformation, a fundamentally different existence beyond the Anglo-Saxon purity and impurity, a rejection of the deferral of pleasure and repression that separates us from our bodies, one another, and the world. But above all festival, fiesta time, is the victory of the love of the body renewed, re-created, redeemed. The spirit of the eternal return rejects the linear one-dimensional search for a future and roots us firmly in the present, here and now. But the here and now is past, present, and future *fulfilled* in a new incarnation of who we are. If a society is essentially defined by its concept of time, there can be no more glaring difference between the Latino and the Anglo-Saxon cultures. The Anglo Saxon, as Philip Slater has written, lives for the future, saving money for the sake of money, deferring pleasure and relationships, and seeing pleasure and festival as a waste because it is a loss of money and power.[17]

It is because of our rootedness in an incarnate spirit that knows itself in festival and erotic connections that we, as Latinas and Latinos, must not allow ourselves to turn against our body as Anglo-Saxon society would have us do. We can be a counter-community, a countersign to a partial and arrested life based on the war of all against all. We need to begin with our selves, with the personal, political, historical, and sacred faces of our being in their wholeness. We have an opportunity to stand as a symbol of what every person is capable of, a new creation. This is the age of *el quinto sol*, the fifth sun, the era of motion, of earthquakes, of the collapse of the pyramid of established power; this parallels the historical situation in which the whole world is living as we deconstruct the systems of oppression. We will be saved not by power and stability but by our capacity for change.[18] We can be a people characterized by resistance, a subversive people that speak and act together with the deepest source of transformation. We can manifest humanity's hope of renewal. We cannot afford to be assimilated, co-opted, absorbed, fused, or bought off. To preserve the best in our Amerindian/Spanish past is to reaffirm festival, the body, death and rebirth, the erotic, the here and now, the love of the other, and the deepest source of transformation within our creative selves.

There are universal resources to be rediscovered in our indige-
nous-European heritage that speak of hope, creation, love, and community. It is our task to educate ourselves to these sources of transformation, both those within our Indian-European roots and those
that are to be discovered here in this country. To bring together
counter-traditions from both cultures is to affirm that the deepest
source speaks in all times and places. We are the crucibles of the
new incarnation of the deepest source. If we lack a home in the system, we have our selves, each other, and the god of transformation
and it is more than enough.

Politics is more than voting in official contests for power, writing a constitution, carrying out the laws, and ruling through govern-
ing parties. Politics is what we can and need to do together with
others to bring about a more human community with love and justice here and now. Nobody gives us permission to be political. We
are political by the very nature of our being human. To be political
is to continuously enact the political face of our being together with
our personal, historical, and sacred faces. The institutions that are
created are the result of the linkages or patterns by which people
have chosen to bind themselves in a social union. Therefore, politics
of its very origin and nature presupposes a human-made network of
relationships that can be put out of business to create new institutions. In this sense we are all and must be political. And now we are
ready, finally, to redefine, to transform our solitude. The quality of
this solitude is fundamentally different from that of docile solitude;
the retreat that we speak of here is temporary not permanent. It is a
creative use of the relationship of isolation, a withdrawal into our
deepest self to find the strength and creativity to return to our communities to act out the vision that was revealed to us in our solitude. This is a fundamentally different kind of isolation because
now it is in the service of transformation.[19] Our time has come not
because we are on the cover of *Time* magazine but because our period of gestation is over. We are called upon to be the fathers and
mothers of the deepest sacred by giving birth to the divine child, our
new self, so that we can be co-creators with the deepest source of
transformation.

The hibernation is over. I must shake off the old skin and come
up for breath. There's a stench in the air, which, from this distance underground, might be the smell either of death or of
spring, I hope of spring. But don't let me trick *you* there is a
death in the smell of spring and in the smell of thee as in the

smell of me. . . . And I suppose it's damn well time. . . . Even hibernations can be overdone, come to think of it. Perhaps that's my greatest social crime, I've overstayed my hibernation, since there's a possibility that even an invisible man has a socially responsible role to play.[20]

This is the essence of alienation: we repress our personal and sacred faces and lose the capacity to change our lives for the better by silencing the political and historical faces of our being. To be political and historical is to take back into our own hands the personal and sacred task of building a more just human community. This is what it means to participate in the creation, nourishment, and destruction of stories, relationships, and ways of life. When the human institutions by which we structure life become destructive, it is our task to put them out of business. We destroy not human beings but the stories and the relationships between us that prevent us from responding to problems. The deliberate and conscious breaking of relationships brings about incoherence, two groups standing in the same place who can no longer agree on how to manage continuity and change. It is the bewilderment that absentee landlords feel because they can no longer make exorbitant profits by withholding heat and hot water. But this is preferable to the violence that destroys both the body and spirit of the tenants. For tenants to organize a rent strike by enacting together the relationships of direct bargaining and autonomy is to destroy the linkages of isolation and subjection that allowed the powerful to use them as a means to their own end; the intent is to break relationships, not the bodies of the landlords or their livelihood. The concrete inherited relationships into which we were socialized in the ways of life of emanation and incoherence that often colluded with deformation are now used in the service of transformation as created patterns. These new manifestations of direct bargaining and autonomy in the service of transformation guarantee the rights and duties of *both* owners and tenants. To create conflict and change, to initiate the breaking and the creating of new and better alternative relationships, is to develop an opportunity for both sides to experience justice. The most revolutionary people in a time of breakdown will be those persons who can create more compassionate and just relationships among strangers. This is the essence of nonviolence.[21]

Whoever shares with us as Latinas and Latinos a consciousness of wanting to build a society based on justice and compassion are members of *La Raza*. In this way the original meaning of such phrases will have been transformed. Once a sense of identity has been achieved, it is necessary to move beyond the initial exclusivity of the original meaning. By redefining the concept to include people who care deeply about others is to demonstrate that ethnic and racial identities are not absolute. El Pueblo and *La Raza*, therefore, are not ultimately statements about color, language, or race as much as they are concepts indicating a community of consciousness, a consciousness of creating linkages with others in justice.

GROWING ONE'S OWN RACIAL AND ETHNIC IDENTITY

In the United States a legitimized violence is still being used to maintain the powerless fragmentation of la comunidad Latina. As the system of domination breaks down, members of the dominant class, primarily white males, face the loss of power and privilege based in great part on the subordination of communities of color. This endangered group responds to its incoherence by conjuring up a mystifying group consciousness based on skin color and/or ethnic heritage. Such aggressive and defensive exclusion of others on the grounds of racial or ethnic differences is racism. The story of racism is an attempt on the part of a group to hold together a chaotic world for its members. In order to block out the threat to their world they create a fantasy based on a fragment that comes to dominate the whole of life. Those who glorify skin color or ethnicity attempt to justify power as their natural right. This is a false mystification that is in reality enacting the story of tribalism in the way of life of deformation that destroys both whites and people of color. Members of allegedly superior groups see themselves solely as extensions of their own ethnic or racial group. Individuals in such a group thus give up the right to critically evaluate or create options. Blood becomes their fate; people are presented with race and ethnicity as permanent facts of life. Such a sense of blood enhances the ability of groups to have internal cooperation and continuity in the limitless security of the mass. But the price is too high: there is no individual self present to dissent or to deal with conflict and change and justice. Outsiders are looked upon with suspicion and confrontation that ends in exclusion and other forms of violence.

Traditional scholarship that merely tells us "what is" perpetuates the racism or romantic claims of ethnic greatness since the conventional wisdom equates reality with the persistence of existing relationships. We need to go beyond description to consciously analyze and uproot destructive relationships and stories to create connections to others that are new and better. One of our greatest gifts as human beings is to refuse to accept the world as given and to enact the political and historical faces of our being to in-form the world, that is, re-create it according to a new creative and imaginative vision of possibilities. Thus in how we approach either the natural or social sciences the scientist is more important than we have realized: "We no longer have a science of nature, but a science of the mind's knowledge about nature."[22]

Until recently Latinas and Latinos and members of other communities of color in the United States lacked the strength to preserve their identity or to win political and economic rights because they remained unconnected to one another. The dominant group continues to develop its power because of the disconnection between and within groups such as Mexicans, Puerto Ricans, and African Americans. Thus, power groups maintain a vested interest in assimilating Latinos and other communities of color into American society. Much too often we as Latina women and Latino men enter white society by joining the powerful at the price of agreeing to avoid conflict or demands for change. Assimilation alienates us from our own communities and our own people often become an embarrassment.

All societies create linkages between people by which they organize daily life. Such links constitute institutions. The bonds of a particular society can be analyzed as the relationships that count. C. W. Mills called the capacity to see and understand these patterns behind the flux the sociological imagination. In U.S. society the dominant relationship is autonomy, a form of encounter in which each self and other is entitled to claim an autonomous zone of power based on explicit principles of law, custom, value, or competence that both share. The United Auto Workers and General Motors would be examples on the group level; on the personal level it can be seen in student-teacher relations or between man and wife in which each party has specific boundaries or an autonomous zone of jurisdiction that is theirs based on mutually accepted rules. In the student-teacher relationship, the course outline serves as the contract that sets down the autonomous rights of each in regard to what they expect from this course. The benefits and duties of each party are spelled out as requirements for the students and the material that is to be taught by the teacher. Both sides need to agree on the boundaries set down. Because of unforeseen circumstances such as a serious illness individual students can also enter into negotiations to change the original agreement. Another important relationship, direct bargaining, that is, the ability to win a better arrangement by direct, face-to-face, negotiations between individuals or groups is also present. On the group level, every three years both the automobile industry and the United Auto Workers practice the relationships of direct bargaining and autonomy by negotiating from within existing boundaries based on agreed upon rules to redistribute wealth and benefits. Both sides bargain with the hope of maintaining or enhancing their own boundaries.

In American society, groups or individuals who are isolated from one another and who are subjected by organized groups will not be able to participate. To survive in the U.S., direct bargaining power and autonomy are essential. Those who control the existing boundaries of power are not at all anxious to share the benefits of the system and in fact work to disable the competitive power of others. This is why the federal government needed to intervene as a mediating force to open the doors through the power of subjection in the form of laws such as Affirmative Action, Title IX, Americans With Disabilities Act, and Equal Employment Opportunity. This is why those who continue to believe in the invisible hand of the market as the equalizing principle are forever opposed to government intervention on behalf of any group except their own.

The Chicanos, African Americans, and Filipinos in California in the 1960s chose to end their isolation and subjection and to organize themselves as the United Farm Workers and thereby enacted the relationship of autonomy that allowed them to bargain with the farm owners. This is an example of enacting the relationships of direct bargaining and boundary management in the service of transformation. The Teamsters, who went through a similar struggle in the 1930s, closed ranks with the growers to sign sweetheart contracts. This latter coalition of autonomous jurisdictions, or boundary managements, was used to preserve power and prevent change. This is an example of the relationship of autonomy as a form of institutionalized domination or autonomy used in the service of incoherence because it perpetuates the economic and political domination by the already powerful and excludes those considered to be not as valuable. And because this domination is based on race and class it reveals how racism and capitalism, the ways of life of incoherence and deformation, collude with one another to preserve power and privilege.

Because of their fear of communities of color that organize around issues of social justice, the dominant have practiced a policy of co-option. The powerful protect their privilege by allowing the "better" members of communities of color as individuals into power positions. They know that the logic of individualism, "I've got mine," works only too well. Those invited to assimilate by joining the powerful are then expected to counsel others to be patient and let the system work. In their own ways marginalized ethnic and racial groups understand these dynamics. But there is a danger that they think that they can work the system for their own good without being corrupted. However, a rational decision made with good will is not helpful in this situation. Capitalism and the way of life of incoherence are rooted in sacred forces that possess us and take us over. Not being aware of the underlying sacred power of the stories and ways of life in which the system is grounded means that we end by being controlled by the consciousness of U.S. society, that is, the same stories and ways of life. In other words, when we achieve our own autonomy by enacting the relationships of boundary management and direct bargaining and the story of capitalism in the service of incoherence we will dominate those individuals and groups that have not yet learned how to survive in American society.

The awakening of racial and ethnic pride led to the Black Power movement and the phenomenon of "good" and "quiet" Mexicans becoming militant Chicanas/Chicanos who began to create conflict and to agitate for change. But the achievement of a power base by a whole group does not guarantee winning the revolution against exploitation. David Gordon has documented the refusal of Muslim men to allow true liberation for women in Algeria.[23] Thus we need to look within a racial or ethnic group to determine the quality of the relationships by which members relate to one another. The liberation of a group cannot be authentic unless the individuals in that group are free.

As stated above, there are qualitatively different ways by which people can relate to that emerging group known as Latinos, *La Raza*, Boricua, or Chicana/Chicano. Some Latinas and Latinos have been disillusioned by their attempt to enter into the embrace of the American way of life. They had to sacrifice too many aspects of their heritage: their color, ancestors, language, and culture, and even themselves in order to belong. During the Civil Rights movement of the 1960s some Mexican Americans sought a newfound security in a total embrace or immersion in the group Chicanas/Chicanos or brown-power people. They were taken over by this new family and identity. To lose oneself in any group is to give up any fresh insight into oneself and to repress change and conflict for the sake of security.

Such is to treat oneself solely as an embodiment of an ethnic group because of the seemingly mysterious and overwhelming source of power of the group.

Other Latinas/Latinos, separated from the American stream of life, grab hold of this new identity so as to be able to capitalize on ethnic "in-ness." They gladly accept being ethnic because it is a marketable commodity. One's ethnic or racial identity is used as a valuable tool in the competition against others. In this way we turn ourselves into a commodity in which we ourselves trade. Identity is another weapon in the service of incoherence.

Some choose to get revenge on white society by declaring that only Latino is valid; white and other communities of color are excluded from the area of mysterious power. Color, language, and ethnic identity help to provide horizons within which people feel secure, superior, and autonomous. An overreaction to the experience of oppression leads them to claim that everything Latino is good. This search for total security in a new identity can put us on the road to destructive death at the exit from the core drama of life in deformation because we consider the others less than we are. We become the victimizers and are now caught by the story that possesses a white consciousness based on superiority, the story of tribalism.

Then there is a fourth choice. There are those who do not want to be uncritically loyal to Latinismo in the service of emanation. They refuse to accept a definition of who they are and do not wish to isolate themselves from other people who are not brown. They believe that they can see the world through other perspectives. These Latinas and Latinos refuse to use their ethnic and/or racial identity as a commodity in the service of incoherence and reject using their heritage, language, and culture to gain revenge for their pain by excluding others in the way of life of deformation. Such Latinas and Latinos are persistently in the process of critically evaluating what it means to be a member of la comunidad Latina. They are growing their own racial and ethnic identity in the service of transformation.

Now we can form coalitions with others because we are able to accept those aspects of our lives which constitute our own heritage.[24] The tragedy of the melting pot continues to be that immigrants, at least by the second generation, ignore, or are forced to ignore, their national and cultural past in their rush to be assimilated Americans. People now need to go back and reconnect to themselves as Chicanos, Cubans, Poles, Swedes, Chinese, Irish, Ecuadorians,

Guatemalans, Costa Ricans, Argentines, or Puerto Ricans before they can form a new American identity. A people cannot create meaningful connections with others until they have connected to themselves. We cannot reach out to love others unless we love our own selves. Too many of us suffered from forms of self-alienation or self-hatred because we were made to feel ashamed of our Spanish-speaking parents and our dark skin. Latina women and Latino men connected to one another can then begin consciously to re-create what it means to be a member of the community. We need to always question, "What do we mean by Latino, Hispanic, Mexican American, Chicana, Ecuadorian, Colombian, Guatemalan, or member of *La Raza*?" Latinos and Latinas come from many different nations and although we share a common language and certain cultural and historical experiences as a group, we do not see the society in which we live in the same way. Specific groups such as Ecuadorians, even though they share a common land of origin, language, and customs, do not agree on many issues. Thus, ethnic groups are constantly in process and evolving because their members are continually redefining who they are. For this reason it is important that not only ethnic groups but also the individuals within that group be liberated as well. Only freely connected individuals can pose new questions as their consciousness of who they are grows.

When we accept who we are, we can then create new connections to others. It makes no sense to create a militant rhetoric that compels people to reject others before they can experience them as a person. Malcolm X spoke of this kind of automatic rejection of whites as "Devils" in his autobiography and felt especially bad that he had sent away a young woman with no hope. When she asked if there was anything that she could do to make things better, Malcolm had answered, "Nothing."[25] To do so is to fall prey to a false vivification that endows concepts with a life of their own and thereby turn our lives into the tools of ideologies.

SELF-IDENTIFICATION

Are we Latinas, Hispanics, Latins, Latin Americans, Afro-Latinos, Chicanos, Boricuas, Nicaraguans, Ecuadorians (naming ourselves by our country of origin), Afro-Quisqueyas (the indigenous name for Hispaniola), members of *La Raza*, Afro-Cubans, Spanish Americans, Spanish, Afro-Caribbeans, Cubans, or what? There are so many different ways by which we as a community and as individuals identify ourselves. The Census of 2000 opened the door to self-identification which on the whole proved to be a good idea since it allowed people to express the diversity within our common heritage. The names chosen to self-identify are also political declarations. We know that Latinas/Latinos can be members of any race and this is obvious for anybody who travels to Latin America or enters the barrios of this country. Nationwide 2 percent of Latinos self-identified as Black. Of those Latinos who identified as Black, 28 percent or more than 200,000 live in New York City. Of Latinos nationwide, 47.9 percent declared themselves as white and another 6 percent chose to identify themselves as members of two or more races.[26] Over 90 percent of those who said that they were of "some other race" on the 2000 Census identified themselves as Hispanic or Latino. Hispanic was favored over Latino by 34 percent to 13 percent. But the majority of Spanish-speaking people, according to a recent poll, identify themselves primarily by their place of national origin.[27] We do indeed come in all colors, sizes, and shapes and with a diversity of perspectives as to who we are.

Yet we need to be aware of the political implications of the names that we use to self-identify. Words are political and carry a message. Because of the virulent racism practiced in Latin America since the beginning of the Conquest and that continues to this day, there is a prejudice in favor of being Hispanic with lighter skin, blonde, and blue eyes. These characteristics give preference to the Spanish aspect of our heritage that is filled with a history of discrimination against the indigenous communities. As a result, to use the term "Hispanic" for many carries with it an elitist preference for things Spanish. The term "Hispanic" has its origins in the Roman colony of Hispania. Spaniards whitewashed their history by tracing their heritage to the Visigoths, Gauls, Franks, and the Romans. Yet for eight hundred years Spain was the land of Jews, Muslims, and Christians, a *mestizaje*, a blending of culture, religions, and peoples. Thus Spaniards are descendants of this great intermingling that until recently they refused to accept.[28]

The term "Latina/Latino" carries a sense of movement and history because it better captures the intermarriage of the European and the indigenous cultures and races. It fits the reality of the majority in Latin America who are clearly mestizas and mestizos, men and women of mixed blood and culture. Some dislike this term because it sounds too much like Ladino, the language spoken by Jews in Spain and preserved by communities of Jews who were dispersed after the expulsion in 1492. Others shy away from this term that denotes being mixed since they want to be "pure" Indian or European. To name yourself was and continues to be a political act of defiance against the dominant culture that named us to fit their views. Second, it is a revolutionary statement that we are here, present, with all of our cultural and historical heritage that we celebrate. In a recent interview Sandra Cisneros said, "People who use that word [Hispanic] don't know why they're using it. . . . To me it's like a slave name. I'm a Latina."[29] The terms "Latina/Latino" also represent a development in political consciousness and liberation that has its roots in the Civil Rights Movement of the 1960s. The use of the terms "Latina/Latino" is analogous to the growth in political consciousness in the Black community who went from being Colored to Negro to Afro American to African American. Each name change signified a development in the community's maturation to full acceptance of who they are.

Terms for self-identification like "Chicana," "Boricua," "Afro-Cuban," or "Afro-Caribbean" are political terms of protest that are specific to a particular group. These terms grew out of a nationalist movement that began in the 1960s as a way of taking one's identity back from a racist culture that rejected these communities. The emphasis is on racial identity, being primarily Indian and African while conceding the presence of the Spanish as that aspect of one's identity that is most painful and problematic.

Other terms of identification like "Latin," "Latin American," "Spanish," or "Spanish American" emphasize a tendency not to be associated with the Latina/Latino community of the barrios. They are terms that are used to emphasize class differences and in some cases to disassociate from a mixed group. These terms are often used by the media and the entertainment industry to depict a kind of flavor and rhythm.

Different regions of the country prefer some terms to others and some say that those in the community who are Democrats prefer "Latina/Latino" while Republicans prefer "Hispanic." "Hispanic" is often considered a safe term to identify all people from a Latin American origin since it was officially blessed by the Census Bureau in 1970. By the 1980 Census, "Hispanic" became a fixture in official government forms for applications for school, employment, and general assistance.

Skin color continues to plague the community both in Latin America and in the United States. As a carryover from our Latin American experience, dark is considered low class and inferior. It connotes "bad blood" meaning Indian and/or African blood. Dark-complexioned Mexicans who were victims of oppression in Mexico and in this country are grateful that they have no "sangre Negra" or Black blood. Cubans until the arrival of the Marielitos in 1980, named thus because of their port of departure from Mariel, Cuba, were assumed to be more white and Spanish than the rest of us. Dominicans can be dark and have African features but they will say that they are not Black; Haitians whom they have been taught to see as an inferior enemy are good only to *cortar caña*, cut cane—"they are Black." For this reason Dominicans to this day refuse to work in the cane fields. White Cubans do not identify with Afro Cubans. Arab Mexicans and Mexicans who have labored mightily to maintain their *criollo*, Spanish heritage, do not identify with the *indigenos* or the mestizos. In Venezuela, the *pardos* who are of mixed blood, Indian and European, are looked down upon by the *mantuanos*, or those with European features, especially light skin. In Guatemala there has been a campaign for years to destroy indigenous languages, culture, and Mayan identity. In Mexico there is a national policy to assimilate the Indians so that in places like Oaxaca the Zapotec Indians are discouraged from teaching their children Zapotec, a beautiful and rich language that has sixty-eight subdialects. Clearly in these cases race and class collude in deforming another group as less human. And in the process members of the community are in denial of their own mingled blood.

What further complicates the matter is that in this country lighter-skinned Latinas/Latinos are given preference. This leads to intergroup jealousy and mutual dislike between, for example, Puerto Ricans and Cubans. In addition it opens la comunidad Latina to accusations by African Americans, who have their own problems with light and dark skin, and who complain that Latinos can pass and therefore are not at risk as much as they are. The dominant white group is aware of this color consciousness in the two communities and makes use of this competition for their own benefit.

Given all of these realities that demonstrate how diverse and indeed divided we are, is it realistic to speak of a Latino community? The divisions are many: race, class, gender, religion, generational, regional, national, sexual orientation, occupation, language, attitudes, and vision. This is why we cannot build a community or consciousness on any of the above aspects of our humanity. We need another way to define ourselves, to name who we are, to create a new kind of Latina woman and Latino man in this country. The irony is that in this nation that has rejected us for so long we have the opportunity to make democracy work and in so doing create an identity based on the truth that each of us in our uniqueness is a valuable member of society.

We can transcend all of our differences based on the characteristics mentioned above such as race, class, and gender and ask ourselves the questions, "Ultimately who am I as a Latina woman, as a Latino man; why do I do what I do; in the service of what way of life and ultimate sacred source do I practice the relationships, the four faces of my being, and the stories of my life?" If we enact our lives in the service of emanation we will get caught in forms of tribal loyalty to a particular Latino national community and not be able to go beyond the differences mentioned above since only my group counts; even if others are from a *herencia Latina* they are not Puerto Rican or Chicano, not indigenous enough, not educated, and on and on. In the way of life of incoherence we could care less about the culture and history of our heritage; all that counts is whether or not the fragments of our culture we hang onto are marketable, whether we are worth more with or without Spanish, with or without whatever in our background is desirable to project. We have the worst choice of all in practicing racism, classism, or sexism in the service of deformation against our own people. There are Mexicans who find the indigenous communities of Mexico repugnant and less than human. This prejudice is just as strong in this country when we see middle-class Mexicans turning their backs on undocumented Mexican men and women, Puerto Ricans discriminating against Dominicans, or Colombians disparaging Ecuadorians. Only those Latinas and Latinos who care deeply about each person they encounter can build a true community. They see the diversity as strength; they see the personal faces of their fellow Latinas/Latinos as sacred and assist them to become strong enough to practice the political and historical faces of their being in the work of creating a community based on love and justice.

The way of life of transformation is the only ultimate choice that gives us the capacity to transcend tribal loyalties, relating to people out of self-interest and hurting others as less than we are based on fantasies of racial, class, gender, religious, or national superiority. The issues raised above that often divide us can be transcended as we set about creating a Latino community in the service of transformation. We need to go beyond the fixation on labels and stereotypes to experience the underlying deeper meaning of our lives that we practice in the service of four fundamentally different ways of life. Only in the way of life of transformation are we truly free to come forth with the four faces of our being to be fully present to respond to the needs of others with justice and love.

The transformation of ethnic and racial groups will mean the conscious and creative breaking of destructive linkages and stories and the creation of new and more just alternative stories and manifestations of the nine relationships. The principal creative force will emerge from the personal and sacred faces of the individual. Instead of being unconsciously embedded in the mysterious power of the group, the individual is set free to enact the political and historical faces of their being to analyze and experience the creation of new and better patterns of encounter within the self and with others. Rather than being the extension of another individual or a group in the relationship of an inherited emanation, either in the ways of life of emanation, incoherence, or deformation, the individual becomes an embodiment of himself or herself in the way of life of transformation. New relationships can now be created, consciously selected, and maintained, but only as long as they give us the capacity to generate a more just and compassionate response in a constantly changing world. Since a person is armed with a new consciousness of self and other and with a willingness to create new relationships, a new kind of wealth is now possible.[30]

An awareness of concrete linkages and stories that preserve racism and destructive ethnicity along with a consciousness of alternative relationships and stories, especially the story of democracy, frees us from attacking abstract systems, a strategy that is tantamount to beating the air. Ethnic and racial groups that have become conscious of their strength can now use their capacity to develop strategies of change within their own community and with other groups. The relationship of subjection can be used in the service of transformation to enforce civil rights laws. Groups can freely withdraw temporarily in isolation so that members can experience who they are and see the others within the group afresh in order to discover how to relate to new problems. New possibilities can be opened by European-American whites, other communities of color and ethnicity, and the professional Latina/Latino middle class who buffer on behalf of those who cannot yet protect themselves. Political coalitions can be formed as relationships of boundary management in linked power to bargain for economic, social, and political rights. Coalitions of caring professionals can be created to provide services and opportunities for people of color and the poor by organizing a new, larger, more coordinated, and competent base from which to turn to the transformation of communities of color and the larger society. Finally, guides using a new and created form of emanation in the way of life of transformation can through the charisma of their own personalities inspire new identities, produce pride, and give rise to solidarity.[31]

> The politics of transformation or if you prefer, permanent revolution, is always taking the next concrete step in the creation, nourishment or destruction of the next encounter. It is a process whereby the Latino worker for the first time opens up construction unions to his membership, comes to recognize what kind of housing he is not helping to build, recognizes through his work and its immediate rewards new aspects of his own being, struggles to alter the leadership of his union, and so forth. Transformation is not salvation but sanctification of human relations; never perfection but ever re-newed movement toward networks of wholeness.[32]

Thus, instead of using the relationships of autonomy and direct bargaining to suppress change and consolidate one's power, the gains won by an ethnic group are an essential step for nurturing more creative ways to give themselves and others new directions. Such a use of autonomy is a strategy of working "within the system" but not accepting its ultimate intent as power in the service of incoherence. It is a process of subversion by which to take our resources within the system and use them to build more just and compassionate alternative institutions open to all groups. In this way autonomy is itself transformed; rather than being used for the sake of incoherence or deformation, autonomy is now re-created in the way of life of transformation. This is the true meaning of subversion: people turn systems around from below by creatively using institutions, not to prevent change but as stepping stones for further development.

Finally, the irony of all this is that my search and efforts to grow my own identity as a Chicano/Latino male who is Catholic was forever affected by a deeply loving man, Manfred Halpern, a Jew born in Germany, and Frank Sullivan, an Italian with an Irish name. What they did was give me confidence in myself so that I could accept and love myself as a Mexican/Latino man. All of my students, together with my Latina/Latino students, at Yale, Princeton, and Seton Hall acted as guides in my life who helped to return me to my self. In the midst of such personal experiences I cannot accept definitions of racial or ethnic identity that exclude my friends or students who profoundly touched my life. We need to share who we are with African-American Blacks, Poles, Jews, Slovaks, Italians, and Irish in order to discover our fuller humanity. I believe with Gandhi and César Chávez that each human group can only know a part of the truth. To pursue and discover a fuller truth, ethnic and racial groups need to cooperate together in the personal, political, historical, and sacred task of transforming American society.

> The victory of any group will remain a success only if it also helps all human beings to link themselves or to change such linkages in order to overcome the common and persisting incoherence of the human species in the modern age.[33]

3. The Politics of the Latino Family

A child is a guest in the home to be loved and respected,
not to be possessed because he or she belongs to God.
—*J. D. Salinger*

The family is perhaps the most important institution for la co-munidad Latina. We have heard and read much about the collapse of authority in the family due to changes in the relationship between men and women, parent and child, and husband and wife. This crisis is seen as a great danger by many Latinos. Yet it is not the family and authority relations per se that are breaking but a particular kind of family and authority. Latina women and Latino men need to hold onto the family but grow a new kind of family with male-female relationships, authority patterns, and cariño, affection, that prepares each of us for selfhood. In this way the family will neither socialize us into the traditional cultural patterns nor assimilate us into the structures of the dominant society, but prepare each of us to be participants in transforming our barrios.

In an excellent monograph David C. Gordon wrote about the status of women in pre-revolutionary and post-revolutionary Algeria.[1] A similar study done by Gregory Massell in Soviet Central Asia described the attempt of the new government to transform male-female relations in a traditional society.[2] These two readings were brought to mind in a conversation with friends in Mexico regarding the changing role of women in Cuba since Castro. There was a remarkable coincidence in all three cases. Three revolutions had gone on record ideologically as well as legally to alter definitively the traditional relationships between men and women which had permanently structured women as inferior. In the case of Algeria it is quite clear that the women at a crucial point took a lead in the revolution. This revolutionary experience served to change the consciousness of

79

the women in respect to their own self-image and led them to question the inherited cultural stories and relationships that had created such a subservient attitude. Yet curiously enough, in spite of the new laws, the rhetoric, the countless confrontations, and the establishment of the new society, too often male-female relationships slipped back into the old world. Any revolution that does not radically alter the human relationships and stories and the ways of life that are constitutive of cultural institutions is not a transformation of society but a coup d'etat, a mere seizure of power that leaves the structure of that society largely untouched. Male-female relationships in a society and especially in the family are a crucial indicator of the radical thrust of a movement. Thus, when in Soviet Central Asia avowed communist youths began to sexually abuse women who had removed the *hijab*, the traditional veil worn by Muslim women, the revolution was clearly not won. After the French were defeated, the Algerian Revolution was incomplete; Algerian men expected the women to return to old authority patterns based upon male dominance. Similarly in Cuba the stories of male domination, patriarchy, and uncritical loyalty in the service of emanation did not end.[3]

Surely in these three cases as well as elsewhere there is no lack of good will, ideology, conviction, or revolutionary ardor. The problem is that all of the above were at best a sincere effort to confront age-old customs and at worst a mere intellectual liberation. But in the final analysis it was not revolutionary enough. People generally have not taken into account the trauma, indeed the death, of the old ego-identity based on sacred stories that have to be emptied out before fundamentally more just and compassionate alternatives can be created. Carl Gustave Jung has taught us that we are not merely the product of our own personal life span. We all carry within us a history embedded in the collective unconscious.[4] The real revolution consequently will have to be fought out in terms of a deep personal transformation or conversion process. There is no attempt here to reduce transformation to an individualized private realm. Liberated communities must be composed of liberated individuals who together with others link themselves in such a way as to move freely and consciously to solve problems. The lively tension between the individual and the group needs to be preserved not for the sake of competition but for mutual fulfillment. Similarly, especially in the modern age, personal, political, historical, and sacred transformation are all a necessary part of the process. When young people raise their voices and say "Enough!" this is not only a personal liberation, but it moves beyond to pass judgment on the society that repressed the political aspects of their being. Revolutionary rhetoric will not free us from the stories and ways of life that possess us that have to be emptied out so that we can create fundamentally more loving and just alternatives. This deeper level of the transformation of our underlying sources has too often been overlooked by the advocates of social change and revolution.

THE FAMILY AS MERCIFUL CONTAINER

This is not a book that will uncritically celebrate the various Latino cultures. We must not project unto others what we cannot or refuse to face in ourselves. We have to take on the courage to criticize ourselves as individuals and as a group. One of the most immature relationships that render us partial selves is that between Latino men and Latina women. What we have done to each other in the name of *cariño*, affection, needs to end for the sake of our humanity and that of our children. For example, my father related to my mother in a way that was blessed by the culture but detrimental to my mother. My father kept my mother in a state of suspended dependence that made it difficult for her to cope when he died. Much of our family life after my father's death was spent helping my mother to survive. In addition to the story of patriarchy, there is racism and classism in our communities. This is partially due to our Latin American heritage. Many of our mothers and fathers and *abuelos*, grandparents, came to this country already wounded by the privilege and alleged superiority of a hierarchical class society. The indigenos in our background also organized their societies in a hierarchical manner, with the nobles, warriors, and priests at the pinnacle of society. Unfortunately this deformational story of tribalism is still very much alive in la comunidad Latina in the United States. The *recien llegados*, the newly arrived immigrants, are seen as a threat not only by the dominant society but also by established Latino groups because they are all too often poor and undocumented. The large numbers coming from Mexico, Ecuador, Colombia, Guatemala, and El Salvador create an ethnic, cultural, and national rivalry between members of these communities and the Mexican, Cuban, and Puerto Rican communities, until recently the three dominant Latino groups. So there is much in our history and culture as well as our current attitudes that we need to question, reinterpret, and struggle with to see if it affirms or harms our humanity.

Our families are crucibles that prepare us for selfhood. Too often our families, even families that have been here for generations, seek to demand an unquestioning loyalty and in return promise security by protecting us. But the basic familial experience we need is one that allows the flowering of the self to take place. To keep us in containers is to prevent us from bringing our sacredness to fruition. Affection, in the service of transformation, is essential for liberation, to prepare us to walk away or to stay by choice. Love that possesses, dominates, or cripples is not love but a possessiveness that feeds on the use of guilt, power, or total domination.

The institution of the family is made up of individuals living stories, the four faces of their being, and patterns of human relationships that they enact in the service of four fundamentally different sacred sources. The family is a pivotal unit in all societies. Although its structure may vary, it has and will continue to play a vital role in the nurturing of persons. It is certainly the key vehicle for handing down or altering traditions. The issue to which we shall address ourselves is the quality of the archetypal stories and the relationships that exist within the family. The family like any other social relationship must be judged on its capacity to free the individual member of the group. Our choice is to transform the family from a sealed container in the service of emanation into a dialectical process of nurturing and liberating its members simultaneously in such a way that the family is preserved yet changed within an atmosphere of affectionate conflict. The family has often been seen and used as the unit of stability that prepares the new generation to repress what is within them and to live a life of virtue, that is, to preserve the status quo.[5] The very term "husband" betrays a prejudice in favor of patriarchal men who fulfill their masculinity by cultivating and securing a safe haven for loved ones. Fixed sexual roles in the family have made the family dependent upon the economic potential of the father, thus removing men from significant political protest. Indeed, for many years insurance companies have made it a practice to favor married men with children in their premium coverage.[6]

In this chapter we shall focus on the changing relationships, stories, and ways of life of people growing their own marriages. This entails men and women confronting the stories of their lives with each other. According to Jung, it is in dreams that the stories of our innermost person, our unconscious self, our journey toward transformation is revealed to us. Dreams compensate for the issues not consciously faced in everyday life. They constitute manifestations of the unconscious elements that seek to be integrated into our personality. The symbols and images carry a message from the depths within.[7] But we need new language, a theoretical perspective to analyze a culture dedicated to patriarchal rationality. Our theory of transformation allows us to ask new questions and to break out of a commonsense, culture-bound knowledge. Theory in its initial inspiration is a kind of ecstasy that allows us to step out of the old consensus and to participate afresh in the shaping of the self and society. We can go beyond merely reporting dysfunctions to pointing out the relationships that are breaking, why they are inadequate, and how to break those linkages for the sake of creating new and more loving stories and relationships. This is what the politics of the family is all about: participation in relationships in motion.

But where will people find the strength or capacity to deal with such a process of uprooting, creating, and nurturing? The source of that strength lies within the context of the human person as another face of the deepest sacred. This is the basis of human transcendence, of creating again, of hope that alternatives are possible. In this realm we enter into the company of the men and women of the counter-tradition of transformation of different ages and of all faiths who sought the deepest source and their new self *simultaneously*.[8] The introduction of religious language should not alarm us. It provides us with a universal language, an archetypal language, that allows us to speak of how we can participate with the deepest source of transformation in creating the world afresh.

THE LATINO FAMILY: CONTINUITY AND CHANGE

There have been some fascinating studies of Latino families; but they did little to help us move beyond a sensitive awareness of what *is*.[9] Often all families of whatever racial or ethnic background were grouped together in studies and discussed under headings that betrayed a white middle-class orientation. We now move to study the relationships and stories enacted in different ways of life of la familia Latina,[10] to evaluate those linkages and to speak of breaking traditional patterns and dramas for the sake of new and better ones. Much of what follows will allow people other than Latinas and Latinos to recognize themselves. Traditional families the world over have remarkably similar patterns of interaction. Our intent is to present a theoretical perspective that is not culture bound.[11]

The Latino family in the service of emanation has provided a strong container for the security of its members, but the cost to those same individuals seeking to grow within and beyond the group has been prohibitive. There is a poverty of relationships available to the members of la familia Latina in the way of emanation. The father is the source of the mystery (in some cases a strong mother, grandmother, or aunt, or the eldest son replaces the father in his absence) and the women exist to serve the needs of the men and the household. The father can coerce, cajole, mediate, demand, and bargain but he will not allow female members of the family to physically isolate themselves or to develop an area of autonomous jurisdiction such as a lifestyle that allows them their own jobs, paychecks, and schedules. But not even the father is free; he is an extension of the archetypal drama of patriarchy enacting a predetermined place in the Latino family that he inherited. The mother often becomes an institutionalized mediator who is dedicated to softening the conflict between members of the family. It is her role to reconcile the children who are in rebellion with the father. Outsiders who appear on the scene are dangerous insofar as they do not accept the repertory of relationships within the family. That is, if a friend was a *malcriado*, a brat, with *malas costumbres*, unacceptable behavior, she or he could undermine the authority of the family as a self-contained entity by contaminating the sons or daughters by introducing them to bad ideas or attitudes. What this means is that they might inject new ways of relating that endanger the sovereignty of the father and/or mother thus threatening the security of the family. For this reason Latino immigrants are alarmed by the culture in the United States which stresses autonomy for children. A veil of sin, shame, and guilt traditionally snuffed out any attempt to question the authority of the parent. But now in this country the guilt is losing its effectiveness. Latino sons continue to be given freedoms denied to daughters. As an extension of the father, the son is expected to repeat the manly exploits of the father. But for many Latino families "a daughter is the jewel of the family, and one cannot be too careful with them."[12] In other words, a daughter carries the honor of the family and by becoming sexual outside of marriage she dishonors the family.[13]

Women from la cultura Latina have for centuries belonged to men: a father, husband, brother, bishop, or other male guardian. Their ability to create conflict or change was minimal. Their lives were limited to cooperating with and seeking to continue the strength of the male who gave them security. Women were unable to create alternatives and exercised only those relationships acceptable to the culture. Women were allowed to withdraw only into a psychic state of moodiness. An aunt or other mediator could intercede on their behalf and win for them some concessions. If the stress and strain of the subjection by a man went beyond all reason, a woman could become bold enough to confront the dominant male in her life and try to negotiate a better situation. Whether she succeeded or failed in getting a better deal, she was left with the only option of returning to normal, that is, seeing herself only as an extension of others and therefore limited to what they would permit. This was their life space: possession and domination softened by a limited isolation, mediators, and bargaining. Women were devoid of the right to be physically left alone, the right to go away to renew themselves (isolation), denied any independence (autonomy), and, ironically, forbidden to rebel in any way (incoherence) lest it cast a shadow on the family image of contentment. People forbidden to feel their own deep discontent cannot generate the conflict and the energy necessary to break the old and to change their lives for the better (transformation). Latina women were traditionally raised to feel ashamed and worthless if they broke with authority. It is these internalized feelings of sin, shame, and guilt together with relationships and stories of dependence that allowed the tradition of male-female relationships based on domination and dependence to be repeated generation after generation. In regard to the four faces of her being, she was prepared to continue repressing her personal face because her desires were not important; with her political face she practiced a politics of uncritical loyalty to her husband; her historical face repeated the past as she lived the stories and relationships of dependence of the women before her, and her sacred face was possessed by the lord of emanation who inspired her to remain loyal to the culture that favored men.

Indian males, following the Conquest, lost much of their confidence in their indigenous culture, which at the very least recognized the complementarity of the masculine and feminine. As a result the Spanish male became a very powerful model of manhood. One of the ways for indigenous men to regain some sense of their lost dignity was by emphasizing their power over women. In many conversations with relatives and friends an outline of the possessiveness and domination operative in the Latino family emerged. Men and women have hurt each other for the sake of stability and *cariño*, affection.

Adjustment, order, and harmony in the Latino family meant accepting one's inherited place. Thus, a woman considered it to be her fate to be married to a male who would do what he wanted.

Often this male freedom expressed itself in a sexual manner. A Latina woman has known and knows that as long as the traditional relationships and stories between them continue she will not be able to relate to her husband as a valued person. In this tradition-bound world women were reduced to using covert manipulation, usually sex and food, the bedroom and the kitchen, to win back his attention. Some men continue to live in two worlds, their life with their family and their life with *la otra,* the other woman. Or if they are not involved with women they feel free to drink and gamble with their compadres. But the wife will have her revenge. To compensate for this loss a wife turns to the son, who becomes the object of her frustrated affection. The son is raised to feel loyal to the mother against the unfaithful father. In cases of abandonment this protective filial role is intensified. When the young man marries, he cannot so readily shake this first loyalty; he ends by accepting the oft-repeated warning of his mother, "Your mother comes before anybody, even your wife." The cycle is put in motion again: the rejected wife will now possess her son (this may be one reason why sons are preferred over daughters) just as her mother-in-law possessed her husband. Herein is a constant process of violence whereby a mother who has been frustrated prevents a son from developing his own selfhood. He becomes an eternal son so that she might remain an eternal mother.[14]

In a similar vein young women in traditional cultures are considered to be disloyal, even on a sexual level, to their fathers when they prefer another *macho* to their father. This cycle of betrayal, revenge, reconciliation, and betrayal again points out the inherent fragility of emanation as a way of life. The people who live relationships, stories, and the four faces of their being within emanation as a way of life cannot respond to new problems. They keep running back to what they know. Since they are not allowed to doubt, to disagree, to experiment, they are incapable of thinking and acting outside the accepted rules and norms. As partial selves they are not fully present to confront issues in a new way. Those who are alarmed by unorthodox behavior feel justified in turning to violence to restore order. Those who are victimized usually hurt themselves and others as they rebel. Since they cannot create new and better responses, their rebellion is usually short lived and they end by accepting the inevitable return to the status quo that began the problem. For this reason, as emanation as a way of life decays, it gives rise again and again to the exit from the core drama through the practice of relationships and stories in the service of deformation.

Many Latino men and Latina women realize at a later time that they have married their own mothers and fathers. Too often in looking for freedom from a dominant parent by marrying, they were not conscious that they had internalized the stories, relationships, and whole way of life of the parent. To break on the concrete level with the mother or father is not enough since the internalized need of belonging to others or possessing others has not been exorcised. Similarly, as we shall see in more detail in chapter 5, the lord of emanation who legitimizes cultural relationships and stories of dependence has not been confronted. Thus we repeat the same old dramas and relationships with new persons. It is these cycles and feelings of loyalty that are now being broken and questioned by Latina women. Women who find sources of mystery only within their sons or families still fail to find it within themselves. Many Latinas see their own life as an extension of a powerful other, as a shadow of their greatness, to avoid facing the failure and unhappiness of life. They might refuse to hear their inner voice in Act I, Scene 2. It is a choice of remaining in emanation in fear of experiencing incoherence, the breaking of the container. The relationship of incoherence following the loss of one's original security might not be transformed but deepened by escaping to find total security in one's children. What makes it painfully incoherent is that they are conscious of using their own children as shields but they either cannot or will not create a new life. This constitutes an attempt to replace the broken container of the way of life of emanation with a form of violence against one's self and others. To deny one's own value puts us on the road to the exit from the core drama of life in Act II, Scene 2, in the service of deformation. As partial selves we cannot respond to fundamentally new kinds of problems. In this context the four faces of our being radically change for the worse. A woman caught in this situation ends by erasing her own personal face since she sees herself as insignificant; she practices a politics of violence against her own well-being; with her historical face she makes life worse the longer she hurts herself, and her sacred face is possessed by the lord of deformation who confirms her in her self-wounding.

Men have always been aware of a mysterious power in women that they sought to control. Taboos arose regarding the menstrual cycle, veiling women as a shield not for women but to protect men from temptation, and purifying women after childbirth. Women were identified with the moon, dark forces, the demonic, and the irrational.[15] Women in traditional societies have learned to cope with male jealousy and dominance through a process of covert manipulation or subversion. Women were allowed to work their mystery, or the relationship of emanation, only in the home. Here the dominance was reversed. It was culturally acceptable for a woman to exercise her mystery over a man and to temporarily overpower him. For a short period he is caught as an extension of her feminine prowess and mystique. This helps to explain why women have always gained concessions or better bargains from men through their cooking and sexual prowess. However, the threat that this domestic power might become a source of public competition is a haunting, irrational threat to many men. For this reason the politics of transformation was restricted to the kitchen and not acceptable outside the home. Even though women might gain power in the family, there was often no transformation since women living without male domination often practiced the story of matriarchy, that is, patriarchy with a feminine face.[16] This means that women who found themselves in positions of authority due to circumstances beyond their control, such as the death of a father, husband, or older brother, behaved like a man. For example, when my father died my mother raised us as if he was still there, giving my brothers and me the usual male privileges and restricting my sisters to traditional female roles. My mother's ascension to power strengthened the system, that is, the existing traditional culture and relationships of dependency for women. My mother practiced the same relationships of emanation and subjection that keep everybody arrested in the core drama of life in its first act and scene. Consequently although the person in power has changed, men and women are still trapped in the same relationships: one is the extension of the other in emanation; the other is controlled by their partner through the relationship of subjection; mediators like aunts or grandmothers are sought out as buffers; and direct bargaining is set in motion to gain a better deal. But when this way of life and the acceptable relationships and stories are in danger of being overthrown, the relationship of deformation that manifests itself as psychological or physical violence is used to return the wayward to the right path. These four relationships together with the relationship of deformation and the stories of patriarchy or matriarchy and uncritical loyalty in the service of emanation are no longer working. It is the breaking of these linkages and stories practiced in this way of life that constitutes the current revolution in the Latino family and in male-female relations.[17]

There is something new happening within Latina women and Latino men. Women are breaking with the inherited connections, stories, and ways of life in some cases with the support of the men in their lives. Such a revolution is threatening the traditional hierarchical structure of the family. The container of the way of life of emanation is breaking, and those lingering fragments of the traditional culture constitute both danger and promise.

Historically the violence of rape against women has been used as a weapon by conquerors to destroy not only male-female relationships but as a means to undermine the family, the manhood of the men, and ultimately destroy the culture of the defeated. The catastrophe of defeat and conquest undid the web of emanation that provided security and a sense of well-being. Men who were forced to look on as their wives, daughters, and mothers were assaulted were filled with rage but could do nothing to show their anger or they would be killed. The rapists knew what they were doing; they were putting a time bomb in the home. Conquered men turned their frustration against women in the home, the only place where they could demonstrate such feelings. The conquerors destroyed trust between men and women and put a doubt into the mind of the oppressed men of historic proportion. This use of rape in the Spanish tradition has been traced to the reconquista of Spain from the Muslims by Christians.[18] This violent tradition was repeated in the New World in the eighteenth century in California. Spanish soldiers under threat of ecclesial excommunication and physical punishment by their military and civilian commanders continued to rape indigenous women.[19] Some see the betrayal of Malitzin, the concubine of Cortés, as the template of the woman as unfaithful and therefore worthy of beatings and even death.[20] To this day in Mexico a "Malinchista" is a term used to refer to a coward, a *vendido*, a sell out, who betrays his own people. This is the kind of cultural context within which Latina women and Latino men were raised. If the women questioned male domination they could be physically assaulted. In this way emanation as a way of life colluded with deformation as a way of life in order to preserve male dominance in the story of patriarchy.

The response of the Latino male to the breakdown of his traditional role is too often a refusal to deal with the problem. Some men respond with domestic violence as an attempt to return Latina women to the old docility, others become apathetic, while still others resort to forms of self-wounding such as drinking. A woman might take over as the bread winner and gain power. But this frees no one; the same relationships are maintained and nobody is free to create a better relationship to each other. There is a mutual hurt: neither men nor women can assert their own consciousness; they

are powerless but to repeat the past. Some Latino men who are facing opposition from their wives see this frustration as the result of
not being able to find a woman who will love them as their mothers
loved them. They consider the failure to achieve total security in
total possession as the core of their problem. They do not know how
to love a woman as an *equal* and not as a projected mother or challenge to the mother. The traditional *macho* relating to a woman
does not see a person but the image of the ideal woman in his mind
that he projects. He envisions the preferred cultural image of the
loving and obedient woman but when he tries to embrace that image
it all ends in a narcissistic nightmare. Such relations reveal with a
vengeance the powerlessness of power. Males have the power to control and command but are reduced to pouting children when it comes
to the capacity to transform their lives and their relationships to
women. The end result of these kinds of sexist relationships cripples
both men and women. Men cannot grow and become full persons
unless they can love women as equals and accept those aspects of
themselves that are feminine. The breaking of the traditional patterns of dependence of women on men creates the relationship of incoherence: they stand in the presence of each other and admit that
they do not know how to relate to each other. To try to reestablish
the old relationships of dependency and stories against the will of the
other and to refuse to create new and better ones is to enact relationships and stories in the service of deformation; that is, a man now re-
sorts to violence in order to end the threat to traditional male power
and authority and refuses to accept the changes in the other or himself. Thus he builds a fortress in a desert, and all have to deny their
new consciousness. But there are alternative ways by which Latino
men and women can relate to each other.

STORIES OF TRANSFORMATION

Archetypal dramas from around the world speak of the journey
of the hero in search of a fulfillment which is achieved through integrating the feminine into his personality. There are many versions,
but the following account contains the main elements. A young man
leaves his ancestral home, often after confrontation with representatives of the tradition, usually his parents. He overcomes their appeal
to love and guilt and sets out. On the road he confronts obstacles
such as dragons, robbers, or a forest. He succeeds after great struggles and resists the desire to return home. Finally he comes to the

last gate or passage. On the other side is the princess or fair maiden whom he rescues from witches or ugly suitors. The hero is now fulfilled: he has found his feminine counterpart without which he was doomed to be an incomplete, disconnected self. Although these stories are not intended to justify the dependence of women on men, there is no denying that given the historical condition of women, these stories were told and written with a male bias.

Our own cultural heritage has much to offer us regarding the complementarity of the masculine and the feminine. In the ancient cosmic mythology of the Nahuas and Mayas in pre-colonial Central America there was the god beyond all gods, the Lord of the ring, known as Ometeotl. This god represented the opposites of the universe: negative and positive, living and dead, light and shadow, male and female. Furthermore, Ometeotl was said to be at the center of the cosmos. To reach such a center of fulfillment, it was required to traverse through passages and rites of initiation involving thirteen heavens and nine hells, all representing a progression to higher levels of existence.[21] The important aspect for our purposes is the awareness that our ancestors had of the integrity of existence, the coming together of opposites, especially the masculine and feminine, for the purpose of wholeness or totality. Furthermore, there is ample evidence of a transforming process which is necessary to achieve selfhood, symbolized almost universally by the birth, journey, death, and rebirth of a hero-guide.

In another story the gods descended into a cave in which a prince was lying with the goddess called Precious Flower. From their union was born a godlike child called the Well Beloved, who immediately died and was buried. Out of the ground, from his body, there sprang many of the plants that were to supply humanity's basic needs.[22] These stories contain aspects of the archetype of the journey that we embark upon to find the source of life within our deeper self. As a tender and emerging reality, the ego breaks from the feminine, maternal hold to assert masculine individuality. But as the myth continues, it is the feminine that is clearly missing in the personality of the hero. When Siddhartha kissed Kamala, and Cinderella was kissed by the prince, there is an awakening symbolizing the coming together of the masculine and feminine in a new way that overcomes the old antagonism and leads to the wholeness of the self. Thus, constantly to project the archetype of the feminine onto women is to seek liberation by possession of the woman, not by struggling with the feminine within the masculine psyche. Similarly, men and women also seek to be possessed in order to find security. The mystery is placed in the other, not in their own selves as women and men confronting the masculine-feminine mystery within. Thus the following dilemma:

> The reward for what his masculinity has become is power. The reward for what her femininity has become is only the security that his power can bestow upon her. How do you call off the game?[23]

Women are now telling their own stories, taking their own journeys, and thereby revolutionizing our understanding of self, male and female, the family, marriage, culture, and the sacred.[24] Ann Belford Ulanov has beautifully and brilliantly written about the search of Dorothy in the *Wizard of Oz* for her masculine counterpart *within* her own psyche which will lead her down the yellow brick road to the center of her own mystery, the self within. Dorothy's quest constitutes the journey of the heroine in search of a fulfillment that is achieved through integrating the masculine into her personality.[25] But traditional male-female patterns do not allow this kind of liberation. Instead, people cling to one another. The male seeks Don Juan's liberation by going from one woman to another, never achieving liberation but simply striking out at the mother-feminine-woman-sex demons that he cannot confront. It is difficult to find and identify the enemy.

> The idea of restricting a relationship with a woman to a purely animal-like sensuality, excluding all feelings, is often enticing. . . . In such a union he can keep his feelings split off and thus can remain "true" to his mother in an ultimate sense. Thus, in spite of everything, the taboos set by the mother against every other woman remain inflexibly effective in the psyche of the son.[26]

THE AUTOBIOGRAPHICAL: THE JOURNEY WITHIN THE SELF

In autobiography, at least for the moment, a writer knows in his or her depths that he or she is exactly as his or her vision suggests, that for the moment one speaks for humanity as a whole. For now I wish to speak autobiographically. I feel that what I have experienced and am confronting with my wife and family has a wider significance that I believe will speak to the lives of other Latino men and Latina women and well beyond our own groups.

> The task of the philosopher [person] is to search himself and to find his own Einsteinian equation against chaos, his own Socratic theory to prevent blindness of the soul.[27]

As a person, as a male, as a Latino/Chicano, as a Catholic Christian, I have and continue to confront all of the issues mentioned above. For years I found myself trying to identify the enemy. I was surprised to see myself and not my father or brother, the representative males in my background, as the problem. I discovered that what I had acquired from them and from the culture were the stories of romantic love and patriarchy and the lord of emanation who inspires us to possess each other. During my struggle with how to relate to my wife I had a series of recurring dreams that gave some direction to the struggle. Recently my wife and I have exchanged our dreams. There was nowhere else to go but within, because we had not been able to find out why we were disconnected. Each crisis had ended in a catharsis, a purging of the emotions, but with no real change. Everything reverted to the way it had been before.

We cautiously began one day to move to a different realm. Casual comments about dreams led to an extended conversation. In our exchange of dreams the following motifs emerged. One dream found me in Toronto where I had attended university and where I significantly failed to face my own sexuality. Zapata (one of my heroes) and I were in a mazelike trap. We escaped together, and as we were leaving a sports stadium, a man asked for my gun, saying that I would not need it. I gave up the gun, and Zapata and I proceeded to leave. I became aware of the presence of another powerful force. Zapata faded away. As I walked, I saw Celia, my wife, walking in the opposite direction. I felt guilty that she was not the one who was pulling me. I feigned trying to call to her and kept going. In the distance I saw the attraction: a young woman from my past. I was filled with a sense of urgency to reach her. I quickly awoke. The young woman in the dream was pivotal in my adolescence. I was afraid of her and saw her as a threat to my neatly packaged image of asexual innocence.

In a related dream I remember being in the basement with the same young woman with my mother in the shadows. Another dream revealed something further. This same young woman whom I had hoped would protect me from sexual chaos because of her strict Catholic moral code appeared in a dream. As I approached her, I saw that she was wearing a black bra; but it was different, it was a nursing bra. I found myself walking down a corridor and saw myself as a young man. I saw the woman with her mother, but I was happy when the mother left. I now felt free to be affectionate with her. She had her back turned to me and as I was walking toward her I awoke.

The dreams point out that I was not able to relate to my wife or to other women as an equal. I was looking for my sexual identity but I was caught by the archetypal stories of patriarchy and matriarchy.[28] As a patriarchal male I was an intellectual liberal who was committed to being in favor of equal rights for women. Deep down I did not believe this but I could not admit it to myself. I had been unable to free myself of the story of matriarchy as manifested by the control of my mother who manipulated me through the use of guilt. The presence of the two young women from my past I recognize as aspects of my own personal need for an erotic relationship based on love and mutuality. What is clear is that Zapata, or myself as a conquering hero, is powerless to win the revolution by domination. All the power in the world cannot bring about a caring and loving relationship between men and women. This is only possible if both are able to participate freely. It is important to recognize that the issue in the dreams is not to look for a particular woman who is expected to solve our problems as men. We need to look to the deeper underlying causes, the radical roots of our problems, in sacred stories that can possess us especially because we are not aware of their presence. So to project onto women what has to be confronted *within* the self and culture perpetuates the problem.

My wife has had similar dreams. She has dreamt of living by the sea alone. As a Mexican young woman, the men in her life, her father and grandfather, never allowed her to have time by herself, especially outside the home. She had been denied the use of the relationship of isolation. Just to be alone, to do and go where you please was a delicious but a forbidden desire.[29] In other dreams she has been with a male friend. I was threatened by these dreams and wanted to make them go away by rededicating myself to her. In one dream I became interchangeable with her father, and she awoke confused. The father-daughter relationship and the son-mother linkage have too often led to arrested personalities since they cannot see the parent of the opposite sex as pointing to a *mutually* fulfilling relationship with a person of the opposite sex. This is only part of the price that we pay for not ridding ourselves of the stories of patriarchy and matriarchy.

The story of romantic/possessive love is another drama that prevents Latina women and Latino men from creating a deeply loving and mutual relationship. What Latino men, and it is safe to say that many men, find almost impossible to accept is that their wives could have meaningful and honest friendships with another man. Like Tolstoy's, character, Karenin, to recognize this is to accept that his wife has an emotional life that he thought could not exist apart from him. She has a life of her own, hidden, perhaps, but nevertheless her own.

> But now, though his conviction that jealousy was a shameful feeling and that he ought to have confidence was as strong as ever, he could not help feeling that he was confronted with something illogical and absurd, and that he did not know what to do. Karenin was face to face with life; he was confronted with the possibility that she might be in love with some other person besides himself, and that seemed quite absurd and incomprehensible to him because it was life itself. . . . For the first time the possibility of his wife's falling in love with someone else occurred to him and he was horrified at it.[30]

Latino males have always accepted friendships with women as a possibility for themselves, yet they denied the possibility to their wives. This is a failure to realize that meaningful friendships with others, for husband and wife, are a risk that is worth taking because it allows them to grow individually and to bring something *qualitatively* new to the marriage.

CREATING THE ALTERNATIVE: THE FAMILY AS RELATIONSHIPS IN MOTION

The family remains a necessary and merciful container for all of us. It provides us with the necessary security, affection, and continuity to begin the process of individuation, our journey through the core drama of life. But we fail to realize that archetypal stories and patterns of relationship emphasizing security and protection should be temporary. In the hostile area in which many of us grew up it was essential to have a close-knit protective family. Yet this has led too many of us in this country to romanticize and to pass over the abuses in the family. As Latina women and Latino men we need to take care that in our resistance against the assault on our communities we do not say that *everything* Latino is good. Revolutions have to remain consciously critical of self and other and not allow a tribal loyalty to hide the problems within. We require courage based on a new consciousness to create our own marriages and families that are neither Anglo-Saxon nor blindly Latino. A family that as a group is dedicated to the liberation of its individual members will never be out of date. We need the family but in a qualitatively different way. Too often love is oppressive. What we need is love that frees us to become what nobody can give us, the decision to create our own selfhood. This is the inner force that begins to demand that the family give us space both internal and external. Thus, to perpetuate relationships of dependency beyond the time that they are necessary and to fail to transform our linkages is to create neurotic personalities.

The danger for Latina women and Latino men as they attempt to act out new relationships that free them from the inherited past in the service of emanation is that they will assimilate into the dominant culture and concentrate on creating power relationships, direct bargaining, and the boundaries of power that come with the relationship of autonomy. For example, a Latina woman who becomes economically independent can have her own car, schedule, career, friends, and money. The relationship of emanation in which she related as an extension and shadow of the lives of others has ended, along with the relationships of subjection and buffering used to control her. She and her husband have become autonomous. The affection used to fuel the story of possessive love has lost its attraction. In a traditional marriage sex is often used as a form of emanation, to solidify a sense of security, as a form of bargaining, and as a buffer to deflect problems. Yet now that the relationship is in trouble none of the inherited patterns satisfy either partner. As a response to the end of a marriage in the service of emanation they live a rational marriage.[31] Both have busy lives, and there is no transformation. To avoid the real price of the end of their traditional marriage and family, Latinos might do what many middle-class Anglo-Saxon couples do: pull yourself up individually by your bootstraps and develop separate but equal lives. This constitutes a refusal to deal with the deeper issues of mutual love, feelings, emotions, and risk. It is a strategy to *avoid* one another. It looks like liberation, but it is not. This is a form of rebellion that ends by allowing love, affection, and caring emotions to die rather than be transformed. The "enemy" has won. The enemy here is the use of contractual relationships, or autonomy and direct bargaining, in the service of incoherence. Both partners agree to stay together usually for economic reasons, knowing that the contract means mutually suppressing passion, spontaneity, and love. This is to participate in mutual fragmentation: they agree to share only a fragment of who they are and not to let their messy, that is, their emotional life show itself.

Before a new marriage and family can be built we need to empty ourselves of the old relationships, stories, and the four faces of our being enacted in the service of emanation, incoherence, and deformation. Transformation is always preceded by the relationship of incoherence, the breaking of the inadequate relationships that were inherited or those used to build a rational, contractual marriage or one that caused hurt to one another in order to bring about a new and better relationship. The answer is not to set up power positions that accept the new gains for women. We need to create another quality of security, love, affection, and intimacy that honors the wholeness of the personal, political, historical, and sacred faces of one's own identity. The family will be free and loving only because its members are free and loving. To create one's own womanhood and manhood is to create one's own marriage and family. Such a task of transformation will demand not set actors but persons growing their own lives with mutual love and respect. The container of the inherited Latino family and the inherited concrete manifestations of our nine relationships are becoming increasingly useless. Rather than remaining the embodiment of the other in the relationship of emanation, each person feels the need to become an embodiment of their own individual self. A man and woman, the members of a family can stand in the presence of one another and admit that they no longer know how to relate to one another; they are experiencing the reality of broken connections, the relationship of incoherence. But they are now free to create new and better relationships with one another. They can consciously select and maintain those relationships that give them the capacity to respond to a constantly changing relationship. They are engaged in the process of growing their own marriage and family.

A husband and wife, a father and mother, children and parents having broken with the inherited concrete manifestations of the nine archetypal relationships are now free to create new forms of the nine in the service of transformation. Previously they were limited to five relationships: emanation, subjection, isolation (limited to psychological withdrawal for women), buffering, and direct bargaining. The possession and jealousy inherent to the relationship of emanation in the service of either the ways of life of emanation or incoherence is based on the need to love and be loved and so can be consciously transformed into an affection and love that mutually liberates and fulfills both men and women. Subjection also has its place, such as when a husband or wife, for example, refuses to allow their partner to go to work when they are sick. Such enacting of the relationship of subjection is now clearly for the *benefit* of the other and not to control. Unlike the inherited or created relationships in the ways of life of emanation, incoherence, or deformation, relationships are now exercised for the sake of persistent transformation and are therefore temporary. Thus, after nursing one's partner with care and affection, refusing to allow them to endanger their health, and mediating between them and their sickness, the time comes for the husband or wife to return to their job wherein they enact their competence and creativity in carrying out her or his own duties and plans. In such a different world of created relationships in the service of transformation, a woman can practice the relationship of isolation by going away both physically and psychically to renew herself, advance her own personal skills that will increase her autonomy, enact direct bargaining with her husband and children for less housework, love her family deeply without possessing them, use subjection for children reluctant to study, admit when she has lost her way, and, finally, be ready to descend into her transpersonal depths again and again to experience herself as a person open to new ways of being a woman, a lover, a mother, and the other possibilities that now belong to her.

There is no ideal family or marriage or relationship to which to return. Men and women have the same rights to create, nourish, and uproot inadequate relationships and stories so as to create again. Both are now wealthy with new relationships available to them. Thus, in addition to emanation, subjection, buffering, and direct bargaining there are new relationships available to Latina women and Latino men: autonomy, isolation, incoherence, that is, the right to be confused, to doubt, to break connections that are no longer needed, and to come out of the doubt with a new and better life in which we practice the relationship of transformation. Nor are there only these nine relationships by which to relate to self, others, problems, and the deepest sacred; we have an infinite number of each one of these archetypal patterns that we can break, uproot, create new forms of each and nurture them until they no longer allow us to deal with the problem at hand. Men and women relating in such freedom can now see conflict and change as positive, as necessary counterparts to continuity and stability. Their newly won justice is *mutual* growth. Neither women nor men need sacrifice their ideas and consciousness; they can seek ways to creatively act out their new insights. Men and women due to their own skills are now able to create new relationships to protect and nourish the emergence of others. Their justice is one of creating shared benefits for all who come into contact with them. The source of this renewal is the deepest sacred source of transformation that was previously blocked by relationships, stories, and ways of life that did not allow them to come forth in their wholeness. Our own sacred face is constantly renewed by the journey through the core drama of life that takes us home beyond our ego to our inner self and the deepest sacred source of transformation.

> Dorothy, like a woman's ego, discovers a central truth, that otherness is located both far inside herself and far outside herself. We are once again confronted with the mystery of the two sexes, both far apart from each other and contained within each other, and the mystery of the divine and the human, both far apart from each other and contained within each other.[32]

In a similar manner parents can transform their relationships to their children. Legitimate authority means to guide a child to herself or himself; a parent's authentic authority is enacted to help their children to become the authors of their own life. In this way they guide their children to the center of their own lives so that they can participate in the process of planting the new, not only nourishing but also learning to uproot the destructive aspects of their lives in order to begin again. This is not a case of liberal permissiveness or tough love. If a parent knows that their life is sacred, then they realize that together with their wife or husband they have been given a temporary task to bring their children to fruition. Thus, all the strategies of transforming used by a woman and man to fulfill each other are also available in relating to their children. For example, one child who has been slow to develop physically must be buffered and given closer attention. Another child who seeks more respect for his or her own growing autonomy may need less attention. Still, the most independent must also have affection to protect and nourish that autonomy. Parents need to be ready to exercise subjection to protect an impulsive or headstrong child against herself or himself. But always a parent must ask: "Do I exercise this authority to keep them dependent in the service of emanation; do I use power and control over them in the service of incoherence; has the authority become a justification for hurting them in the service of deformation; or does the use of the relationships and my authority allow them to be able to discover their own self in the service of transformation?" True authority leads each child toward selfhood. The role of the parent is to be a guide, and authentic guides can only lead a person if they, too, are on the journey. This is what raising and nurturing children is all about, not lectures but the capacity to practice relationships in motion: the creation of new and more loving and just concrete manifestations of the relationships in the service of transformation that allows us to respond to the emergence of new problems in the nitty-gritty of everyday life.

A wife, husband, and each child have as their goal to be at the center of their own mandala, where they are free to create the relationships that are necessary wherever they find themselves in order to respond to any particular person or problem. To be restricted to enacting only a certain group of relationships at home, to another set at work, and to another repertory of relationships with friends is to be fragmented. Freedom means to have available all nine possible relationships and an infinite number of concrete manifestations of each. We need to avoid enacting the skills and competence inherent in the relationship of autonomy in the office and returning to inherited patterns of dependency such as emanation and subjection at home. Our fuller freedom heals the split between the personal and political realms of our life. Each of us has the right to be fully who we are whether in our homes or the public realms of our lives. In enacting any of the archetypal relationships we also have the freedom which is both moral and political to enact our relationships in the way of life of transformation and consciously to reject the ways of life of emanation, incoherence, and deformation.[33]

This is what constitutes a true politics of the family: consciously, mutually, lovingly choosing how to relate to one another, freeing ourselves of disabling relationships and stories and creating afresh in the service of the way of life of transformation. What better way is there to prepare children to grow their own personhood? How better to relativize the power of inherited or imposed institutions and to demonstrate that our marriages, our families, our schools, churches, culture, and society consist of our relationships to one another? Institutions are human ways of relating and therefore belong to us to be uprooted when inadequate so that new ones may take root and grow.

Latina women and Latino men need to be about the business of growing their own peoplehood. As I understand this process, it means the refusal to be assimilated and socially adjusted into white, middle-class culture. Boricua, Latina/Latino, Afro-Cuban, *La Raza*, and Chicana/Chicano are words that represent a political decision to create an autonomous and self-determining life for our communities. If this is so, then we need to resist adopting a married and family lifestyle that represses our spontaneity, our affection and warmth. As marriage partners, a woman and man can have their autonomy and self-development *without* sacrificing the best that is within their heritage. Let me give an example. La cultura Latina is permeated by affection. But there are four fundamentally different kinds of love and affection. One mother or father kisses their children tenderly with great affection but with the intent to bind them ever closer and thus to possess them in the way of life of emanation. This kind of love and affection arrests the children in the first act and scene of the core drama of life and prevents them from pursuing their journey of transformation to wholeness. A husband hugs his wife but in such a way that they both know that it is a mere formality that masks the power struggle between them. Or the hug might be done with such force that it is intended to send a message of domination. These two latter scenarios are examples of love in the service of incoherence wherein neither men nor women are free to be vulnerable for fear that they will be controlled by the other. This kind of relationship arrests our lives in Act II, Scene 1, of the core drama of life wherein we are locked in contests for power at home and in the wider society. The worst misuse of love and affection is that of a man or woman who asks their partner to prove their love by having unprotected sex or taking drugs together or sex without consent that becomes rape. This leads both into destructive death and exits them from the core drama in Act II, Scene 2, into the abyss. Affection in the service of deformation always ends in violence against the self and other.

Then there is the hug of love and affection that ends with liberation. A child loved for her own self gains the courage and strength that prepares her for the day when she listens to her inner voice that tells her it is time to leave. Love and affection in the service of transformation heals us. It leads us out of the abyss so that we can begin to love ourselves enough to rebel against those who loved us in the wrong way. We now have the capacity to empty our lives of the stories of the wounded self, patriarchy, possessive love, and capitalism and send them into the abyss instead of ourselves and others in Act II, Scene 2. Now freed from destructive relationships and stories that distorted the four faces of our being, love and affection liberate me to be myself, to hug myself for the first time. This is an experience of wholeness in Act III, Scene 1, of the core drama of life wherein we have experienced the fullness of our being in at least one aspect of our life. Once we have known this joy as a personal and sacred experience of liberation, we can now reach out to others with the political and historical faces of our being in the second scene of Act III in order to guide others to their own realization as a self.

In the above examples the exact same exterior acts are involved, a hug and kiss. But the quality of the relationship involved is radically different depending on the way of life in which the act of affection was practiced by the mother, father, or lover. The uses of affection are to possess, overwhelm, cripple, or liberate the other. This demonstrates the ability of the theory of transformation to do both empirical analysis and to be normative. The theory helps us to analyze our practical choices but also to know whether these choices are just or unjust. We do not have to accept the gap between what is and what ought to be. We are enabled to point out what kinds of affection are inadequate and that kind of affection that does justice to the four faces of our being. This awareness of relationships, stories, and the four faces of our being enacted within four fundamentally different ways of life allow us to examine and test this theory first of all in our own lives. This theory allows us to make the following statement: Unless we take the risk of breaking with the relationships and stories of our lives enacted in the service of ways of life that arrest our lives as partial selves, we will not be free to transform ourselves or our society. The revolution needs to take place in our underlying depths. Mary Lou Espinosa, a young Latina in Milwaukee, Wisconsin, put it this way in her poem, "La Madre de Aztlán":

> Creative solution to social change comes with people who have creative life within themselves, a free woman can creatively contribute with radical solutions because she knows life from within.[34]

William Blake, the great English poet, expressed a similar idea when he wrote that creative union between people was possible only when we have achieved creative unity within ourselves.[35]

Symbols of Transformation

Within our indigenous-Christian heritage we need to rediscover symbols of transformation that have been buried under the de-
bris of fetishism. We have to search out our ancient stories which
carry within them the seeds of a sacred process.[36] Let us consider one
example from the Catholic history of Mexico, La Virgen de Guadalupe. In spite of the recent controversy over the canonization of Juan
Diego to whom la Virgen was alleged to have appeared in 1534 and
whether or not he ever existed, the key issue is the power of her symbolism. For centuries la Virgen was co-opted by a clerical interpretation intent upon perpetuating the image of the Church as our
mother from whom we seek help, thus making the people permanent children dependent upon the official Church. This was an attempt to keep us in the way of life of emanation enacting the stories
of patriarchy and matriarchy together with uncritical loyalty. But La
Virgen can legitimately be interpreted in a different way. Like the
White Buffalo Woman who appeared to Black Elk,[37] La Virgen appeared to a poor Indian. She was dark and Indian, *La Virgen Morena*,
and she spoke *Nahuatl*, the Indian dialect. She appeared on the very
hill where for generations the Indians had worshipped Tonantzín,
the Mother earth goddess. The goddess, Tonantzín, was now re-
created in a new *mestizaje*, or blending of the old and new world, the
Spanish and Indian, the Christian and Indian religions. The new Virgin affirmed the indigenous world while transforming it, something
that the official priests and elites failed to do. She came representing the feminine principle of liberation. La Virgen can be interpreted
as the feminine goddess, the counterpart of the masculine god within
the sacred, who does not preserve the status quo but dissolves violent structures in order to build afresh. Furthermore, Mary's virginity was never meant to be a mere biological intactness but a
person who was *at-one-with-oneself*. Thus virginity symbolized a
psychological transformation, a new wholeness in both men and
women. La Virgen brought about the mixture of the human and the
divine that gave birth to the pilgrim servant, Jesus Christ, the guide
on the journey of transformation and the beginning of a renewed humanity.[38] She is the liberating mother of marginalized indigenous
communities who were the victims of racism and economic exploitation.

It is no accident that in 1810 Padre Miguel Hidalgo carried the
banner of la Virgen de Guadalupe into battle against the Spaniards in
the campaign to free Mexico from Spanish rule. Mary, the Mother,

earth goddess, as a symbol of liberation continues to inspire the personal faces of our being to awaken and ask new questions that lead us to action. We enact the political faces of our being by asking what it is that we can and need to do together to bring about a society based on compassion and justice and then to fight for that very justice that protects our brown faces that had been excluded. When we embark on such a task we practice the historical faces of our being by changing history for the better. The personal, political, and historical faces of our being are renewed again and again because now the sacred faces of our being are connected to the deepest source, the god of transformation. Together we participate in finishing creation. This is what it means to be pregnant with our own inner mysteries: the marriage of the human and the divine, the feminine and the masculine within each of us that results in the birth of pilgrim servants, new manifestations of the god of transformation, other selves, new daughters and sons of the deepest sacred. Such persons will be able to create fundamentally more loving and just marriages, families, and cultures so as to grow new lives for old.

GAY, LESBIAN, AND BISEXUAL RELATIONSHIPS AND FAMILIES

We need as a community to speak openly about gay, transgendered, bisexual, and lesbian relationships and families. I, like many of us, was raised in a virulent homophobic culture both in la comunidad Latina and in the wider society that diminished the humanity of gays, lesbians, the transgendered, and bisexuals.[39] Everything that was said above about heterosexual relationships between men and women and the relationships that we can create in transforming our relationships between one another in our families and marriages is equally applicable to Latino men and Latina women who are gay, lesbian, transgendered, or bisexual. Within the context of transformation we cannot stereotype and we need to go beyond labels just as we did when discussing love between a man and a woman. We need to ask the same questions, "In the service of what way of life do you love as a gay, lesbian, transgendered, bisexual, or heterosexual man or woman; in the service of what ultimate way of life are you relating to each other in your family? Can you enact all eight beneficial relationships in the service of transformation when responding to problems? Have you emptied yourselves of the stories of possessive and romantic love, patriarchy and matriarchy, capitalism, the wounded self and uncritical loyalty to others? Are you able to practice in their fullness the personal, political, historical, and sacred faces of your being and to choose to live new and more loving and compassionate stories such as transforming love, the guide, mutuality, and the political innovator in your family and relationships?"[40]

A gay Latino who cares deeply about his lover and refuses to possess him in the story of romantic love can practice the same relationships in the service of transformation as do those who are lesbian, heterosexual, or bisexual. But also a gay or lesbian who is jealous and seeks to isolate their lover from others is acting with the same kind of destructive behavior as a possessive heterosexual woman or man.

In regard to raising children what counts is that they are loved and nurtured in a deeply caring family so that they have enough confidence in themselves to make their own decisions about their sexuality and identity without the poison of homophobia. Children throughout the world and in the United States are at risk. Many adults who are unhappy with their lives project their anger on children and hurt them. It is a blessing for a gay, lesbian, bisexual, or heterosexual couple who love each other to raise children. Let's keep our eyes on the prize.[41]

4. The Politics of Transformation in the Latino Community

The Latino communities in the barrios have been hampered by internal conflict as well as by discrimination and economic exploitation by the double devil, the stories of capitalism and tribalism in the wider society. Strategies for being political are necessary so that the stories and relationships enacted in partial ways of life that impoverish the four faces of our being can be broken and new ones created in their place. To be political is to move beyond transforming our life in the personal and family realms to reach out to assist in transforming our wider family, the community, that is, the public realm.

A culture is said to be a total way of life encompassing the stories, values, feelings, beliefs, and traditions of a people. Different cultures, therefore, structure life in a variety of ways. A people patterns, shapes, or institutionalizes its values and ideals that are in turn shaped by geography, historical necessities, religious myths, and age-old traditions. United States society, or mainstream United States culture, socializes its young from a variety of ethnic and racial backgrounds into stories and relationships enacted within ways of life largely constituted by Anglo-Saxon and Western European patterns. In order to compare any two cultures, we need to name these ways of life, stories, and relationships, to identify them, and to spell out their logic. Familiarity with these relationships and stories gives a person the ability to survive and succeed in a particular society. They are linkages providing a person with the capacity to deal simultaneously with the five issues of everyday life: how do I live in such a way as to *continue* my relationships with people yet *change*; how do I *collaborate* with my parents' ideas and society's priorities yet *conflict* with them in such a manner that there is mutual benefit and thus *justice* promoted for all involved? By the same token, the lack of such relationships by which to relate to self, others, problems, and our deeper sources constitutes a unique kind of poverty, a poverty of relationships. Each relationship available to us provides us with a different capacity to respond to issues arising in our daily lives. Some relationships emphasize continuity and collaboration at the expense of change and conflict. This means that stability is often purchased at the cost of repressing the justice of one's own ideas and experience.[1]

NAMING THE LATINO RELATIONSHIPS

Why are Latinas and Latinos often stereotyped as being passive, easygoing, and quick to show deference? Certainly these are stereotypes, but there are patterns of relating that Latinos share that lend credence to the perceptions of others. Every group socializes its young into a repertory of usually four or five relationships, of which one is a dominant relationship with two or three subdominant patterns of encounter. Latinas and Latinos have experienced emanation as a dominant relationship, a powerful sense of belonging to a mystery outside themselves, usually focused in the father or mother. Out of respect the children are raised to be reluctant to create conflict or change and to find the justice of security in the strength of the family that is maintained by giving it their continuous cooperation and support. The relationship of subjection is employed to enforce the stability of the container. Buffering is a relationship through which a third party or mediator, such as an uncle or *padrino*, godfather, can bring about change or conflict on our behalf. The relationship of buffering can take our experiences and filter them through a web of clichés by which to rationalize life as it is. For example, the phrase, *¡Ay Bendito!* Good Lord! when it refers to the lord of emanation, reconciles us to our fate. When persons living in the way of life of emanation undergo great stress, they can enact the relationship of direct bargaining with the source of their mystery, such as a father, mother, or spouse, to gain a more tolerable situation. Finally, Latino culture also allowed men the right to isolate both physically and emotionally, but due to the burden of carrying the honor of the family, women were not allowed to practice the relationship of isolation. Whenever the stories of patriarchy, matriarchy, and the relationships described above were in danger, people in authority could and continue to practice the relationship of deformation as they employ the use of violence to keep the container of emanation intact. The use of deformation is a sign of the inherent fragility of emanation as a way of life because people who are caught in this way of life cannot respond to fundamentally new kinds of problems.

When young people marry, they socialize their children by relating to them in these same patterns. Why this emphasis on continuity and cooperation with an inherited past? The stories and the relationships that we live in the service of underlying ways of life are sacred forces that possess us especially when we remain unconscious of them. And since the personal face of our being is repressed and our creativity hobbled by sin, shame, and guilt, our political face can only practice a politics of loyalty to what already exists. The historical face of our being is incapable of bringing about a new turning point in our history because our sacred face is possessed by the lord of emanation who says: "Just believe and don't ask questions." The sons and daughters now become the fathers and mothers but the same stories, relationships, ways of life, and the four faces of our being remain as the sacred roots of the traditional family. This is how and why traditional patterns are repeated, generation after generation.[2]

Relationships with others outside the family in Latin America often emphasize direct bargaining as the dominant relationship, such as a father bargaining with a landowner or *patron*, the boss, to exchange labor for crops as in sharecropping. Middle-class families in Latin American countries are middle class precisely because they have acquired other relationships, that is, the relationships of the international business community, especially autonomy. This new way of relating gives them their status, power, and prestige especially when competing with their fellow Latinas/Latinos.

Literature by authors such as Oscar Lewis provide a descriptive analysis of Latino culture,[3] but this portrayal is inadequate because what it did was analyze in detail what many of us already knew, that the Latino culture is different from the American culture that is presented to us for emulation. Educators have told us that the Latino child does not look into the eyes of the authority figure out of respect and that they find it hard to compete. These points we have heard time and again. But what has been missing are three key ingredients: first, naming and identifying those relationships by which the different Latino cultures and the American culture shape everyday life; second, the alternatives open to Latinas and Latinos by which to create a new culture in this country; and, finally, the way

of life in which these relationships are being enacted. Too many social scientists merely report the world. A living culture is always on
the move and responds to change through a healthy self-criticism.[4]
Our task is to search out a process by which we can go beyond description to participate in a process of resistance to the dominant
culture or beyond an unquestioning loyalty to our inherited culture
by uprooting stories and relationships and then creating and nourishing new ones that make life more just and compassionate. This is
the open-ended process by which each of us can participate in transforming our lives and society.

United States and European-American Patterns

Autonomy is the dominant relationship in the United States,
Western Europe, and increasingly in Japan and other countries seeking to industrialize. Autonomy is a relationship in which both sides
are entitled to claim and occupy an autonomous zone or area of jurisdiction. The basis of this principle may be custom, competence,
ethics, revelation, or a rationalized legal system. What matters is
that this principle needs to be made clear enough to all so that each
participant in this relationship can enact it freely, for example as a
member of a union or as a fellow citizen. This relationship defines
the checks and balances of our federal system of government—the
executive, legislative, and judiciary—and allows us to link all three
through both collaboration and conflict. For example, the executive branch accepts and collaborates in the agreement set down in
the Constitution that it cannot declare war but reserves the right to
conflict with the legislative branch in the president's duty as com-
mander-in-chief to urge the Congress to act. This relationship also
dictates the separation of church and state, each with its own autonomous rights of jurisdiction that are seen as inviolable by each other.
On the personal level, it stresses the ability of a person to put himself or herself forward as a competent, aggressive, mobile individual.
This relationship is practiced by ambitious men and women who are
dedicated to establishing, maintaining, and enlarging their personal
boundaries (upward mobility) by fulfilling the expectations of the
corporate world. There are three subdominant relationships that
usually accompany autonomy: direct bargaining, subjection, and isolation. Direct bargaining power, or leverage by which to enlarge
one's zone of autonomy, is achieved through isolating oneself and

deferring pleasure, subjecting oneself and others in order to gain more power. But as we shall see, there are ways to enact these archetypal relationships other than in the service of incoherence.

When the Latino patterns of relationships and the patterns of American society clash in the United States, there is no doubt as to which will win. This unequal competition begins in the schools. The majority of those who are arriving from Latin America have been brought up with relationships stressing respect and deference which cannot compete with children who have learned aggressive behavior in the relationships of autonomy and direct bargaining in their home environment. This also holds true among Latinas and Latinos and helps us to recognize the class conflict between, for example, middle-class Cubans and migrant workers from Mexico or Puerto Rico. The majority of Cubans who fled Castro's Cuba in the period 1959–1965 arrived with a working knowledge of the relationship of autonomy, having learned this pattern of behavior and corresponding skills before coming to this country. Thus, although they share a common language and religion with the migrant workers, this learned relationship put them in a different socioeconomic class.

Alongside the language barrier is the painful awareness on the part of Latinos that they are being outmaneuvered and used without knowing why. This leads to a growing sense of fear, anger, apathy, or cynicism. In any case, it creates incoherence, a breaking of connections with one's own culture and tradition which is now identified by many Latinos, especially the young, with powerlessness and defeat. The incoherence increases with the inability to relate to one's past in Puerto Rico, Ecuador, Guatemala, Mexico, Peru, or the Dominican Republic. They perceive U.S. society as baffling and as rejecting them. The result literally is a group of people *sin raices*, without roots, in either country or culture. At this point some Latino men and Latina women rebel against their past, reject it, and assimilate into the dominant American mores, relationships, and stories with a vengeance. Some act out their anger and turn to violence against themselves in forms of self-wounding with drugs or alcohol; others take out their anger by hating whites or turning to underground capitalism by becoming involved in the drug trade. Still others choose to remain aloof from the dominant culture and see any attempt at accommodation as selling out because only the culture of their national heritage has the answers. Many Latinas and Latinos end in a kind of schizophrenia: wanting to make it here but rebelling against the heavy cost of repudiating their cultural roots.

Since it is a rebellion, their life now becomes dominated by that against which they rebel, but in an unconscious way. They swallow their past without being able to confront it or to transform it.[5] As one Puerto Rican student related recently, he saw his own culture as "weak, non-progressive, and inadequate." He became so serious that he could not play or enjoy anything lest he lose the initiative in showing white society that he could beat them at their own game. He did. But this was done at a very heavy cost—his identity.

We cannot romanticize la cultura Latina and condemn American culture as the enemy. Freedom in this context means the right to critique both cultures and to create relationships and stories in the service of transformation that allow us to enact the four faces of our being in their wholeness. As we have seen, the politics of freedom involves participation in uprooting of relationships and stories practiced in the service of partial ways of life in order to respond to new problems in the way of life of transformation.[6] This is not about pragmatically mixing together several relationships or stories from both cultures. The quality of our lives will depend upon what way of life we serve when we enact the stories, relationships, and the four faces of our being in relating to ourselves, one another, and the issues we confront. The relationships of the dominant society and our inherited Latino cultures are in trouble because they do not return people to themselves as creators but to an ever-widening search for power and possessions in the service of incoherence that locks us all into an insatiable competition or a renewed effort to attain security in the service of emanation. The irony of American culture and institutions is that with all their power they end by being powerless to create afresh. On the other hand, for Latinas and Latinos the inherited relationships of dependency practiced in the service of emanation as a way of life described above and in chapter 2 cannot provide us with the necessary insight or capacity to respond to new problems in a time of personal awakening and political upheaval.

Structural Violence against la Comunidad Latina

Many Latinas and Latinos have been assimilated into white society on a selective and individual basis. They were not promoted, hired, or selected as members of a group but as exceptions who could be made tokens. Often people of color are isolated from their own communities as a result of being separated by class due to their upward mobility and identification with their new colleagues and status. A tacit agreement is made to avoid conflict or demands for change because one's interests are now vested in a respectable position. There is a basic assumption that everybody will eventually make it. Advancement is considered automatic based on a belief that meritocracy is at work as long as people work hard, go to school, and follow the system.

But structural violence cannot be so easily covered up. Some have a vested interest in maintaining their boundaries at the expense of others. Thus when a dispossessed group such as A.T.A., Asociación de Trabajadores Agricolares, a Puerto Rican migrant organization, attempted to enter the mainstream of American political and economic participation, they were excluded. Puerto Ricans and Chicanos, two of the older Latino communities, together with the *recien llegados*, the newly arrived, and the *esquineros*, those who stand on the corners looking for work, continue to be isolated and subjected in relationship to the greater society. By sitting down together they can agree to end their mutual isolation so that they can enter into a direct bargaining agreement to set up an organization, such as a union, protected by the principle of autonomous jurisdictions. By organizing they can end these debilitating relationships and create a direct bargaining relationship that can lead to the formation of an alternative autonomy, a new form of capacity, linked creativity that cannot be carved out of existing zones of autonomy. Connected in this new way through the relationship of autonomy they are now prepared to bargain with the corporations or school systems, that is, other autonomous jurisdictions, in order to achieve justice.

In New Jersey, for example, as well as other states throughout the country, Latino immigrants face an array of institutions that are often not prepared to welcome them: law enforcement personnel, local politicians, a powerful farm lobby, schools, banks, and a public with ambivalent feelings toward them. In the past mediators who have sought to intervene on behalf of those who were voiceless have been criticized and even physically attacked, such as Representative Byron Baer of Bergen County who had his arm broken by a guard while he was attempting to investigate abuses of farm workers. This kind of response constitutes structural violence, since it demonstrates the extent to which the already powerful will go to protect their autonomous zone of power by excluding others from the very opportunity to gain human standards of living. In this case law and order becomes a mask for violence that goes beyond the pursuit of power in the way of life of incoherence. The use of violence demonstrates the fragility of incoherence as a way of life; since the powerful are caught by the story of capitalism that arrests their lives as partial selves in Act II, Scene 1, of the core drama of life they cannot respond with compassion and justice.[7] By turning to force and violence to protect their privilege, they exit the core drama of life and now practice the story of capitalism in the service of deformation. The above example is an excellent way of seeing how persons enacting autonomy in the way of life of incoherence are always in danger of entering the road to deformation. In addition we can see from this example how the double devil, stories of capitalism and racism, collude with one another to justify the exclusion of Latinos as people of color. Yes, we all need the relationship of autonomy by which to shape daily life in this country but it makes all the difference in the world whether we practice the relationship of autonomy in the service of incoherence and deformation or we create new forms of autonomy in the way of life of transformation. We shall return to this process of transforming relationships in the society around us in chapter 7 in our discussion of Latina/Latino professionals as a transforming middle class.

Let us consider some other examples of "invisible violence" presented to us by our "best and brightest" boundary managers: it is invisible violence because it has become part of the fabric of our everyday life.[8] In 1972, when negotiations were being carried out by the State Department and North Vietnam, the Pentagon continued to bomb because bureaucrats had a mandate to expend their ordinance (bombs and rockets) so that they would be able to justify a larger share of the budget. The American Medical Association has consistently stifled legislation in favor of national health-care insurance to maintain a scarce medical delivery system, thereby assuring the medical profession's inflated salaries. The pharmaceutical companies' lobby, one of the most powerful in Washington, protects their power to control the price of drugs by resisting the transition to generic drugs from the more expensive brand name. Like the Pentagon some law enforcement officials develop a vested interest in promoting false crises to justify bigger budgets. These are acts of structural violence against all of us. Like Big Nurse in *One Flew Over the Cuckoo's Nest*,[9] the power of so many people in our society rests upon keeping other people weak and dependent. Within Nurse Ratched's boundaries she creates a turf, with no limits, through a deliberate mystification of her authority and person. At this point bureaucrats cease to be efficient, rational managers and become obsessed with their area of jurisdiction as a personal fiefdom. It is no longer a detached professional enterprise but autonomy in the service of incoherence, the way of life of fragments, that now holds us in an irrational emanational embrace; the office is now an extension of one person's views and whims. This is one reason why so many hardened bureaucrats fight change: it is viewed no longer as an attempt to change an office procedure but rather as a personal attack. The irony is that they become irrational and turn their boundary of authority into a turf that they are prepared to defend against all comers even with violence. As a result, defending one's autonomous zone of power can become a relationship in the service of deformation. This is why when McMurphy, her main protagonist, refuses to conform to her system the Big Nurse does not hesitate to turn to violence.

Let me give an account of an example that I observed. Several years ago an Anglo student who was in charge of a several-thousand-dollar budget for student entertainment approached a Puerto Rican student and asked him what he would consider appropriate to fit the cultural needs of Latino students. The Puerto Rican student was offended and suspicious. The Anglo student was hurt at this reaction. This is a perfect example of the relationship of incoherence: two people stand in the presence of one another and do not know how to cooperate or continue, everything is conflict, and they do not know how to change so as to relate meaningfully. Both feel there is an injustice. Now who is the enemy here? Certainly it is not initially either of the two students; it is the hidden agenda of U.S. society. That hidden agenda consists in the following: those with positions of power, the relationship of autonomy, believe that they have achieved it legitimately and that they have every right to wield that power. Those who have no access to practice the relationship of autonomy or power will have to get it like everybody else—by hard work and other legitimate means. But the Latino student knows when he confronts an Anglo student with power that it is not merely one Anglo that he confronts face-to-face but "the establishment." This student has all manner of benefits at his disposal: he has a strong fraternity as a base; he has the keys to the Xerox machine; his father, a lawyer, knows the dean on a first-name basis; he knows the ins and outs of setting up a concert and carnival; he is usually a full-time, resident student; in short, the Anglo student at that point *is* U.S. society. The Anglo student saw a "deprived" minority student and wanted to reach out. But he extended himself as one with power to dole out privileges. The word "privilege" here is most significant; too many whites do not consider people of color to have a right to good health, employment, adequate education, and decent housing. As far as the dominant are concerned these benefits for Latinos, African Americans, Native Americans, and Asians are privileges which may be distributed by whites, but to which whites feel they have an inherent right since their ancestors earned them for them.[10] Ultimately the term "privilege" is a racist term. The privilege here is to be white, and since all the tricks in the world will not make people of color white, too many Anglos see people of color as their burden living on the edges of white beneficence and power. Power of its very nature is power because it is scarce: you find out how much power you have by comparing yourself to those who have no or less power. Power in this logic can never be shared. The incoherence here is that the good intentions of the Anglo student in a cultural context dominated by competition, power, and an institutional racism were reduced to condescension and humiliation. In the final analysis what Puerto Ricans and other Latinos want is the capacity to affirm themselves and therefore zones of autonomy become important *because* they protect the task of creating alternatives. As long as power is in the hands of the dominant and benefits are subject to the whims of those who hand them out, a relationship of subjection is perpetuated, which is made more tolerable by occasional flashes of paternalism.

The confrontation between these two students has its carbon copy in the whole welfare mentality. Welfare payments do not end the relationships of isolation and subjection. Welfare often deepens the despair by hiding or buffering the real issues. In Alan Paton's superb novel of South Africa, *Too Late the Phalarope,* Japie, the social worker, is a buffoon.[11] He prevents and puts off the confrontation with the real causes of crime, unemployment, and bad housing. He tinkers with the fringes of the system when the real cause is racism. But his duty is not to expose but to preserve the illusion that people are poor, ill-fed, and badly housed because it is their own fault. This public relations façade hides the real cancer of such a society: when one group of human beings systematically practices violence against another group, they brutalize themselves in the process. There are no victors, only victims. This is the real meaning of how absolute power corrupts absolutely.

The logic of gaining strength by uniting and negotiating for autonomy is a risk. Power politics in the way of life of incoherence has been reproduced in the various social service agencies in Washington to the effect that as a community of color earns recognized power relationships of autonomy and direct bargaining, it then dominates the groups arriving later on the scene. A hierarchy has developed among communities of color. African Americans promote from within their own community; Chicanos do the same for other Chicanos; and the Puerto Ricans are often at the bottom of the pecking order. This is the logic of individualism on the societal level. The system has had its revenge. Those who sought to beat the system and to tell others what they wanted to hear end by themselves being controlled by the present consciousness of U.S. society. When previously dispossessed groups achieved their own power, they closed out the group that has not yet learned to survive in America. Thus rather than opening new opportunities for other communities who are experiencing the same oppression, a group assimilates into the story of capitalism in the service of incoherence and thereby joins the powerful.

THE POLITICS OF TRANSFORMATION

We need a politics of transformation. Politics is what we can and need to do together to bring about compassion and justice. We do not need permission to be political; it is part and parcel of being human. The meaning of our lives is not to be found in the secure embrace of mysterious others or in the efficiency of systems that end by reducing us all to victims. The search for meaning is within individual persons who discover that their inner self is the source of creativity. People can take patterns and relationships into their own hands and transform them. Now when a Latina *chooses* to use autonomy or direct bargaining, it is a temporary choice that fills our needs here and now but remains open to respond to change. The relationships of autonomy and buffering enacted in the service of transformation raises up men and women with professional skills who protect human dignity. A lawyer can now use legal skills to protect rather than exploit. The liberal agenda of living with incoherence allows an entrepreneurship that exploits the needs of others for personal gain. Autonomy in the service of transformation demands on the personal and group level people acting autonomously with competence and skill for the good of those who are in need. Emanation is also transformed not to contain and possess others but as a temporary relationship to nourish us until we are strong enough to begin our own journey of transformation through the core drama of life. Parent and child, lovers, husband and wife are now free to become friends and mutual guides. This enables us to face problems with a new consciousness, creativity, new relationships, and a mutual justice, made possible because our sacred face is connected to the deepest source of transformation.

To be political in our communities consists in empowering ourselves to use eight of our nine archetypal relationships in the service of transformation rather than the three or four which most societies employ in order to relate to self, others, and problems. The ninth relationship, deformation, almost always cannot be used for the sake of transformation. We have nine archetypal patterns but an infinite number of different ways of enacting these relationships. How better to relativize the power of institutions and to demonstrate that our political organizations, schools, churches, economies, and neighborhoods, the barrios, consist of our relationships to one another. What changes in every use of the relationships, stories, and the four faces of our being is the intention, the quality, the ultimate way of life in which we enact them.

EMPOWERMENT IN THE LATINO COMMUNITY: THE HELPING PROFESSIONAL

The modem age comes to a society when there is a breakdown of the linkages by which a people have dealt simultaneously with continuity and change, cooperation and conflict, and justice. This is the experience of incoherence. We live now during such a period characterized by separation and the inability to communicate with or understand each other. We are all in trouble. Both Latino and American cultures are inadequate. Latino and Anglo alike are now equal in their mutual need and vulnerability.

Latinas and Latinos in need of services approach agencies with a sense of their subjection and isolation. Social welfare agencies constitute large zones of autonomy that were established to buffer on behalf of those who could not create change to better their lives. Too often the roles created by these patterns establish a power relationship. Bureaucrats usually take on the consciousness of defending the system. Some genuinely desire to help but find themselves frustrated and eventually embittered by the red tape. The bureaucrat and the citizen are both victims. To insist on standard operating procedures that are often inflexible in a situation demanding compassion and openness demonstrates that bureaucracy is based on repression. Agency personnel who wish that they could reach out and who have genuine compassion must repress such sentiments because they would wreck the system. The system, or ways by which people are trapped in relating to each other, takes on a life of its own and turns the service personnel and the clients into things. And yet what is this system, this thing but our own relationships, our own institutions that have taken over our lives. But many seek to press on, thereby avoiding the truth of how they feel. They continue to work as if there was nothing wrong. "Lifers" are found in all agencies who believe that if you keep the rules, the rules will keep you. This loyalty to a system, or fixed way of organizing life, is an example of autonomy initially in the service of incoherence because it freezes people into power relationships, but then descends to deformation because it diminishes the humanity of the social worker and the client.

Yet there are those helping professionals, such as public health nurses, teachers, social workers, welfare workers, and other community aides, who have liberated themselves from an inherited reliance on bureaucratic methods by which to process people and have set about creating new and more compassionate relationships in order to confront the problems of daily living. Our theoretical perspective does not allow us to stereotype. Two women walking into a government agency may look like two hardened bureaucrats with the same job description, but one might be prepared to use her personal skills to create structural change that makes life fundamentally better for those whom she serves. We need allies everywhere. Do we need social workers? Yes, but in the service of what way of life do they relate to the community is the question that always needs to be asked.

Authentic helping professionals are "wounded healers."[12] Only those who realize their own pain can reach out and help heal others. It must be a mutual therapy. This attitude removes the power relationship and introduces a different kind of nurse, teacher, or social worker. This type of helping professional does not give people anything nor reach down in condescension; he or she, by enacting the story of the guide, is always ready to seize the opportunity to put themselves out of business in the lives of others so that new relationships of mutual healing might be wooed into being. They realize that poverty is more than financial difficulty; poverty is also the absence of vital connections. The broken connections in our lives to our own self, others, problems, and the deepest source of our being together with the lack of new and better alternative relationships destroys our wholeness as persons. Consequently they ask what relationships are missing and what linkages are essential to provide us with the necessary kind of capacity and performance to renew our lives. These sensitive and caring people can be appropriately called political innovators.

An example of such transforming people at work was a conference in New York City on "Mugging and the Senior Citizen."[13] At first it seemed like the typical approach: protect your purse, carry a whistle, and so forth. But the conference listed seven muggers, and heading the list of perpetrators was the Social Security system itself. Last on the list was the youth who was himself considered a victim of high unemployment and poor educational opportunity. This was a remarkable program that allowed the seniors to identify the enemy as the culture that sanctioned the stories of capitalism and competence often in collusion with racism and ways of relating that led to a society attempting to buy itself out of their lives by sending them a check once a month. Senior citizens came to recognize that their own personal situation was caught up in a broader systemic context. This helped them to become radical, that is, to get to the roots of the problem, the causes and not the symptoms. In this example social workers did not function as buffers to prevent conflict and confrontation but provided a political analysis leading to reflection and action.

Let us analyze what took place here. Social workers, aware of the process of transforming relationships, used their professional position in a structure, or their relationship of autonomy, in a subversive manner. They used their official status to buffer or mediate on behalf of senior citizens not to perpetuate but to end their isolation and subjection. Senior citizens met one another, discussed their common problems, and established linkages that now allowed them to create their own zones of autonomy, senior citizens' organizations, which empowered them to bargain with politicians, state agencies, universities, and others. This is a transforming autonomy that was shared in a context of community that allowed caring relationships. Here the nuclear family was extended to include a larger family of people sharing the same concerns and vision. This kind of strategy has freed many senior citizens from self-pity on the intrapersonal level, liberated them from dependency on their children, and brought them to a keen political and social awareness of American culture and society. In this way senior citizens who were victimized as isolated individuals were now politicized. They practiced the personal, political, historical, and sacred faces of their being to create an environment that took into account their value as persons. Thus, their poverty had consisted in more than lack of money and services; they also suffered from a lack of relationships to each other. This is why it is so important to know which relationships are present, what relationships need to be broken, and what relationships to create in the way of life of transformation in order to enable ourselves and others to confront problems. This is the kind of creative imagination by which to challenge health care professionals. Our capacity to participate in creating, nourishing, and uprooting in order to create again demands social workers who go beyond job descriptions and who are still creating what it means to be a helping professional, that is, they are in the process of growing their own relationships to real people.

The condition of Latino senior citizens is a similar one, being trapped in debilitating relationships of isolation and subjection. Their isolation is often increased by their lack of knowledge of English. Fear of being mugged or robbed and of arson leads to increased isolation because they are afraid to leave their homes and apartments. The strategy described above is an excellent example of what can be done in all of our barrios to end the relationships of isolation and subjection. And this is exactly the strategy used by Chicano/Latino organizations such as Communities Organized for Public Service (COPS) and United Neighborhood Organization (UNO) in the Southwest, especially Texas and California. COPS is probably the largest neighborhood organization in the United States. In fact, COPS has had a lot to do with transforming the Valley in Texas and even the rest of the state from an Anglo political reserve to one where Chicanas/Chicanos are now a force both politically and economically. Organizations like COPS, UNO, La Raza Unida, the G.I. Forum, the League of United Latin American Citizens, and Valley Interfaith have given voice, hope, and real accomplishment to Latinas and Latinos who were unable to participate in their society as valued citizens.[14]

In all of these examples we see empowering relationships being created in a new context of transformation. People are now able to change and create conflict with others, whereas before they were limited to cooperating in their own loneliness and powerlessness. To confront politicians and bureaucrats as a group and to realize successful intervention on at least one issue led to a new kind of consciousness of what they can do together in other aspects of their lives. They creatively set about establishing new institutionalized forms of power by establishing organizations. This institutionalization of linked power assures that they will not be sent back to their solitude by being a one-issue, overnight phenomenon or a one-act drama of transformation. To be successful, they had learned to share their ideas, resources, and lives. This is a new kind of justice that allows everybody to participate in the cost and the fruits of a common struggle. The process was initiated by activist organizers or helping professionals acting as guides. However, it was the people themselves who discovered their ability to risk, to begin life anew by drawing the strength from their own personal depths. Furthermore, these are examples of people enacting new concrete forms of the nine relationships, with the exception of deformation, and especially creating for the first time in their lives relationships like autonomy. But this is not assimilation, since the people enacting this relationship were not pursuing *individual* power and self-interest according to the way of life of incoherence; this is the liberal American agenda. They enacted the relationship of autonomy on both a personal and group level in order to connect themselves to each other in an alliance to achieve *common* goals. The people created fundamentally new and more just concrete manifestations of the relationship of autonomy in the service of transformation.

Let us now turn to consider another area of extreme importance to the Latino community's empowerment, education, specifically bilingual/bicultural education.

CREATING NEW CONNECTIONS: BILINGUAL/ BICULTURAL EDUCATION

Our phrase "bilingual/bicultural education" needs to be taken seriously. It already implies and demands a synthesis, a coming together of different cultures and languages out of which emerges a third enriched reality that was not there before. To lose either one of these cultural expressions as a result of racism, colonialism, or other forms of subspeciation is to impoverish everyone. We who are both members and representatives of the various Latino communities in the United States need to intervene to prevent the permanent wounding of our people. It is estimated that prior to 1940 only 1 percent of Chicano children growing up in the Southwest were enrolled in school.[15] Mexicans were seen as and continue to be viewed as a permanent source of cheap and docile labor. A Texas superintendent of schools left no doubt as to the reasons why Mexicans were not to be given an education, "If a man has very much sense or education either, he is not going to stick to this kind of work. So you see it is up to the white population to keep the Mexican on his knees in an onion patch. . . ."[16] This helps to explain why we have so few persons from that generation who were prepared to protect the community with legal, educational, and medical skills. They were consciously crippled by an Anglo attitude of superiority and an economic policy that sought to create a permanent illiterate and unorganized work force. The story of tribalism was practiced here: the Mexican people were treated as invisible, then allowed to work if they accepted their inferiority in wages, housing, health care, and education. Those who were the "better" Mexicans were invited to assimilate, to join the powerful; if they proved to be disloyal they were exiled from the privileged realm, and finally they could be killed or exterminated as a last resort. Some find this last aspect of the story of tribalism too harsh. But we need only to recall the US-Mexico War of 1846–1848 that was fought to expand slavery and take lands from Mexican people who were in the way of American Manifest Destiny as the nation stretched itself from sea to shining sea.[17] The story of the lynching of Mexicans in the Southwest between 1848 and 1928 is just now being told.[18]

From 1848 to 1968, a period of 140 years, the Mexican/Latino community suffered from a continuous and conscious strategy of marginalization. Mexicans were the primary targets. Their exploitation was justified with a racist rationale: "Who cares? They are only Mexicans." In this way the double devil, the collusion between the two stories of capitalism and tribalism in the service of deformation, did immeasurable harm to the Mexican/Latino community. Thousands of Mexicans were lynched during this period for resisting Anglo power. The story of Anglo brutality against Mexicans in both California and Texas after all these years is finally being revealed in all its details.[19]

This is why the plight of the undocumented has struck such a nerve; the return of these two stories in their most blatant form threatens to wipe away much of the gains achieved by the Chicano Civil Rights movement, La Causa, and the struggle of the Puerto Rican community for justice. Undocumented workers employed in Immokalee, Florida, were threatened with having their tongues cut out if they tried to leave their jobs. They were treated as if they were nothing, objects with no rights who were brutalized by the double devil of capitalism and tribalism. Hundreds of workers were held hostage by contractors and forced to work without wages. Since

1996 six cases of involuntary servitude, that is, slavery, resulted in convictions in Florida with many more probably going undetected. The state of Florida did almost nothing to intervene. This was largely due to the coalitions forged between the powerful agricultural industry and many legislators who have close ties to the growers. The combination of autonomous zones of power were enacted in the service of deformation since they erased the humanity of the workers. It was only through the intervention of community organizations, the Coalition of Immokalee Workers, using their autonomous power in the service of transformation that alleviated the plight of these workers. Yum Brands, the parent company of Taco Bell, agreed after boycotts and demonstrations to put pressure on the growers who supplied them with tomatoes to increase the workers' wages and to provide guarantees that their human rights would be respected. The workers were given a pay raise of a penny for every pound of tomatoes picked. This is effect doubled their salaries.[20]

The dropout rate among Latinos in our schools, due in part to a lack of bilingual resources, is alarmingly high. It is no wonder that, given the lack of English skills together with other factors, the dropout rate for Latinas/Latinos in the country hovers around 50 percent. In order to prepare our youth for the relationships that are necessary to survive in U.S. society, we need first of all to provide them with the tool of language. Recently a young man from the Brookings Institute who represented a Latin American nation in its dealings with a multinational corporation spoke of how he could have cried in reviewing past contracts that put them at a disadvantage. It was a twofold language problem: the Latinos did not know English nor did they know the legal language of contracts. English allows our people to participate in recognizing how established power manipulates them. The ideal is to educate simultaneously in English and Spanish. Our desire is to maintain our Spanish language, culture, and history, while acquiring new cultural traits and English. But wherever bilingual programs exist, we must be equally serious about the bicultural dimension, that is, Latino history and culture. However, we must not forget that bilingual/bicultural programs carry the philosophy of the funding agency, the Department of Education.

As a bureaucracy, the Department of Education is not committed to the transformation of our society. Federal programs are primarily intended to alleviate the social and political pressure brought to bear by groups who are essentially excluded from American society. Government programs in the service of incoherence are intended for the good of the powerful and buy time in order to mask the real issues of dependency and powerlessness. In fact, federal programs strengthen the system; they are not intended to transform it. This is an example of buffering in the service of incoherence because it allows most of U.S. society to pursue power as individuals while fending off the poor. This is the liberal and conservative agenda although they differ in how far they are willing to go to fund the safety net. The guidelines for establishing federal poverty programs give us an insight into their ultimate direction. Those guidelines stipulate that professionals or boundary managers are to initiate, organize, and implement the programs. Thus a stronger middle class too often emerges at the expense of people who remain in hopeless impoverishment. It can become a class issue that splits our community because some people increase their status, power, and prestige, while members of the same ethnic community remain behind. We have to remain critical of these programs and learn how to subvert them so that they are in fact used to make the lives of people new and better.

Our basic hope lies in establishing linkages between the practitioners responsible for and students enrolled in bilingual/bicultural programs and the community. It is necessary to *subvert* the intentions of bureaucrats whose conscious or unconscious aim is to assimilate and to extend the doctrine of individualism to our students. The term "subvert" is taken from the Latin, which means to turn (*verto*) from below (*sub*). The strategy of subversion means to do the direct opposite of what was intended: rather than allow bilingual/bicultural programs to assimilate students into the mobile, competitive stories of living with incoherence, we need to prepare our youth to excel by teaching them both Spanish and English and simultaneously assist them in finding the sources of creativity in American culture, in their own cultural background, and within their own selfhood.[21] We shall return to a more detailed discussion of a strategy of subversion in chapter 7.

Bilingual/bicultural programs can truly politicize our people. First we need to remain critical of programs by asking questions: Do we have the resources to teach English and Spanish simultaneously? If not, then which language should get priority, and why? What is necessary for our people to succeed here and now in this situation? Second, our community must have the right to critique *both* cultures, not just the Anglo. And finally, through a return to our own inner self, as a source of creativity, we can now set about truly being political by asking the question: "What is it that we can and need to do together to achieve a just resolution facing the community in regards to this problem here and now?" In this way we can participate in the shaping of our daily lives and society. Perhaps the greatest danger to avoid is the isolation of our community from the rest of society. It is possible to argue that the French in Quebec helped to structure their political and economic subordination in a predominantly English-speaking nation. Their official language and cultural policies to an extent helped create a political climate of separation. Feelings of powerlessness were aggravated by not knowing the English language, which is the vehicle to more economic, political, and social participation. Too many French responded with a permanent posture of going it alone over and against an allegedly hostile, English-speaking Canada. African Americans in the United States did not make the same mistake when some tried to romanticize and teach Black English in the schools. Some Blacks saw this as a subtle form of racism, because it would prevent them from communicating with others in a mutual struggle for justice in a world of power. African Americans are bilingual and bicultural. They have their particular colloquial forms of communicating, as all groups do, but they also understand the necessity of knowing the language of the market economy. However, it is essential to understand the complexities of the market economy in another sense in order to transcend it, that is, not to allow the mentality of competition to dominate our consciousness. Thus, persons well schooled in the intricacies of the market can also establish viable cooperatives that economically and politically allow people to participate in their own advancement.

Nevertheless, given all of these objections and warnings, bilingual/bicultural education has become a rallying point for Latinas and Latinos throughout the United States for several reasons. First of all, the large influx of recent immigrants, *los recien llegados*, into a society and economy that is increasingly becoming more dependent on information technology makes the learning of English essential. When my father arrived in Detroit from Mexico and was hired at Ford Motor Company, it was not necessary for him to be literate in English to get and hold a job. He made a relatively good wage and never learned to read or write English; he understood English but spoke it only when necessary. But these kinds of jobs are no longer available. Millions of jobs created in the last decade are primarily in the service area, that are generally low paying, non-union, often without benefits, and with little chance of advancement. The new generation of Latina/Latino children need ESL or bilingual/

bicultural programs to avoid becoming a permanent economic underclass, or what Mario Barrera has called "a colonial labor force" with ranks filled by Latinas and Latinos whose needs are made subordinate to the dominant society.[22]

Another reason for insisting on bilingual/bicultural education is to heal the wounds of the past and to avoid repeating them. We continue to be a people at risk; our children are labeled as "disadvantaged" "culturally deficient," or "linguistically deprived" and are often placed in E.M.R. (Educable Mentally Retarded) classes, remedial classes, low-ability groups, and vocational tracks. I.Q. testing is usually done in English and so results in lower scores. Transfer students from the different nations of Latin America are often placed in lower grades. These policies based on an attitude of indifference or racism are one of the causes for the high dropout or failure rate. Latinos are the youngest and one of the fastest growing populations in the nation. Therefore, what happens in the schools is of fundamental concern to our community and should be to the rest of the country. We will return to the issue of education as the priority for la comunidad Latina in chapter 9. Many of the children of the *recien llegados* speak only Spanish or are not proficient in either language. Language problems together with discriminatory attitudes are devastating our students.

In 1980 the U.S. Census reported that a mere 44 percent of all Latinos in the United States had completed high school. It is not much better more than twenty years later. In 2004 the high school completion rate for Latinos and Latinas over twenty-five was 58.4 percent whereas for European Americans it was 85.8 percent and for African Americans it was 80 percent. In 1980 the Latino graduation rate from college for those over twenty-five was 7.6 percent and in 2004 it was 12.1 percent in comparison to European Americans at 28.2 percent. Furthermore according to the 2000 Census of the 18 million Latinas and Latinos twenty-five and over nearly 13 million have no college degree.[23] In 2000, 74,963 Latinas and Latinos earned a bachelors degree in comparison to 107,891 African Americans and 928,013 whites. In 2003 Latinos had a median family income of $33,000, only 69 percent of the median of European-American families. In fact, the Latino median family income actually declined 2.6 percent between 2002 and 2003. Overall the poverty rate for Latinos in 2004 was fully 21.9 percent while non-Hispanic whites was 8.6 percent. These figures clearly highlight the correlation between educational achievement and socioeconomic well-being. For these reasons Latinos are adamant that this kind of educational discrepancy shall not continue.[24]

To address this risk to the Latino community and its children, the community became politicized on the local and national levels. For the first time on the national level Latinos were politically successful. The passage of the first Bilingual Education Act in 1968 was largely due to Latino political pressure. This law and the Lau vs. Nichols decision, primarily involving non-English-speaking Chinese, made the retention and advancement of language and culture a political right.

The creation of bilingual/bicultural education provided access for Latinas/Latinos in many areas of the country to city, state, and federal jobs. It opened up a whole new area for the creation of a professional class in teaching, administration, grant-proposal writing, consultant work, publishing, and law. For the first time Latino parents were elected or appointed to school boards. Federal monies funded bilingual fellowship programs and bilingual teacher training grants; many states opened offices for Hispanic Affairs as a direct response to the influx of federal and state grants and political pressure. The result was a gradual closure of the gap between the demand for bilingual/bicultural programs and the availability of personnel to provide the services. There was much progress and solid gains were achieved.

But today some thirty-eight years since the passage of the Bilingual Education Act it is déjà vu all over again. Many of the battles that were fought and the gains achieved over the past generation and a half have suffered a great setback. Since the 1980s there has been an amazing influx of newly arrived Latinas/Latinos into the United States. This latest migration is comparable to and even surpasses the waves of migration that the nation experienced at the end of the nineteenth and the beginning of the twentieth century. This has happened at a time when segregation in the schools throughout the nation is growing. Courts have been reluctant since the 1980s to force integration usually by redistricting and the inevitable solution sought by busing children to schools outside their neighborhoods.[25] In addition Latinos are arriving daily in small towns, villages, and cities throughout the nation that have not had to face mandated ESL and bilingual programs. This has led to a great deal of discrimination especially against students who are undocumented. We need strategies by which to respond to this old yet new phenomenon. We shall return to this issue in chapter 9.

There continue to be the inevitable arguments over whether bilingual/bicultural education is or should be compensatory, transitional, and ultimately assimilationist. Some Latinos demand complete bilingualism on all grade levels; others are not sure if this is desirable. Such a policy should be decided by the local Latino community, who know their own needs and the resources available to fulfill them. The bottom line is that some form of bilingual/bicultural education is a non-negotiable right to help our children acquire the educational development necessary to succeed in the United States. It should not be as it was for many of us as children, a question of either Spanish or English, but of *both/and*; we can be both Mexican and American, Ecuadorian and American, just as much as the Irish and the Italians are both Irish and American, Italian and American. Bilingual/bicultural education is not separation but an affirmation of *mestizaje*, the blending and enrichment of cultures and linguistic expression. The other goal of bilingual/bicultural programs is to provide enrichment for a monolingual and culturally impoverished society. A foreign language should be universally made available in grade school, especially Spanish. Three out of every five persons in the Western hemisphere are Spanish-speaking. By 2025 Latino births will be 13 percent of the national total and in 2050 fully 25 percent of the U.S. will be of Latino heritage.[26] Finally, to be at the very least bilingual provides opportunities for all students to become participants not only in the nation's economic, political, and social life but also to be contributors to a global consciousness in both vision and politics.

For all of the above reasons bilingual/bicultural education has become a symbol of both the gains made by Latinas/Latinos in this country and their hopes for the future. For the foreseeable future people from Latin America will continue to come in large numbers to the United States regardless of how many walls are built and how much money is spent on the Border Patrol. Because of continuing migration, bilingual/bicultural or ESL education is essential for Latina/Latino students to be able to succeed in their education and become full participants in the development of this country.

The real creative task remains: How shall we continue what is best in la cultura Latina while accepting what is best in the American experiment? Both cultures are needed to be authentically bicultural. It is conceivable that our youth will simply assimilate as some have and continue to do.[27] There is cause for great hope. Our concerns can be addressed from within our heritage. It is precisely our cultural re-

sources that have largely been forgotten, within which we can rediscover age-old symbols and stories of transformation.

LATINO SYMBOLS OF TRANSFORMATION:
A PEOPLE OF THE SUN

Whereas the first half of the night, when the westering sun descends into the belly of the whale, is dark and devouring, the
second half is bright and bountiful, for out of it the sun-hero
climbs to the eastward, re-born. Midnight decides whether the
sun will be born again as the hero, to shed new light on a world
renewed, or whether he will be castrated and devoured by the
Terrible Mother, who kills him by destroying the heavenly part
that makes him a hero. He then remains in the darkness, a
captive. Not only does he find himself grown fast to the rocks
of the underworld like Theseus, or chained to the crag like Prometheus, or nailed to the cross like Jesus, but the world remains without a hero, and there is born, as Ernst Barlach says
in his drama, a "dead day."[28]

A symbol or story of transformation points us toward the underlying and deeper grounding of our lives and puts us in contact
with the rhythm of the universe; we are the carriers of such a living
rhythm. We participate in the rhythm of creating, preserving, and
uprooting so that we might plant new roots, create afresh. The sacred face of our being in the way of life of transformation is connected to the deepest sacred source in a new way. If we do not participate in this process, we impoverish ourselves, our deepest sacred
source, and the world. The lords of emanation, incoherence, and deformation cannot lead us to the fundamentally new and better but
only inspire us to repeat the status quo, dominate others, or practice
fantasies of destructive death. Symbols found within our heritage
have the power to elicit and reawaken in us the sacred within, our
selfhood, which is rooted in the deepest sacred source of transformation. The best of our *curanderos*, healers, shamans, *espiritualistas*,
those who could divine evil or benevolent spirits, and *brujas*, women
with creative imagination, were aware of this mystery of the human
and divine intercourse in the depths of the self. Our many gods and
goddesses are a religious realization that the sacred is expressed in
an infinite number of ways. Our lives become the vessels within

which the sources will come to intermingle with us. But we need to wrestle with these forces to determine if they are manifestations of the god of transformation.

> "After all," he said, "we are a people who live on the roof of the world; we are the sons of the Father Sun, and with our religion we daily help our Father to go across the sky. We do this not only for ourselves, but for the whole world. If we were to cease practicing our religion, in ten years the sun would no longer rise. Then it would be night forever."
>
> I then realized on what the "dignity," the tranquil composure of the individual Indian, was founded. It springs from his being a son of the sun; his life is cosmologically meaningful, for he helps the father and preserver of all life in his daily rise and descent. . . . Knowledge does not enrich us; it removes us more and more from the mythic world in which we were once at home by right of birth.[29]

Taíno, Aztec, Maya, Aymara, Inca, Tlahuica, Puebla, Moor, Jew, African, Basque, we are all people of the sun. From time immemorial our people have watched the heavens and daily participated in the death and resurrection of the sun. Our rituals, lifestyle, religion, and culture have largely revolved about the sun-god-hero. The sun brought warmth, hope, growth, and life itself. For our ancestors it meant the essence of existence. Marvelous associations grew up centered around the sun. What a magnificent scene it is in *The Blood of the Condor*, a film set in the 1960s in Bolivia, when Ignacio, the Quechua Indian leader, goes to the top of the mountain to "fill himself with the light." For to be enlightened was not to be able to see the externals but to perceive the internal threat to their way of life by the presence of the Peace Corps members who were sterilizing indigenous women without their knowledge. Ignacio was filled with a new consciousness as a result of placing his own source in touch with the source of all life. This experience with the sacred led to a personal decision to become political by confronting the threat to the community.[30]

We are certainly also people of the moon. Among the Indians of Mexico and Central America gold was considered to be the sweat of the sun god, whereas silver was said to be the tears of the moon goddess. The poverty of the Christian God was that there was no struggle with the feminine, no competing opposites, only an avenging masculine lord that knew all things. The Indians of our heritage realized that every god had his counterpart goddess. The masculine alone was not human, but totality of selfhood was feminine and masculine. Thus the pyramid to the sun god at Teotihuacán in Mexico is intimately related to the pyramid of the moon. The dark side of the moon was the unknown or dark side of the sacred. Whereas the sun represents the magnificence of the divinity in all its splendor, it is the feminine moon that symbolizes the deepest sacred source that invites us as we struggle to bring the dark into the light.

Let us look at two specific examples of the role of the sun in our heritage. First of all, let us consider the myth of our participation with the deepest sacred in finishing creation. A Pueblo Indian tale, *Arrow to the Sun*, as adapted by Gerald McDermott,[31] is extraordinary in its beauty and simplicity. According to this tale we are sacred offspring of the Sun as father who seeks and needs our cooperation in the building of the world. It is essentially a creation myth that tells us of our divine origin.

Long ago the Lord of the Sun sent the spark of life to earth. As in the biblical tale of Jesus' miraculous conception, the hero is born of a virgin with the Sun as the father. All heroes are god-begotten. But when the boy grew up, he was unhappy in the world of mortals. He was anxious within himself to know his father and his true origins. To prepare himself for the struggle of life, he sought his source. He traveled about, asking for help until a wise man, the Arrowmaker, realized his divinity and reshaped the boy into an arrow. The Arrowmaker as guide fitted the boy/arrow to his bow and flung the boy to his father/Sun. When the boy landed, he cried out with great joy, "Father, it is I, your son." But the Sun would not accept him without testing him. The boy was given a fourfold test: he must pass through the four Kivas of lions, serpents, bees, and lightning. By passing through this second birth the hero is twice born. When the boy came forth from the last stage, the Kiva of Lightning, he died but was transformed with a new life. Anyone who has suffered a double birth must be regarded as a hero, a child of God. Consequently, the father and son rejoiced. By having entered into the devouring jaws of death, the hero now won the right to be called the Son of God. The Sun-God now flung the son back to earth in the form of an arrow to bring the spirit of the sun, participation in divinity, to the people. When the son appeared, the people celebrated his return with the Dance of Life. As Jesus on the Mount, the boy was transfigured and showed forth his father in the radiance of his face. Like the Buddha and Jesus, our Pueblo Indian hero lives among the people to bring them the message of all heroes, that you must find the deepest sacred, your

own hero and heroine, within your self. This story of the hero portrays the possibility of all conscious development and the four Kivas,
or rituals, represented here symbolize the development and journey
of every child. The boy has put himself, and we through him, in
touch with a participatory self, so that *together* with our deepest sacred source and others we can cooperate in building the world with
love and justice.

> Now I know what it was, and knew even more; that man is in-
> dispensable for the completion of creation; that, in fact, he him-
> self is the second creator of the world, who alone has given to
> the world its objective existence—without which, unheard, un-
> seen, silently eating, giving birth, dying, heads nodding through
> hundreds of millions of years, it would have gone on in the pro-
> foundest night of non-being down to its unknown end. Human
> consciousness created objective existence and meaning, and
> man found his indispensable place in the great process of
> being.[32]

The Sun Dance

The sun dance religion of the Shoshones and Utes of the Central Rocky Mountains and Great Basin of North America was
born of misery and oppression in the early reservation period
(circa 1890–1900). It persisted in a context of misery and oppression, and in the late 1960's it flourished as the major religious movement on the Wind River Shoshone reservation in
Wyoming, the Fort Hall Shoshone-Bannock reservation in
Idaho.[33]

In his book on the sun dance Joseph G. Jorgensen points out
that the dance was rediscovered as a result of the sense of loss and
incoherence in which the Indians were caught. They knew that the
days of freedom on the Plains were gone forever, yet they did not
know how to proceed beyond the abyss. The dance was in many
ways a call to the depths, a profound desire to return to sacred
sources for the necessary courage to transform their lives. However,
there are times when the author misses the importance of the sun as
a symbol of transformation. Jorgensen saw the sun dance as a sign of
rebellion in the face of the white world that forbade such rituals. But
it is more than rebellion; rebels are dominated by the consciousness

of those that they attack. There was the possibility that the old lords/ gods might reappear in new clothing and simply try to restore a dying world through rituals or warfare. The sun dance represented the emergence of the sacred, that is, the numinous experience of a sacred process that was being reborn in the Indian. The brave dancers knew that they were suffering not only for themselves as individuals but for their people and for the whole of creation. The dancer was tied to the center of four poles and understood that the four directions met in his body, so that he himself represented the center.[34] It was essentially a dance of faith that allowed the individual to be vulnerable to the penetration of the sacred that would destroy the old sloth and renew the individual as well as the face of the earth. Often the new vision that was given was unacceptable precisely because it was threatening since it was not a return to the old world and known gods. The deepest source of transformation was entering into a new participation with the personal, political, historical, and sacred faces of the individual who would then carry the message to the people. Each was asked to participate in the new rituals that linked the individual to the sacred in a new conversion.

Perhaps one of the most remarkable aspects of the sun dance is its ability to symbolize the reconciliation of opposites that is an inherent characteristic of Indian culture. We have spoken of creating a new understanding of the individual in U.S. society and the demands of the deepest sacred that we discover the inner self. U.S. society has chosen as its goal not the individual but individualism in the service of incoherence to the exclusion of communal well-being in the way of life of transformation. This highlights the importance of the Latino culture rediscovering the source of transformation. The sun dance was not a means to achieve power but capacity, or linked power; it was a ritual that affirmed the personal, political, historical, and sacred faces of the individual and of the community *simultaneously.* Individual power is an Anglo-Saxon trait that is based exclusively on conflict and competition. Capacity, or linked power, is fundamentally and qualitatively different because it asserts the fulfillment of all through mutual commitment.

The attainment of power through individual and collective effort, through individual and joint suffering, should not be minimized. Each living thing sacrifices its power—the trees, the bushes, the earth, the flames of the fire, the singers, the dancers, the committeemen, the spectators—so that others may live. The synthesis of death with life, the passing of power from one form (dying) to an opposite form (the living), is made complete in the sun dance.[35]

The Sun as Mandala

Our forebearers performed all their dances and rituals, built their lodges, passed the sacred pipe, and constructed their villages in the form of a sphere, circle, or mandala. Their most important symbols, the sun and the moon, were spheres radiating their blessings in the six directions: north, south, east, west, upward toward the highest heavens, and downward to the deepest depths. The center was simultaneously the center of the individual, the tribe, the universe, and the sacred. To be at the center of the mandala was to be in touch with the deepest source of transformation and one's own sacred face.

Among the symbolic representations of the self, one finds much emphasis on the four corners of the world, and in many pictures the Great Individual (self) is represented in the center of a circle divided into four. Jung used the Hindu word *mandala* (magic circle) to designate the "nuclear atom" of the human psyche. The Navajo Indians by means of mandala-structured sand paintings bring a sick person back into harmony within the self and with the cosmos and thereby restore wholeness and health.[36]

The mandala is a symbol of totality and continuous transformation. What occurs in the inner cosmic psyche of the human spirit has its counterpart in the cosmos without. An ancient alchemical text entitled *Amor Proximi* tells us that:

> Ye see that the earth turns to the sun but the reason ye know not . . . so this turning around shows us that the world was once renewed, and in its beginning, as sun is punctum, it desires to return, and its rest will be alone in that; therefore the soul of men is also similarly gone out of the eternally divine sun, towards which it also yearns.[37]

In this creation myth the deluge signals the beginning of the work of rebirth. Similarly, in pre-Colombian Puerto Rico the Indians of Borinquén, the Taínos, believed that following the destructive spirit of the wind and flood that accompany the hurricane, Huracán, the transforming god of fire, Yocahu, or the sun, whose throne was in the high mountain, would appear to renew the souls of the people and the land.[38] The mandala as magic circle, sun wheel, sphere, symbolizes the totality and wholeness of human beings and the cosmos. Each day the rising sun encompasses the awakening world in its sunburst.

There is a danger that symbols and stories of transformation that are usually masculine in their imagery will be used to distort our inheritance. Some people would use these symbols of renewal to lull us into a world of an allegedly golden past. Our culture resides within us, and our symbolic treasure has the power to elicit from us again the creativity that has lain fallow. In the final analysis I have not presented these stories of transformation to develop a mystique of passive reflection. The culture belongs to us as men *and* women who have the right to re-create it. Here I return to the theory with which we began. The symbols for our theory are a journey and a sunburst, a mandala that returns us to the realization that together with the deepest sacred source of transformation we can participate in the building of a new culture and world.

This means that we need to be personal, political, historical, and sacred people who are capacitated by the deepest source to break the hold of demonic forces, the Huracán, and to be reborn with Yocahu, the rising sun. As centers of creation *we refuse to be links in a long chain of tradition that merely repeats the past.* Rather than living on the fringes of the mandalas of others as extensions of their mystique as satellites, we need to become interconnected as we weave the fabric of transformation in creating the fundamentally new and more loving. Thus Mexicans, for example, do not need to be trapped in an Aztec heritage that taught that the daily return of the sun was dependent upon sacrificing human hearts to the god of the sun and lord of war and deformation, Huitzilopochtli. We must not allow the gods and goddesses of our past to rule us. As sacred persons our tradition is to struggle until we win a new blessing from the deepest source of all sources. Our sacrifice shall consist precisely in dying to those stories, relationships, and ways of life that arrested our lives as partial selves and to experience the resurrection of creating the fundamentally more loving and just in all aspects of our lives.

5. Latinas/Latinos and the Sacred

To be a self, to be political and create a new and more just history is to be nourished and renewed by being rooted in the realm of the deepest sacred source. Latina women and men have always been a deeply religious people but at times our religious fervor goes astray and we accept the false lords of a fixed truth, power, and violence who legitimize a dependent relationship with the sacred that denies the struggle between the human and the divine which is necessary so that we and our deepest source can be mutually transformed. Our perspective of the sacred in this chapter is one that rejects a world that is bifurcated into the secular and the sacred or the mundane and the religious. The sacred permeates the whole of creation.

The sacred is discussed throughout the pages of this book; this is as it should be since the sacred permeates our lives and as one of the four faces of our being is always an aspect of our response to the world around us. We enact all of the stories of our lives, our relationships, and the four faces of our being in the service of four fundamentally different sacred sources.[1] But because we are not conscious of the sacred in our lives it can possess us, especially through the stories that we practice such as romantic love, uncritical loyalty, machismo, the warrior, capitalism, tribalism, the wounded self, patriarchy and matriarchy, the state, and other such dramas. These are all sacred stories that derive their deeper meaning and their ability to hold us from the lords in whose service we perform them. There are also stories that we enact in the service of transformation such as the guide, participatory democracy, transforming love, the transforming self, education, and the political innovator.

To be personal and political is also to participate in the historical and sacred drama of completing creation. The Muslim mystical tradition names every person as another face of the deepest sacred. This is an ontological statement, an affirmation of our own sacredness since we participate in a relationship of bi-unity with the deepest sacred source in order to finish creation. Such a philosophical understanding adds urgency to our becoming full selves who participate in re-creating our world. The new cannot come from partial selves who are mere carbon copies of the roles that others play and give to us. To repeat the truth given once for all whether in religion or politics is to impoverish our selves, the world, and the sacred.

The deepest sacred source of transformation continues now at this moment in history to become human through us as other Christs, as we seek to reveal the deepest sacred in our daily lives. We save the savior in the depths. The deepest source becomes concrete and present in the world by flowing through us.

All of us can discover within our own tradition the archetypal journey of transformation. We are all taught the difference between good and destruction, but we are often not aware of the ultimate grounding of what we call evil or good. Is evil merely what one group considers bad or is there a normative means to determine the creative or destructive source behind the use of words such as good and evil? For example, in the way of life of emanation it is evil to express dissent from the truth given once for all by one's parents as representatives of the sacred tradition. But in the service of transformation it is necessary to break with those who would hold us in containers of an alleged final truth. Therefore we need to know why ultimately we are doing what we are doing. The root of knowledge means *gnosis*, knowledge of the process of transformation.

Latinas and Latinos have always been deeply religious people. Certainly our indigenous forebearers recognized the presence of the sacred as is witnessed by the pyramids, gods and goddesses, and prayers to the divinity found throughout Latin America. The Spaniards did not introduce the sacred. They contributed a particular, historical, although very important, manifestation of the sacred as found in the Catholic religion. The sacred is always more than its manifestations and has to be pursued and struggled with in whatever way the sacred sources choose to reveal themselves. Both the Spaniards and the Aztecs, for example, attempted to domesticate the sacred by preserving it in formulas, rituals, an official priesthood, and theology. Such institutionalization, although a necessary part of the process of culture-making, often malfunctions through relating *recipients* not to the sacred but to mediators who claim that the ultimate truth was already delivered to them. Rather than leading us to our inner selfhood to experience the deepest sacred, priests and ministers often pointed us toward false lords who possessed us. Such alienation from the deepest sacred is also an alienation from the self and leaves others to play god. And this they do with a vengeance. Social and political arrangements are no longer only the domination of a class or oligarchy but the will of an all-powerful sacred source. After generations of this kind of religious indoctrination, people internalize their own perceived inadequacy as sinfulness, powerlessness, and a sense of uselessness: "No sirvo para nada," "I am not good for anything."

For historical and cultural reasons most Latinos have been Catholics. From the time of the Conquest the Church became an institutionalized buffer for the Indian and mestizo population. Eventually this became a negative relationship because the Church considered it a duty to protect the indigenous peoples from greed and cruelty without questioning the hierarchical system that oppressed them. Thus the Church never challenged the legitimacy of the system itself, only its excesses. In this way the official Church became part of the problem. At different times due to internal political upheavals liberal groups turned against the Catholic Church. These conflicts occurred after the wars of independence that ended Spanish rule. New political groups fought against the Church because it controlled much of the land and education and exercised a heavy influence on the law courts. This was not an antireligious or anti-sacred position, but it was anticlerical. The liberal reformers refused to allow the cleric to be the final arbiter in the realm of the state. There is a similar trend today. Latinos in this country are not antireligious or antichurch, but there is a growing resistance to the efforts of the hierarchy to consider themselves as the final arbiters of the sacred.

Recently there have been a series of attempts on the part of the Catholic Church to evaluate the condition of Latinos throughout the United States. Since the 1960s the church hierarchy has opened diocesan offices for Hispanic ministry. However, for various reasons the bishops were not able to develop an indigenous Latino clergy, sisterhood, and hierarchy. In addition the attitude toward the community was characterized by a condescending paternalism. These studies have a pragmatic basis; almost 40 percent of Roman Catholics in the United States are Latinas and Latinos. That number will continue to grow, so that by the year 2020 it will be fully one half. The Catholic hierarchy has suddenly discovered us. We have always been here but not so vocally or in such numbers. But we need also to point out a growing consciousness in the community following the spirit of Vatican II that the Church is not constituted by the official hierarchy or only the clergy but that the Church is the people of God, laity and clergy together. In addition there have always been many deeply caring parish priests who devoted their lives to serving the Latino community.

Another factor in the recent interest in la comunidad Latina by the Catholic hierarchy has been the growing success of evangelical Protestantism among Latinos. There are many reasons for their appeal to Latinos: the ministers often come from a Latino background, speak Spanish, share the daily hardships of the community, and have more of an egalitarian church service based on scripture. The success of the evangelical groups in attracting a growing number of believers from the Latino community makes the Catholic Church's efforts look at times as if it is now competing with the evangelicals and attempting to win back their "fallen members."

In 1972 and 1977 Encuentro Nacional Hispano Pastorals were convened by the bishops to discuss the needs of the Latino community in the United States. The U.S. Catholic Bishops' pastoral letter, *The Hispanic Presence: Challenge and Commitment*, issued in January 1984 convoked the third encuentro held in 1985. Taken together the first two encuentros raised a series of questions that for the most part were not adequately addressed. *The Hispanic Presence* was on the whole a very cautious, almost apologetic, statement that can at best be charitably considered a beginning. One of the bishops who participated in writing *The Hispanic Presence* stated that the Latino bishops did not want to be too bold or outspoken lest the rest of the bishops be disturbed and reject the draft of the letter. This attitude exposes the effect that the Church has too often had on Latinos. We do not speak of struggle or demand political rights because we have been socialized to be patient, work through the system, and to be thankful for what we get. This socialized passivity and ritualized avoidance is a disservice to our people because it denies the depth of the suffering and the urgency of our needs. We have a right to be filled with *coraje*, anger, and to refuse to defer our needs. Conscious efforts were made to avoid words such as "liberation" and "political" or "institutionalized violence" as they were considered too provocative. When the pastoral letter meant to say "political," it used such traditional ecclesiastical language as "social justice," "social action," and "temporal needs." Voting rights, discrimination, immigration rights, status of farm workers, bilingualism, and pluralism are referred to as "social concerns." In spite of the fact that since *Rerum Novarum* Catholics see it as their right to form workers' unions, nowhere did the bishops support the right of Latinos and Latinas to organize, to struggle for their rights, nor did they urge other Catholics of goodwill to help Latinos empower themselves.

But in the third encuentro the Latino community found its voice. Many of the conclusions and commitments that arose out of the group discussions are truly outstanding. They are clear and distinct statements declaring the rights of Latinas and Latinos to be political in shaping our own lives. And in total contrast to *The Hispanic Presence,* there is an unequivocal declaration of making a preferential option for and in solidarity with the poor and marginalized. The document goes on to reject assimilation, affirms and promotes the value of women, and speaks of education as necessary if one is to participate in transforming society. Latinos are urged to be the subjects of history and to condemn institutionalized injustices. It speaks of continual conversion and advocates for the undocumented, the farm workers, and the marginalized.[2]

> The experience of solidarity leads us to affirm in faith that all material means and technology must be at the service of the transformation of society and the confirmation of human divinity, rather than being used for materialistic and individualistic ends. . . . The experience [of the third encuentro] helped our people to understand that the Kingdom of God, announced and inaugurated by Jesus . . . implies not only a change of heart but also overcoming the structural exploitation our people suffer and an end to perpetuating and maintaining situations and structures that are contrary to the plan of God.[3]

In the follow-up to the third encuentro the document produced by the participants, *The National Pastoral Plan for Hispanic Ministry,* is truly a remarkable endorsement of a politics of liberation and transformation that reminds us of the documents of Vatican II and the Consejo Episcopal Latinoamericano (CELAM) II documents that resulted from the meetings of the bishops of Latin America in Medellín, Colombia, in 1968. The plan, after endorsing all of the commitments to the poor and the marginalized, moves to implement the goals of the encuentro. The goals of the transformation of persons and society are to be achieved within and through small ecclesial communities that are in daily contact with people. This is based on the model of the Basic Christian Communities, Comunidades de Base, in Latin America that instilled in the people a theology of liberation and that worked toward the goal of religious and political transformation. The plan emphasizes the church as community rather than as a hierarchical institution and speaks of an authentic church that carries out the mission of Jesus by entering into the cultural, religious, political, and social reality of the people. In its critique of the Latino culture it deals a devastating analysis and rejection of perhaps the most deformational story in the cultura Latina, the story of patriarchy.

Within this reality women suffer a triple discrimination:

- Social (machismo, sexual and emotional abuse, lack of self esteem, exploitation by the media);
- Economic (forced to work without proper emotional and technical preparation, exploited in regards to wages and all kinds of work, bearing full responsibility for the family, lacking self-identity);
- Religious (her importance in the preservation of faith is not taken into account, she is not involved in decision making yet carries the burden for pastoral ministry).[4]

Two more documents issued in 2002 and 2003, *Encuentro and Mission* and *Strangers No Longer*, offer more examples of the intertwining of the personal and the political, the historical and the sacred. Some years ago the Archdiocese of New York sponsored a study, *Hispanics in New York: Religious, Cultural and Social Experiences (Hispanos en Nueva York: Experiencias Religiosas, Culturales y Sociales).*[5] The fundamental flaw in the study was the separation of the sacred from the political. The writers neglected to focus on the political dimension that flows from the sacred face of our being. This study left the impression that the main concern of the archdiocese was not for the development of Latinas and Latinos as members of the community but for the benefit of the institutional church and its continuing influence and power. But in these documents the Church is portrayed as above all the people of God as a community that takes a political stand to support the most vulnerable by optioning for the poor and in *Strangers No Longer*, a joint pastoral letter from the bishops of Mexico and the United States, they bravely and boldly declare their support for the poorest of the poor, undocumented immigrants, in declaring that national sovereign borders are not absolute.

While recognizing the right of the sovereign state to control its borders . . . this right is not absolute . . . the needs of immigrants must be measured against the needs of the receiving countries. . . . The Church recognizes that all the goods of the world belong to all people. When persons cannot find employment in their country of origin to support themselves and their families, they have a right to work elsewhere in order to survive. Sovereign nations should provide ways to accommodate this right.[6]

Both documents begin with and conclude with a political statement that the Catholic Church in its commitment to justice is willing to identify itself with and to support Latinas and Latinos both as a group and as individuals in their struggle for jobs, housing, health care, bilingual/bicultural education, immigration reform, access to legal services, and participation in all the benefits of our society. In these two remarkable statements the Church becomes a source of hope for the new immigrants especially for our undocumented community. As a result of these kinds of declarations throughout the country many Catholic parishes are returning to the courage and commitment of the early church of the catacombs as they provide a sanctuary for the most vulnerable in our community. This is the Catholic Church at its best.

In the latter documents the Church did something very important: rather than support a particular political party it urged the Latino community to *be* political. Furthermore, the statements address the persistence of structural violence and systemic injustice rather than individual sin. They support the Latino community in seeking institutionalized justice, not selective charity as a handout that perpetuates dependence. The documents teach that the Church as a community is committed to the work of transformation in all aspects of our lives. This refreshing and liberating ecclesiology that is rooted in the experiences of the Latino community is "a model of church that seeks to respond to the needs and aspirations of the poor, the undocumented, the migrant workers, the incarcerated, and the most vulnerable, particularly women and children. . . . This prophetic model calls for a strong commitment to social justice, for advocacy and action in favor of new immigrant families and young people for the empowerment of Hispanics and all Catholics to enter into the full life of the Church and society."[7] This empowers the new Latino communities to realize that they have not come to the

U.S. only for a better life for themselves but also to serve as members of a prophetic community that intends not to assimilate into either ecclesiastical or social structures but to challenge the Church to help them in the task of transforming their adopted country.[8]

A word of caution is appropriate. When the bishops of the world returned to their home dioceses from the Second Vatican Council and the Latin American bishops from their Consejos, many of them did not implement the reforms that they were urged to carry out. But they did initiate a process of *conscietización*, consciousness raising, that could not be recalled. Now Latinas and Latinos in the U.S. can refer to these wonderful and empowering documents to remind members of the Church who are slow to put them into practice that the politics of liberation are here to stay.

It is not enough to assert the relationship between the personal, the political, the historical, and the sacred as we have seen in the documents discussed above. The quality of the relationship between the personal and the sacred must also be addressed. This has a lot to do with the guides we find in our churches. So the issue is not the name of the church, theological degrees, the documents that are issued, or the use of scripture. The point is whether the religious community, Catholic or Protestant/Pentecostal, other world religion or religious sect, relates the individual to the sacred in a redemptive way. Some Catholics and some Pentecostals seek to give security above all else to Latinos and so relate to us in such a way that they try to possess us and to demand our loyalty in exchange for security in a harsh world.

FOUR FUNDAMENTALLY DIFFERENT SACRED SOURCES

Surveys that give us information about the numbers of people who go to church, synagogue, or mosque, or who read the scriptures of their religion or participate in religious ceremonies are not that helpful. When examining the relationship of Latinas and Latinos to the sacred, we need to ask the question: "To what sacred source am I relating at this moment in regard to this problem?" The answer to this question reveals whether we are free to respond to problems with the wholeness of our being.

The sacred has always been with us but since the age of the Enlightenment religion was discredited as the enemy of reason and science. Historically every civilization and culture has created rituals and religions, literally links to the sacred. Gods and goddesses were given human or animal characteristics so that humans could contact a quality or virtue with which they could identify. Symbols and symbolic stories also pointed us beyond the concrete, tangible world to the unseen sources of our lives. People have always had visions, heard voices, received messages in dreams, or have fallen into trances. People who had such special gifts were considered blessed by the community because they communed with the sacred sources of the spirit. These gifted individuals were set aside by the people and called shamans, witch doctors, *curanderas* (healers), *espiritistas* (spiritual mediums), rabbis, guides, mullahs, priests, or ministers. They were honored because they could put the community in contact with the sacred. They became mediators between the human and the divine.

But what we have not been able to do theoretically is to distinguish among those sacred sources. Three of the deeper sacred sources are destructive, the lords of emanation, incoherence, and deformation, yet we have referred to them as "God" with a capital G and assume that "God" is always good and benevolent.[9] Every time people want us to back down on a controversial issue they make appeals to "God." But which god are they praying to? The answer to this question is of utmost importance since we have people who are diametrically opposed to each other calling on the same "God" to help them defeat the other as the manifestation of evil. What "God" indeed did the French Catholic bishops ask to bless the tanks of the French army during the First World War and was this "God" different from the "God" that the German Catholic bishops called upon to protect the German tanks?

Our theoretical approach allows us to recognize that bitter enemies such as the Wahabbi sect in Islam, the religious ultra-right wing in Israel, and extremist fundamentalist Christians actually worship the same tribal lord of emanation who tells the flock that they have the truth and that all others are wrong. In their dealings with those outside the parameters of the saved, the outsiders are considered as lesser human beings who are invisible, inferior, worthy only of assimilation if they are converted and seen as better than the rest of "them," subject to exile if as the converted they prove disloyal, and, ultimately, if they are considered dangerous they can be exterminated. In this way the lord of emanation collaborates with the lord of deformation to kill the infidels within the community and those outside the community of final truth. It is so ironic that without being aware of it the three religious groups mentioned above are actually inspired by the same destructive lord who leads them from the fallacy of possessing "the" truth to the fantasy of having the right to kill those who oppose them. We need a perspective that will allow us to determine if the sacred source from the depths is to the good or destructive. This is the main goal of this chapter.

Gods waxed and waned; they came and they went depending on the needs of the people and their own maturity. Tired lords were retired, and often new competing sacred lords came with conquering armies. Competition among gods also took place. Greek and Roman gods became angry, fell in love, became irrational, and fought each other. The gods were often playful. The Aztecs, Mayas, Taínos, and Aymaras had gods for the sun, death, water, fertility, hurricanes, rebirth, and transformation. The German god, Odin, ruled the primeval forests. Quetzalcoatl got drunk and was expelled; he went on a journey to recover his powers and promised to return. The alchemists attributed divine power to their alchemical experiments; they spoke of and practiced a process of transformation whereby sacred elements like quicksilver and sulfur transformed base metals into gold. Alchemists participated with the sacred in the ancient alchemical process of transformation: *coagula et solve,* that is, creating and nourishing and dissolving in order to re-coagulate to give new form to the underlying realities. The people of the Middle East had temple virgins who served jealous gods. At times the priests had intercourse with the virgin in the name of their gods in order to fill the virgin with the power of the sacred. Often this divine-human intercourse became a mere cover for lust and passion. The Jews were always on their guard against the false lords of the surrounding tribes because Yahweh was a jealous lord. Christians spoke of the one, true god in a triune mystery of Father, Son, and Holy Spirit, yet Mary and the saints were often revered as gods and goddesses who substituted for regional deities, that is, local deities were baptized by being given a Christian name. After knowing all of this we are not much closer to being able to tell which of the sacred sources mentioned above are arresting our humanity and which stories contain indicators of a sacred source that needs us to finish creation with love and justice.

Often gods with different names were adopted gods and so were actually the same lord. The Muslims were especially tolerant of other people's gods as long as they were considered to be lesser gods than Allah. Intolerance sometimes led to murder and slavery in the name of the sacred. A move toward strict monotheism in Christianity, especially medieval Catholicism, resulted in an emphasis on the only true religion. The Inquisition was established to determine doctrinal purity, and "God" became an avenging lord: people were killed. The Spaniards brought the Catholic religion to Latin America and declared the religion of the indigenous to be idolatrous. The codices of the Aztecs were burned because they were considered demonic. When Cortes arrived in the mountains overlooking the splendor of Mexico City the Spaniards concluded that such a beautiful city must be the work of the Devil since the Aztecs were ignorant of the one, true faith. In these examples the powerful used the sacred, the lord of emanation, as a tribal lord and the lord of deformation as the sacred source of legitimization for their conquest, enslaving, and killing.

The Bible is a story of the relationship between the divine and the human that clearly points out the presence of four fundamentally different sacred sources. The Torah and the New Testament contain the stories of the human-divine struggle. In Deuteronomy 2:26–36 we learn of an avenging lord who commands the Jews to kill all the inhabitants of Heshbon and to plunder the towns and take the livestock. This is an example of the tribal lord of emanation in collusion with the lord of deformation who together justifies the killing of others in the name of Yahweh. This cannot be the same sacred source as the god of transformation who is described as a passionate lover of humanity in the Song of Songs. Thus even in scripture we need to be able to distinguish when the term "God" is used in place of false lords to justify horrific violence against strangers.[10] Some lords did what Marx and Freud criticized: they left us childishly dependent, passive, and afraid and therefore unable to participate in the building of the world. But not all the stories in the Bible speak of sacred sources that demand docility. The Book of Genesis 1:26–30 tells us that we are made in the image and likeness of God. That image is not a physical description but a symbolic one, of a divinity busy creating. If we are of the same image, it must be as co-creators of the world, together with the deepest sacred source of transformation.

If human beings are to be more than the playthings of sacred lords, subject to their every whim, how can we participate in the creation of a new and better world? Moreover, what really is the significance of the human-divine struggle, what is the purpose of it all? What we have already seen above and in earlier chapters is that we are moved from the depths by four sacred sources who are responsible for the ultimate ways of life. These four ways of life are fundamentally different ways within which we interact with the sacred. Moreover, it is by struggling with only one of these sacred sources, the god of transformation, that we can give expression to fundamentally new and more loving stories and relationships.[11]

The sacred is present to all of us by virtue of our humanity and is expressed in an infinite number of different ways. All the gods referred to above come from the same undifferentiated source, or the deepest source of sources. It is up to us to distinguish between the different sacred forces that emerge from the depths. Ever since we left the realm of the concrete we have been talking about a realm of living forces that is not ours to command but which can command us. They are forces that move through us. If we are not strong enough to contend with them, we will become possessed by them; we can even become psychotic. If we are strong enough to repress these forces but not strong enough to deal with them freely, we are likely to turn neurotic. In order to prevent our being inhibited or undone by these living forces, our knowing participation with them is crucial. Our full participation as co-creators with the deepest source of transformation is open to us if we prove to be at once receptive and struggling in helping to give concrete shape to the fundamentally more compassionate and just.

Our theory of transformation allows us to ask new kinds of questions that more adequately address how we relate to the sacred. Max Weber, Emile Durkheim, and Karl Marx all did us a great service by showing the dialectical relationship between religion and society.[12] These men took the sacred and its impact seriously; it was a fact of human life whether they agreed with its influence or not. Lately too much of our study of religion has been just that, the study of *religion*, that is, the institutionalized residue of the religious factor. Weber and Durkheim, perhaps more than Marx, recognized the dynamic aspect of the sacred and traced its objectification in specific cultures. It was the frozen residue of tradition that Freud primarily referred to in his critiques of religion.[13] Ernest Troeltsch, in his classic work on church and sect, wrote about the human tendency to canonize, legalize, and routinize original religious insight and creativity once the fervor of the initial experience of the sacred had cooled.[14] Wilfred Cantwell Smith wrote of the distinction between religion as object or thing, as residue to be analyzed, and the religious as adjective, as a quest for the sacred within the context of human life.[15] But none of these pioneers succeeded in telling us when the sacred is destructive and when it liberates our humanity.

Our theory always points us toward the realm of underlying forming sacred sources and asks the question, "In the service of what ultimate sacred source and way of life am I living my life here and now?" The quality of our relationship to the sacred is the heart of the matter. The encounter with the deepest sacred is dialectical, that is, it involves a mutual interpenetration of self, other, the world, and sacred sources.[16] In terms of the methodology that we use to determine the quality of our encounter with the sacred there can be no such thing as a value-free, detached analysis that is a characteristic of quantitative studies, or participant observation that allows us to be neutral. Our method is based on an understanding of the sacred as fulfilled in the experience of transformation that takes place only in persons.[17] The sacred is not to be ignored or passed over to other disciplines. Our problem is not with social science but with inadequate social science paradigms.[18] Our theoretical perspective allows us to analyze the religious experience of persons not only on the level of the concrete but also to explore our connection to the underlying sacred in the depths without doing violence to human inquiry or to the experience of the sacred.

Traditional social scientists merely report the residual categories of religion in an empirical, positivistic, behavioral manner. With questionnaires and statistical correlations they turn our vibrant encounter with the sacred into an abstraction. They never tell us anything about the struggle in our depths. Consequently they miss the revolutions because they see the new only in terms of the old. Inadequate and destructive connections to the sacred inhibit our humanity; a mutually fulfilling alternative is participation with the deepest source of our being, the god of transformation. From time immemorial we have archetypal stories and symbols that tell us that life is a journey on which we encounter the rhythm of the microcosmic and macrocosmic as a dialectical process. In India the encounter is symbolized by a three-headed god/goddess: Brahma the Creator, Vishnu the Preserver, and Shiva the Destroyer.[19] The alchemists realized that base metals could be dissolved in order to be re-created, *solve et coagula,* into gold.[20] The heart of the Christian teaching was the birth, death, and resurrection of Jesus that is practiced now, today, by Christians. The moon waxes and wanes, all of the cosmos follows this rhythm.[21]

According to this perspective of the cosmos, reality is of a piece but with an infinite number of different expressions. Native American Indians were aware of a cosmic unity. The Oglala Sioux, for example, believe that wherever they pitch their tepee, there is to be found the center of their own being, the center of the tribe, the universe, and the sacred simultaneously.[22] This is a felt and experienced philosophy and epistemology of being. Being is synonymous with reality.[23] God, the religious, the sacred, the deepest source of our being, the undifferentiated source, the holy was always considered an integral part of life. But due to reductionist and positivist trends, especially since the eighteenth century, the sacred and mystery became an embarrassment. The traditional social scientists, eager to quantify like their colleagues in the natural sciences, cut us off from our underlying sacred sources. Thus, when social scientists say that they know something, they know only a fragment of reality. They know, for example, how many go to church but they cannot tell us anything about the quality of our relationship to the sacred.

Subjectivity and inter-subjectivity are the touchstones of reality to which there is now a fruitful return. To trust one's own experience and encourage others to pay heed to their experience is to participate in searching for the sacred. But how do we come to know our being, our reality? In the Muslim, Jewish, and Christian mystical tradition the way that people experience being and reality is encapsulated in a beautiful proverb: "To know yourself is to know *your* god, not God or *the* god, but *your* god." Thus if you discover what source moves you to do what you do, then you will know what lord or god you serve.[24]

The wholeness or fragmentation of the personal, political, historical, and sacred faces of our being can be determined by the quality of the connection that we have to our sacred source. For example, as a young man who was living the story of uncritical loyalty to the Catholic Church, I repressed my personal face by denying my own feelings, ideas, and desires. With my political face I practiced a politics of unquestioning obedience to the Church and her representatives. My historical face sought only to repeat the commitment to the past tradition of the Church and my sacred face was taken over by the lord of emanation who inspired me to forget my doubts and believe. I was a living incarnation of this false lord that I called "God" and gave concrete expression to this partial sacred source through practicing the relationships of dependency, especially emanation and subjection, and the stories of patriarchy and uncritical loyalty. I did not know that this was only one of the four sources to which we can relate. For years I prayed to this false lord of emanation asking this "God" who threatened me with damnation if I left the true path to preserve me from temptation. Anyone who undermines this way of life is in danger of being given over to the lord of deformation for punishment.

If we repeat the manifestation of the sacred for generations in the service of the lord of emanation, or choose the partial lords of

incoherence or deformation, then we cannot create a dialectical relationship of mutuality with the sacred. These lesser lords possess
us, thus robbing us of the ability to participate in creating new forms
of compassion and justice. Institutionalized religion loses its authority when it no longer connects us to the deepest source of transformation. For example, taking communion can become a legalistic
banquet detailing the disposition of exactly how to perform the ritual. This reduces Jesus to a lord of emanation. This linkage needs to
be broken in order to reaffirm the authenticity of Jesus as a transforming god who seeks a new incarnation of justice and love. For
this reason, even in the midst of the most inquisitorial conditions
there arose a counter-tradition, that is, the recognition that human
beings had the right to question and re-experience themselves, the
universe, and the sacred by participating in *gnosis*, or knowledge of
the process of transformation. Dogmatic orthodoxy in the service of
the lord of emanation, if we call it Christianity, Islam, or Judaism,
only knows how to preserve the tradition and is inherently incapable
of allowing us to re-experience life or experiment with the truth because it would mean the death of the tradition which legitimizes unquestioning obedience within established social, cultural, political,
and religious structures.

We miss the deeper meaning of all aspects of our lives when we
fail to see the sacred as integral to our being. The scientific community turned to philosophical and religious questions when the prevalent scientific view was no longer able to respond to the emergence
of anomaly, that is, something outside the norm of the prevailing
scientific perspective. Niels Bohr underwent a religious conversion
that provided him with the courage and creative imagination to
plumb the depths of the atomic mystery. But he needed first of all
to re-experience the reality of the sacred in himself and nature and
to go beyond his own personal depths to a more profound transpersonal mystery.[25] If scientists as the practitioners of inquiry and experimentation merely mirror the world, they can never participate
in their own or the world's transformation. He or she becomes arrested in the previous transformation that has now become "the"
only way to do science. We have ample evidence that scientists have
discovered parallel phenomena in nature by creatively playing, imagining, and seeing new possibilities.[26] The implications of this are
crucial for human participation and creativity. It gives a necessary
significance to the scientist which is of ultimate importance. She
does not repeat nature or other phenomena; she as a scientist actually creates, together with the deepest underlying sacred source, a

fundamentally new way to see the world. The scientist participates in giving direction to forces within and outside her self.

> What really landed him in trouble was that he saw the concrete archetypically. He saw the motions he saw as necessary relationships. The Pope objected that Galileo was necessitating god, so that god ceased to be all-powerful. God himself thus becomes subject to the laws of creativity through which he expresses creativity. The science that grows out of this position is an inquiry which liberates, energizes and gives significance to the scientist.[27]

Religious and symbolic language points us to underlying depths and frees us from the superficiality of rationalism and positivism that only examines the empirically concrete. Fixed faith, in whatever area of human knowledge, ends with sterile orthodoxy or dangerous expressions of fundamentalism that do not permit any new personal experience of the deepest sacred. For example, once Muslims began to look only in the Koran for the truth of science rather than heeding the command of the Koran to seek the sacred in the world around us, religion, politics, and science were profoundly wounded. One of the reasons for the weakening of Muslim science and scholarship was the increasing emphasis on rote learning and memorization of the Koran during the past millennium. "The notion that all knowledge is in the Koran is a great disincentive to learning. . . . It's destructive if we want to create a thinking person, someone who can analyze, question and create."[28] Relating to Allah as the lord of emanation made it impossible to question and experiment. The intrusion of Islam in the service of emanation into science has been an "effort to 'Islamicize' science by portraying the Koran as a source of scientific knowledge. . . . For example, it was not Islamic to say that combining hydrogen and oxygen makes water. You were supposed to say 'that when you bring hydrogen and oxygen together then by the will of Allah water was created.'"[29] Ibn Arabi said that one of the worst mistakes made by Muslims was the creation of Shari'a, Muslim law.[30] Arabi advocated that people acknowledge what Allah said. But that was then, in that situation, so what does Allah say to us now as we confront a new problem? God continues to reveal the truth through the questions that we ask and looking to nature to reveal the mystery of the deepest sacred source. In the same way Kabbalistic Jews said that all that Yahweh revealed was the Aleph, the beginning point; all the rest is interpretation.

ARCHETYPAL ANALYSIS

We know the fix of stereotypes, not the movement of archetypes.[31]

Everything has two faces, its own face and the face of God.[32]

Some sixty years ago Arthur O. Lovejoy delivered his famous lectures on *The Great Chain of Being*.[33] Lovejoy's study criticized the Catholic Church that sanctified a frozen, permanent, fixed chain of being. Everything flowed from on high and was created once for all. The course of human history was fixed and irrevocable. The eternal ideas manifested themselves as a continuity of an already finished scenario. Human beings merely received the world and its final truth. But what Lovejoy did not understand was that the *Aurea Catena*, the golden chain, was a dogmatic reinterpretation of a continuous transforming process. In contrast to the ways of life of emanation, incoherence, and deformation, the god of transformation needs our participation in a process of continuous creation of our self, the deepest source, and the world. Our dialectical process tells us that there are three stages to being or reality: destruction, re-creation, and nourishment. To create once and for all is to deny that anything fundamentally new can emerge.

Any religious ritual, dogma, or prayer that cuts us off from the deepest source of our being, the god of transformation, and allows us to be possessed by the false lords of emanation, incoherence, or deformation is demonic. This is the essence of idolatry. To consider the world as a particular lord's final revelation makes it impossible for us to participate in bringing about the new and more loving. We reject the orthodox chain of fixed creation in the way of life of emanation primarily because it posits fatalism as a pre-established plan for all time. Human freedom is of ultimate significance for the following reason: the deepest source, the god of transformation needs us; there can be no concreteness in the source and no differentiated consciousness without our participation. Human beings, because of their consciousness, are necessary to the source to participate, not in the fatalism of a divinely fixed plan, but in the destiny of finishing creation together with the deepest source; if humankind needs the source, then the source in its turn needs us.[34] This gives us a more relational and dynamic insight into revelation. Revelation has been defined as god's entry into man's making of man.[35] But our theoretical perspective allows us to restore the full impact of the experience of revelation as transformative, that is, that revelation is dialectical and mutual in that it is also humankind's entry into god's making of god. Whenever this archetypal process of transformation is re-experienced, we can participate in the creation of new forms of love and justice with the transforming god. This is the essence of personal, political, historical, and sacred therapy that seeks the healing of wholeness in all aspects of life.

The implication of this understanding of revelation is that neither humankind nor the undifferentiated source is complete. Galileo and all the members of the counter-tradition speak of necessary forms in which any concrete relationship must express itself. In their understanding the deepest source is not all-powerful but is subject to the laws of a cosmos in continuous creation. God also, therefore, ceases to be fixed and is still flowing forth with creativity.[36] Human beings become creative in the realm of the concrete through participation with the sacred. This perception of the human role in building the world by participating with the divine further underlines the bankruptcy of detached, value-free, quantifying science carried on by many social scientists who merely report the world but make no effort to transform it. Our theory allows us to be dialectically connected to our source and to the concrete world. We can empirically ask whether the *quality* of this connection to the sacred allows us to change yet continue, to cooperate yet free to disagree so that we can bring about new forms of justice. *Our* choice is crucial. Our freedom is rooted in the following:

- We are free to choose that sacred source that guides us in transforming our life.
- Our freedom of choice is based on the realization that there are competing sacred sources from which to choose.
- Our choice is archetypal, otherwise we would not be able to move beyond our own concreteness; this is the basis of our transcendence rooted in our own selfhood.
- All archetypes are not finally established; if they were, our freedom to participate in transforming would be an illusion; archetypes can die and others are born.
- If human beings are to be freely creative, the god of transformation must be imperfect, i.e., unfinished.
- Finally, we must be able to participate in the creation of new archetypal relationships and stories, which posits ourselves and the source as co-creators.[37]

Rediscovering Truth in the Personal Encounter: The Latina/Latino Catholic/ Christian Experience

We would be of no help to the deepest source of our being or to ourselves if our arrival in Act III were based on no new experience. If either we or our deepest source knew the outcome in advance it would be calculated manipulation instead. We both participate in transforming both of us. . . . The deepest sacred source needs all four faces of our being to discover and test in concrete practice what is indeed fundamentally better than what exists now.[38]

The majority of Latina and Latino Catholics were raised to believe that in religious matters they were not to follow their own interpretations. They had to agree with "the mind of the Church." Dreams, visions, speaking in tongues, and other religious experiences were denied validity. Heresy was always a threat. The Catholic Church was a powerful container that answered definitively all of the perennial questions: life, death, heaven and hell, meaning, hope, love, the divine, the world, and the whole of reality. This was fixed faith in the way of life of emanation.

The crisis of this perspective came quickly following Vatican II.[39] The challenges to authority are familiar to us all: the birth control controversy, celibacy, collegiality, liberation theology, the authority of the hierarchy, reproductive rights, unjust wars, the demand for married and women priests, and more recently the loss of credibility of the institutional church in its failure to protect the young from pedophile clergy. This conflict brought about an awakening in Act I, Scene 2, of doubts, inspirations, and new ideas. Many were caught off guard by this upheaval. But the breaking of the secure container ended once and for all the monolith of the Church. The question to ask now is: What is the quality of the connection that those of us who call ourselves Roman Catholics and/or Christians have to the sacred and to our own tradition? Are we, as Latinas and Latinos in the process of nourishing, uprooting, or re-creating our relationship to the sacred and to our tradition? In the service of what sacred source are we enacting the stories, relationships, and the four faces of our being? We cannot make this determination once for all. A Latina/Latino who has been secure in a religious tradition in the service of emanation in Act I might find herself or himself driven out of it by the exigencies of responding to specific concrete problems that they are facing. We can choose to reject our pain and to submerge ourselves deeper in the inherited past in order to escape the incoherence. We can assimilate and join the powerful in the second act in the way of life of incoherence. We can hurt ourselves and others in deformation and enter into the abyss or we can choose to build more loving and just communities together with the god of transformation. We only know that we cannot stereotype Catholics, Pentecostals, Muslims, Jews, atheists, or any other group; we need to go beyond the label. For example, if we observe four Latina women going into a religious service we cannot assume that they are praying to the same sacred source. One prays to the lord of emanation to free her from temptation and to help her become a more loyal servant of the Church; another asks the lord of incoherence to send her a few more stocks and bonds as a sign that she is living a worthy life; the third prays to the lord of deformation to punish her enemy with misfortune; the fourth woman prays to the deepest source of transformation to guide her to empty her life of all those stories and relationships, to die to everything that prevents her from being able to live a life of compassion and justice. To those doing positivist social science these women were all praying to the same "god," belong to the same religion, attend the same church, hold more or less the same beliefs, and perform the same rituals. We need to analyze on this deeper level to see the quality of our connection to the sacred and go beyond the concrete assumptions we daily make.

The sacred is an integral part of the Latino community in this country that cuts across religious lines. A Latina/Latino theological reality is emerging within the community and is one that transcends religious denominations identified as a mestizo consciousness. We have gone beyond the Marxist phase that saw religion as a means of escape and of exploitation. Marx did all of us a great service by reminding us of the importance of political and historical challenges but in the process he ignored our personal and sacred faces. Theology at its best is a reflection on the lived faith experiences of a people as they confront the political and historical situation.[40]

Our task as Latina/Latino scholars who seek to rediscover the sacred in our community is to go beyond discussions about popular religiosity, methodologies, or institutionalized religion versus a more personal and culturally free expression of religious rituals. It is about recognizing that all of us by the very nature of our humanity can participate together as a community in the sacred story of transformation in all aspects of our lives. With this as our criterion we are then free to ask what expression of the sacred, what rituals, what kind of organization, which forms of popular religion will enable us to transform our selves, our community, and our society.

Roman Catholics and Protestants of mainline churches like the Episcopalians and Presbyterians were for the most part taught to look down upon the Pentecostals as members of a storefront religion without much credibility. But we miss the deeper significance of the lives of any member of a faith community when we violate them with stereotypes. We need to ask the same question of all religious groups, "To what sacred source are you praying?" The answer to this question allows us to see the deeper significance of a faith community. There is a Chicano/Mexican-American Pentecostal congregation located in East Los Angeles that offers us an excellent example of a new and different way of examining the religious experience by reflecting on the ritual constructions and deconstructions of the human body. The centrality of the person as sacred both in body and spirit provides new and innovative ways of relating the sacred to the lives of Latinas and Latinos that go beyond the usual religious service. This particular faith community does something that I never experienced in any other religious service; they take the actual, concrete bodies of men and women seriously. The rituals practiced in the church emphasize that it is personal, political, and sacred work to reclaim the bodies of the people that have been historically violated and battered daily in the world of racism and capitalism.[41]

We need also to see how their lives are liberated beyond the Sunday service to take back our bodies, our selves. This personal and sacred affirmation needs to have real concrete political and historical results in our society during the rest of the week in the world of family and work. Expressions of the sacred can be co-opted since they often provide a temporary respite for the people. If at home and in the workplace people return to the same stories of oppression, racism, patriarchy, and capitalism after a Catholic mass or Pentecostal service, the process of renewal is derailed. It is necessary to continue to undermine and subvert the systems of oppression after our services and healing rituals. The powerful use reform and incremental change, that is, system-maintaining change, that indefinitely delays the uprooting of destructive stories which actually strengthens a violent social system. Transformation is radical change beyond reform that demands preference for the poor *and* structural, system-transforming change that will affect the totality of our personal, political, historical, and sacred lives.

Almost one-fourth of the Latino community in the United States, 22.5 percent, lives in poverty in comparison to 8.2 percent for

European Americans.[42] We cannot as people who care deeply about our community lose our way by arguing over names and labels like Catholic, Santería, Pentecostal, popular religiosity, or methods of how to count numbers of people who are practitioners of religion without asking the question, "In the service of what sacred source do we pray and practice our politics?" We need to look for evidence in the community for those religious communities that encourage and enable us to fully participate with the four faces of our being in the transformation of our community and the wider society. In this way we will be able to choose between those sacred sources that are destructive and the one that is creative. We are required to be prophetic in our ability to discern which sacred source inspires us here and now. Each of us as a Latina woman, as a Latino man, has a unique, personal face and story of transformation to be lived; each of us is political through our participation in daily shaping a more human and compassionate environment; each of us together with our neighbors can create new turning points in the history of our communities.

THE SACRED AND THE POLITICAL

In the current political atmosphere la comunidad Latina is surrounded by a Catholic and Christian revivalism that borders on being fundamentalist.

A fundamentalist Christian is one who holds the Bible as infallible, historically accurate, literally true, and decisive in all issues the Bible is believed to address. Fundamentalists have a pessimistic expectation of the world's future and see what is called secular humanism as the work of Satan to deceive us from the true path. Political power is the tool for prosecuting the Fundamentalist war against unbelief, even among Christians.[43]

Both Catholics and evangelical Christians express a need to return to original sources in order to cleanse their flocks of the sins and temptations of the modern world. We have a president in the White House who expects his advisors to attend Bible study groups and who believes that, "There is only one reason I am in the Oval Office and not in a bar. I found faith. I found God. I'm here because of the power of prayer."[44] Of course this perspective precludes us from asking whether the vote of the United States Supreme Court and the irregularities of the vote in Florida had anything to do with it. George W. Bush chose to run for president because he believed that "God wants me to run for president" and has spoken of a messianic mission to invade Iraq.[45] Just prior to the War in Iraq Mr. Bush stated at a National Prayer Breakfast: "We can also be confident in the ways of Providence, even when they are far from our understanding."[46] He believes that "He has made it clear he feels that Providence intervened to change his life and now is somehow an instrument of Providence."[47] This is a man who sees himself as the leader against the axis of evil: Iraq, Iran, and North Korea. This, of course, means that he is in the axis of good. This is a holy war against evil and those who disagree with him are in danger of identifying with evil.[48]

But we can and need to ask: "What lord is Mr. Bush referring to when he claims to be the instrument of Providence?" Is he witnessing to the lord of emanation who seeks to return us to the beliefs of our fathers? Is this an envoy of the lord of incoherence who justifies the powerful in their domination? Does he appeal to the lord of deformation to gain revenge against terrorists for 9/11 who ironically pray to the same lord? Or is Mr. Bush claiming to be inspired by the god of transformation who does not favor a citizen of any nation or a religious hero who belongs to any denomination? The deepest source of our being calls upon us to see every person as sacred. Based on the evidence of how Mr. Bush uses religion and the sacred for political gain it can be argued that we have a person who is responding to the promptings that come from the source of emanation as he appeals to our patriotism without question, who asks us to trust him as he pursues the privilege of the powerful, illegally spies on American citizens, condones torture of suspected terrorists, and uses the resources of the nation to spread the gospel of capitalism as the answer to the world's needs even if it means using violence in the service of deformation.

As an undergraduate at the University of Toronto I learned an important lesson about imperialism that helps to explain how the powerful in Washington view American citizens and the rest of the world. As a student I understood that imperialism consists of a powerful nation extending its control beyond its borders to conquer another nation, state, or people. This results in economic, political, and cultural domination and exploitation of the riches of the conquered people for the benefit of the imperialist nation. Because they won, the powerful begin to believe in their natural superiority and the defeated start to believe that they lost because they are inferior. This creates a colonial consciousness in the oppressed and the oppressor. The conquering nation reaps the benefits of the combination of cheap labor and raw resources.

Empire or the imperial is an idea that needs to be constructed by the powerful to justify and legitimize the exploitation of others. The powerful at the center of empire need to sell the idea that empire makes even the life of the ordinary citizen better. What they cannot do is admit to the people that the dominant group uses the resources of the entire nation for the benefit of the already powerful. It does this by encouraging and instilling in their citizens a sense of patriotic grandeur and pride in the imperial power that all share. Imperialists are adept at sending men into battle and consuming the wealth of the nation in the name of the people. This obscures the real intent of imperialism: the further enrichment of the dominant who wave the flag of patriotism and nationalism and declare that the good lord is on our side in order to provide the final legitimization in their deception of the people. Because it is an idea everything needs to be done to shield it with an exaggerated rhetoric of being in the nation's best interest, the good of democracy, spreading freedom around the globe, and delivering us from tyranny and other such slogans. It is all for god and country. But the young who live on the edges of the society and who are not yet committed especially need to be won over by a sense of mission, a purpose that can fire up their enthusiasm. Today, as in the days of the last generation of the British Empire, the powerful in the United States are selling a political idea hoping that it will capture our imagination. The dominant want their idea of the world to be seen as both a challenge and a promise.

Although it may make much of reason, it is not reason that acts as its dynamo. Finally it must have an obvious quality—summarizing in itself something that men have hitherto felt, but have not known how to express.

An idea fulfilling these conditions will be strong enough to force circumstance itself to obey its dictation.

In the last generation of the Victorian era, many men thought they had found just such an idea. It became their faith, that it was the role of the British Empire to lead the world in the arts of civilization, to bring light to the dark places, to teach the true political method, to nourish and to protect the true liberal tradition. It was to act as trustee of the weak, and bring arrogance low. It was to represent in itself the highest aims of human society. It was to command, and serve, a status and prestige shared by no other. It was to captivate the imagination and hold fast the allegiance of the million by the propagation of peculiar myths. . . . While encouraging and making profit from the spirit of adventure, it was nevertheless to promote the interest of peace and commerce. While it was to gain its greatest trophies in war, it was to find its main task in serving the ends of justice, law and order. It was an idea that moved, an idea that expanded, an idea that had to continue to move and to expand in order to retain its vitality and its virtue.[49]

This is what our lords and masters are up to these days as they try to sell us a glorious image of the United States as the hope for the world. This renewed sense of manifest destiny and the thrust of imperialism inherent in the Pax Americana was a result of the United States being the only superpower after the collapse of the Soviet Union.

We are in the midst of a period in American history that is being referred to as the Fourth Great Awakening. In a recent Gallup Poll, even if we are skeptical as to how much we can learn in this way, there are some interesting and sobering results: 46 percent of those polled defined themselves as born-again Christians, an astonishing 48 percent believe in creationism, and 68 percent claimed belief in the Devil.[50] In a special report, *Spirituality in America,* based on a major poll we learn that everywhere there is a flowering of spirituality among Catholics, Muslims, Pentecostals, Jews seeking the meaning of life through Kabbalah, a rebirth of pagan religions, people looking for God in Zen and other forms of Buddhism. Of those polled 79 percent described themselves as "spiritual."[51]

But in the midst of this renewal we are also witnessing the phenomenon of fundamentalist Christian evangelicals allying themselves with right-wing orthodox fundamentalist Israelis in their fight to prevent the return of biblical lands to Muslim Palestinians. At first glance this makes sense because both groups are dedicated to the literal interpretation of the Bible. But this is an amazing alliance because evangelical Christians believe that Christ is the only means to salvation and at the Second Coming there will only be two kinds of Jews, those who have converted to Christ and those who refused and are therefore condemned for all eternity. And yet members of these Christian groups who visit Israel and give their support are welcomed by many Israelis. Evangelical Christians for their part want to use their support of Israel to get back at Muslims for the attack on America and because America has a tradition of being a Judeo-Christian nation. Mr. Bush, who needed this constituency and looked and hoped for the Jewish vote to be re-elected in 2004, is constantly pressured by evangelicals not to abandon parts of the Holy Land that were given by Yahweh to the chosen people. Tom DeLay, Republican from Texas, who was until recently the majority leader of the Republican-controlled House of Representatives, also happens to be an evangelical of the Christian Zionist movement, a formidable bloc of conservative Republicans whose support of Israel is based on biblical interpretations. "I recognize that my faith came from that part of the world. And in my faith, fighting for right and wrong, and understanding good and evil, is pretty apparent and pretty straightforward."[52] These are the words of a zealot who is so convinced of possessing the truth in his religious beliefs that he is willing to fight and presumably kill in defense of those beliefs.

Islam has been referred to as a religion that is regressive, fraudulent, and violent by among others Pat Robertson, Jerry Falwell, Jerry Vines, and Franklin Graham, the son of the world renowned evangelist, Billy Graham. There is a supreme irony in the struggle between the three monotheistic world religions. Ultra-right-wing fundamentalist Christians and Jews are worshipping the same sacred sources, the tribal lords of emanation and deformation, as do fundamentalist members of al-Qaeda, the terrorist group that claims allegiance to Allah. In each case there is a shockingly cynical use of the sacred to achieve their political goals. Another ironic twist is that they are not manipulating the sacred; on the contrary, the sacred sources of emanation and deformation have possessed their lives and driven them to further violence. Violent believers from whatever religious heritage serve the lord of deformation; their view of what is revealed by their lord makes those who are not believers worthy of death. Observers of religious behavior, because they do not have a solid theoretical base from which to compare and make normative judgments, have missed the insight that all fundamentalists—whether the Muslim Taliban, al-Qaeda, Christian Zionists, far-right members of the Likud party in Israel, or Sikh extremists—enact religion in the service of destructive death.[53]

In Naples, Florida, the first Roman Catholic college in forty years, Ave Maria University, was founded by a wealthy lay Catholic, Tom Monaghan, who made his fortune as the owner of Domino's

Pizza. He spent $200 million to achieve his dream. His reasons for building a new university and not giving money to existing Catholic colleges are very clear:

> The reason why God created us was to earn heaven, so we could be with Him, and my goal is to help more people get to heaven. You can't follow the rules of God unless you know what they are. At some Catholic universities, students graduate with their religious faith more shaky than when they arrived. . . . 75% of Catholics don't practice their faith right now. I hope to do something about that.[54]

As in the case of Muslim and Jewish fundamentalists Monaghan wants to restore Catholics to a pristine tradition that has been lost. He wants Catholics to return to the lord of emanation in order to be saved.

The Hispanic Project at the New Democrat Network conducted a poll of eight hundred Latino voters with almost half the interviews in Spanish. Issues that hurt the Republicans are immigration, especially the flow of undocumented workers, jobs, and social welfare concerns. Sharon Castillo who oversees the Hispanic outreach for the Republican National Committee stated that the Democrats are worried about their continuing appeal to Latino voters. It is evident from this activity on the part of both political parties that the Latino vote is considered crucial to their future election plans.[55] There is a battle going on within the ranks of Republicans over the thorny issue of immigration. The proposals put forth prior to the election of 2004 for amnesty were so cumbersome as to discourage application and the safeguards to protect the rights of the guest workers were inadequate.[56] A draconian piece of legislation passed by the House of Representatives would make illegal entry into the United States a federal crime and give heavy penalties to anybody hiring or aiding undocumented workers.

What are we to make of the above comments and how can they help us to see the connection between the sacred and the political faces of our being? We find a president praying for guidance to wage war; a coalition between Evangelical Christians and right-wing Israelis; fundamentalist Jihadist Muslims waging a holy war; a new Catholic university being planned to return Catholics to the true faith; the Latino community being wooed by both Democrats and Republicans. All of the above are issues that are permeated by the sacred and the political. We now ask the question, "In the service of what sacred source are those in the events being political?"

If we read the comments of Christian fundamentalists carefully they all have to do with proving that all that is good and right belongs to the United States. There is no room for dialogue or disagreement when looking at the complexity of issues. Born-again Christians desire to return to the faith of their fathers and imply that this is the only way for all people of good will. Like Tom Monaghan and Jerry Falwell and the leaders of the Taliban they want to make sure that the lost are redeemed and saved. They all want to return us to a golden past of true believers wherein all accept the word of the lord. But what lord is this, what is the tradition, to what fundamental truths are they taking us? The road is one that takes us back to the way of life and the lord of emanation. Conversion for them is a return to the truth given once for all from which Christians, Jews, and Muslims have deviated. My personal life was a mess and god saved me and now I have a mission to clean up the mess in the country and the world is what Mr. Bush is telling us. Mr. Monaghan uses the politics of education to return us to the straight path. In what way is this different from Wahabbism, the fundamentalist religious ideology of the madrasas, the religious schools in Saudi Arabia and elsewhere in the Muslim world, that teach the young to see Islam as the only true religion and the West as the enemy?

We cannot know what is in a person's heart but we can discern from their words and actions what ultimate sacred source they serve when they do what they do. In the service of the lord of emanation we are given a plan for life and we cannot question it. There is only one correct way. There is no experimenting and moving beyond established boundaries. We are asked to be loyal, to trust, and to obey. If we disagree we are seen as enemies of the truth; we are the fallen. This makes the dissenters vulnerable to retaliation. At the very least it means having doors closed to opportunities for advancement with the rewards going to those who are in agreement. The early Christians were seen as enemies of the state by the Romans; the Church served as a permanent source of judgment against the power of the state. But this all changed with the Edict of Milan in 313 A.D. Since that time the Church as the official church of the Empire allied itself with the state in the service of the lord of incoherence. Religious authorities were obligated to support the state and legitimize its power and in return received the support of the state against its enemies. Because the Roman Empire saw religion as a useful tool to preserve the unity of the polity, the dominant were ready to use violence against those who were threats to the state and religious institutions. This demonstrates the inherent fragility of emanation and incoherence as ways of life; neither can respond to fundamentally new kinds of problems that might undermine their authority. Those living in these ways of life inspired by the lords of emanation and incoherence always put us on the road to destructive death in the service of the lord of deformation. This triangular relationship between these three sacred sources has nothing to do with the deepest source, the god of transformation.

There can be no coercion, psychological or physical violence of any kind, in the way of life of transformation. We can and need to disagree with authority whenever there is an appeal to blind patriotism and obedience, a campaign to assert our power or a war of revenge. These kinds of appeals are a clear indication that the three partial lords of emanation, incoherence, and deformation are present. This allows us to identify these lords in whatever guise they take. Fundamentalist extremists whether they are Christian, Muslim, or Jewish are all serving the same sacred source, the lord of deformation, because they are prepared to kill others in the name of this lord.

Given this normative perspective of transformation we can see that much of what is going on in the politics of the country is inspired by the demands of power in the service of incoherence. By calling on our patriotism the powerful use the lord of emanation to hide the ugliness of the fist that is prepared to enter into deformation to protect their interests. Everything from the tax breaks of 2001 and 2003 and extending the tax cuts to 2010 that favored the rich and the attempt to make these tax breaks permanent, the Wall Street scandals, the lies regarding the weapons of mass destruction to justify war in Iraq, the cynical use of unqualified judicial nominees to placate the conservatives, the stand against affirmative action, raping the environment to curry the favor of the mining, oil, gas, and lumber industries, sloganeering about no child left behind and then not allocating the funds to achieve the goal, providing tax breaks for small companies of up to 85 percent for the purchase of high polluting SUVs, cutting the budget of OSHA, attempting to privatize Medicare drug benefits to boost the profits of the pharmaceutical companies, starving the treasury so that there is little money left for the social safety net, all of these policies have nothing to do with compassion and justice. It is all about the story of capitalism in the service of incoherence and deformation that arrests our nation in the pursuit of power and the retention of power by the privileged at any cost.

We need to do this kind of analysis to smoke out the real intent of the powerful when they invoke the name of "God" to bless their work. God Bless America? America is hated around the world because we worship the lord of power while we preach the blessings of freedom to others who cannot afford our version of capitalism. The developed countries continue to give out an astonishing amount of money in the hundreds of billions in farm subsidies that dwarf the money given out in development assistance. These subsidies allow farmers from rich nations to grow an abundance of products and then dump them on the world market that depresses prices on the commodities market so that farmers from poor nations in Africa, Latin America, and Asia cannot sell their agricultural products. In addition the developed nations impose high tariffs that raise the cost of imports from the developing nations. According to the International Monetary Fund a repeal of all tariffs and subsidies by the rich nations would improve global welfare by $120 billion. An increase of only 1 percent in Africa's share of world exports would bring in $70 billion a year, five times the amount that African nations receive from the developed countries in aid and debt relief. The main player in the world economy is the United States that preaches free trade to gain access to foreign markets for our goods but then turns its back on the neediest in the developing world.[57] A case in point is the growing of cotton in African nations where cotton is literally their life line. Nations like Chad, Benin, Mali, and Burkina Faso have sent a proposal to the World Trade Organization that calls for an end to unfair subsidies given by the developed nations to their cotton growers. For example, 25,000 cotton growers in the U.S. received more in subsidies, some $3 billion, than the entire economic output of Burkina Faso where two million people depend on cotton. U.S. subsidies are concentrated on just 10 percent of its cotton growers. Subsidies to approximately 2,500 wealthy farmers have the unintended effect of impoverishing some ten million people in West and Central Africa.[58] In the area of textiles and agriculture the barriers to trade by the rich nations continue to be a roadblock for the developing nations. The developed world provides nearly $1 billion a day in subsidies to its own farmers which drives down commodity prices so that farmers from poor nations cannot compete with the resulting lower prices even in their own countries.[59] These subsidies do much to undermine the image of the United States as the protector of human rights and democracy around the world. Crushing poverty is a breeding ground for terrorism since it leaves those within its grasp without hope.[60]

There are many who want to seal the border with Mexico in order to stop the flow of undocumented workers coming into the country. But these advocates for secure borders have no idea that subsidies we pay to our farmers who grow corn has led to a growing economic crisis for Mexican farmers and workers who rely on corn for their livelihood. Since 1994 when NAFTA took effect, the price of corn in Mexico has dropped 70 percent reducing the incomes of fifteen million people who are dependent on the growing of corn. Mexico is the birthplace of corn; corn was considered the food of the gods by the indigenous people; corn is the staple of the Mexican diet. But now the United States is flooding Mexico with cheap corn. The U.S. is now the biggest exporter of corn to Mexico so that nearly one-third of the corn used in Mexico is from the U.S.[61]

Through a series of editorials *The New York Times* has been unrelenting in its criticism of the U.S. and the thirty developed nations of the Organization for Economic Cooperation and Development for its system of high tariffs and subsidies of its own farmers that is directly related to poverty around the world.[62] Through a policy of subsidies and protectionist tariffs the developed nations of the world dump their agricultural products on the world market depressing prices to the point where farmers from Guatemala, South Africa, the Philippines, Mexico, Berkina Faso, Brazil, and Vietnam cannot sell their products and make a living. For example, "If the US terminated its cotton subsidies, commodity prices would rebound to more realistic levels, allowing the third-world cotton farmers to compete and earn a profit on their crops. And by terminating trade-distorting farming subsidies, Washington would defuse a potent source of feverish anti-Americanism."[63]

Our involvement and indeed leadership in maintaining this system of high tariffs and subsidies leads many to consider the U.S. as an arrogant nation, the bully of the world who says to others, "Either you are with us or against us." We tell the world that we are going to do whatever is in our best interest and if you do not agree, we do not care. The war in Iraq, for example, had nothing to do with justice, the truth, compassion, freedom, democracy, human rights, or ending dictatorship. It was all about power, American power, oil, our hope to dictate what the world should be like, to favor the state of Israel, to intimidate the Muslim world, to impose a Pax Americana as the only superpower. American corporations, like Haliburton, that are closely linked to members of the current administration are reaping a financial windfall from the rebuilding of Iraq. What a terrible tragedy it is for the families of those killed in Iraq to face the possibility that their loved ones may not have died to keep this country free and to bring the blessings of democracy to the rest of the downtrodden world. They cannot allow these thoughts to surface. As is made clear from the articles and editorials cited above, the United States can do more to address the poverty and despair that are the true weapons of mass destruction by leading a movement to drop agricultural subsidies paid to U.S. farmers and those in the developed world. President Eisenhower at a National Security Council meeting in March 1953 asked why we can't "get some of the people in those downtrodden countries to like us instead of hating us."[64] We still ask this question and yet the answers are available for all to see.

So when we as members of the various Latino communities hear politicians asking for our votes we need to know that our choice is never a so-called secular one. The sacred permeates our lives and everything that we do as an individual or as a nation is enacted in the service of a sacred lord and way of life. In all situations we need to ask the question. "Why ultimately am I, is this nation, doing what we are doing?" Are we asked to be loyal beyond question, is our main concern as a nation to increase our power, are we living a fantasy, or are we victims of a fantasy based on lies of alleged superiority to justify hurting others because they pray, look, dress, and live differently, or do we care deeply about others so that we are willing to risk our own well-being to assist them to achieve a better life? These kinds of questions allow us to wake up to what we are doing and why. Once we answer these questions we have a choice. We can choose to empty our lives of those lords and ways of life in whose service we have been enacting the relationships, stories, and the four faces of our being and choose to bring about concretely the fundamentally new and better in all aspects of life. Let us turn now to an analysis of our journey through the core drama of life that successfully continues only in the way of life of transformation.

THE ARCHETYPE OF THE JOURNEY: THE CORE DRAMA OF LIFE

Our quest is a sacred journey. It is a journey that takes place both within the depths and without in the everyday world. In prehistoric times people consciously enacted rituals that involved traveling to almost inaccessible caves which they transformed into sacred spaces by adorning the walls with representations of animals upon which they were dependent for life. The journey was a hard and dangerous one. Christ reenacted this same archetype in his *via cruces* (way of the cross). Through this way comes redemption, "I am the way, the truth, and the life" was a conscious utterance on the part of Jesus which transformed the archetype, and shaped the attitudes of all the ensuing generations of Christians who have reenacted this road of conversion and salvation. Christianity, Buddhism, Judaism, Confucianism, and Islam all represent religious formulations of the archetype of the journey that either arrest us in a fixed way of life, in partial ways of life, or move us toward the deepest sacred.[65]

The journey, as we have seen in chapter 1, consists of traveling through the core drama of life that has three acts and two scenes within each act. Erich Neumann traced this movement from a condition of being immersed in others to the emergence of the individual by writing of the gradual separation of consciousness out of the unconscious.[66] The process of differentiation, of separation, was necessary so that human beings could initiate the journey of transformation by becoming aware of their personal and deeper sacred sources.

The source of sources in Act I creates a merciful container that nourishes us in emanation. The child is not yet fully conscious of its own innate abilities nor is the child aware of living as an extension of others. The individual lives in a pre-ego stage because he or she is not aware of alternatives; they can only live within the givens of their world. If a child remains in this stage because of fear, a sense of sin, shame, or guilt, or possessive relationships then the source that possesses and arrests its life is the lord of emanation. The connecting link with the deepest source is broken and the lord of emanation becomes the only lord and thereby freezes the flow of relatedness in a one-way divine monologue. This constitutes an arrested and partial manifestation of the sacred. An example of this lord of emanation as a tribal god was the Aztec god, Huitzilopochtli, the god of the sun, war, and the chase that needed to be given nourishment by human blood. This is a classic example of a lord of emanation that becomes a lord of deformation when the tribe is challenged by outsiders who are threats to tribal security and therefore worthy of death.

Act II is initiated by an original sin against the orthodoxy of the fathers. A sin committed against the parents is also an offense against the lord of emanation who punishes us with anxiety attacks permeated by guilt. The Spanish word for guilt is a very powerful and image-provoking term: *remordimiento,* a word that is derived from the verb, *morder,* to bite. Guilt is intended not only to bite but to continue to gnaw at us again and again as a form of psychological torture. Resistance entails freeing ourselves of guilt and releasing the energy locked up in the repressed self. The energy can take the form of a creative anger, *coraje,* in order to make us bold enough to rebel against those who would hold us in emanation.

Once we cancel the guilt, the old web of meaning begins to lose its power over us. But this is a dangerous period. What now will hold us together in common cause with others? The shattering of the container of emanation and the weakening of its lord allows us to enter the first scene of Act II. The new lord of incoherence takes us over. Although we protest that all that we want is the freedom to pursue our own best self-interest, we know neither who we are nor what is best for us. We can arrest our lives here but we also have the choice of continuing on the journey to Act II, Scene 2, and become open to transformation as well as to deformation.

At this point of the journey we can either empty ourselves of the false lords and the relationships and stories practiced in their service or we can exit the drama into the abyss as we make life worse. The lords can take on new forms so that we believe that they are dead when they are still present. The sacred is always present, but the more we ignore its presence the more open we are to being possessed. Even allegedly "secular" men and women, atheists and agnostics pursuing power are serving a sacred source, the lord of incoherence, who links us to a partial sacred in a way that cuts us off from any creativity intended to transform our fragmentation. In deformation the lord of nothing binds us in the depths at the exit from the core drama of life.

> In Act III of the core drama of life, our new concreteness comes also to be newly connected—in bi-unity—with our deepest sacred depths. This is our most important choice in life. Whereas we have three different Lords inspiring us to remain with a fragment of the core drama of life, and commanding us to be a partial self, the deepest source of our being guides us through the core drama of life so that in fact we come to understand and love ourselves and to be with and love our neighbors as ourselves.[67]

In Act III there is, for the first time, a mutual interpenetration of the human and the divine. The deepest source is free to reveal itself because we have chosen to participate as we enact the story of the transforming self. Our symbol for Act III shows a mutual activity that involves a new qualitative link to the sacred; we together with the god of transformation create a chain of transforming links in which the sacred and the participatory self can respond to new problems. We are now free to place something new *concretely* in the world that was not there before.

> The god of transformation is never omniscient or omnipotent. The god of transformation is perfect only when we are prepared to participate in order to create. . . . Our task is to help god into wholeness ever more often and covering an ever larger network of life. . . . The source of sources has incomparably more power than anyone else but the source of sources has complete capacity only when it connects to the god of transformation and also manifests itself thus in human beings.[68]

We ourselves participate in divinity in the sense that each of us can be a manifestation of the deepest source.

IN THE SERVICE OF WHAT SACRED SOURCE DO WE ENACT MINISTRY

Knowing that there are these four sacred sources allows us to distinguish between four kinds of priesthood and ministry. A priest or minister is a guide to show us the way but they can only guide us to the sacred lords in whose service they practice the stories, relationships, and the four faces of their being. Consequently, some will lead us to give ourselves totally to the church as the voice of Christ. This understanding reduces Jesus to being the lord of emanation who legitimizes religious structures and institutions and places them above the people. This incapacitates us because we take no action to give flesh to the sacred in fundamentally new and more loving ways. These priests and ministers prepare us to ignore the incoherence by masking, repressing, and distorting our concrete problems. They urge loyalty to a fragment of the core drama, the way of life of emanation that is losing its ability to explain the whole of life.

Other ministers preach an accommodation with the culture: we are urged to work hard and to pray for success. This integrationist or assimilationist approach is taken by many white clergy whose own ethnic group has been brought into the mainstream. We are urged to see the lord of incoherence as the source of our blessings and to pray to this lord for further benefits. Megachurches that accommodate up to as many as 5,000 to 15,000 people are mushrooming around the country. They preach how to do everything from how to reach your professional goals and discipline your children to how to invest your money. "If Oprah and Dr. Phil are doing it, why shouldn't we?"[69] The lord of incoherence legitimizes the pursuit of power; it is this lord who "helps those who help themselves." Serving the same lord of incoherence are those ministers who preach the "prosperity gospel." These ministers tell their flocks who are often poor people that when the collection plate is passed "It's opportunity for prosperity." This message was given by a pastor who is wealthy urging people who make about $30,000 a year to be generous.[70] Clergy of all denominations are prone to this approach. Some urge changes to let people into the system, while failing to critique the very foundations of a society that created and maintains a lower class based on the story of capitalism in collusion with racism and sexism. So these ministers teach us to live with incoherence. Years ago I witnessed Mexican families in South Texas sitting in the back of a Catholic church while a white family sat alone in the front pew. All of us, both clergy and lay, Latino and Anglo, had come to accept living with incoherence on the road to deformation since this exercise of power connected to racism was an act of violence that turned the Latinos and Latinas into lesser human beings.

Ministers, mullahs, rabbis, and priests as leaders of fundamentalist groups deny that the web of life guarded by the lord of emanation has broken. They promise a return to unity and security in a hostile world. If this tactic does not work, theocratic societies use legislation to force all to obey traditional laws that dictate a fixed morality intended to return the people to the purity of the past heritage. Women in Afghanistan who were oppressed by the fundamentalist beliefs of the Taliban were still beaten after the Taliban were defeated for wearing Western-style clothing that revealed the shape of their bodies. The men had freed themselves from the Taliban but not from the sacred stories of patriarchy. The tribal lord of emanation continued to inspire Afghan men to believe that they needed to impose the authority of Islam over the women lest they be contaminated by the West. In the shroud of militant Islam the lord of emanation now colludes with the lord of deformation, the lord of nothing, who promises a return to a pristine past by violence if necessary.

This is a vindictive lord who justifies a repetition of the power that men have traditionally exercised over Muslim women. The same fantasy of male superiority blessed by Allah is repeated. This is not transformation but deformation.

What has been lost sight of is what ministry is all about. Priesthood in the service of the god of transformation recognizes no such thing as gender, age, race, sexual orientation, class, or formal education. Those who care deeply for others and are committed to love and justice are ministers of the deepest source of transformation. To love others is to shape a society so that all might share in the fruits of human endeavor. To recognize my own sacredness is to recognize the sacredness of my neighbor. To put people in contact with their own self and sacred source is to function as a minister of the sacred regardless of public or institutional ordination. In the way of life of transformation all of us are called to be ministers of the sacred. So in fact we already have Latino and Latina priests who do the work of the god of transformation as celibate, married, or single persons. We need compassionate clergy in the present situation who are outsiders and insiders, that is, ministers in the service of transformation.

The ministers of the god of transformation are ordained by the Spirit. Their ministry is created by responding to the deepest source within and by their own response to meet the needs of the community. Ib'n Arabi wrote about the ritual of processing around the Kaaba in the Holy Mosque as an opportunity to open one's heart to the new revelation from Allah that needed to end in a new transformation. As he circumambulated he heard a voice "The Temple which contains Me is your heart." The temple around which the pilgrim walks is his own heart that contains and reveals the god of transformation. In the temple which contains them both is revealed the secret of the Adamic theophany which structures the Creator-Creature as a bi-unity, He knows Himself in you and through you.[71]

> The fulcrum of the pilgrimage is also the essence of life: a caring heart fired by the imagination. For instance, after paying homage to the two women Eve and Hagar in the rites of pilgrimage, how can some Muslims still violate the rights and dignity of women in the name of Islam? Is this not a contradiction? If the pilgrimage is done not by rote but with imagination, honor killings become unthinkably loathsome, a curse to be condemned like the Satan just stoned. The truth of the imagination pertains today . . . who still believe the imagination is the healing balm for our deeply troubled world.[72]

This is an extraordinary and beautiful example of Islam in the service of the god of transformation. It is proof that we cannot stereotype any religion. There are indeed four sacred sources that can guide us but only the deepest source of transformation inspires a caring heart fired by the imagination.

Gandhi understood his own ordination in this way. He felt that he had been raised up by the Spirit to answer the call of the sacred *and* of his people. His self-realization was fulfilled by a life dedicated to the service of others.[73] *El Payaso,* the clown in Federico Fellini's *La Strada,* ordains Gelsomina by placing a gold medal around her neck after urging her to love Zampano, a man dedicated to power "who will not love, you who cannot love." Gelsomina decides to stay with Zampano as her commitment to love as the purpose and meaning of her ordination. Many of us have intuitively understood this kind of ordination in our bones when we have witnessed our own elders, parents, grandparents, and others take command at decisive moments of spiritual and emotional crises. We knew that the official priests were not the only ones who could bring the Spirit or the transforming god into our situations. In the Latino community we observe an ancient tradition of asking for a blessing, the laying on of hands, from our parents and *abuelos,* grandparents, before leaving the house; we kissed their hands out of respect for their sacred place in our life and we prayed the rosary with them in a sacred space set aside as our home altar.

Christians do a disservice to the priesthood by creating and preserving a privileged, clerical caste that is called the priesthood of Jesus. This reduces Jesus to a lord of emanation for the uncritically loyal, or the lord of incoherence for the privileged, or the lord of deformation for those who kill in the name of Jesus when in fact Jesus' entrance into human history was a pivotal and grand moment because he was one of the world's most profound and influential incarnations of the god of transformation.[74]

> His example gives us faith that any of us is capable—not of copying Christ's life: his human life was uniquely his own— but of living our particular life as a transforming life, which is also to say, to live it like Christ as the incarnation of the god of transformation.[75]

It is in this sense that Christians participate in the ministry of Jesus Christ, as incarnations ourselves of the god of transformation. In our own community I think of people like Dolores Huerta and

Susan Casillas, strong Chicana women who have consciously chosen a life of struggle and poverty on behalf of farm workers. In this
way they fulfill their own vocation to be a full person in the very act
of struggling for the humanity of others. There are many others like
Dolores and Susan, from all ethnic and racial backgrounds, who
labor daily with our people. Many Anglo parish priests working as
their allies have used their clerical and institutional resources to
help them challenge the realities of everyday racism and poverty.
Both women have experienced the transforming sacred in their commitment to farm workers; they are women growing their own ministry and Catholicism in the service of others. They have very little
in common with Catholic growers who deny a living wage to migrant workers. They have the same religious label but they are in the
service of radically different sacred sources.

Jesus is a crucial and axial event in human history. Jesus is not
the only manifestation of the transforming god, even though he may
be the highest manifestation of this god. Similarly, the priesthood of
Jesus is a priesthood among many that puts us in contact with the
transforming god, the deepest source of all. The refusal of many
Christian priests and ministers to recognize this plurality of priesthoods makes them intolerant of each other's Christian priesthood
and the ministry of those who are non-Christian. There have always
been holy men and women in all traditions who mediated the sacred
in an extraordinary way. Indeed, transforming priests and ministers
have recognized the validity of the priesthood of other denominations and faiths, as will be discussed below in the case of a Maryknoll missionary in Bolivia. Those who serve the lord of emanation
attempt to domesticate the sacred. Virgilio Elizondo wrote a fine
book on Mexican Americans in which he develops a theological interpretation of *mestizaje*[76] as a blending of cultures. Elizondo correctly sees the blending of European and American forms of culture
and religion. The sacred was here before the Spaniards arrived. We
need to distinguish true from false gods lest we implicitly or unconsciously accept the prejudice against unknown manifestations of the
sacred as superstitious and pagan. For example, Quetzalcoatl, the
plumed serpent, is a symbol of the transforming god. He was for centuries used as a lord of emanation but can be rediscovered as a god of
transformation. He is very similar to the god Mercury, who holds together the opposites, sulfur and quicksilver, two of the main ingredients by which the alchemists dissolved and re-coagulated the base
metals symbolic of the fragmented human personality in order to
transform the dissolution of the old into the precious gold of a new

and sacred self.[77] Both Mercury and Quetzalcoatl originally represented death and rebirth, incoherence and transformation, destruction and creation. Both gods represented the possibility of an infinite number of new forms, possibilities, and creations.

> Wherever the night sea voyage in pursuit of the sun is undertaken, by the gods of the human soul, it signifies this development toward the relative independence of an ego endowed with such attributes as free will. This tendency, which we have found in the Old World and in Malekula, can also be demonstrated in Aztec Mexico. It achieves its highest form in the myth of Quetzalcoatl, the Mexican hero figure. He is not a hero who transforms the outside world, but one who transforms himself by atonement. He is the dying and resurrected god, but he is also the hero king and the culture bringer, the earthly and divine representative of the principle of light and humanity. In his dual nature, he combines the western, deathly aspect and the eastern aspect of life: he is the evening star and the morning star. As morning star, he is the positive symbol of the ascending power belonging to the male-spiritual aspect of heaven and the sun. For this reason he is associated with the symbol of the east, the plumed serpent. He is the wind-ruach-spirit aspect. He is the god of knowledge and the ascending spiral tower is one of his attributes.[78]

There are other gods and goddesses in the Latin American tradition that can be rediscovered as manifestations of the transforming god. In a similar vein, Black Elk, a holy man of the Oglala Sioux, was ordained by the Spirit and received a vision from the White Buffalo Woman. For years Black Elk resisted his priesthood, his call to show the face of the sacred to the people, because he was afraid.[79]

In *El Señor Presidente* by Asturias[80] and in Dostoevsky's "The Grand Inquisitor" of *The Brothers Karamazov*[81] we find the same struggle between possessive lords and the deepest sacred source and their priesthoods. A Catholic cardinal as the Grand Inquisitor promised the people security and in exchange for their freedom he offered them passive obedience and bread; the Grand Inquisitor cheated them out of their humanity. For Dostoevsky he is, therefore, really the anti-Christ who leads them to the prison of a fixed fate, they will be forever children who serve the rich. In this instance Dostoevsky pierces through the title of cardinal and shows us a priest in the service of the lord of emanation who has made an alliance with the lord of incoherence, the sacred source that legitimizes the state and the lord of deformation. This very logic forces him to jail Jesus because even though the cardinal carries the title of priesthood of Jesus, it is merely to deceive the people. He must imprison Jesus Christ as a god of transformation. The cardinal who represents the alliance of church and state serves sacred sources radically opposed to the god of transformation.

El Señor Presidente tells the story once again of the alliance between the three lords of emanation, incoherence, and deformation in an alleged democratic state. The president, as a minister of the state, is democratically elected. But if the state and his power are threatened he is prepared to practice the deformation of killing and dominating the people as the old rulers did. He fails to possess the people through loyalty as totally as the old priestly, warrior class had done. He lacks the old legitimacy and for this reason uses the Church and "God," the lord of emanation, to bless his regime. Asturias is forewarning us of the future because he recognized how the Latin American state with all of its democratic trappings was really the return of the pyramid symbolizing power and privilege for the few. The state in Latin America is a direct descendant of the ancient pyramid upon which the clerical warrior classes both indigenous and Spanish preserved their status with the blood of its citizens. People no longer experience the truth or security of the web of life of emanation and the state sees that its power in the service of incoherence is failing. Since the people do not accept its legitimacy, the state responds to their rebellion with violence in the way of life of deformation. It is precisely for this reason that the theology of liberation is so dangerous to both church and state in Latin America. On the one hand, the advocates of liberation theology refuse to legitimize the power of the state and thus leave it naked in its ruthlessness and illegitimacy. On the other hand, the followers of the theology of liberation also refuse to allow the church to use the state as an instrument of power in order to force people back to the orthodoxy of the lord of emanation. Thus as the alliance between the lord of emanation and the lord of incoherence is being undermined, they turn increasingly to the lord of deformation as the national security state that kills anybody who opposes it. This places the practitioners of liberation theology in the service of transformation at total odds with some but certainly not all the agents of the hierarchy of the church and state.

The *Comunidades de Base,* or Basic Christian Communities (BCC), found in the Philippines and throughout Latin America, especially in Brazil, guided by a theology of liberation are extraordinary manifestations of the god of transformation. These communities provide us with another example of ministry that considers service as constituting an option for the poor. The BCCs represent an attempt to ground us in and return us to our deepest source and origins. Theologians like Gustavo Gutiérrez and Juan Luis Segundo[82] speak of the economic system and the national security state as demonic instruments that point out the alliance between the lords of emanation, incoherence, and deformation. In the late 1960s the BCCs in Latin America took a revolutionary step in choosing to identify with the poor. This conversion from the lords of power and uncritical loyalty to the god of compassion has cost many lives, even that of Archbishop Oscar Romero, the bishop of San Salvador in 1980. Romero followed in the brave tradition of Antonio de Valdivieso, the bishop of Nicaragua who was murdered in 1550 by Spaniards who were angry with his denunciations of their treatment of the indigenous people.[83] The proponents of liberation are feared by the privileged of both church and state who serve their own interests. The BCCs organize people as equal participants and use the scriptures as the basis for their acts of liberation. They form cooperatives to end their dependency on the powerful who exploit them. They also speak as equals with the priests who work with them. It is the Spirit who speaks where it wills and who is no respecter of titles. Priests earn respect by struggling with the people and arriving together with them to a deeper understanding of how to live their faith for the good of all.

This understanding of ministry and its rejection of hierarchical control threaten those in church and society who want to continue to treat the people as ignorant children in order to control them.[84] Since traditional values are dissolving, the powerful seek to build fortresses in a world that they cannot understand or control. Nevertheless there is great potential for liberation. The people are free now to re-experience the deepest source without the traditional religious filters that excluded as heresy their personal experience of the source of all sources.

The emphasis on personal experience helps to explain the rise of groups such as the Pentecostal and Charismatic movements among Latinas and Latinos. The authenticity of the *carismaticos* depends on the quality of their connections to the deepest source and the faithfulness with which they participate in creating new and more loving forms of justice. Some are responding to the god of transformation. But others may be seeking another container to encounter the traditional lord of emanation to provide security. It is possible that the Catholic Church has allowed the charismatic movement to grow so that it can compete with the various Protestant evangelical groups, especially the Pentecostals, for the loyalty of the community. Latinas and Latinos can create a new and more compassionate alternative by reaching out to others with the political and historical faces of their being to create a community that values each person. If they find that they cannot validate their own experiences due to religious interpretations or structural authority, then they need to question that teaching and authority. Latinas and Latinos ask that no church use our vulnerability for their own institutional reasons. For any group to seek to embrace us in a new kind of security is to provide a false community and to profit from our vulnerability.

Churches, mosques, and synagogues can help build community. The community is neither an addendum nor an afterthought; community follows from the very essence of selfhood that can only emerge in creative relationship to our neighbor, the world, and the deepest source of transformation. A religious institution can serve as a community of transforming persons who provide us with a temporary container. We need to mature and to have the courage to listen to our inner voice that leads us away from the web of emanation in order to discover who we are on the journey. Following this new inspiration from the depths we need to discern which sacred source is present. Because of this understanding of the sacred and of our life as a journey of persistent transformation, it is inconceivable that any religion in the future will ever be able to sustain the kind of permanent emanational embrace of its members that the Roman Catholic Church once did and that fundamentalist movements in Islam and Judaism are trying to revive. All religious institutions are being challenged to practice a conversion based upon a process of emptying out false lords and undergoing a rebirth to embark anew on the journey of transformation.

As we ask these new questions, we come to see that there were indeed women and men who belonged to the counter-tradition, that is, that tradition of journeying with the transforming god, who refused to be silenced; who sought to break through to contact the deepest source. To live the tradition afresh then is to re-experience these women and men in a new way: Plato, Socrates, Moses Maimonides, Ib'n Arabi, Ignatius Loyola, the young Hegel, Marx, Nicholas of Cusa, Master Eckhardt, John of the Cross, St. Teresa of Avila, Sor Juana Ines, Peguy, and Teilhard de Chardin. They all realized that tradition had begun as a revolution; the mystery of the source was revealed to us in a new incarnation. They also knew that there was no final transformation as a magic formula. They witnessed to the presence of the Spirit who makes possible an infinite number of new incarnations with our participation. It was the risk of conversion that allowed Loyola and his colleagues to renew themselves and others through *The Spiritual Exercises*.[85] In their annual retreat Jesuits seek the hidden *gnosis,* or knowledge of the process of transformation. Loyola practiced the "heresy" that the god of transformation continues to reveal itself. Tradition, then, is not only what we remember but also what we forgot or have not yet brought into the light. We need to see that tradition is created, nourished, and uprooted and planted based on a new experience of the sacred by the persons living that tradition. We are free to continue what liberates us, to re-experience ourselves and the holy, *and* to free ourselves of freezing the holy and our lives in formulas that trap us in fixed faith and repress any new insights.

This crisis of fixed faith and authority in the service of the lord of emanation is especially painful for Catholic missionaries. They are symbolic of an understanding of the crisis of a Church triumphant which seeks to impose its truth by embracing the world through conversion. Born-again Christians preach conversion to the one true lord as revealed in Jesus and his church as the road to salvation. But the name of Jesus is often used to mask the real lord that is present, the lords of emanation and incoherence that collude with the lord of deformation.

Let us consider the example of the Maryknoll missionaries working in Latin America and more particularly in Bolivia and Peru. They came to baptize, teach, and serve the native population. They have been for some time now questioning the authority of their teaching. What has led them to such a crisis is a personal awareness that many have known for a long time, that the people whom they came to assist had a relationship to the sacred centuries before they came and goes on living side by side, often in a hidden manner, with the sacred sources brought by the Catholic Church with the Conquest. In an excellent documentary film, *El Curandero,* The Healer,[86] the Maryknoll Fathers told the story of one of their own, Father Salazar. He baptized, preached, said Mass, and felt that he was making progress in strengthening the Catholic faith of the people. But one day by accident he discovered hidden rituals. He found potatoes around the base of a statue of the Virgin Mary. When he inquired why they were placed there he found out that Mary was being worshipped as a version of the Earth Goddess, Pacha Mama. Since time immemorial the people dedicated fruits of the harvest to thank Pacha Mama for her mercy. He was shocked and dismayed and preached against this residual "paganism." It did not go away. The people ignored him. After centuries of indoctrination, Roman Catholicism was not the only vehicle of the sacred. He sought out the meaning of the strange amulets and rituals. At first he was angry, then curious, and, finally, genuinely moved by what he discovered. Eventually he took an extraordinary step into the other world: he became an apprentice to an Aymara Indian *brujo*, male witch or shaman, who performed services for the people to the earth goddess, Pacha Mama. Father Salazar participated in the services. In the midst of this encounter the Aymara priest's son died. Both faiths were incapable of adequately explaining or soothing the harshness of death. That is to say, both religious expressions had to admit their inadequacies. It was a remarkable example of two men forced to leave behind their religious formulas in the face of death. What is more noteworthy was the young priest's awareness that he no longer had the answers. His recognition of the validity of his friend's priesthood helped him to free himself of the absolute claim of Catholicism. As the film ended, Father Salazar narrated his determination to resolve his crisis of faith.

Both the Aymara and Catholic religions in this situation had turned the sacred into an avenging lord. Their lords were terrifying in their use of power. Marcellino, the shaman, could see death only as a punishment from a lord who would now make it up to them by giving them cattle. Father Salazar felt helpless in his attempt to console his friend. Some of the Indians in the film considered their sacred lord cruel and death as a total end to everything. For almost five centuries the Catholic missionaries preached their understanding of the sacred. The indigenous population quietly resisted the lords of the European white world by nourishing their threatened lords. The lord of the missionaries was an imperialist deity and the Indians cultivated their lords as rebel sacred sources. Missionaries and Indians were locked in a fruitless struggle. Catholic and Indian were possessed by the lords of emanation in collusion with the lord of deformation that justified the cruelty of their suffering since the Conquest was inevitable. Pacha Mama may have begun as a manifestation of the god of transformation but now this sacred source was unable to respond to the new problems facing the people.

These gods, however, were able to engender and reiterate only a single act of transformation—a cycle of their own. They can therefore only connect themselves to our primitive consciousness. . . . These gods have also emanated angels and demons, spirits and matter of their own, but, left to themselves they and their hosts and their works can only repeat themselves.[87]

We need to struggle with the sacred until we are blessed with a new understanding. Jacob wrestled with the angel; Job attacked Yahweh as unjust; Elie Weisel rejected a divinity that turned its back on innocent suffering; Jesus sought that the cup be removed; Prometheus stole fire from heaven; Antigone disobeyed Creon, the lord of the state; Tevyev in *Fiddler on the Roof* rejected his traditional lord by responding to a new face of the sacred when he saw the love in his daughter's face. In order to respond to the fundamentally new we need to experiment and step outside of the known boundaries and thereby create conflict and change. A passive acceptance of reality incapacitates us from recognizing that reality, our lives, and the source are unfinished. The deepest source of our being provides us with opportunities to see hidden treasures, revealed anew at every moment.

Problems with authority will arise for women and men open to transformation. The Latin American advocates of liberation theology such as Juan Luis Segundo of Uruguay, Gustavo Gutiérrez of Peru, and Leonardo Boff of Brazil all recognize the role that religion has played in condemning millions of people to permanent poverty by preaching that their suffering is the will of an all-knowing lord. A theology based on a process of creation, nourishment, and uprooting in order to plant again paralleled by a politics and education of liberation calls for a new community, a new society, and a new kind of politics. Juan Luis Segundo encapsulated the relationship between the sacred and the political in the service of transformation when he stated that any sacramental activity not directed to the transformation of the world was irrelevant.[88]

We begin, then, by acknowledging at last our heresy. Not heresy, in its usual, limited meaning as a sharply dissenting version of a particular orthodoxy . . . I mean to acknowledge heresy in its original meaning, as choosing only what one can grasp one's self and thus opposed to any knowledge or practice imposed solely by the authority of others. It is the story of our unfinished relationship with an imperfect god. In the spirit of heresy, however, I am telling no myth except the one which I can grasp myself through the myth . . . but none of the tellers of this myth, nor I, are trying to establish the officially sanctioned canon of this story. There can be no final version of the story of continuous transformation. The task for each of us, including the reader, is to retell this myth of creation as he or she has learned to make their way on a consonant journey.[89]

Latino men and Latina women have a primary commitment to build a society based on love and justice and not to any fixed tradition. We are the living members of our communities and the traditions live in us. All religious communities are in process and constantly evolving because the members who compose those groups are continually redefining who they are in relationship to their sacred sources. It is only liberated individuals who can pose new questions as they encounter the sacred in their lives. The most creative religious people in a time of crisis are those who can create new relationships to the deepest underlying source.

We need to take our stand somewhere. Our religious traditions and communities can be a rare blessing in difficult times. We need a base from which to build a counter-community.[90] This is why the recent commitment of the American bishops to support small ecclesial communities to reach the Latino community was so welcome. We owe an authentic response to our fellow Latinas and Latinos; we have to relate to them where they are. The churches as community can serve us all in the following ways depending upon our progress on the journey through the core drama of life: it can protect those still coming to birth; provide a nurturing community for those who have unfinished work within it; be a home for those who have no strength to leave; offer a home to discover new understanding of the sacred and the political in our daily lives; serve as a place wherein people can prepare for the next concrete step toward transformation; and, finally, it can serve as a liberated zone to renew those who are daily involved in the struggle for justice.

Conclusion

Finally, I want to end this chapter by giving an example of the kind of freedom open to Latina women and Latino men and others to reinterpret their relationship to the deepest sacred.

Our perspective allows us to recognize in the symbols of dogmatic faith frozen moments of transformation. . . . [O]ur relationship to symbols is a persistent test of how alive we are at
each moment to the transformation of that unity which is ourselves, our yearning and our source. . . . As before, not all of us
have the power to create symbols that inspire millions, but as
never before, each of us will need to find out for himself and
herself which symbols most inspire them along the way of
transformation.[91]

As young men and women we were taught that the Eucharist
was a cure for concupiscence that we usually interpreted as illicit
sexual passion or lust. The Eucharist was reduced to being a guardian of a dispassionate chastity. Furthermore, communion was a way
of surrendering ourselves to Jesus as his followers. But there is another way of seeing the Eucharist as participation in the life, death,
and resurrection of a god. In primitive religions this drama involved
a sacred banquet in which the god was eaten. The strength passed
from the god to the person who ate the sacred food. Mandalas, magic
circles, or sun wheels were among the oldest religious symbols used
to point to the unity of creation.[92] Black Elk spoke of the circle at the
center of creation that sustained the self, the tribe, the world, and
the sacred simultaneously.[93] The Eucharist has always been represented by the symbolic mandala that archetypically pointed to the
self and the sacred simultaneously. C. G. Jung and Hermann Hesse
both referred to Jesus as the symbol of the archetype of the self.[94]
Theologian Bernard Cooke helped to free me from my earlier understanding by reinterpreting concupiscence as dishonesty and the Eucharist as a transformative healing and not a remedy for sexual
problems. This new understanding converged with my personal
search for meaningful symbols of transformation. I re-interpreted,
re-visioned, and re-discovered the Eucharist. It now signified standing in the presence of Jesus as someone who became a self by being
totally open to the deepest source of all. He was the Savior, as D. H.
Lawrence has said, because he was able to initiate a new connection
between humankind and the universe.[95] He was the man for others
who lived a life of creation, nourishment, and uprooting. By rebelling against the lord of emanation in a fixed Mosaic law and the
Roman state legitimized by the lord of incoherence and defeating
the lord of deformation in the abyss by his resurrection, he became
the new experience of the deepest sacred source himself as the temple

of the divine. He is the new Adam, the Anthropos, the transforming god, the symbol of the new humanity and incarnation divinized.

Thus, for us as Latinas and Latinos our conversion does not consist in giving ourselves to Jesus but to save the savior within ourselves, that is, the call to authenticity, the vocation to become the new temple of the deepest source through our own humanity and thus, like Christ, become another concrete manifestation of the transforming god. Jesus is too important to leave to the fundamentalists of whatever religion; Jesus belongs to the artisans of a new humanity. Finally, Jesus left us his Spirit as our guide. The Holy Spirit is known in the counter-tradition as the feminine principle of liberation that represents an infinite number of new creations. The source of all sources did not begin by creating entities, neither human nor spiritual, but by creating the core drama of life that it is our vocation to travel again and again as we respond to new challenges. The masculine and feminine aspects of the deepest sacred give rise to a dialectical relationship that allows for encounters from opposing positions creating the movement within which the new cosmos can emerge.[96] The cost of the story of patriarchy to our personal, political, historical, and sacred faces has been the deprivation of the creative dialectic of the masculine-feminine.[97] Healing this rupture within ourselves can be accomplished by rediscovering a whole human being as both masculine and feminine and emptying ourselves of stories that violate both men and women.

Surely in all of this the Holy Spirit, our transforming connection to the deepest source, is leading us to the creation of new manifestations of love and justice that will allow us not only to say *Padre*, Father, but also *Madre*, Mother, of us all. A transforming community as church is one that helps us to distinguish between the false lords of emanation, incoherence, and deformation and the god of transformation. As members of various religious traditions, and in my case, the Catholic Church, we need to resist any church or sect that seeks to possess us. We have to become mothers and fathers ourselves by struggling with, conceiving, and giving expression to the sacred impulses that come to us from the deepest sacred source of transformation. We cannot become the means of revealing anew the deepest source in our own lives unless we struggle against and reject partial lords and their representatives. It is in this way that we are the Church, the vessels of the deepest sacred. Our sacred vocation is clear and urgent: to participate in the transformation of the deepest source, our selves, our neighbor, and the world.

6. The Politics of Liberation versus the Politics of Assimilation

Assimilation is a profound kind of self-wounding because it forfeits our personal, political, historical, and scared uniqueness. We are not allowed to be authentically American and Latino but are forced to be either an excluded minority or an assimilated individualist. As Latina women and Latino men we choose liberation, which means to be both Latina/Latino and American and to participate in fulfilling the principles upon which this nation is founded. Perhaps our greatest contribution will be to witness to the right of each person to be a self in a community of equals who are committed to each other's advancement because they love others as themselves.

THE POLITICS OF LIBERATION VERSUS THE POLITICS OF ASSIMILATION

For Latinas and Latinos to be political is not limited to joining the Democratic or the Republican Party or some other national or local political organization. To think in these terms is to look to others to be political on our behalf and to give us permission to be political once every two or four years. To be political means much more than participating in official contests for power, the usual interpretation of politics. The political is one of the four faces of our being by which we choose to create responses to life. Political activity is a radical, fundamental human right that has always belonged to us by the very nature of our being human but that was taken away from all of us, people from communities of color and from the majority community. To be political is to continuously ask the question, "What is it that we can and need to do together

185

to achieve justice and compassion in regard to this problem here and now?" The political face of our being leads us to participate and struggle with others on a plane of equality to create and nourish and also uproot inadequate institutions to build new ones. Politics has been reduced to legitimizing systems based on hierarchy that control us; every two or four years we vote and allow others to determine what is best for our society. Thus because we live in a society permeated by the way of life of incoherence, we abdicate our right to control our lives and world for the sake of being left alone to pursue individual dreams based on consuming more and more fragments: better houses, cars, PhDs, appliances, and other indications of wealth and power.

Yet real work and real political participation is to re-create our selves as species-being and the world according to our newly discovered selves. Political work means creating fundamentally new and better relationships to self, others, problems, and our deepest sacred source. "Middle class" or "professional" need not be defined only by status, power, or money but by where you stand in regard to the value and meaning of four fundamentally different kinds of work: preservation of the truth given once for all in the service of emanation, the pursuit of self-interest and power in the way of life of incoherence, giving in to fantasies based on race, class, gender, religion, or some other aspect of our life that allegedly makes some superior to others in the service of deformation, or the creation of justice and compassion in response to all issues in the way of transformation. We need as Latinos and Latinas to recognize individuals who act out of fundamentally different kinds of consciousness in regard to their political choices. We have in our community, as is true in all other communities, opportunists or brokers for a system that will reward us with new positions of power so that we can help to police our own people. They are interested in creating movement in a system but only to the extent that it will open up new opportunities for themselves. They will then call for a halt to further change in order to protect their newly acquired power. There are also individuals who are angry and bitter and look for revenge against those who treated us as inferior. And finally, we see in our midst members of a group who choose to participate in a constant process of breaking with destructive relationships, stories, and ways of life so that with the personal, political, historical, and sacred faces of their being they can participate in renewing our society for the advancement of all people.[1]

THE POLITICS OF ASSIMILATION

Education is political. Education has always been one of the most powerful assimilating agencies of all societies. Socialization is never neutral or apolitical. Socialization may be defined as a process whereby a society, that is, the members of a group who share values and ideas, prepares their young to desire what they, the society, wants them to desire. Thus socialization acquires the same definition as repression: repression is an intrapsychic force that people use against their own desires.[2] Our desires are called subjective, that is, unreal, unfounded, personal, and emotional so that we will concede to objective truths which are actually the subjective personal experiences of powerful others. These powerful others succeed in shaping all life according to their perceptions and interests. After generations of this kind of conditioning, people are assimilated into an all-powerful, objective system. New generations now bow down before the system as a lord that sustains them. But what they cannot do is question, doubt, or reject that lord. Socrates was killed for political and sacred reasons: poisoning the minds of the young by causing them to doubt and question the traditional gods and truths.

To assimilate is to make one's self over in the image of others and to fuse one's self with the desired group. Why would anyone want to do that? To join the powerful. People with power have things that we do not, expensive goods, security, travel, money, and respect. But assimilation also presupposes discontent not only with what we lack but also with who we are. We begin to believe that we are powerless to influence and shape our lives. Many of us concluded as children growing up in a hostile environment that this inability is our fault, yet much of this had to do with something over which we had no control, our ethnic and/or racial identity. We did not want to be identified with our community of color, the Latino people, who were made invisible and inferior, so we assimilated. To succeed we had to become like the dominant: white European American, affluent, and powerful. Our background was one of painful poverty. So we rejected our heritage, stripped ourselves of anything that would hinder us, which meant reject our parents, our culture, and ultimately crucial aspects of our own selfhood.

To assimilate is to arrest our lives in Act II, Scene 1, of the core drama of life and choose the way of life of incoherence that strips us of spontaneity, vulnerability, emotional depth, creativity, and imagination that are all rooted in our deeper self. Assimilation involves acquiring not only power but also anxiety; we see others as threats. We fragment ourselves and strip ourselves of feelings that might prevent us from gaining power. Our personal face is suppressed, consciously calculating what is best for us. We enact the political face of our being by practicing a politics of power by asking, "Who can help me and who can hurt me in my quest for power?" Our historical face is reduced to turning time into a period for gathering more power. Our sacred face is taken over by the lord of incoherence who inspires us to practice the stories of capitalism and competence that possess us as we insatiably search for privilege and self-interest. Is this really what we want? We should be grateful for this? Ultimately what the system wants is for us to choose our un-freedom by loving Big Brother, spontaneously to give our consent so that the will of the master and the will of the subject are one.[3]

Because assimilation is filled with self-loathing it places us on the road to deformation. Assimilation is a stage in the story of tribalism that begins with being invisible and inferior. People assimilate to try to escape this condition of being nobody in a world of power. But then when we think that we are safely assimilated we wake up one day and begin to ask questions. The powerful consider this an act of disloyalty (they let us in because we were one of the "better" Mexicans), and so we are exiled. Finally, if we prove to be too much of a threat we face the possibility of extermination.[4] Assimilation erases our personal face because we see our skin color and facial characteristics as ugly; we practice a politics of self-wounding by making our hair good by straightening it and we try to make our face acceptable by using special creams to make it more white. As time goes on our historical face gets worse as we descend deeper into self-denial and our sacred face is sucked into the abyss by the lord of deformation.

Institutional religion often lends its power to the politics of conformity/assimilation. When we criticize social, political, economic, and religious practices or values we are socialized to experience sin, shame, and guilt, the trinity of repression, one of the most primitive forms of people controlling or denying themselves. All of us in this country face this kind of repression which is in reality a sacred force. As Latinas and Latinos we are members of a group that has been systematically excluded from participating in shaping our lives, and so the powers that oppress all Americans are even more deadly for us. Not only are we deprived of participating in our destinies, but the very core of authentic resistance, our selfhood, has been seriously wounded.

To be political, to ask what is it that we can and need to do together to shape our life, to plant, nourish, and uproot in order to plant anew in order to achieve love and justice, means to be a self, a person connected to one's self, to others, to problems, and to the deepest sacred source of transformation. To suffer segregation, racism, and powerlessness is damaging enough, but then to have one's own identity undermined is even more damaging. And yet, ironically, this very assault on our ethnic and racial self can be the basis of our hope. To be white and blue-eyed is to be able to merge and fuse oneself into the dominant culture and to be accepted and rewarded. But it is a terrible trap. Those who choose assimilation also have a self, a destiny, but it is so completely bought off by the system's rewards that the combination of repression and suppression is almost total. Whereas for us even if we try to be white, Anglo, European-American, Gringo, Spanish, or Irish Catholic, we know in our souls that we shall never be. It sticks in our throat; we feel it in our bones. We ultimately resist going under for good. At times the real pain of the memory of being called a dirty Mexican, a greaser, or spic keeps us from assimilating. At other times it is the legacy of struggle of our mothers and fathers and the generations before us. When we realize what has happened to us we are overcome with sadness that we have been ashamed of our own color, blood, language, heritage, and of our Spanish-speaking, often poorly educated parents.[5] We then feel anger against the white people who have caused all the pain, while we fail to realize that they, too, are victims of a society and way of life that does not want anybody to be a self, a participating, creating, nourishing, dismantling, and re-creating self. Powerful others want us to forget who we are. To refuse to forget where we came from and to insist on being somebody is what gave rise to the movement for Civil Rights, the gay and lesbian resistance, the feminist movement, the student uprising, and the struggle for Chicana/Chicano civil rights. We are a people who resist, who are members of a counter-tradition, the tradition of transformation. To belong to our selves is to profoundly threaten those who have purchased their power by negating who they are and what they feel. It is so ironic that to be a self is such a radical revolutionary, political decision.[6] "Yo soy Joaquín" is more than just a cry of defiance; it is a personal, political, historical, and sacred grito de dolores, a cry of pain, that precedes revolution, declaring to all that we are here, ¡Presente!, prepared to take on all necessary challenges.[7] The denial of our presence tells us something about the way of life in which we are all involved; the one thing a society that is based on the anti-self agrees on is that we can assist others and sacrifice for them, but we must not love and desire ourselves.[8] What a tender scene in Tom Robbins's novel, *Even Cowgirls Get the Blues*, when Sissy caresses and blesses her over-sized thumbs because although they are a freak to others, they are a symbol of her unique mystery.[9]

THE ALTERNATIVE: THE POLITICS OF LIBERATION

The politics of liberation begins with you and me *reacquiring* who you and I are. We take ourselves back from the stories of capitalism and competence enacted in the service of incoherence that hide behind the label of democracy. They want us body and soul. But just as you and I fought against our mothers and fathers who wanted us to feel guilty for leaving home, we are locked in the same archetypal drama with a society dominated by the way of life of fragments. We did not leave our families in the Bronx, El Paso, El Cajon, Lima, or San Juan to give ourselves to a possessive system. We journeyed to find out who we are. We got an education not only to acquire skills but to put them at the service of our rediscovered self and others. Now we have an opportunity to reacquire the personal, political, historical, and sacred aspects of our being that were used in the service of ways of life that did not allow them to come forth in their wholeness. The greatest joy that we can have is that of transforming our own lives.[10]

The following are characteristics that constitute emptying ourselves of a colonial mentality, the story of assimilation in the way of life of incoherence, and choosing to reacquire the personal face of our being, our self, as the first step of liberation in the way of transformation:

- To ask the question: "Who am I?" is a political and sacred act.
- To create fundamentally new and more loving relationships and stories is to cease to be an object defined by others, a thing to which something is done, and to see oneself as a subject, a person who defines herself or himself and who acts on the world for the better.
- To realize that there is no such thing as a dumb or neutral fact; there is no fate unless we give up and become ahistorical; there is destiny that is brought about by people willing to intervene to bring about something new and better. The world is not

given; it is created by men and women like you and me in the service of four fundamentally different ways of life.

- People become conscious through separation and conflict; outside of the container of emanation that shrouds institutions and systems in a fog of mystique we can analyze, critique, and choose in the service of what way of life we will act.

- One begins to ask the key question: Who benefits from our lack of personal, political, historical, and sacred participation in regard to any particular problem?

- Economics and politics go hand in hand; an actual laissez-faire economics never existed but its idea serves as a shield for the powerful to use the state for their own enrichment.

- The repression inherent in emanation as a way of life becomes the oppression of deformation when the game is over and people refuse to control themselves out of love for the master; the master must turn to violence to force people back to "normal," that is, to be docile and passive. Conscious people who awaken to their inner self in Act I, Scene 2, cannot go back to the past; something irrevocable has happened.

- Women and men recognize that they were not born dull and passive; they were made that way as the result of stories and relationships practiced in the service of ways of life that arrested them as partial selves in a historical and political situation. Thus people no longer blame themselves; they inherited a violent system that they have the right to change for the good.

- The self-hatred and group hatred inherent in assimilation give way to archetypal analysis to find out how we ended up in such a bad way: "Where am I in the core drama of life, what stories and relationships am I practicing that arrested my journey, in the service of what way of life was I doing what I was doing and how have the four faces of my being been affected?"

- Latent racism is made manifest and is exposed; in its latent non-conscious form the dominant culture succeeded in socializing another group into the story of tribalism that led them to believe in and to accept its own inferiority and incapacity for political action.

- To take our self back is to see the mystery in our own life; no parent, system, lover, or even lord has the right to possess us. Now we are ready to enact in their wholeness the personal, political, historical, and sacred faces of our being on the journey of transformation.

The Role of the Sacred in the Politics of Liberation

Freed through liberation from the demonic power of systemic enchantment in the ways of life of emanation, incoherence, and deformation, we can now journey with the deepest source, the god of transformation. Orthodox systems and institutionalized religion cannot prevent the spirit from blowing where it wills. The deepest sacred that constitutes the goal of the journey of life is encountered in our lives and in the community of a pilgrim church. But where shall we begin? We need to go home: home within ourselves to rediscover our connection to the deepest sacred source, the god of transformation, and, second, home to our historical and cultural communities wherein we are now ready to create new forms of justice and compassion. Within our own persons we are locked in a struggle with competing, sacred forces. Richard Wagner tells us in his opera *Parsifal*, through the words of the chorus, that the purpose of the journey is *"Erlösung dem Erlöser!"* the redemption of the Redeemer or the salvation of the Savior.[11] The goal of the journey is twofold: to liberate one's own sacred face and, second, through the self, which is another face of the deepest sacred, to free the source of sources who calls to us for help from the depths. In a similar vein Marguerite Yourcenar in a simple yet beautiful way redefines and stands on its head the traditional relationship between saved and Savior:

> What if we are mistaken in postulating that God is all-powerful, and in supposing our woes to be the result of His will? What if it is for us to establish His Kingdom on earth! I have said to you before that God delegates himself; now I go beyond that, Sebastian. Possibly He is only a small flame in our hands, and we alone are the ones to feed and keep this flame alight; perhaps we are the farthest point to which he can advance. How many sufferers who are incensed when we speak of an almighty God would rush from the depth of their own distress to succor Him in His frailty if we asked them to do so?
>
> Such a notion ill accords with the dogmas of the Holy Church.
>
> No, no, my friend; for I abjure in advance anything I have said which might further tear that Robe without Seam. God reigns omnipotent, I grant you that, in the world of the spirit, but we dwell here in the world of flesh. And on this earth,

where He has walked, in what guise have we seen Him except as a babe on the straw, just like the innocents left lying on the snow when our moorland villages are devastated by the King's troops? Or as a vagabond, with no stone whereon to lay His head? Or as a man condemned and hanged at a crossroads, asking, in His turn, why God has abandoned Him? We are indeed weak, each one of us, but there is some consolation in the thought that He may be even weaker than we, and more discouraged still, and that it is our task to beget Him and save Him in all living beings.[12]

The term, "God," has usually carried a positive connotation for la comunidad Latina. But what is important is the quality of our relationship to the sacred. Only the god of transformation is a guide who invites us to journey together to participate in re-creating the face of the self, the earth, and the face of the deepest source. The lords of emanation, incoherence, and deformation want us to remain committed to the sacred that inspires a once-for-all believer, a person dedicated to the pursuit of power, or to the fantasies of total power that lead to destructive death for us and others. These are very powerful sources with all the necessary allies to help enforce their will. We cannot alone resist these sacred forces. To struggle against these lords it is necessary to call upon a guide, the god of the transforming journey. By appealing to the god of transformation we ask to be accompanied by a creative spirit on our unique, personal journey. The partial gods impoverish the deepest source because they either stress manifestations that are true for all time, or declare that there is no ultimate truth, or demand extremism in the pursuit of truth, their truth. But the god of transformation leads us back beyond the morning star to the depths where the lords have their origin. Here we need to steal fire from heaven to give new form to our self, the cosmos, and our deepest source. We together with the god of transformation participate in creating, nourishing, and uprooting in order to bring about the fundamentally new and better.

When I was a boy, my mother used to say to me, "*Eso es castigo de Dios*," That is a punishment from God, whenever anything bad happened to me. This was intended to keep me a good boy, to force me to come back and ask for forgiveness for daring to be disrespectful or choosing to do something of which she did not approve. My mother also said to me, "*¡Que Dios te castigüe!*" May God punish you! whenever I disobeyed her. These were harsh words. Now to what sacred source was my mother appealing? This was the false lord of emanation who gave my mother security and buffered her suffering. My mother saw herself as an extension and agent of this lord. To disobey her commandments was rupturing the relationship not only with her but with a whole way of life that defined the sacred, church, culture, family, nature, and life as given once for all. There was only one remedy: come back and ask for *perdón*, pardon, make your peace with the lord, with me, with the church so that the good feelings of unity and peace will be restored. But now more than ever before there can be no going back.

So the lord of possessive emanation will punish us, send us anxiety attacks, and condemn us as will the people who serve this lord. This false lord does not want us to save the Savior, or the sacredness within us, or to reveal the true source of sources in the depths, or to be political and therefore make history on behalf of others. I love my mother and my people, *La Raza*, but I recognize the need to struggle against the tendency in myself and in our community to return to the lord of emanation and there to commiserate with each other about the temptations of the world that threaten the container of orthodox truth. The answer is not to reject our parents or our culture but rather to rediscover them and remind them that they gave us the tradition of journeying. They came to this country seeking a better life. Latina women and Latino men need to go home within ourselves to become co-creators together with the deepest source of transformation to finish creation. It is to be like other Christs, making compassion and justice concrete in our selves and in the world. This is why we pray to the Spirit to free us from the lord of the world so that we can leave secure assimilated flesh pots and journey into the desert for redefining and renaming ourselves. We earn the right to redefine ourselves through struggling. This is the political and sacred significance of the terms "Chicana/Chicano" or "Boricua" or "Afro-Cuban." Now rather than repeating worn-out prayers and rituals, our lives become a new prayer. We cannot accept being defined, named, numbered, assimilated; rather we enter the promised land by transforming, naming, defining, becoming, and experimenting outside the boundaries of what is given to us. Each of us is a sacred drama of stories, relationships, ways of life, and the four faces of our being in motion.

To return from the struggle in our own personal and sacred depths to the everyday tasks of our lives is to reach out to others to make real in the world the truth that we learned on the journey within. We are no longer the same. So we cannot continue to allow others to relate to us as if nothing has changed. We are home, and yet our home is not the same because we have changed. I am firmly convinced that if we act for the sake of transformation, then it will also be for the good of others. The suffering involved will be not for its own sake but with a purpose, with hope because out of it will come our new selves. Now we are free to break or uproot relationships and empty ourselves of stories and partial ways of life that cripple all of us. We are not rejecting our mother or father, *abuelos*, grandparents, the Catholic Church, the Pentecostal community, or others who care for us, but rather we reject the stories such as patriarchy, possessive love, matriarchy, uncritical loyalty, and relationships of dependency by which way they relate to us, and we reject the false lords that bless our arrested personalities. We also reject the false and partial lords of the American way of life that inspire the stories of capitalism, tribalism, false patriotism, and conquering heroes. We are calling those related to us and ourselves to participate in a new drama of transformation. When we go to church, we celebrate the presence of the deepest source of transformation within our own self and within our neighbor. This sense of our personal self-worth rooted in the sacred face of our being means that we can politically and historically shape a world that manifests in its structure the reality of each person's dignity and worth. Our indigenous ancestors and the Catholic Church were wrong to terrorize the population with an avenging lord, the lord of deformation that would punish us for asking questions or experimenting with the truth.

The sacred is not up in heaven, a lord to whom we sacrifice human beings or construct pyramids and cathedrals; the transforming sacred is the deepest depth of our depths. To seek and manifest our own mystery is to make real both our selves and the god of transformation that we reveal through our creation. For a jealous husband, or father, or lover, or church, or state, or system to possess us is a sin. We are free to re-create all our institutions: marriage, family, educational, economic, political, and legal and to deconstruct systems that cripple us and to create again and again. At this point the political and the sacred converge. The commandment not to create false idols before Yahweh certainly applies to the greedy institutions and systems that seek to arrest our lives. Our task is to struggle with the inspirations that come up from the depths to test whether or not they are manifestations of the god of transformation. We need to test these sacred sources and ourselves in a community of people. Sacred sources are always present to us and moving through us; we need to be aware of their presence and the choices that we make in their name in all that we do. We need to wrestle with these forces until we discern which sacred source is present. We are still in formation, in process on the journey. We are a people on the move. We are members of the counter-tradition, that is, men and women who have always known in our bones but now realize more clearly that the world is unfinished, that we are unfinished, and that the god of transformation is unfinished.

We are a people still growing our own identity as Latina women and Latino men, constantly creating, nourishing, deconstructing so that we can take the next step on the journey of transformation. Our task is to help the deepest source of our being into wholeness evermore often and covering an ever-larger network of life. So the deepest source, the ground of our being, is not distant, nor perfect in a masculine aloofness, but our *dios/diosa*, god/goddess, is the god of transformation and is only perfect in relationship to our willingness to participate in the task of creation. Thus, when we create political organizations to enable us to confront racism, sexism, and classism, when we see men and women as equals, when we form unions to protect the dignity of our work, when we take control of our own school boards, then we and the god of transformation are being personal, political, historical, and sacred as we build the world with love and justice.

CONCLUSION

And so now we see the ultimate sin of assimilation by allowing ourselves to be possessed by demonic stories and ways of life. The sin is to lose the self and to cause others to lose themselves. What about our white, European-American or Anglo brothers and sisters and our brothers and sisters from other communities of color? We must not end with a narrow, stingy view of our ethnic and racial heritage that celebrates us at the expense of others. On the contrary, we owe it to other communities not to assimilate but to continue to resist a system that victimizes everybody by forming coalitions with them to confront oppression. We need to step forward aggressively to say that we do not identify with this system, but we do not in any way reject the individuals who are caught in the system. We have felt the worst of this system. Thus we need to speak out, to serve as a people who resist, who are part of the community of saints, the men and women of the counter-tradition, who spent their lives witnessing to the creation of more compassionate and loving alternatives.

We cannot avoid moral decisions; we have to choose. Paulo Freire, the Brazilian educator associated with the movement *concientización*, or education as political consciousness, has taught us that we live in a thematic universe, that is, each of us needs to face the fundamental moral issues of our age. We live at a time in which the most fundamental issue is the confrontation between liberation and oppression, between deformation and transformation.[13] As Latina women and Latino men we need to take a political stand: we opt for either liberation or the domination of others; either we help maintain a situation of systemic hierarchical inequality or we help to prepare our fellow Latinas and Latinos and others to participate in transforming all aspects of our life. Nor can we say that we shall wait until later when we have our credentials. We are all presently being socialized by the system, especially our educational institutions, to take power, prestige, and status for granted as our birthright *because* we have now been graduated, that is, moved up in society. We need to remind ourselves always that all education is political; it is never neutral. Education in the service of the politics of emanation prepares us to be the loyal disciples of powerful others and not to ask fundamental questions. In the service of incoherence, the politics of education reduces the whole of our schooling to preparing us to dominate others. The politics of education in the way of life of deformation leads us to believe in the fantasies of our own inferiority or in our superiority over others. In the classrooms in the service of transformation we are guided to our creative imagination that capacitates us to create a new and better society. We can allow ourselves to be prepared according to set roles or we can be people who become the authors of their lives and help others to determine their destiny. Plato saw the Academy as a preparation for political life. He sought to prepare his pupils for public service by having them contemplate the *Eidos*, the eternal ideas, the archetypes, the underlying forming, sacred sources that need to be made concrete in the world through political action. Moreover, no person could participate in this dialectic between contemplation and action without having a *daemon*, one's own deeper self that came from the deepest source, that is, one's own realization of self through pursuit of a particular life choice. This presence of the sacred at the core of our lives was the source of resistance against commercializing this gift of a life's calling that is intended to serve others through the use of our skills.[14]

Only persons connected to themselves, each other, and the deepest sacred can create the vision to build a society of equal participation. Like the Invisible Man, we realize that our dilemma need not remain a private crisis of conscience.[15] Even Latinas and Latinos who have been given visibility by the system have to come out of hibernation. We need no longer play the game as defined by white America that reinforces in the minds of the powerful the stereotype that they have of us as a mañana-oriented people or who mock us with "José, Can You See" sung to the tune of "The Star-Spangled Banner." We need to put the phrase in the form of a new question, José, can you see what they have done to us? Do you realize what has become of our people? Are you awake now to realize that to see means to see with knowing eyes? These questions serve as a hammer on the anvil of our hearts and minds. We can no longer be bought off by our occasional Latina doctor or congresswoman. Our authentic invisibility is the self within. The only way that our invisible authentic self can become visible is in the concrete world around us if we decide to risk ourselves. Without the possibility of action all knowledge comes to nothing. It is not possible to transform the personal and sacred faces of our being without also engaging the political and historical faces of our being that allow us together with others to uproot injustice and plant fundamentally more loving and just alternatives. Our gifts have set us aside, dedicated us for others. I feel that we as Latina women and Latino men have been ordained by history to be pilgrim servants alongside the god of transformation to take up the challenge of these times. Power, prestige, and money cannot fulfill our desires. We need to listen to Ralph Ellison, recently chosen as one of the best American novelists of the twentieth century, and refuse to make passive love to our sickness, the sickness that tells us there is nothing we can do, that the system with all of its lords is too big. But even restructuring an entire society can only be accomplished by transforming our daily stories and relationships now, today, with those closest to us. No, there is no escape from the responsibility that we carry of participating in the journey of sowing the fundamentally new, uprooting destructive institutions, and nourishing those that are conducive to justice. We as Latinos and Latinas might not be interested in transformation but transformation is interested in us.

7. Latina/Latino Professionals: A Transforming Middle Class

We need skilled and competent Latina women and Latino men. But we need deeply caring professionals who use their skills for the well-being of the community and not for the sake of the market where our personal gifts and competency are turned into commodities. We ask that our middle class be of a particular quality: a group dedicated to transforming institutions. This means to reserve the term "successful" for members of our middle class who practice their expertise in the service of transformation, creating fundamentally new and compassionate linkages to themselves, their work, their community, and their deepest source. Professional and middle-class status need not be determined by income or prestige but by the character of women and men passionately committed to a new wealth and quality of human work: establishing new forms of justice and compassion that allow all to share and benefit from the production of goods and services.

A professional is someone who professes values of truth, justice, love, and wisdom, someone who stands passionately for life. The term "professional" has been distorted and narrowed to signify a holder of a scarce skill: technical, legal, medical, business, administrative, or bureaucratic who can now sell his or her services on the open market.

In the metropolis, where men were both more and less equal than ever before, the most intimate relationships were determined by calculations of advantage. Marriage was seen as an instrument with which to acquire, consolidate and increase wealth and power. Young men and women were treated—and were taught to treat themselves—as commodities for speculation in a human market. "Has my father sold me, then?" Julie cried. "Yes, he had made his daughter into a piece of goods (merchandised) . . . and profited at my expense! He had paid for his life with mine!" (I, 28, 94) Thus marriage served to initiate innocent youth into the primary experience of modern society. They began their lives as adults by being sold; thrown into a universal market place, they would learn gradually to sell themselves. Modernity had liberated the self, only (it seemed) to transform it into capital. The modern development of individuality and of *sensibilité* opened up new dimensions of personal intimacy and love; yet any genuinely personal relationship was forced to go underground, and to define itself against all the institutions and values of modern society. Social relations were split into the dualism of "public" versus "private"; an individual could be himself only by leading a double life.[1]

MARKETABILITY FOR THE TWENTY-FIRST CENTURY

Latinas and Latinos often anguish over their inability to merge the private world of their poverty-stricken background and shy Spanish-speaking parents with their newfound public existence that finds them drinking orange juice and eating croissants while discussing the arcane value of medieval literature with Ivy-League colleagues. They feel fragmented—they are. When a person or cultural group is cut off from its own feelings, personal sources, and intuitions, it is also cut off from its creative depths. Thus some Latinos gain an identity by holding on to a past, by romanticizing it out of all proportion, which leads to an ethnic chauvinism or a strident nationalism. Others attempt to forget their past by assimilation, which is a form of self-alienation and self-hatred. Assimilation is a question never of both/and but of either/or, with the element of power dictating the choice of the predominant culture. Assimilation creates fragmentation. Deprived of our personal feelings and emotions, we accept the real, "objective" world of the others. This creates the guilt-ridden schizophrenic/amnesiac walking-wounded who have dropped out of their consciousness their own emotional heritage. The therapy of the Chicano, Boricua, and other Latino movements was intended to lift such repressed and suppressed consciousness back into place. Latinos are angry because they now know that their oppression is more than political or economic; it is cultural. We were all deprived of more than money or position; we were stripped of a self. Without a self there is no basis by which a person can resist what is being done to them. I agree with Rousseau when he wrote that the peasants were not born dull; they were made that way. Rousseau would disagree with those who speak about a silent majority. There has never been a silent majority by choice; people were *silenced*, somebody violated us so that our dissident voice would not lead to a destabilizing of democracy for the few. Similarly, Paulo Freire refuses to accept the stereotype of Latinos as passive or fatalistic, as if we chose to be violated. Freire correctly points out that perceived fatalism is the result of particular historical and sociological conditions. The truth of the matter is that one group has a vested interest in *making* others passive so that they can control them.

Beginning with the personal leads us to the political and historical realms, however, because to be a person is to be political and historical. We become who we are by asking the political question: "What is it that we can and need to do together to create a new turning point that is more compassionate and just?" Yet if the others in the greater society reject us until we become like them or assimilated, we enter into society as lesser beings. In addition, we are depoliticized or deprived of being political, that is, we cannot shape our environment or create a new history on a basis of equality with others. Every individual has the inherent right to participate in creating an environment to nurture and enhance society but also to dismantle or deconstruct institutions that have turned against the creators by taking on a destructive life of their own. One turn in the spiral is complete when an alternative creation is substituted for the old. This understanding of revolution, politics, and the intimate relationship between being personal and political demonstrates that not only Latinos and Latinas are victimized; all of us in this society are deprived of shaping our personal and political lives through an alarming trend toward a hierarchical society. Many European Americans or Anglos do not realize when they feel threatened by our participation that a system based on power and privilege depends on a declining participation by all groups, including their own communities. American voters do not participate; we unfortunately help to legitimate the growing inequality every two or four years. This is largely because many of us define wealth as consuming more and not as participating with others to take risks in building new institutions or consciously nurturing those that continue to serve us well.

Thus, when Latinos consciously take themselves back from a society and culture that wants to redefine us as honorary whites, provided they "behave," it is viewed as both a personal and political act. It is a personal act because it presupposes an act of resistance that can only come from a center, a self, who is capable of imagining alternatives and of acting to implement a different life. It is a political act because it is the rejection of having "superior" others shape life, attitudes, and values for us. As self-conscious political beings we insist that we can participate together with others to establish institutions that reflect our needs. This is revolutionary stuff. This insistence on an inherent right to shape one's own life and environment together with others was behind the transformation of Mexican Americans to Chicanos, of Puerto Ricans to Boricua, and of Spanish Americans to Latinos and of Hispanic women to Latinas and Mexican women to Chicanas. It is the desire to define oneself, to create oneself anew according to a new vision. Al Pacino, playing the role of Tony Rome in *Scarface,* tells us what United States society is all about. Tony crudely figures out the philosophy of life in his new home. By constantly using the four-letter expletive for "making" somebody, meaning that you have to get somebody before they get you. Unfortunately, such a statement only masks rebellion; it is a stark capitulation to the power games of U.S. society. What one cannot do with all the power in the world is shape, make, or love your own selfhood and demand respect for your person *as* a person. For Tony the whole society is a brothel, and whoever moves fast achieves the prize. Everybody is a threat in this Hobbesian view of life, and so to win you have to be better at the game than those who devised it. He outsmarts his tutors but tragically comes to ask, "Is that all there is?" This is the ultimate question for all of those who at the cost of the self are successful at assimilating by joining the powerful. Nothing new is created, only the assertion that the system is right. What I, and I believe many others, seek is not power over others but the capacity to change not only our lives but the system of power itself.

Many of us have gotten to be marketable, that is, to the point of being or becoming professionals, because the government and private industry made a concerted effort after the upheavals of the 1960s and 1970s to recruit the top members from all potentially troublesome racial and ethnic groups to help police their own people. "Police" is not used here necessarily in a repressive manner; the science of "policing" consists in regulating everything that relates to the present condition of society. But the usual aim of policing is to strengthen and increase the power of the state and likewise or thereby allegedly serve the public interest.

As a result of programs like Affirmative Action, which remains a very important access program and that will be further discussed in chapter 9, Latinas and Latinos, especially Chicanas/Chicanos, Cubans, and Boricuas, have for the past thirty years been recruited by some of the top universities in the country. As a people, Latinos were for generations excluded and wounded by racism, classism, and sexism. The most recent Supreme Court decision on Affirmative Action has kept open the doors of opportunity by allowing race to be one of the considerations in admitting students.[2]

But rather than a commitment to justice and compassion there are some who want us to use "Chicana" or "Chicano," "Boricua," "Hispanic," or "Latino" as a new power prefix to get ahead in the system. And some of us do, forgetting that there is a history of suffering that earned the right to create our opportunities. So we have new prefixes in the community: a Chicano lawyer, an Ecuadorian policeman, a Latina doctor, a Boricua or Puerto Rican superintendent of schools. But we need to take care that this is not another face of the story of capitalism allowing our best and brightest to join the powerful in the service of incoherence by co-opting their personal gifts along with a group's history of past discrimination.

It would be useful at this point to give a fuller definition of professional and to review the historical context of the professions.[3] Most social scientists speak of professionals in the following terms: a professional is a person who practices a skill that gives him or her special power and prestige. Society grants these rewards because professionals are considered to have expertise in specialized bodies of knowledge linked to central needs and values of the social system, and because professionals are viewed as persons who are devoted to the public, above and beyond monetary gain. For the time being let us accept this definition. Professionalization of the professions developed as an integral part of the bureaucratization and specialization characteristic of a mature nineteenth-century capitalism. The esoteric skill and knowledge of a particular group became a new kind of property. These special skills and expertise were translated into another scarcity, social and economic rewards. To enforce scarcity and thus control rewards, monopoly was essential. The rewards that could be demanded depended on the public's perception of the value of the skills. If this value perception was high, then the profession had a high degree of marketability. Thus professions consciously organized themselves to attain market power. Once a market was obtained, it had to be controlled. Yet such striving for monopoly based on marketable expertise is a crucial element in the structure of modern inequality.[4] The professionalization movements of the nineteenth century prefigured a structural social inequality. Professions are the heart of an occupational hierarchy wherein legitimacy is founded on socially recognized expertise or on a system of education and credentialing. As Latinas and Latinos we need to be conscious that the very essence of professionalism is both effect and cause of a structure of inequality.

Professionalism and its growth are made possible by the openness of the American university to new areas of expertise and the widespread access to higher education in American society. Our universities play an essential part in furthering and accelerating the hierarchical and unequal nature of U.S. society. Since the nineteenth century the professions have gone through a fundamental change. The predominant pattern is no longer a free practitioner in a market of services but that of the salaried expert in a large corporation. Yet the earlier model has been retained as a public relations gimmick, so that it constitutes a veil that obscures real social structures and power relations. This mystification has led to a false consciousness, so that even the poor or those on the lower-class levels of society accept the legitimacy of inequality by giving deference to people that they consider morally and intellectually superior to them. This superiority is founded on schooling and credentialing. Those who do not make it into the professions blame themselves, thus helping by their self-inflicted repression to justify inequality and closure of access to higher mobility. The professions have succeeded beyond their expectations in having an image of themselves fraught with ideology accepted as a value-free sociological ideal type. This makes it easier for the professions to veil the element of power.

> Professions ultimately depend upon the power of the state, and they originally emerge by the grace of powerful protectors. The privileged position of a profession is thus secured by the political and economic influence of the elite which sponsors it.[5]

Structural Violence and the Politics of Professionalization and Autonomy

According to our theoretical perspective the process of carving out zones of autonomy based on competence is an enactment of the relationship of autonomy:

In this form of encounter, the occupant of each pole claims an autonomous zone of jurisdiction based upon explicitly rationalized grounds of revelation, morality, law, power, or competence. . . . Autonomy is the dominant polarity of contemporary American society.[6]

By means of acquiring the relationship of autonomy based on professional expertise, a group shapes a boundary of power in which they are the experts and from which they can protect their interests and look toward the consolidation and enlargement of their area of jurisdiction. Such zones of autonomy give a group a power base by which to bargain with other jurisdictions in order to achieve benefits. This combination of the capacity to bargain from a base of professional competence is the key for achieving power in U.S. society.

Many groups in our society that have not yet achieved the relationships of autonomy and direct bargaining as a base for power are locked into the two relationships of isolation and subjection in relating to the powerful. In isolation continuity and cooperation are purchased at the cost of giving up the right to create conflict or change. Both parties agree to leave one another alone. The justice in this relationship allows persons the right to be left alone but the cost is the inability to effect change in one's living conditions. In subjection, domination is exercised by one person or group over another. Change takes place only with the consent of the more powerful. Conflict must be suppressed, since the subjected do not have the ability to exercise options of which they may be aware. The justice of the relationship of subjection is survival. Because we have not been able to name and identify these relationships we have used a rhetoric that is tantamount to giving systems a life of their own. Statements such as: "You can't fight city hall" and, "That's the way the system works" are examples of comments made by people who know that there is something wrong but who do not have the analytical language to expose the connections that count. Too many see the answer through simply defining themselves in terms of the present power relationships; they join the system. What is necessary to achieve the American Dream is to get out of isolation and subjection and achieve relationships of direct bargaining and autonomy. Those who cannot do so are considered to be lazy, weak, or defective in some other way.

By applying this theoretical language, for example, to the health professions, we can see that organized medicine led by the American Medical Association is a formidable example of the use of the relationship of autonomy that has fused a coalition of boundaries with other groups such as pharmaceutical companies, insurance companies, legislators, and hospitals. Together this coalition has determined the cost, direction, and quality of the health delivery system. Within these boundaries such organizations exercise power over their personnel. Nurses among others were for a long time, and to a great extent still are, isolated from one another and therefore unable to create meaningful change or conflict. As a group and as individuals they were subjected by a coalition of largely white, male professionals who jealously guarded their prerogatives. There is no doubt that many of these men sincerely believe that what they were and are doing is in the best interest not only of themselves but also of the American public. What is at question here is not their sincerity but their narrow interpretations of what constitutes quality health care.[7]

Institutions are essentially human relationships. The political face of our being in the service of transformation practices a politics of participation in the creation of institutions that allows us to respond to problems with love and justice. To be deprived of such participation due to exclusion by others constitutes a violation of our human rights. It is an impoverishment that prevents us from taking the direction of institutions or our own human relationships into our own hands.

In U.S. society we assume that upward mobility consists of climbing out of relationships of isolation and subjection and gaining the necessary relationships to succeed, direct bargaining and autonomy. We allegedly pull ourselves up through a system of meritocracy to achieve negotiable positions and competence. Upward mobility is determined only by a willingness to work hard and seize the opportunities available. Yet we often fail to recognize that there are organized groups which have achieved autonomy that have a vested interest in preventing others from achieving their own autonomy. Despite all of their rhetoric to the contrary the one thing that the powerful fear is competition. The power and stability characteristic of the managerial class has been possible because it is prepared to defend its boundaries by restricting innovations to those which maintain the status quo. This is the use of autonomy in the service of incoherence which can quickly become a relationship in the service of deformation if depriving others of access to this relationship leads to their inability to survive. Violence does not have to be directly physical or overt to be violence; whatever prevents people from achieving the opportunity for a more human life, such as using one's bargaining power to maintain the boundaries of power by lobbying against legislation that regulates dangerous working conditions in order to increase profits, is an act of violence.

A glaring example of the relationship of autonomy that is exercised to organize the workplace for the sake of profits over the value of human life is the case of the McWane Corporation which has experienced one of the worst safety records in recent history. It was clearly stated in corporate memos that in order to increase profits the corporation needed to cut back on its work force and yet maintain the same level of productivity. This was done at a shockingly high cost paid by the number of injuries to the workers. Between 1995 and 2000 there were 1,200 accidents and nine fatalities, most of them attributable to poor equipment, unsafe working conditions, and the exhaustion of the workers that made them more prone to injury. Just as the corporation was about to be fined and cited, another powerful institution stepped forward to prevent any meaningful punishment and demand for reform. The New York State Attorney General's Office had jurisdiction in this case and the Attorney General, Mark Jackson, was a personal friend of the McWane family. In addition another autonomous zone of jurisdiction that was also supposed to protect workers, OSHA, was slow in investigating and determining blame as well as the penalties to be handed down. When the issues were resolved it amounted to a slap on the wrist. This is a classic example of how within the story of capitalism the autonomous jurisdiction given to corporations by law uses their connections to other autonomous jurisdictions or boundaries of power to form an alliance to protect themselves from prosecution at the expense of workers who are considered expendable. The brutality of the McWane Corporation also demonstrates how the way of life of incoherence colludes with deformation as a way of life when profits, power, and privilege are at risk. An ongoing investigation finally found the McWane Corporation liable for serious violations of the safety code and this time the fines were in an amount that came closer to being a real deterrent. An agreement was also signed to make a serious effort to establish a safety system that was committed to the well-being of the workers.[8]

The dominant relationship in U.S. society, autonomy in the service of incoherence, often leads to the legitimization of institutionalized violence as we saw in the example of the McWane Corporation. The relationship of autonomy in the way of life of incoherence means giving social and political approval to the pursuit of power after power. Persons who are taken over by the story of capitalism refuse or are unwilling to stop violating others. Violence is inherent in the way of life of incoherence so that the few might continue uninhibited to pursue wealth and power.

Because of their very position in the social hierarchy, the professions provide access to its members to the connections and leverage necessary to make things happen or not happen. This access to the system is made possible by the relationships of autonomy and direct bargaining. Many of us believe that if we can get into positions of power through the professional ranks, we will be able to do something about the powerlessness of la comunidad Latina. Again we need to remind ourselves that professional education prepares us to give individualized service, which is a personal remedy for ills of a social nature. We, even as members of a community of color, can become co-opted as mediators for the system by practicing the relationship of buffering that places a veil over the fist of power. In this way we knowingly or unknowingly become buffers for a brutal system that does not know or respect you or me as persons. So we are prone to ignore political action and analysis for more individual therapy. Our power as professionals is usually individual power that is intended to be used to increase our status and prestige. Our very education emphasizes specialization to the neglect of the whole. The technocratic ideology of science and objectivity buffers those of us who are engineers and natural scientists from the political and social consequences of our work. We are told that we cannot be responsible for the whole world, so we develop a sense of limited ethical responsibility. Furthermore, our humanity is desensitized by this fragmentation; we consciously suppress our personal face, our so-called private self, that refuses to become emotionally involved with others and our political face practices a politics of joining those who can help me and avoiding those who are a liability. Our historical face, in the service of incoherence, is reduced to seeing time as money; our sacred face is dominated by the lord of incoherence that blesses the pursuit of power. Ironically, we wake up one day and recognize that we might have a great deal of money but we are personally and politically powerless to change our lives or that of others as long as we remain in the service of incoherence.

> Paradoxically the same ideology of the 'expert' which gives the technician a certain autonomy within his or her own specialty, simultaneously prepares the technician to execute blindly the designs of others.[9]

The universities are part and parcel of this fragmentation. In an increasingly credentialed society, education serves as the central legitimization of the new forms of inequality. The dominant ideological apparatus of the system is the school.

> The various units in the system of higher education have themselves been relatively standardized and arranged in a recognized system of hierarchical prestige. This system operates as a switchboard to the world of work, but as a switchboard that would, at the same time, determine the distance and the speed of the trains. The trains are the different classes of colleges, universities, and professional schools at which the passengers arrive after having been filtered by a number of other switchboards.[10]

The ivy-covered walls of academia provide a mystique of privilege and superior authority for the professions within its embrace.

> The setting of the training process within the environment of an academic community with primary concerns in the dispassionate profession of knowledge itself serves to extend the range of legitimation, to add luster and super-authority to the ideals of detachment, public rather than self-interest, service to an ideal and ethic. The universities have gained a legitimation of a utilitarian kind by the demonstrable needs which are met by those it certifies as competent—this allows the continued presence of many faculties whose contribution is demonstrably non-utilitarian in character.[11]

Thus the humanities that should provide us with a vision of how to re-create the world are turned into the poor relatives, the flunkies of the affluent practical professional courses of study, and are used to give the aura of academic prestige to the more technical areas of study.

The professional schools in the universities, in order to give the impression of "all-aroundness," insist on courses in philosophy, ethics, history, and literature. They bow toward the rhetoric of creativity and the search for meaning in one's work and initiative. But all of these laudable goals are *defined* in such a way that they are compatible with the requirements of production in advanced industrial capitalism. All discontent is treated as an individual problem to be dealt with by the conflict resolution provided by still another professional, the industrial psychologist. It is his or her job to treat symptoms, not the underlying problems, the system itself, so that the wounded can return to their jobs re-energized. The protests of insubordinate professional workers can be managed by offering them more of the same: *individual* privileges. This approach coincides with professionalism's own ideological emphasis on individual career goals and individual solutions. The politics of power isolates the individual malcontents and thereby renders them impotent.

> The ideology of professionalism deflects the comprehensive and critical vision of society which is necessary to reassess the social functions of professionalism. In this sense, professionalism functions as a means for controlling large sectors of educated labor and for co-opting its elites.[12]

We find it difficult to challenge this privilege because society has convinced us that we must first become legitimate, must achieve power on society's terms before we can confront the system. But this individualizes the protest because the only solution is too often purely personal, that is, individual hard work so that you can make it to the top and change things. Once you are at the top, the system usually wins. The best of our people, by getting to the height of their profession, often legitimize inequality and elitism; they are living proof that knowledge is beneficent power. They made it so why can't everybody else? All you need to do is work hard to achieve the American dream. Latinas and Latinos, like the rest of society, unconsciously absorb this hierarchical vision of politics and society, thus making it easier for those in power to exercise privilege and power without even having to prove special ability.

CREATING ALTERNATIVES: MIDDLE-CLASS LATINA/
LATINO PROFESSIONALS AS POLITICAL INNOVATORS

Education is often considered only as a preparation for a career goal. We establish priorities in relationship to a particular marketable profession. But we cannot afford to forget that education is political, that is, it is preparing us either to become permanent disciples, to sustain a way of life based on power, to exercise power over allegedly inferior others, or to create fundamentally new and more compassionate alternatives to what does not work. Unfortunately, most of us do not realize that education is a mirror of the culture and so schooling prepares us to *preserve* rather than critique, uproot, and re-create. Most of our education is therefore socialization, and university education is a more sophisticated level of preparing us to agree or to want what the powerful in society desire for us. This kind of education borders on repression: the dream of every state is to achieve a political victory over its subjects without the weapons of threats and promises. The aim of all political masters is to base their power upon the spontaneous consent of the governed. If the people can be made to duplicate spontaneously within themselves the will of the powerful, so that what the system wills the people desire, then the will of the master and the will of the ruled are one, and now it is no longer necessary to base the power of the society on force but on getting the people "to love their own slavery."[13] This is why so much time and effort is spent on appealing to love of country, patriotism, democratic principles, and nostalgic genuflections toward a glorious past.

Education also means a *critique* that presupposes conflict and the rise of consciousness that breaks the spell and separates us from the embrace of the society. It is this understanding of education that places those of us who profess a vision of compassion and justice on a collision course with the marketability of Latina women and Latino men in the twenty-first century. White, liberal America wants to be perceived as having good intentions and wishing us well. But what they really want to do is to save their free-enterprise system by giving some of us, but not all of us—only the best who have made it through the gates of their tests—access to the same tools that are available to them so that we can all legitimately and as equals compete with each other. But we know that not everybody will have equal access and so we search and search for ways to rationalize our privileges. We know that the great majority of our people will never make it in the system's understanding of success. We have to buffer away this harsh reality through rationalizations because we have accepted the dominant understanding of professional, that is, acquiring the relationship of autonomy as an area of competence such as computer programmer, physicist, doctor, lawyer, or professor which now allows us to enact the relationship of direct bargaining as we demand and enjoy status, power, and money.

There is another path. A Latina/Latino professional middle class can play a radically different role in our community. But what kind of middle class; what does it mean to be middle class? In keeping with our theoretical perspective it is possible for us to re-vision old and static concepts of class. The poor are seen as the lower class or subclass of a hierarchical society. The middle class, usually the professional class, is considered as the climbing class who escaped poverty and who are on their way to the upper echelons of power and money. The middle class is often mistrusted as the group that advances at the expense of the poor. Many of our people either resent or envy the middle class. These feelings also have their roots in Latin America, where "la clase media" that is usually lighter skinned and oriented toward Spain and Europe, is considered by many of the poor and indigenous population as their enemy. This view of society is based on stereotypes of class antagonism and therefore fails to analyze what is actually and potentially present. We may distinguish four kinds of middle class in the service of four ways of life: a middle class in the service of emanation that inherits its power and money from the previous generation and that seeks to continue the personal elements of doing business based on a family model; in the way of life of incoherence a middle class works to develop more power and to enlarge its area of control over resources and accumulating more capital; a middle class that wants to use its education and skills to maintain an alleged superiority over the lower classes who are viewed as less than human; and, finally, a group of men and women in the service of transformation who build a middle class that shares a common task, to employ their skills to create a more just and compassionate community. Therefore, class, and especially middle class, must not be perceived merely on grounds of property or wealth, prestige, power or authority, or professional standing.[14]

We cannot say that because people are poor or wealthy, they will be revolutionaries or conservatives. Regardless of what class people have been born into or have achieved, it is their *choice* that is decisive in regard to helping to maintain the old, preserve power, use violence to maintain power based on fantasies of race, class, or gender superiority, or create a new and better alternative. Rich and poor may at times have a common desire to preserve the status quo, with the poor hoping to be rich some day. Some poor people consider reformers and revolutionaries alike as dangerous people who threaten their dreams. They will therefore resist change. In this way the powerful, the less powerful, and the powerless are all caught by the story of capitalism in the service of incoherence and deformation that arrest our lives as partial selves. On the other hand, there are those who want to destroy the system as evil and beyond repair. All their efforts are bent upon bringing down the system, with nothing to replace it. Others who become conscious of the need for transforming society become aware precisely because they have succeeded in subverting the opportunities afforded them by "middle-class" education and professional training that is intended to make them defenders of the status quo. Instead they subvert, they turn things around from below, by becoming simultaneously insiders and outsiders who see fundamental injustices in their society. They hope to create and implement ways to eliminate human poverty *structurally*, that is, by changing the institutions and conditions of society so as to guarantee the incorporation of new generations of excluded people into the benefits of society.

The threat and the promise are side by side. The danger is that as middle-class, some Latinas and Latinos will only be eager to embrace the goods, values, and styles of life characteristic of the middle class worldwide. The great potential is that a professional and salaried middle class will occupy positions that provide the most effective leverage for transforming a society. Latina and Latino middle-class professionals will have to decide if they are interested in participating in the preservation, destruction, or transformation of a society. Within such a perspective of middle class, professional women and men do not need to suffer from success guilt or allow themselves to be called *vendidos*, or "sold out." To be successful or to make it is radically changed to mean men and women, regardless of background, who share the same commitment to implement fundamentally new and more compassionate changes in all areas of life.

We spoke earlier of professionals who passionately speak the truth, who care about justice and love in the political as well as in the personal realm. This pursuit must be made real and concrete in the everyday world. Plato taught us that the Academy had a practical meaning; its goal was to look after the condition of the state, not only the world of ideas.[15] The purpose of education is to shape one's society, one's *polis*, the city state, according to a vision. To be political is to know the deeper relationship between the realm of *Eidos*, eternal ideas, and the concrete realm. After all, we can only dissolve the concrete and re-create it if we have some understanding that humanity is rooted in the realm of underlying forming sacred sources with which we can participate. For example, the archetypes of justice and compassion become concrete and therefore personal, political, historical, and sacred when a Latina lawyer uses her skills, with the newly acquired relationships of autonomy and direct bargaining, to protect the civil rights of children to a good education so they can participate in shaping society. Yet winning the case is not

enough; what remains is to involve oneself in the quality of education, the construction of schools, the role of the community, the preparation of teachers and school administrators, and on and on. A
transforming politics always takes the next step to shape the ever-
emerging newness of life. Such a lawyer together with other professionals can form task forces to create new and more just alternatives
for others, that is, to help them become political so that they can
sustain, dissolve, or give rise to new institutions. This is what it
means to subvert a system constructed with the relationships of autonomy and direct bargaining in the service of incoherence. Now
rather than using the relationship of autonomy to preserve power
through alliances of the powerful, it is being used to link others in
a common cause to bring about fundamentally more just and compassionate change in the service of transformation. This is what it
means to change systems: actual concrete manifestations of relationships such as autonomy and direct bargaining that connect
people together in the service of a way of life are broken so that new
and more compassionate manifestations of the same relations of autonomy and direct bargaining relationships can now be re-created in
the service of transformation to respond to the needs of the previously excluded. What is being shaped and broken and created again
are human relationships and stories enacted within ways of life that
belong to all of us. Politics is what we can and need to do together
here and now to make life more just and compassionate. Latina and
Latino professionals with this view of politics can use their position
in society on behalf of others so that everybody will be able to *profess and practice* their vision of the truth through acquiring skills. In
this sense our professional status enables us to become simultaneously an outsider and an insider; an outsider because we do not share
the perspective of power of the institutions that we attended; an insider because we look to turn around a system from within, so that
we use the relationships of autonomy and direct bargaining acquired
through our education to become caring professionals as the best
doctors, engineers, lawyer, teachers, or accountants who open doors
for those who have been excluded.

In a discussion with my students at Princeton in a seminar on
Chicana/Chicano politics, we entered into a heated discussion on
"What does it mean to be *in* Princeton but not *of* Princeton?" Several students who were mesmerized by the very fact that they were
at Princeton with all of its prestige were quite upset by this question. They considered it to be disloyal to the institution that was
giving them a privileged education. The seniors were strangely quiet

for a while and then they spoke up with a depth of anger that was surprising. They commented that since they first arrived they often discussed what Princeton was all about. They came to the conclusion that Princeton was about power and that they felt that they did not really belong. They believed that they had gotten an excellent education but did not share Princeton's values. As the dialogue went on, the point was made that they all had the right to be *in* Princeton but they did not have to be *of* Princeton, that is, agree with the elitism of the university.

As Latina/Latino professionals and members of a transforming middle class, we need not perpetuate the same power relationships in the service of incoherence. Previously we used the term *inherited relationship of autonomy* to describe the usual search for power within zones of autonomous jurisdictions such as the professions. We have already seen above that there is another way to enact the relationship of autonomy, and that is in the service of transformation. Rather than using a zone of autonomy to prevent change and preserve power, a professional can use her or his power to create liberated zones within which new approaches can be envisioned, implemented, and fostered. But to believe that Latina/Latino professionals will automatically be more loving than white professionals is naive. Our professionals can be taken over by the archetypal drama of capitalism in the service of incoherence that possesses our lives and disconnects us from the community. Power is seductive and is made into a scarce commodity; nothing has changed except the skin color of those who wield power. We need linked power as the capacity to transform our lives and our society; this entails recognizing that we are not atomistic individuals but a community of people who need one another to realize our humanity. Capacity has five aspects: a new consciousness, creativity, linked power in community, a shared justice, and a new connection to our deepest sacred. To pursue power is to be driven by an insatiable individualism which makes others a threat. Freedom for rugged individualists means the right to be released from responsibility for others. Freedom in community entails the joy and suffering involved in creating new and more loving relationships with others.

Latinas and Latinos as professionals need to separate the transforming human meaning of one's work from the ideological function committed to power inscribed in one's role by society. This process begins as a task of personal, political, historical, and sacred liberation. Challenging the structure of inequality requires a fundamental redefinition of the self.

Instead of the self remaining embedded unconsciously in the mysterious power of the other, the relationship of incoherence breaks the spell and, in this case, leads to the free experience and analysis of opposing selves and their patterns of encounter within the individual and with others. The relationship of emanation itself is then recreated in the service of transformation as an embodiment of the remaining true mystery of one's own self, and no longer of one's own unexamined self or as the extension of the mysterious power of others.[16]

Professionals cannot successfully challenge the structures of power as fragmented individuals:

Breaking with ideology, finding new norms for the social production of knowledge and the social uses of competence, demands passion, vision, and hard work. This major historical task can only be sustained by a solitary collectivity, aware of its past and of its place in the overall struggle for human liberation. In a historical perspective, abandoning the "subjective illusion" and the seduction of bourgeois individualism becomes the premise of personal freedom.[17]

Thus the passage from seeing problems in a purely personal perspective to an evaluation of their structural causes begins to heal the split between the personal and the political faces of our being. This phase of political and historical consciousness involves the development of new norms and new criteria that are alien to the logic of the individual pursuit of power.

Institutionalized power that serves to maintain an enduring capacity to generate and absorb persistent transformation may take the form of procedures linking individuals in community as among scientists, or as between government and opposition in a legislative assembly. Individuals may be linked by commitments to common tasks of individual, social or political therapy, by intellectual collegiality, by love-always, by shared consciousness and creativity for collaborating in the worldwide task of transforming unintended, uncontrolled change into justice.[18]

For a professional to be rooted in the way of life of transformation in the community is to have a different concept of wealth.

Rather than the zero-sum total, the bottom line, we can see wealth from a different perspective that allows a broader understanding based on human relationships. The joy of seeing people organize and change their environment because they are now free to practice the relationships of autonomy and direct bargaining and the personal and political face of their being is priceless. This is the deeper meaning of *respeto* that our culture insists upon. We want not a system that will respect our right to achieve power after power but a system that will respect our persons *as* persons. A society based on power cannot respect our personhood. Friends in a competitive situation are always prospective masters over each other, and victory will come to him or her who marshals the stronger weapons with greater skill. The other is the enemy. People in such a system cannot afford to love one another. Success in terms of power only serves to highlight their failure in terms of friendship. To cover such an emptiness and loneliness people strive for more power in order to compensate for the loss of intimacy. *Respeto* for la comunidad Latina means giving every man and woman his or her due, that is, to give each one respect because as a person each is sacred. A system that is based on ways of relating that is incapable of ensuring a respect for persons as persons does not deserve to exist.

So we come to see that professional marketability within the story of capitalism means unceasing competition for power that arrests our lives as partial selves unable to respond to new kinds of problems. Transforming men and women can implement a new truthful vision through their insights and acquired skills. For this reason we need to see our education as being political. Many of us received our education largely *because* we are the members of an excluded group. It would be a supreme irony if we then allow the agenda of others to make us the policing role models for our Latino communities. What we can do is to be persons *for* and *with* the community. This entails creating strategies together with others to solve common problems on a plane of equality. To be a guide in our community means to escort people to their own authentic selfhood. Octavio Paz, a Mexican philosopher and poet, has argued that one of the characteristics that distinguish us from European Americans is the cult of the festival. Paz sees the festival as a religious celebration because every true festival is communion. Festival for the Latino community represents not separation but participation, not individualism but joining together.[19] For Rousseau the most important reason for citizen participation was not efficiency but authenticity; to be oneself meant to shape one's destiny, to unite thought and action, to guide the forces that shape one's life. Rousseau also used the image and reality of festival to signify a new politics, participatory democracy: the people in the festival are not spectators but become themselves actors in their own right.[20]

Finally, let us reflect on another aspect of what it means to be a professional. Truth, love, beauty, and justice are archetypes that can be made concrete in the world in an infinite number of different ways; this is our personal, political, historical, and sacred participation. Some will choose to participate as lawyers, nurses, doctors, engineers, teachers, or social workers. Underlying each of these helping professions is a calling. Plato and Socrates both stressed that a person had to find one's life's calling by being in touch with one's inner self or *daimon*, that is, destiny.[21] A professional connected to one's life's calling and not the manipulation of the market is a person called by one's own *daimon* to serve as a guide for others. A guide is someone who assists others to come into contact with their self, or mystery. Only those who are in touch with the deepest source will be able to guide us. Thus the presence of a personal *daimon* in Socrates was what determined his educational and political mission: to heal the split between possibility and reality. It is precisely the essential life choice, or *daimon*, of the professional that must protect our legal, medical, engineering, and teaching tasks from becoming a mere economic pursuit. This presence of a non-rational underlying reality, the sacred, is always involved whenever we participate in one another's lives. Moreover, it is the presence of the deeper self, our destiny as a transforming self, that gives professionals their authority. Thus when they speak out on behalf of medical rights, legal access, building humane cities, or the protection of children, they do so not because of a desire to protect a vested interest but in the interest of others. The Latin verb, *augeo, augere,* means to increase the other, to guide a person to become their own author. Anybody not interested in this kind of transformative authority holds an illegitimate pseudo-authority based on degrees, laws, competence, or other justifying mechanism.

Now it is precisely our *daimon*, our gift to reach out and shape the world, that is exploited by the present economic system. Responding to our inner self through work is what constitutes our labor. This understanding of our labor as fulfilling our self helps us to realize why the profit motive is really a kind of poverty. This profit-seeking economic system wishes to possess and dominate our labor, that is, our inner gifts, for its own profit. As an alternative we can create new forms of justice and freedom as we participate in building a new and better world. This is the opposite of alienation, the loss of the self. Moreover, it was Marx who wrote that a human being becomes human or a species-being to the extent that the other as a human being becomes a need for us. In other words, people become human *because* of their necessary relatedness to one another, not in spite of or in competition with each other. Moreover, mutually fulfilling relationships constitute the new man and woman as wealthy or rich.[22] Transforming middle-class Latina/Latino professionals have an inner drive or necessity to create wholeness; by expressing this inner need they become truly free.

One might legitimately ask if there are professionals who actually choose the commitment spoken of here. We need to know if this is possible. There are individuals who have decided to be a different kind of professional, a professional in the service of transformation. Dr. Joseph Kramer had a lucrative medical practice in the suburbs when he realized that he wanted to do more with his life.[23] He moved quickly and established a new practice in a barrio in New York City where his clients were almost all Latinos and African Americans. The community accepted him and trusted him. He made home visits and treated his patients with respect and concern; he counseled people having emotional problems. Dr. Kramer, who learned Spanish, cared deeply about people to the extent that he made a conscious personal, political, historical, and sacred decision to limit his income to one-half of what it had been before. We need stories of this kind with regard to the reality of transformation. People have to be asking the right questions and be open to seeing and creating alternatives. We need people to do this in all walks of life. Dr. Kramer is an Anglo or European American, not a Latino. This forces us to face our tendency to speak about Anglos as a monolith of unconcerned people. Dr. Kramer is a white male, but he does not have a white, male attitude, that is, a belief of superiority. Furthermore, he serves as a hope to all of us that racial and ethnic wounds can be healed.

CONCLUSION

Latina and Latino professionals in the twenty-first century are in a challenging situation. As the welfare safety net continues to be dismantled by powerful interests, especially the right wing of the

Republican Party, there is a considerable threat to the opportunities available for our communities. But because of the political realities of future elections both political parties will be looking to win a larger share of the Latino vote. If Latina women and men along with African Americans and women continue to vote in the same percentages as they did in the 2004 election for the same candidate, issues, and party, they can together profoundly influence the future of American politics. This fact haunts the powerful. Even the possibility of nominating a Latino to the next opening on the U.S. Supreme Court was corrupted by a cynical strategy. Alberto Gonzales, now the Attorney General, and Miguel Estrada were said to be candidates in line for the nomination to the next seat on the Court. Democrats successfully filibustered the nomination of Miguel Estrada to the federal appeals court thus preventing this as a step on the way to the Supreme Court. The White House accused them of standing in the way of sitting the first Latino Supreme Court Justice. The administration hoped as a result to win Latino votes; the Republicans blamed the Democrats for playing ethnic politics hoping to erode their Latino support. This had nothing to do with diversifying the Supreme Court to look more like America, nothing to do with democracy at its best, nothing to do with who is more qualified, and nothing to do with any notion of justice for a formerly excluded community. This was all about power in the service of incoherence that continues to arrest our nation in the pursuit of self-interest and privilege. It was furthermore a ploy by which so-called minorities are cynically used to achieve the ideological goals of the conservative religious right wing that is the heart of Mr. Bush's constituency. At the top of this list are finding Affirmative Action and abortion to be unconstitutional. We can be sure that any future Latina or Latino nominated will have to pass through the gates of the religious fundamentalists before they are nominated. Roberto Gonzales was said to have hurt his standing with the religious right by urging Mr. Bush to be more moderate on his stand on Affirmative Action.[24] Those in power always need to be vigilant as they maneuver to take advantage of the game.

    This is why it is not enough to say that a Latina woman or a Latino man nominated or appointed to an influential position will touch the lives of all of us for many years to come. Yes, we want Latinas and Latinos to be at the highest echelons of government, but in the service of what way of life will they exercise their authority and power? To refuse to take advantage of this power for personal aggrandizement will demand a new kind of Latina/Latino professional. Such professionals will have an opportunity to enact a new kind of politics that can make history as a new turning point for the better in the life of the community. Only persons connected to their personal, political, historical, and sacred faces in the service of transformation as whole persons can create the vision and build a society based on love and justice.

8. Choices for La Comunidad Latina: Creating the Present and the Future Now

Each of us has choices; we cannot be neutral. Latina women and Latino men have four fundamentally different ways by which to build the present and our future. The four choices for Latinas and Latinos will be discussed: the traditional, the assimilationist, the destructive, and the transforming models. The traditional model corresponds to the way of life of emanation; the assimilationist or fragmented model represents the way of life of incoherence; the destructive choice is to choose the way of life of deformation, and the transforming model is grounded in the ultimate way of life of transformation.

In this chapter we shall be concerned with developing strategies for Latinas and Latinos based on the theoretical view of life represented in this book. The theory of transformation that has been developed and tested throughout the book allows us to participate in transforming the four faces of our being in both theory and practice as we respond to fundamentally new kinds of problems.

Now that we know the theory and have seen its application in many dimensions of our daily lives, I would like to broaden our dialogue with some reflections and symbols that point us toward the choices available to us as we build a present and future. As we have seen, we have four fundamentally different choices, four ways of life within which to enact archetypal stories and the nine archetypal relationships and the four faces of our being. I would like to speak of four models that are another way of speaking about our four ultimate ways of life and that I believe will help us to understand where we have been, where we are, and what we can and need to do together to build a more just and compassionate future. These four models are the traditional, the assimilationist, the destructive, and the transforming model.

THE TRADITIONAL MODEL: IN THE SERVICE OF EMANATION

In daily conversations we often use terms such as "traditional," "assimilated," or "transformation." I would like to reinterpret these concepts and to see them in the light of our theoretical perspective. The traditional model points to a whole way of life that hangs together. Authority begins with the lord of emanation and flows downward from the top of the pyramid to the head of state and the religious elders, then to the father and elders of the family and community. Love, sin, the divine, death, meaning, virtue, marriage, and sex are all explained, understood, and lived as a total fabric of life. Everybody knows their place in such a scheme of life. The young are raised to prepare them to turn over, hand on, *tradeo, tradere,* the word taken from the Latin for tradition, the teachings to the next generation. Suffering and anguish are given meaning to the extent that they end by reconciling a person to the will of an all-powerful sacred lord. Conflict is successfully confronted and overcome when the rebel returns as the prodigal child thus reinforcing the ultimate truth of the society. It is truly a sacred overarching way of life since everything is endowed with an overwhelming mystery given once for all. People not within the container are outside of the pale of the truth. The household comes to symbolize in its architecture and authority patterns the workings of the entire cosmos. The customary high walls that surround the traditional living quarters of Latin American countries protect *and* contain the inhabitants. Here you are safe and can enjoy the mystery of *Dios,* "God," father, mother, and significant others. Outside the walls there is fear and insecurity from which one has to be buffered and isolated, especially women. Beyond the fortress of one's ethnic community, and even within one's own community because of race and class, outsiders are looked upon with fear and suspicion.

Within one's family, ethnic, religious, kinship, or national container, persons are usually limited to practicing five relationships in which they were socialized: emanation, subjection, buffering, direct bargaining, and deformation. Deformation is available to all traditional societies and families and is used to maintain and restore people to the traditional relationships within the overarching way of life of emanation through the use of violence. Sin, shame, and guilt are very powerful as containing factors. Conflict and change are severely limited and practiced only by the male guardians of the family, clan, and culture. Continuity and collaboration with those in power was held up as the ideal and was often found in warnings to obey your elders and have respect. Archetypal stories such as patriarchy, matriarchy, possessive love, and uncritical loyalty, as we have seen in previous chapters, arrested our lives and contained our journey in Act I, Scene 1, of the core drama of life.

This world works only as long as people do not raise fundamental questions based on their own experiences. You cannot question because you cannot even imagine an alternative world. The personal face of our being is repressed since our desires are not important. The self is therefore absent as a source of resistance and there can be no fundamental change without listening to our inner self in Act I, Scene 2. The political face of our being practices a politics of uncritical loyalty and with our historical face we repeat the history of the past as a recipient never as a creator of new turning points. Security is the justice of this model. To feel trapped is not necessarily painful if one sees it as the will of the lord of emanation that possesses the sacred face of our being and thereby cuts us off from the deepest source of transformation. A sense of resignation can also provide one with great energy to work within the given limits.

Caught between Ways of Life

When Latinas and Latinos arrive in this country and have to face strangers outside of their world, they experience incoherence: they stand in the presence of others and really do not know how to relate to them. To resort to the relationships of dependency puts them at a great disadvantage since the members of their adopted nation do not share the same web of life. The dominant society does not respond to the *respeto* inherent in the relationship of emanation except to see it as weakness that causes some to take advantage of us. How can traditional Latinas/Latinos bargain with people who have fixed prices, laws, and boundaries for everything? In this context the web of life cannot be sustained. The children especially no longer feel secure when they see their parents hesitant and silent in front of authority figures. This breaking of the traditional culture creates a crisis of having to live in two worlds. This dilemma of being suspended between two cultures, societies, sets of values, and ways of life has always brought confusion and suffering to immigrant groups. At home we were to speak Spanish and uphold the inherited relationships in the way of life of emanation. In school we had to learn how to survive by being like the others, that is, learn new relationships of behavior, especially direct bargaining and autonomy and, more importantly, a new way of life, that of incoherence. To solve this crisis some parents tried to enforce the traditional way of life of emanation by use of the relationship of deformation, physical intimidation. Subjection was used to try to shore up a way of life that was unraveling. This is the use of subjection in the service of emanation because it constitutes a refusal or inability to deal with the breakdown of the old. My mother romanticized the traditional world of Mexico and tried to relive it here, since it was the golden age of her life. She practiced the relationships of buffering and emanation to create nostalgia for the only culture she knew. Children everywhere look to authority for security. If they see their parents preserving a world and culture that does not in fact give them a sense of well-being here and now, they begin to call their parents old-fashioned and out of touch with the new world. But more seriously, the children who need security to grow are attracted to the symbols and persons of authority in the new culture. A comparison often leads many young people to consider our Latino culture and parents as stigmas, as cause for embarrassment, and a heritage that perpetuates a lack of opportunity.

Understanding the ways of life or the underlying patterning sources of life by which all of our relationships, stories, feelings, values, and ideas are given ultimate meaning helps us to appreciate much more profoundly classics such as *Five Families* and *La Vida* by Oscar Lewis[1] and *La Carreta* by René Marqués[2] as well as books such as *A Welfare Mother* by Susan Sheehan and more recent books like *Caramelo* by Sandra Cisneros and *Random Family* by Adrian Nicole LeBlanc.[3] When the families described in these books left their rural birthplace and migrated to the cities of Mexico or Puerto Rico and then to the United States, they did not simply exchange muddy roads for paved streets; they literally went from one ultimate way of life, emanation, to another, that of incoherence with the presence of deformation as a way of life that colludes with emanation and incoherence as they break apart. The two ways of life of emanation and incoherence although they can collude with each other, they are fundamentally different and meet in conflict: *el choque de las culturas*, the collision of cultures; it is a radical confrontation, a grim struggle.

People who are not restrained by seeing the world as resting in the fate handed out by the lord of emanation see those who still live by such a morality as naive. Latinas and Latinos who know how to work the system can be more dangerous because they are recent victims and so understand how to exploit the incoherence of the *recien llegados*, the newly arrived, either with or without documents. An example of this is the recent death of nineteen people near Victoria, Texas, who were locked in a truck carrying seventy-seven people; they died from the oppressive heat and lack of water. This was the nation's deadliest experience of human smuggling. They were being illegally transported into the United States by an organization that was run by a woman from Honduras, Karla Patricia Chávez, who herself had entered the country guided by immigrant smugglers, or coyotes, a decade earlier when she was merely fifteen years old. Ms. Chávez had only a sixth-grade education and was already a veteran of the assembly lines of blue jeans factories in Honduras. All of her accomplices in the loose network of the smuggling ring were Latinas/Latinos from the contact persons, to the coyotes, to the suppliers of safe houses, to those who arranged travel to points north. The driver who was to be paid $5,000 to transport the people from Harlingen to Houston was the only non-Latino and not a regular member of the group. Comments made by her family after she returned there following the tragedy showed a young woman determined to make it at any cost. Her father commented that she probably came back to Honduras on a visit to try to find out who she is because she no longer recognized nor liked the person she had become.[4]

The plight of the *recien llegados* without papers is the situation poetically and yet painfully depicted in the film, *El Norte*. A young undocumented Guatemalan is betrayed by a "pocho," a derogatory term given to Mexicans who are not considered real Mexicans by their relatives in Mexico and who are not accepted as Americans by many in this country. The pocho character, as he is depicted in this movie, is an example of a Latino who sought his identity through achieving power in this society. The Guatemalan *expected* loyalty because both were Latino victims in an Anglo world; the pocho acted according to a new set of rules that negated the loyalty of emanation to be found among fellow Latinos, or *paisanos*; he betrayed the Guatemalan young man to the hated *migra*, the immigration authorities. Actions that began in the service of incoherence in both situations were based on making money at the expense of others and defeating a competitor for power at any cost. Both the pocho and Ms. Chávez ended by using others in the service of deformation wherein life is made fundamentally worse and often results in destructive death.[5]

There is an economic culture that has sprung up throughout the country similar to that which began in California twenty years ago, *los esquineros*, the men on the corners, looking for work. Groups of as many as a hundred men gather on busy thoroughfares and parking lots with signs advertising their specialties: landscaping, laying concrete, carpentry, plumbing, and other assorted skills. It is estimated that there are seven to nine million undocumented workers in the country. (Altogether there are twelve to thirteen million undocumented persons but not all are in the work force.) Since 9/11 there has been a great ambivalence on the part of the public toward immigrants, both legal and undocumented. Recently two Mexican men were lured by two white men to a remote area in Farmingville, Long Island, where they were beaten and abandoned. These workers are facing the same problems confronting Mexican workers of a century ago who were exploited as a source of abundant cheap labor. Undocumented workers receive no benefits and are in addition often underpaid, cheated out of promised wages, face poor working conditions, receive little or no respect, and if they are hurt on the job they have no insurance.[6] Local groups have emerged to form organizations to intervene on behalf of the immigrants. In order to respond to the public's fear of large groups of men standing on the corners, some communities in places like Morristown, New Jersey, and in Montgomery County, Maryland, have moved to establish hiring halls that also serve as a place to learn English, address health concerns, and receive counseling services and other social services. Other cities and counties are discouraging the arrival of more immigrants by issuing tickets to contractors who hire them, limiting the number of people in a room, and passing anti-loitering ordinances. Because of this atmosphere of hostility Latina women immigrants are vulnerable to sexual abuse and assault. DeCoster Farms paid out a $1.5 million settlement to five Latinas who were raped and abused by their bosses. At Chef Solutions Bakery in Connecticut workers were threatened with deportation if they voted for a union. At a company called Quietflex in Houston, Mexican workers were paid $80.00 a day while the Vietnamese were paid $110.00 per day, a difference of $5,000 over the course of a year.[7] This latter is a classic example of dividing one community of color against another and winning the loyalty of the better paid who voted against a union to repay the company.

Many complain that the newly arrived are costing too much. Yet the workers pay billions into social security and unemployment insurance but receive no benefits from these payments. They also keep the cost of living down. Los Angeles County faces the greatest task of reconciling the benefits versus the costs of the *recien llegados* since it is estimated that there are 1.1 million undocumented immigrants residing there. The most stressed social services are health care, law enforcement, and education. More than 2.5 million people receive treatment and of these it is estimated that 800,000 are undocumented. Because of the budget crunch facing the State of California and local governments the cost of responding to the needs of the recently arrived has become a bitterly divisive issue. In regard to whether the benefits of undocumented workers outweigh the costs, a 1997 study by the National Academy of Sciences, the most comprehensive although flawed study yet conducted, concluded that immigrants over their lifetimes pay out more in taxes than they collect in services, but it also found that immigrants with less than a high school education over their lifetime cost the economy $13,000 and most immigrants tend to fall into that category. This last point indicates why it is so important for the children of the *recien llegados* and the society at large to provide a good education.[8]

Why they come daily and face the dangers of passing through the deadly west desert corridor between Mexico and Tucson is summed up by Eric Carreto, a twenty-two year old from Guatemala, "I come for a better life."[9] It is a forty-mile walk from the northern desert of Mexico through the west desert corridor into Tucson. The temperature goes as high as 140 degrees in the summer. Because of the attack on America, the Border Patrol has been beefed up from 4,000 agents in 1994 to 10,000 in 2002. Charges have been made that the Border Patrol has actually planned to funnel people into this death zone in order to discourage them from coming. Most of the 134 deaths in 2002 took place in this area. Regardless of how many police there are the people will continue to come looking for the American dream, "the five dollar-an-hour version." In the final analysis this is a schizophrenic policy. On the one hand, there is the fear of terrorism and of immigrants pounding at the gates. Yet we need cheap labor without which thousands of small companies would fail and the entire agricultural industry would be severely hurt if not crippled. Our policy is to seal the border, criminalize those who make it into the country, attempt to arrest them, but if they get away eagerly hire them to do our dirty work. The irony of this policy is captured in the personal life of one of the arresting officers, Mr. BeMiller of the Border Patrol. The children of those who escape from him end up in one of the local schools where his wife, Michelle, teaches them ESL. This kind of cat and mouse game that often ends in tragedy is repeated hundreds of times a day on the 1,950 mile border separating the United States from Mexico. This highlights the need for a new approach: decriminalize the migration of people by initiating an amnesty program for those undocumented already in the country who can prove residency and have a work record for five years, create a worker guest program that would allow Mexicans to work and reside in the country six or seven months a year, make provisions for people to cross into the country for day jobs and return home in the evening, expand the visa program, and guarantee the civil rights of Mexican and other Latino workers either documented or undocumented by enforcing the law.[10]

In the meantime many Latina and Latino undocumented workers are especially vulnerable. They find themselves without the relationships of direct bargaining or autonomy necessary to protect themselves. They come without documents and live in fear that they will be deported. They are caught in powerless relationships of subjection and isolation, relationships that are no match for the power relationships of direct bargaining and autonomy enjoyed by their bosses. They are afraid of joining together to form their own zones of autonomy such as a union, lest they be fired or reported to the authorities. A union such as the UFW could provide for them a zone of autonomous power within which they can link together in common cause over a sustained period of time to make possible the bargaining power that they need to enter into negotiations with the companies that employ them. Because of their vulnerability many undocumented workers experience sexual harassment, low pay, poor working conditions, dangerous use of pesticides, and other forms of abuse. This kind of treatment of vulnerable workers by the powerful means that the use of direct bargaining and autonomy are no longer in the service of incoherence but are now enacted in the service of deformation that makes life fundamentally worse for all involved.

But as recent events show, the day when the undocumented immigrants remained in the shadows and accepted being victims is now over. Beginning in March 2006 there have been a series of marches across the nation demanding justice for undocumented workers. In Los Angeles more than 500,000 demonstrated, another 200,000 in Chicago. The marches culminated with a worker and student boycott on May 1, 2006, that was very successful in attracting large numbers of people and in capturing the attention of the American public. Not since the Civil Rights era and the anti-Vietnam War marches from the mid-1960s to the early 1970s has there been such an outpouring of direct democracy, people going into the streets to make their voices heard. The question of what to do with the undocumented immigrants in the country has split the nation. These marches were intended to influence the passage of a comprehensive immigration law advocated by the McCain-Kennedy Senate Bill that would, among other things, open up an avenue to legalization and eventual citizenship for the estimated twelve to fourteen million undocumented immigrants in the U.S. Others simply want to send them back and to militarize the border by building walls, bringing in troops, and prosecuting employers who hire them. Many manipulate the fears caused by 9/11 and speak of terrorists pouring across the border. In December 2005, the House passed a bill, HR 4437, sponsored by Representative James Sensenbrenner, a Republican from Wisconsin, that declared those without documents to be federal felons and considered anybody who assisted an undocumented person with, for example, health care or rent assistance as guilty of breaking federal law. In a remarkable statement Cardinal Roger Mahony of Los Angeles defended his instruction to the priests of the archdiocese to defy the proposed law that would criminalize church workers who assist undocumented immigrants.[11]

By marching the undocumented community also galvanized the support of many in the Latino community who had previously not been that involved. When Latino U.S. citizens learned about the harshness of the proposed new law it made them angry and they began to identify with their undocumented brethren as never before. Many undocumented have young children born in this country who, within a few years, will be voting—they will not soon forget how they and their parents were treated in this case by the Republicans. As they marched, they chanted, "Today we march, tomorrow we vote." Given that the Republicans were beginning to make real progress in gaining Latino support that had been traditionally given to the Democrats, this anger caused great concern in Republican ranks. They know the demographics as well as anyone and so they remain fearful of the future power of the Latino vote. It is so ironic that the President found himself in a situation of needing comprehensive immigration reform to help save his presidency. Given the open wound of Iraq, the failure of Social Security reform, and the debacle of the new Medicare prescription bill, the President bet much of his remaining political clout on achieving immigration reform.

But beyond these immediate political concerns there are deeper issues involved here, especially the issue of identity. As a nation the U.S. has always considered itself to be a compassionate and fair country as a nation of immigrants with a tradition of welcoming new groups. That sense of welcome and inclusion is at risk with this latest outbreak of xenophobia. In addition many European Americans are worried about the future. America was always synonymous with being white, but by 2050 communities of color taken together will make up 47 percent of the population and by the year 2100 white Americans will be the minority with only 40 percent of the population.[12] Thus as Americans we now need to ask ourselves what kind of country we want to be and who is an American. The undocumented have answered loud and clear that they want to be American because they share the values of this nation and want only to have the opportunity to achieve the benefits of immigrant groups before them.

The recent effort to provide a comprehensive immigration bill was announced by the President in an address to the American people from the Oval Office on May 15, 2006. His main concern was to assure his conservative base that he remained dedicated to securing the border as the top priority. In a scathing editorial the *New York Times* critiqued Bush's plan.

> Rather than standing up for truth, Mr. Bush swiveled last night in the direction of those who see immigration with delusional clarity, as entirely a problem of barricades and bad guys. His plan to deploy "up to 6,000" National Guard troops to free the Border Patrol to hunt illegal immigrants is a model of stark simplicity, one sure to hearten Minuteman vigilantes, frightened conspiracy theorists, English-only-Latinophobes, right-wing radio and TV personalities, and members of Congress who have no patience for sorting out the various and mixed blessings that surging immigration has given this country. . . . It is still possible that a good bill will emerge this year, but . . . [i]t means overcoming the latest contribution from the ever-unhelpful president, who could have pointed the nation toward serious immigration reform last night, but instead struck a pose as Minuteman in chief.[13]

Until a compassionate and just immigration bill is passed, undocumented workers and their families will continue to be victimized by a double devil, the stories of tribalism and capitalism. Undocumented Latino men and Latina women together with Latino citizens have made it clear that they are appealing to the best in U.S. society, the story of democracy that declares that each of us is valuable by the very nature of our humanity.

> A good immigration bill must honor the nation's values and be sensible enough to work. It must not violate the hope of deserving people who want to work toward citizenship. It must not create a servant class of "guest workers" shackled to their employers and forbidden to aspire to permanent legal status. It must give newcomers equal treatment under the law and respect their rights of due process. It must impose rigorous enforcement of labor laws, so unscrupulous employers cannot exploit illegal workers. And it must clear the existing backlogs of millions seeking to enter the country. . . .[14]

Those who practice the story of capitalism and are taken over by the logic of this sacred drama come to a point where they care little or nothing about compassion and justice. For this reason workers in Latin America or in this country face a grim reality. American corporations and businesses of all sizes are prepared to exploit workers for profits. But because of the brutality of capitalism throughout Latin America, which is usually unimpeded by laws to protect workers many people are desperate to come to the U.S. where wages are higher, working conditions are safer, and the future of their children is far better. But let us look at an example of an American business that is just as callous as it reaches across the border for profits and shows no concern for working people. Here is the ad used by Calyx and Corolla Florist in Miami, an importer of exquisite roses from Cayambe, Ecuador:

> Cayambe is a place where Andean mists and equatorial sun conspire to produce roses that quickly burst into extravagant bloom, then hold their glory long after lesser specimens have begun to droop.[15]

Of the 50,000 workers employed by 460 growers that produce these roses of "extravagant bloom" 70 percent are indigenous women poisoned every day by pesticides that are sprayed while they work.

In a study conducted by the Catholic University and the International Labor Organization, it was found that the women suffer from an abnormal number of miscarriages, headaches, nausea, fatigue, and blurred vision. Two women who were interviewed, Soledad and Petrona, have an elementary education and make $156.00 a month. Unfortunately they are forced to make money to eat first and deal with labor conditions later. They suffer from loss of hair, loss of appetite, their kidneys throb, and they are growing old before their time. Of the 460 companies only dozens provide protective gear, health care, and training about safety. As a result of the fumigation of the rose stems there is a high incidence of conjunctivitis, rashes, respiratory problems, and nausea. And because the roses are sold over the internet, the money does not help to build the local economy. The rose industry grew to be the fourth largest in the world largely helped by the Andean trade Preference Act of 1991 that created tariff free access for Bolivia, Colombia, Peru, and Ecuador to the U.S. market to create a substitute for coca and poppy production. Although there are some benefits, helping women to win economic freedom from men and providing an education for their children, the price is very high. In a classic response of those who feel no sense of responsibility for others when it comes to profits, James Pagano of Calyx and Corolla responded to criticism of the company: "We buy what we think consumers will perceive to be a high quality rose at a competitive price." The environment "is not an issue we have any business being in."[16]

Meanwhile in Bolivia in the mining industry we have another good example of why people are leaving everyday for the U.S. For the past three hundred years boys ten to sixteen years old have been working the mines in Potosi, a mountain city of 145,000 in the Bolivian Andes. The Indians were forced to work there by the Spaniards who called it la Montaña Rica, Rich Mountain; the Indians who know better called it the Mountain that Devours Men. By the age of forty most miners are dying from lung disease and by fifty most of them are dead. They began their work life as young boys with twelve-hour workdays in mines where there is no lighting, no pumped oxygen, no rail cars, no safety regulations, and no overseers. There is no equipment to speak of: no gloves, boots, or masks, just a little charcoal for lighting their headlamps.

The mines are almost exhausted; they no longer yield enough to support the miners. The members of whole families all need to work to survive. Fathers take their sons to work as early as the age of ten where the deadly cycle of work, lung disease, and an early death is the only future that they have. The young have no schools and only pure alcohol and coca to chew as an escape from a dreadful life. There are 10,000 miners who belong to co-ops who barely make $100 a month. There had been 30,000 miners in a government-sponsored co-op until the collapse of world market prices in 1985. As a result the blessings of steady employment, health benefits, housing, and food subsidies ended. Although the Spaniards are gone, the deadly heritage of the Conquest remains: the Quechua Indians are still dying in the mines 350 years after hundreds of thousands, perhaps millions, of their ancestors died of illness, starvation, and overwork as they mined the silver that financed the Spanish Armada.[17] This kind of desperation replicated throughout Latin America pushes people to this country, the *recien llegados* of today and tomorrow. These conditions of a relentless, crushing poverty are the real weapons of mass destruction and the producers of violent cataclysmic outbursts filled with despair that feed the rebellions.

The recent election of Evo Morales is the first Amayra Indian to ever serve as the president in Bolivia's history. He was elected largely because the people lost faith in the white Spanish ruling class. They were angry that they were treated as children and exploited with many condemned to die before their time. In his inaugural address Morales made it very clear that his election was a victory for the oppressed indigenous community of Aymara and Quechua Indians who make up the majority of the population: "I want to say to you my Indian brothers concentrated here in Bolivia, that the 500 year old campaign of resistance has not been in vain. . . . This democratic, cultural fight is a part of the fight of our ancestors, it is the continuity of the fight of Tupac Katari, it's a continuity of the fight of Che Guevara."[18]

Elena Padilla in her excellent book, *Up from Puerto Rico*, written a generation ago but still applicable today, clearly understood the underlying struggle going on in the life of a person displaced from her or his roots. She knew that something had profoundly altered Puerto Ricans after living for a period of time on the mainland. Padilla was able to perceive the change by carefully observing the interaction between newly arrived Puerto Ricans and those who have been here for a generation or those who were born on the mainland.

> Soon after settling in New York, Puerto Rican migrants find that many of the expectations they have nursed about New York and their future lives here have begun to shatter. For example, the norms and values they hold concerning "proper"

and "correct" behavior are not the same as those held in New York, even among other Hispanics. Individuals who left the island as adults and have been in New York for many years do not conform to their expectations either; they act differently and have learned to look at and weigh things differently from the ways in which such things are done in the island. . . . Puerto Ricans in New York do not help each other as they do in Puerto Rico and are not "united." New migrants speak frequently of the lack of consensus and solidarity among Puerto Ricans as reflected in the weakening and lack of recognition of mutual obligations among friends, relatives and countrymen.[19]

Puerto Ricans with a common heritage had become strangers to each other because they were relating to each other in the service of different ultimate ways of life. This is something for all of us as Latinas and Latinos to keep in mind when we are automatically delighted to see a fellow Latina/Latino appointed, elected, or hired for a position. As we have seen throughout the previous chapters, it depends on in the service of what ultimate way of life he or she is living. Perhaps terms such as brother and sister, *hermano* or *hermana*, *carnal*, blood brother, *país hermano*, fellow countryman, and *raza*, the people of the community, should be reserved for those who share with us a dedication to the creation of a fundamentally new and better life.

In *La Carreta, The Ox Cart*, a campesino family is torn between dreams of a golden future characterized by the good life in the cities and the pristine past that linked them to the sacred, the land, each other, and the common values of hard work, sharing, and love. The two sons, Luis and Chaguito, are eventually lost in the jungle of the cities, and it is the women, Doña Gabriela, the mother, and Juanita, who seek to return to their sacred roots by returning home to Puerto Rico *and* by going home within themselves to renew a world gone dead. This play is a contemporary reenactment of the journey of transformation that speaks poignantly to the experience of all Latina women and Latino men who migrated to the United States: "Ehtoy como sin raiseh. No encuentro tierra. No encajo en ningún sitio." "I can't catch on anywhere. I can't find my footing. It's as if I have no roots," declares Luis, one of the main characters in the play.[20] A generation later, Tato Lavierra takes up the theme again in his provocative book of poetry, *La Carreta Made a U-Turn*. He rejects a romantic return to Puerto Rico as the answer and points out that many Puerto Ricans are here to stay and so need to establish themselves here. However, he qualifies the meaning of return by writing that a return to Puerto Rico is possible if return means to affirm one's Afro-Caribbean heritage and to reject the white upper-middle-class Hispanophile ideal.[21] Certainly it is the three aspects, Afro-Caribbean-European, that the Puerto Rican needs to incorporate in creating an alternative here and now.

In *Five Families* the husbands and wives are often at odds because they are living in different ways of life.[22] A man who has built his self-understanding on a relationship to a particular woman quickly knows his identity is threatened when she enacts relationships previously forbidden to her. They are now living in different worlds. Latino men who controlled their wives on the *rancho* because the lord of emanation, the culture, and society gave them the perennial right to do so are at a loss when wives work to support them. Her economic power, due to a move to the city, gives her not only direct bargaining leverage and autonomy but actually allows her to be the dominant person in the relationship of emanation. She is now the source of mystery rather than the recipient; she now has a source of legitimacy that used to belong only to men. Some husbands fight the change by using violence while others slide into a quiet passivity that ends in violence against themselves as they turn to drugs or alcohol or carousing to assuage their sense of loss. Others hang onto fragments of the web of emanation while accepting the new way as inevitable. Others believe that the old world is gone when a woman supports the family while the previously dominant male is still present. Some Latina women see the change in themselves, in their relationships to men and to the culture, and might or might not like what has happened. But most men and women go on without understanding what is really happening to them.

THE ASSIMILATIONIST MODEL: LIVING IN THE SERVICE OF INCOHERENCE

The assimilationist model that we confront in the United States undermines the loyalty characteristic of our traditional heritage; to assimilate is to accept the way of life of incoherence, that is, the permanent rebellion against the powerful so that we can take their place and the constant shifting of alliances in the search for power. We find ourselves in a new place, in a permanent state of arrest in the story of capitalism in Act II, Scene 1, of the core drama of life. The pursuit of power cannot bring back the security that was lost with the breaking of the inherited container in the first act. In fact, it is not possible to be secure in a society based on permanent rebellion. A society living stories and relationships in the service of incoherence is not intended to give security but the opposite, permanent insecurity, so that people will continuously be "forced to be free" to compete for power. We soon learn that this system cannot provide security, so we are disillusioned. Many of us cannot make it here. The failure of the assimilationist model in the public realm forces us to compensate our partial lives with aspects of emanation in the personal realm. This is why many of us continue to hang onto fragments of the way of life of emanation. This inability to make our lives whole by being connected to our neighbors and to the deepest source of our being in a new way is to live with incoherence.

Still many of us made the second choice, the assimilationist model, because we did not know of any other option that was better. We wanted to be accepted, to be like the Anglos because they had clout to get things done, they had power and many consumer goods that seemed to prove their superiority. Of course European Americans did nothing to discourage this attitude of superiority. We fed their prejudice with our need to belong, to be accepted, and, sadly, with our growing self-hatred. Lighter-skinned Latinas and Latinos could always pass, intermarry, and merge into the dominant group. The *morenitos*, or dark-skinned among us, had a more difficult time and always had to prove themselves by being better. Better at what? Better at the white, male game, which meant it was still their game, their definition of life that dominated all of us. So we fought with the white boys on the school grounds, out danced them, and even took their girlfriends.

At home we argued that the Americans let their daughters go to parties, stay out later, and have boyfriends and on and on. Our parents called us *malcriados*, brats, sassy children, because we lost the respect characteristic of emanation as a way of life. Some of us refused to speak Spanish and sometimes mocked our culture. Thus many of us, because we felt there was no other way, assimilated into the European-American patterns of living: competitive, individualistic, virile behavior so that we could be somebody and be accepted. We wanted to be successful in this society. Some changed their name, others began to call themselves "Spaniards" or even to claim, "I'm American." The sadness is that although we were moving toward greater personal autonomy by developing skills and pulling ourselves up by the proverbial bootstraps, it was now a new system giving us our identity. New roles were defined by a system in which occupational skills told us if we were somebody. Some of us were high school graduates, others dropouts who ended as blue collar laborers, construction workers, and field hands. The majority of us came from working class backgrounds. There were a few professionals among us but most of were still close to poverty. Upwardly mobile Latinas and Latinos at times looked upon the others with contempt and felt that they were better. Class became a serious dividing line in the community. Self-hatred was now projected onto the group.

Get out of the barrio if you want to make it because your people will pull you down was the slogan of teachers and counselors. You are one of the "better" Puerto Ricans, Ecuadorians, Colombians, or Mexicans. Better because you are self-reliant, hardworking, and motivated. But really you are better because you are like us. Assimilation is really the search for power that will make us the envy of others. It is public opinion, society that tells us who we are. But this is not like the traditional way of life of emanation where we knew who we were and had security. Exactly. This search for power after power in its own way is a new search for security but without the ability to ever achieve it. Liberal white society is a cheat because it is really trying to tell us that a system called free enterprise can give everybody a good life. The cost of the way of life of incoherence is a combination of suppression and oppression. Many of us will never make it, are *intended* to never make it, so that the game of running in the same spot will continue. The powerful, the less powerful, and the powerless are all caught in the story of capitalism in the service of incoherence, the way of life of fragments that keeps us a partial self. The less powerful are reduced to a special interest group that rebels against the power of the dominant, not to achieve justice and compassion for all, but to become the powerful themselves. This game of replacing one group by another perpetuates the system of oppression.

Nor does life hang together in this assimilationist model. It is living with insecurity. How can I be sure of anything when the upward climb has caused me to be disconnected from myself, my community, my past, my parents, and a loving sacred source? Many of us realized this but we were not aware of any other option. Many Latinas and Latinos did resist as we can see from the various nationalist movements such as the Chicano Brown Berets and Puerto Rican Young Lords. These groups at times responded to the disillusionment with a nationalism that intended to restore the glory of the indigenous peoples. Yet this is the creation of a pseudo-emanation because it takes an aspect of our life, racial and ethnic identity, and invests it with total meaning. It promises not just security but this time total security because life in the system of power is so precarious. Since the old way of life is decaying and we cannot make it in the world of incoherence, we are tempted to create fantasies based on ethnicity or race that make us vulnerable to leaders who lead us into destructive politics in the service of deformation. There are many shades of meaning and disagreements, but I think that many Latinas and Latinos are looking for a kind of purification or redemption, a justification by asserting our past. This is a kind of rebellion because we know what we do not want, European-American cultural and political domination, but we do not know what to put in its place except a vague sense of returning to our *raices,* or roots. In response to an attempt on the part of Anglos to give us a competitive system that does not work for us, we retreated to a total way of life that once gave meaning to the cosmos but which since has been shattered. We cannot go back yet we try to do so. This approach deepens our sense of loss and can lead us to deformation.

THE DESTRUCTIVE MODEL: LIFE IN THE SERVICE OF DEFORMATION

The anger arising out of the dilemma of living between two ways of life, neither of which was working for us, gave rise to another way of life, deformation, that many of us experienced and continue to experience. Deformation is a whole way of life in which our humanity is wounded by fantasies based on racial, ethnic, class, or religious superiority. We are hurt by the story of tribalism that tells us that we are nothing, invisible people. If we make enough noise we are allowed to participate in the society as long as we accept our inferiority: lesser pay, poor housing, inferior health care, and poor schooling. To get away from this discrimination the "better" among us are invited to assimilate, to join the powerful, since we are judged by them to be like them. If we awake and begin to question a system that rewards us at the expense of the community we are then exiled or excommunicated for being disloyal to our bosses. Finally, the powerful can and do practice extermination by refusing us access to enough of the necessities of life to survive. This story in the service of deformation erases our personal faces, teaches us a politics of violence, revenge, and exclusion that embitters our political faces, takes our historical faces and turns our history and theirs downward into the abyss by making life worse as time goes on, and feeds our sacred faces to the lord of deformation.

We need to get out of deformation at the bottom of the abyss as victims. So we go to school, become professionals, enter politics, achieve success, and enter the mainstream of American society. Isn't this what it is all about? But the only alternative offered to us is to live in incoherence as a way of life. We are allowed only to be a fragmented person and to make it by accepting the story of capitalism and the competition for power. All of the relationships with the exception of transformation are now enacted in the service of incoherence. We suppress or hide our personal faces since we cannot afford to be intimate in a world of power; our political face knows only the politics of power and with our historical face we use time to acquire more of the trappings of power. Our sacred face is inspired by the lord of incoherence to see the meaning of life as the acquisition of more and more. We are forced to develop strategies of survival by becoming "streetwise." For example, after having figured out the system, we basically decide that we are going to tell people what they want to hear so that we can live a life of promotions with a minimum of hassle. That is our competitive public life. In the private realm Latinas and Latinos attempt to hold on to a way of life that connects them to their past. Often there is contempt for the *Gringos* and their culture but it is not allowed to surface. There is a constant doubt about our own ability. At times we feel superior because we are surviving and even doing well in spite of the Anglos. But again it is all a defensive comparison with powerful others upon whom we depend to tell us if we are making it and therefore a tacit assumption that Anglos just might be superior.

We cannot go on living this kind of self-wounding without corroding our very souls. It means that we cannot be who we are; based on a fantasy of racial superiority the dominant determine our limited choices. Latinas and Latinos are caught between ways of life, one promising security by holding on to fragments of the dying way of life of emanation and the other the insecure rewards of power in the way of life of incoherence, and since many cannot make it in either world, they are not intended to succeed. We become increasingly vulnerable to deformation that leads to violence by self-wounding as we lose our pain in drugs, alcohol, food, or work and commit violence against the community by dealing drugs or by turning to revenge against others. The Anglo world provides the fragment of power that rewards people with consumer well-being, while the Latino world promises another fragment of the remnant of a golden age to which we can escape to find security in a world of discontinuity. But we cannot be fully who we are in either fragment. Many of us try to juggle these worlds, feeling uneasy and defeated when we cannot reconcile them. Both ways of life fail to give us the necessary means to respond to the problems of our lives.

A *Welfare Mother* referred to earlier is an excellent study of life in the service of emanation and incoherence that ends in deformation.[23] It dramatically and graphically portrays the attempts of a Latina to survive through welfare "cheating." It tells the story of the dying of emanation as a web of life as bits and pieces of a past rural life fail to give her respite from the guilt she feels in having had to become like the rest of society in order to protect herself and her children. There is no longer any ultimate grounding to her life that allows her to respect herself as a person. Initially she is embarrassed but then cheats because "everybody cheats." Her life is further demeaned by having to travel from one agency to another simply to acquire housing and food. Whole days are consumed in visiting and waiting for caseworkers. She is not angry or impatient, merely sullen and more passive to protect herself from anger. She is very affectionate toward her children, but it is a losing battle because the society at large does not care about them. She lights candles to favorite saints and asks for help. Throughout the book the only hope for Mrs. Santana is loyalty to the family. It is her one, if not only, bulwark, an island, a fragment of emanation, in a world of betrayal and broken connections. Her affection and love for family is a desperate act surrounded by relationships devoid of caring, compassion, or concern. Such a situation exposes the reality of living in deformation because she and her children are treated as lesser human beings, burdens of the society with no intrinsic value of their own.

Random Family is a brilliant but haunting study of the collapse of the traditional values of the way of life of emanation.[24] As in A *Welfare Mother*, the author tells the story of an extended Puerto Rican family, men, women, and children who juggle their lives in the jungle of daily life under capitalism in the Bronx. Their lives are filled with fragments of a traditional life that no longer works for them. *Familia* is at the very heart of Latino culture. This book chronicles the journey of a family that in the midst of its members' fight for survival attempt to remain loyal to each other. When there is no money left they still manage to share what little they have. They are willing to spend their last dollar or go into debt to make sure that a birthday party, for example, is celebrated with some degree of luxury. But the larger society that sees them as burdens and drags on the public purse helps to break their lives as they encounter the machine, the system that devours you, spoken of by René Marqués in his classic work, *La Carreta.* We watch as the family disintegrates under the pressure of not being able to make it in a highly competitive society, indeed, are intended by the powerful not to make it. To compensate for their loss of respect the members of the family turn to forms of escape in taking drugs or searching for their share of the American dream by drug dealing. The author, Adrian Nicole Le-Blanc, is a brilliant writer who takes us into the minds and hearts of the members of several families whom she has come to know and care about after ten years of observing their struggles and earning their trust. What concerns me about the book is that it is a study in fatalism. LeBlanc takes us into their world but then leaves us with little or no hope until the end when she speaks of how Boy George and César who are in prison for dealing drugs are beginning to change for the better and Coco is beginning to reevaluate her life after giving birth to five children by four different fathers.

The heart of the book is about a world of broken connections: multiple sex partners, pimps who are connected only to drugs and money, children alienated from their usually unmarried parents, women with children from several different fathers, the younger generation disrespectful of their elders, the broken promises of urban education, multiple dwelling places that are no longer a home, people crying out and nobody hearing them. It is really a study in deformation wherein violence permeates everyone's life from the violence of poverty, poor housing, inadequate health care, and terrible education to the constant physical violence of men asserting their physical and sexual domination of women. But there is almost no hope because there is no change for the better. The book tragically shows us three generations of Puerto Rican women repeating the same stories of patriarchy, romantic/possessive love, and the wounded self, stories that are enacted in the way of life of deformation. For example, Coco has children by four different fathers. She continues to have children and yet has no way of providing for them. Her lovers are all wounded by drugs either as consumers or dealers. César, her first lover, goes to prison and continues to dominate her life. He was repeatedly unfaithful to her and she returns the treatment by sleeping with other men to her own harm. Nobody seems to wake up and at least protect their bodies by taking birth control precautions; nobody wants to go to school to change their lives; nobody considers moving away, except for Coco who vacillates between living in Troy, New York, and returning to the Bronx to be closer to family; nobody has a sense of hope, only survival counts; nobody wants to be different from their parents; nobody takes control of their lives. Power, sex, drugs, money, and violence or their opposites, a life of being helpless, loveless, and a crushing poverty consume their lives and take them over. This is a disturbing book that while it takes us into the lives of some remarkable people, it leaves us bereft. Their traditional world of loyalty has failed them and they cannot make it in the world of power and brutal competition so they have turned to various forms of self-wounding and wounding of others. And yet transformation is a possibility as we see especially in César who is determined to turn his life around when he gets out of prison.

But on the whole the book tells a very sobering story that borders on despair. There is indeed, as the author states in her Author's Note at the end of the book, insight and generosity, stimulating conversations, lives of unusual hardships and gifts, and Jessica's life as a witness to an existence of extraordinary highs and lows.[25] LeBlanc became a friend who remained in close contact with the various members of the family for ten years as they endured one disaster after another. I wondered as I finished the book if she ever challenged them to change their lives. Their friendship and encounters stimulated her to think and to see the big picture and changed her life and perspective, but did she change theirs?[26]

Fragments of emanation make it difficult for the women in *Random Family* to see themselves as an equal of a male. Their culture, which is still deeply embedded in them, both personally and historically, pulls them back to being women who look to men to complete them; they have children to justify their lives. Motherhood further reinforces a sense of self given to them by their traditional past in the way of emanation. The women continue to live the inherited relationships of dependency. But trouble is inevitable. For long periods of time the men are absent either because of a lack of responsibility for the family or time spent in prison. Women without men need to learn to be aggressive, independent, and confident, that is, practicing the relationships of autonomy and direct bargaining as they maneuver their way through the labyrinth of the welfare system. The women were living in two broken ways of life, the world of emanation and incoherence. Sooner or later this kind of life ends in depression or explodes into confrontation. Attempts to maintain two partial worlds will continue to fail because the women are not fully present and therefore cannot respond to new problems. Violence occurs precisely because of the inability of people to be wholly present to themselves, others, the deepest sacred source, or situations.

Thus, living caught between the demands of two worlds, the dominant Anglo society and the traditional Latino past, is doomed to failure. There simply is nobody home except a fragmented self who continues to create a fragmented world running from one fragment to the next.[27]

This kind of life in which we are suspended between two ways of life is not a rational compromise for living but points out the reality of deformation, an underlying sacred way of life that has possessed us so that we have lost control of our lives. Many Latinas and Latinos get caught here. They have not really figured out the stories, relationships, and the four faces of their being enacted within partial ways of life that prevent them from being able to transform their lives. Deformation is a reality regardless of salary or status; this kind of poverty affects the rich and poor alike. This inability to shape our lives leads to anger and ambivalent feelings about what we are doing with our lives. So we get caught up in rhetoric about "the damn system," playing the game, and so on. There is a dull satisfaction in being numb and ignoring the cost of either illusion: the pursuit of power or looking for security in powerful others. These two illusions feed on each other. When we are weary of being aggressive and competitive, we can retreat to the home front to be compensated for the brutality of the story of capitalism and feel the security of possessing and being possessed in the story of romantic love. Conversely if a person cannot exercise domination on the job, they will seek it over others at home. This kind of existence, living between two ways of life, opens the way for the violence intrinsic to deformation that erupts again and again because we cannot be fully who we are in either way of life. As a result our life is diminished as human beings.

THE TRANSFORMING MODEL

A growing number of Latinas and Latinos are looking for a way, for good talk, to help them to go beyond the shattered container of the traditional way of life of emanation, to overcome the temptation of assimilation into the way of life of incoherence and the descent into the abyss in deformation. The only viable response to the inability of the other three ways of life to respond to our problems is the way of life in which we persistently participate in transforming ourselves and our relationships with others and with the deepest sacred. For the first time, as our symbol of the mandala indicates, the participatory self is at the center of her or his life. This is no longer mere subjectivism as in the search for self-interest justified by the story of liberal capitalism. The participatory self is a person related to one's self, to one's neighbor, to common problems, and to the deepest sacred in a fundamentally more just and loving way. Relationships in the other three ways of life are intended to possess the person, dominate others, or cripple others whereas in the service of transformation relationships, stories, and the four faces of our being are practiced in order to bring about a new and more loving justice. This is a very important point. It helps to explain why even though a Latino might have achieved the relationship of autonomy on the personal level as a doctor, he is still not free to care for others as a priority since the A.M.A. defines who he is as a professional, what kind of fees he can charge, and what his upward mobility depends upon. He is hampered in his responses to patients by enacting relationships with his patients practiced in the service of incoherence.

Many practice the relationships and the stories of their lives in the service of incoherence without being aware of it. This is because U.S. society with its emphasis on status and power lives in an emanational relationship to incoherence as a way of life. We do not analyze our relationship to incoherence as a way of life. We believe that there is no other or better way to live. It is the way things are. We are taught to be in emanation to the role of doctor or lawyer such that we are an extension of a mysterious knowledge that gives us identity and power. We are assimilated and absorbed by the power of being a doctor. Who are we to question this mysterious realm of power that will place me at the pinnacle of respect and power? When Latinos realize this, they work for a compromise between their good intentions to work for the community and the system's demands. But no system of inherited or officially sanctioned relationships can give us justice. It is only a person making personal, political, historical, and sacred decisions to choose justice and compassion rather than power and income that will bring about changes for the good. Moral women and men make moral decisions. He or she can grow their own doctorhood and enact all eight relationships to respond to the well-being of patients. The tradition of medicine endowed with emanation as a mysterious force can only be challenged by a self who decides what to do with medical skills; medical competence belongs to a Latina/Latino doctor and not the doctor to the profession. Likewise the Latina or Latino who has chosen to acquire legal competence can now help to defend Latinos seeking to create the relationship of autonomy by organizing a union that links workers together in common purpose to protect their rights as workers, men and women who are establishing health clinics, civic societies to protect undocumented workers from exploitation, and to incorporate a coalition of other professionals to create a scholarship fund. There is no end to what can be done once people are connected in the relationship of autonomy in the service of transformation to create liberated zones within which to respond to injustice. The practice of autonomy in the service of incoherence places us on the road to deformation because decisions are made by the powerful for the good of the powerful as to who deserves health care and who is to be excluded. This is why we always need to ask the question: "In the service of what way of life, of what ultimate sacred source, are we enacting the relationships, stories and the four faces of our being?"

Let me give some examples of what it means to be free to relate to others in the service of transformation. One day at home I noticed that my youngest son, Matthew, was sad. I asked him if he was one of my best friends, and he said, "I'm not a friend; I'm your son." Matthew needed a lot of protection, affection, and security before he could be a friend, an equal, a strong person on his own. He still needed the relationship of emanation enacted in the way of life of transformation to prepare him to participate in a wider range of life. Later that same day I met with a student who was reluctant to write a paper because he did not like to write. I told him that he would fail the course. This is the use of the relationship of subjection, but it needs to be employed for the purpose of pushing him to learn how to write so that he can walk away from me and the university with skills that prepare him to participate with others in shaping a better world. This is what the way of life of transformation is all about: persons connected to self, their neighbor, and to the deepest sacred can persist in creating, nourishing, breaking, and then re-creating new just and compassionate forms of the eight archetypal relationships to confront the issues of life.

So what do we end up with? Latinas and Latinos who, as a result of being radically linked to others and to the sacred as deeply caring people, can employ their skills in the relationship of autonomy on behalf of others, exercise the relationship of subjection in demanding obedience, who know when to buffer and protect, know when to practice the relationship of isolation by withdrawing, who are aware when they do not know in the relationship of incoherence and who are open to experimenting and risking themselves so as to transform their lives and situations.[28] Within the way of life of transformation whatever strategies we create to solve issues always involve the enactment of the four faces of our being. We create new concrete manifestations of the eight relationships because we care deeply about the people who walk into our lives. In this way of life we mutually fulfill each other.

Our goal in relating to others is to guide them to a new kind of participation with their neighbors and the god of transformation. This is true empowerment. Anything else is the perpetuation of dependence. To illustrate this point, I would like to recount a session with a group of welfare workers, many of whom were Latinas and members of other communities of color. They were speaking of how they helped people week after week so that many became perpetual clients. They realized that this institutionalized a dangerous dependency based on power, so that the clients buffered their true feelings, exchanging the required docility necessary to receive benefits in the mode of direct bargaining. Clients experienced the relationship of subjection by uncaring case workers and generally felt trapped in a poverty that was endless. Burnt-out social workers enacting the relationship of autonomy merely processed the people, which meant that they perpetuated relationships that kept the clients in their place, dependent, poor, and humiliated. This kind of bureaucratic treatment often led to angry encounters, because people being served experienced a sense of injustice. They feel that they were being paid off by the system in exchange for good behavior. This awareness of manipulation caused many to question why there have to be poor people. Not to accept a sense of inherited inferiority is to ask where did our powerlessness come from and whom does it benefit. Such awareness brought about tensions that could not be addressed by more money and quicker services; some people angrily questioned the whole system. This is an example of the relationship of incoherence; there is only conflict and change, no cooperation, no justice, no sense of direction, and no agreement with the agents of the system. Efficient bureaucrats protest that they are only doing their job, but they refuse to or cannot see that their job includes detaching themselves from their feelings, so that they can process people and turn their clients' hurt into an abstraction. The welfare worker is angry because he or she is fragmented since the system reduces them to being functionaries so that caring is out of the question. Any concern for their clients cannot be translated into effective action, as it is blocked by the myriad rules of the system and hope for advancement. Caring professional social workers have been hustled by slick welfare recipients who have figured out the system and merely want to rip it off. To those who become disillusioned welfare people are now considered as potential cheaters. People on each side turn themselves and the others into an abstraction: us versus them. In the meantime the poor sink deeper into becoming an underclass, another abstraction. This places the welfare worker and their clients on the road to deformation.

During the session we spoke of how it was the goal for welfare clients to take charge of their lives. But we are speaking of Latinas and Latinos, some recently arrived from Latin America who have little or no skills or money and who are not aggressive with authority figures. The strategy has been to work on providing job training, welfare subsidies, and bilingual education. Still the people remained unassertive. The treatment was perpetuating the illness. Nobody thought of the importance of their sense of selfhood, of the necessity of being treated with respect, of being a people in need of being connected to others and to a source of mystery within themselves. Nobody had thought of building a sense of confidence and of skills as expressions of who they are and what they want to do and be. This is because gaining power in U.S. society involves acquiring the relationships of direct bargaining and autonomy that enable you to gain competitive skills so you can be independent. This allows caring agencies to close your case and to be free of you. That is how the social workers saw their own lives. So they sought to make others tough and independent by providing skills. As a result, the poor become "successfully socialized" when they learn conforming behavior or how to compete, hold a job, and gain power. This is assimilation into the way of life of incoherence.

In the dialogue that ensued many of the social workers were surprised when it was insisted that they look at their own lives, the stories, the relationship and the four faces of their being and to ask themselves in what way of life they were living their lives and where they were in the core drama of life. How could they counsel, assist, or advise others unless they knew where they were guiding people? Success has too often been identified as helping a person to assimilate into the values of power. Whereas before he or she was considered to be a productive member of society, that very society at one point caused them to lose their job because it was part of the acceptable cost of fighting inflation or saving the bottom line for a company in trouble. Unemployment can be created by small groups of people making political decisions that affect all of our lives. Given this impersonal system, how do social workers prevent a sense of powerlessness and cynicism in their lives and in the lives of their clients? There is no other place to start except to see the self as a member of a community who can link with others to create new forms of justice. As the conversation continued, some of us came to recognize that personal awareness of how systems work, that is, the particular relationships needed to keep the combine going, are specifically dependent upon the roles that people unquestioningly follow. A conscientious person asking questions and caring deeply about others can indeed accept responsibility for dismantling a system, keeping in mind that a system can only continue when we fail to understand that our relationships in the service of a particular way of life is what gives it life. To dismantle a system also carries the opposite task of creating an alternative. This can be done if we accept the risk. A social worker can organize with other colleagues, administrators, lawyers, members of the legislature, and the community to replace regulations that hurt the poor. This is using the relationship of autonomy in the service of transformation: directing one's skills, authority of the office, connections, and obligations owed, not for personal gain, but to change the quality of peoples' lives. We can in this way create institutions that bind us together over a sustained period of time in a common task in the service of transformation and substitute this for the power that disconnects us in the way of life of incoherence.[29]

GOING HOME: THERE'S NO PLACE LIKE HOME

We cannot bring about any change for the better unless it begins with the personal face of our being; we cannot be political or create a new history or encounter the sacred afresh unless we know who we are. People who know who they are have in at least one aspect of their lives journeyed through the core drama of life to discover the self. They are now free to participate again and again in helping to bring about the fundamentally more loving and just in all aspects of life. We need then to give birth to and nurture the deeper self in the wombs of our inner lives. Each of us is pregnant with our own story, our own unrealized self. Like a woman whose time has come if she does not deliver the child both she and the baby will die. "If you bring forth what is within you, what you bring forth will save you. If you do not bring forth what is within you, what you do not bring forth will destroy you."[30] This quote, attributed to Jesus in the Gospel of Thomas, demonstrates the centrality of the individual person of faith for the Gnostics, a sect that was radically opposed to hierarchical authority dictating the truth. Leslie Marmon Silko touched us with the beauty of her feminist imagery reminding us that we need to go home first of all to our own inner life by acknowledging our pregnancy, that we are big with our own story and the stories of the community. Her novel, *Ceremony*, is a testimony to the disintegration of the individual and therefore of the community when the stories of transformation are lost. The novel is permeated with a personal, political, historical, and sacred pedagogy. In Tayo's journey we see our own task for self-discovery and transformation. At the end of his journey after great turmoil and near disaster Tayo has succeeded in bringing about the new and more fruitful.

> He would go back there now, where she had shown him the plant. He would gather the seeds for her and plant them with great care in places near the sandy hills. The rainwater would seep down gently and the delicate membranes would not be crushed or broken before the emergence of tiny fingers, roots, and leaves pressing out in all directions. The plants would grow there like the story, strong and translucent as the stars.
>
> His body was lost in exhaustion. . . . He dreamed with his eyes open. . . . Josiah was driving the wagon, old Grandma was holding him, and Rocky whispered "my brother." They were taking him home.[31]

In *José, Can You See?* the author brilliantly demonstrates the power of the art of the theatre, both on and off Broadway, to tell the story of Puerto Ricans/Latinos going home and the transforming strategies necessary to overcome the damage done to our souls by assimilation.[32] He begins by demolishing Puerto Rican/Latino stereotypes and then takes us into the search for redemption by the characters who are suffering from the loss of their four faces due to the seduction of the dominant culture. The awakening comes to characters found in various plays when they discover that they are *homeless* and cut off from the living waters of their heritage. As tokens in a white society the various characters from different plays like Javier and Marisol have lost their guardian angels and feel alienated and disconnected in the jungle of competition. They have no idea who they are as they pass back and forth between two cultures at war with one another. Their renewal begins as they return home, *homecoming*. The characters in Dolores Prida's plays, *Coser y Cantar*, *Beautiful Señoritas*, and *Botánica*[33] provide us with strategies by which to navigate our way through the demands of both cultures, Anglo and Latino. Millie, Milagros, in *Botánica* learns how to cross boundaries between both worlds and to create a new identity at the crossroads of her new location. She learns how to transform her life by taking the best of both cultures and nurturing these together in a new identity that is her new home both within and without. Now that she knows who she is, Millie is prepared to participate in *home-making*. Camila in Roy Conboy's play, *When el Cucui Walks*, realizes that the art of homemaking is to re-experience one's cultural heritage that was frozen in an amnesiac state. By going home to her deepest depths, Camila reconnects to the symbols of transformation in her indigenous past.[34]

Like the main character in *Doctor Magdalena*, many Latinas/ Latinos want to forget their past and assimilate. Doctor Magdalena is troubled by dreams that move her back and forth between Houston, the city of glass and stone, and the *mercados* of Mexico City filled with the mystery of her cultural past. Her inner voice will not let her ultimately go under for good. She needs healing and finds her answers through the intervention of *brujas, curanderas,* healers, physicians of body and soul, who guide her on how to live in the new world of science without giving up the ancient forms of healing. She needs to reconcile the old antagonisms between the Spaniard and the *indígeno*, the old world and the new, the city and the barrio, the concrete and the unseen underlying meaning and the different interpretations of the sacred. In other words she needs to conquer the Conquest, the ultimate experience of destruction for the Native Americans throughout Latin America, and to find in that destruction of a world a new *raza cósmica*, a new *mestizaje*, a new beginning.[35]

Going home is a continuous transforming journey. Sandoval-Sánchez speaks of *mobile homes*, a people on the move, a pilgrim people who are not at home in any system or society as an ultimate answer. One of the places where he found to call home is the theatre. I would add that together with U.S. Latino theatre, our education, poetry, music, and art of every kind along with a loving family can provide us with a therapeutic place both deep within ourselves and around us in the physicality of the home that "functions as a location for retracing, recovering, recollecting, recycling, reconnecting, negotiating, and reconciling the cultural, ethnic, familial, communal, and national past."[36] A process of the persistent transforming of the four faces of our being demands Latinas and Latinos who are able and ready to create new homes for old, new selves for old wherein

"an identity politics of location reproduces at given historical intersections new ethnicities, in the borderlands, the margins of previous, partial, residual, present, and emergent conceptualizations of
home."[37] Gloria Anzaldúa in her work also teaches us that we are
living on the moving frontier between the borderlands.[38]

Perhaps the most powerful border is not the one marked off by
barbed wire or fences patrolled by dogs and armed agents; rather it is
the borders that exist in our psyches. For years I thought of living
caught between different cultures as a traumatic experience. Then I
came to realize that a person who learns how to navigate the terrain
separating various aspects of her or his life and then as a result of
this struggle creates a bicultural and even multicultural self demands a very strong and deeply caring individual. To create a new
cultura Latina and unity in this country takes people with two
strong legs firmly planted and rooted in each culture who know how
to take the best from both cultures and give birth to a new, inclusive, and more compassionate culture.

We Latinas and Latinos cannot go back home to the old web of
life; we do not need to settle for less and live fragmented lives and to
consider assimilation as the only option; violence against self and
others is a dead end; we need to take our anger, our hurt, and turn
them into the necessary energy to change for the better. To go home
to one's deepest self is to allow the emergence of new consciousness,
creativity, new linkages to others, and new forms of justice by staying in contact with the deepest sacred source that can speak to us at
any time. To be a participatory self enables us to continue to collaborate yet to disagree and change for the sake of remaining open to
the demands of life. To respond to life in this manner is to put into
full play the four faces of our being. To persistently shape life in the
way of life of transformation means to leave our lives open to the
realm of the deepest sacred and as co-creators participate in bringing forth the fundamentally new and better. The mutual interpenetration of the human and the divine is what transformation is all
about.[39]

DEMOGRAPHICS AND THE LATINA/LATINO VOTE

One of the ways to reach our potential as a community is to
participate in official contests to elect those who best respond to the
needs of the community. But throughout the nation it is a serious
problem to organize Latina/Latino voters. Even though we share a

common language and historical ties to Latin America as well as the Christian faith, there is no one Latino community. As we have pointed out, the issue is not whether you are light or dark, Catholic or Pentecostal, lower middle class or high middle class, educated formally or not; ultimately what counts is how we answer the question, "In the service of what way of life are you as a Latina woman or Latino man living your *Latinísmo*?" If members of our community become involved in electoral politics we have no guarantee that they will not join the powerful and even end by assisting in the domination of our own people. Politics in the service of incoherence appealing to our sense of identity with phrases like "all of us are Hispanic" can be used as a rallying cry to seduce us into power games. As in chapter 7 on professionals, we need to practice a politics of subversion. Yes, we will run for public office at every level but we do not have to be of the powerful for the powerful in order to be in the realm of politics. Politics in the service of incoherence is committed to acquiring power after power in order to protect the already powerful from those who would rebel against their power. Politics in the service of transformation is interested in asking "What is it that we can and need to do together to bring about justice and compassion in this situation here and now?" To achieve new forms of justice we do not need to be official, professional politicians; each of us of the very nature of our humanity participates through the political face of our being in shaping a more equal and compassionate society.

The numbers are important, but we need people who care deeply about the community. We know that by 2050, 25 percent of the population of the U.S. will be Latina/Latino. The political implications of this are tremendous.

> For example, in 25 years 40% of the nation's population will reside in states like California, Texas, Florida, New York and Illinois. Latinos will be the single largest population group in California and Texas (outnumbering Blacks and Whites) and the second largest population group in Florida, New York and Illinois. These five states combined will elect 40% of the Congress of the US and control 68% of the electoral votes needed to be elected President of the United States. The political implications are obvious. Many of the federal, state, and local officials elected in these states, including senators, governors and other statewide officials, members of Congress, legislators, mayors, and local/county officials will be Latino.[40]

These numbers are indeed impressive. The growth of the Latino vote means that we will have a great deal of bargaining power within the system. There will be a significant increase in the number of Latina/Latino elected officials but it will be difficult because those who hold power will only share it when it is inevitable and maybe not even then. I think the Latino vote will be pursued by the political parties and thereby give us increasing leverage on behalf of the community. Never again will anybody be elected president of the United States or to many other local, state, and national offices without the Latina/Latino vote. It is for this reason and no other that candidates are speaking their broken Spanish and promising to include us. Politicians from both parties will be making similar promises regarding immigration reform, employment, education, health care, and housing. Even though the Latino communities do not have the full potential of their voting power because many are undocumented, and others are permanent residents but not yet citizens, the future impact of the Latino vote will be enormous. We now have within our hands the capacity to not only determine elections but to run candidates who care about the community.

In a series of polls taken by the *New York Times* and CBS News prior to the 2004 presidential election, we gain an insight as to what concerns us. What is immediately clear is that there is more than one Latino community present; there is no monolithic comunidad Latina. Although they favor Democrats on most domestic issues such as education, the economy, and job creation, they gave high marks to Mr. Bush for leadership and backed the Republicans on tax cuts, opposition to abortion, and gay rights. Latinos have traditionally supported government programs as a safety net and to provide a bulwark against the excesses of big business. The results of this poll testify to that faith in government, 75 percent were in favor of larger government as opposed to 40 percent of the general population and a surprising 46 percent said they trusted the government in Washington to do the right thing. On issues like school vouchers and tax cuts rather than balancing the budget and Mr. Bush's leadership, they were favorable to Republicans. The favorable rating of Mr. Bush, 52 percent compared to 38 percent unfavorable, was good news for those planning his re-election campaign. In 2000, Mr. Bush received 34 percent of the Latino vote; advisers to the campaign say that Mr. Bush needed 40 percent of the Latino vote in 2004.[41] In fact Bush received 37 percent of the Latino vote in 2004.

This poll was a good indication of how the powerful can succeed in shaping a political message so that even the less powerful and powerless believe it. It is difficult to see how a majority of the Latina/Latino respondents backed tax cuts over a balanced budget given their tax bracket and income. An amazing 47 percent of the respondents reported incomes of under $30,000 in comparison to 27 percent for non-Hispanics—they will get almost nothing from the tax cuts. According to Citizens for Tax Justice using data compiled by the Congressional tax staff and the IRS, despite Mr. Bush's claims that the average family would get a $1,083 tax cut, 80 percent of families will get less than $1,000 and most will receive less than $300. Between the years 2001–2010, the richest 1 percent will receive a tax cut totaling $477 billion. This averages out to $342,000 for each of the best off during this decade; if the tax reductions are fully in place 52 percent will go to the top 1 percent whose average 2010 income will be $1.5 million. All of this is happening at a time when 75 million Americans have been without health care some time during the past two years. In addition the latest public relations ploy of sending out millions of tax rebate checks of $300 per child never mentioned that millions of children of the poor who pay no taxes were excluded.[42]

We Latina women and Latino men are not immune to the power of the story of capitalism and its ability to take us over. The powerful, the less powerful, and the powerless are all caught in the same sacred story of capitalism in the service of incoherence. The poor want what the rich have and they will continue to dream of America as the land of opportunity.

We need Latina women and Latino men who are not the usual politicians but political innovators. A political innovator is someone who is rooted in their own authentic self, the deepest sacred source, and in the community to assist in bringing about a new and more creative turning point in the history of our community by enacting a politics of justice and love. In this sense they are radicals, people connected to the underlying sources, the roots of reality. They know the flow of archetypes, not the fix of labels. Terrorists throw bombs out of despair; radicals get to the source of the problem by uprooting the causes of hopelessness. They can discern the signs of the time as prophets who know in their bones that there is something amiss and warn that we need to step forward now. They are also philosophers who interpret the signs of the time and provide guidance for us. Finally, political innovators are those women and men who respond to a situation that challenges our humanity by bringing to fruition new forms of justice and compassion.

9. The Politics of Education: The Most Important Civil Rights Issue Facing La Comunidad Latina

We are now as a nation in the midst of the largest wave of immigration in the history of the United States with the majority coming from Latin America. Demographic estimates are stating that by the year 2050 due to a high birth rate and high numbers of immigrants fully 25 percent of the population of the United States will be from a Latino background. This is truly an astounding demographic projection. This causes concern for some in the African-American community who see their status as the primary community of color being eclipsed and their place taken by la comunidad Latina. Many, but by no means all, European Americans find this development to be unsettling since they will no longer be the dominant majority when compared to communities of color taken together. Many Latinas and Latinos take pride in their growing numbers and strength.

At the same time that we are witnessing the amazing growth of the Latino community there are urgent civil rights issues that require our immediate response. The most serious civil rights issue that touches all aspects of the community is that of education. We know that nationwide the failure of Latino children to finish high school hovers around 30 percent. This lack of educational achievement is taking place at a time when the U.S. has gone from experiencing the greatest rate of sustained economic growth in our history to an economy nervous about reliable oil supplies, scandals in the business community, and the uncertainties brought about by possible recession, war, and terrorism. The $1.35 trillion tax cut voted in 2001 and the $356 billion tax cut passed in 2003 as requested by Mr. Bush favor the upper 5 percent of American citizens. There was no money in the budget for 2004 to assist the states that were facing

256

a collective shortfall of $45 billion and a projected gap of $60 to $85 billion for next year. This fiscal crisis is hitting the poor the hardest. Two-thirds of the states are cutting Medicaid benefits, increasing co-payments, restricting eligibility, and even removing poor people from the rolls due to soaring costs and low revenues.[1] For the first time since the government began to measure poverty the country experienced four consecutive years (2000–2004) of an increase in the rate of poverty. The poor grew from 31.6 million to 37 million. In 2004 the poverty rate for Latinos stood at 21.9 percent in contrast to whites at 8.6 percent.[2] These facts highlight the underlying inability of capitalism to respond with justice and compassion to the needs of our citizens and, in this case, the needs of the Latino community. The hi-tech aspect of our economy continues to eclipse the manufacturing sector and opens up more jobs in the service sector that usually bring lower wages, little or no benefits such as health care, and little or no job security. This means that education, especially higher education, is the highest priority for la comunidad Latina in the U.S. It is not just any kind of education that I am speaking of here, but rather that kind of education that not only provides us with skills, but also raises fundamental questions about who we are as a community and where we are going as a society.

La Comunidad Latina and Educational Levels

During the past twenty-five years the numbers that tell the story of educational levels for Latinas and Latinos are discouraging. In 1980 according to the U.S. Census Bureau, 44 percent of Latinos twenty-five years of age or older had completed high school and in 2004 it was only 58.4 percent. This is in comparison to 85.8 percent of whites and 80 percent of African Americans. Latinas/Latinos with a college degree or more only grew from 7.6 percent in 1980 to 12.1 percent in 2004, while whites went from 17.1 percent to 28.2 percent and African Americans went from 8.4 percent in 1980 to 17.6 percent between 1980 and 2004.[3] In 1998, 8.9 percent of those enrolled in college were Latinas/Latinos, 1,316,616 students out of a total enrollment of 14,791,224. Of the Latino students enrolled in college, 40 percent were enrolled in junior colleges and it was discovered that Latino students who began their college career at a two-year college were more likely to drop out. Ninety percent of Latina/Latino students require remedial courses in math. In its most recent report the American Council on Education cited immigration status, language barriers, migrant worker family, lack of finances, family responsibilities, and insufficient ESL and bilingual programs in elementary and secondary schools as reasons for the low rates of higher education completion by Latinos.[4]

The educational levels of Latinas/Latinos twenty-five years of age or older remain very low. If we take the number of men and women with less than a ninth grade education (5 million) together with those who have a ninth to twelfth grade education (3,600,000) but no diploma, and those with a high school diploma or equivalency (4 million), we end up with almost 13 million out of a total number of 18 million. This means that 13 million or 66 percent of Latinas/Latinos who should be at or nearing the top of their earning power have no college education. This translates into considerably lower wages and a dramatic lessening for possibilities of promotion.[5]

Throughout the nation because of the initiatives set in motion by the "No Child Left Behind Act" of the current administration school districts are feeling the pressure to do well in test scores to avoid having their schools labeled as failing. According to the guidelines sent out by the Department of Education when a school fails to show improvement after it has been given corrective funding, its students can choose to go elsewhere taking valuable dollars with them. In order to hide falling graduation rates and dropouts, school districts in Miami and Houston are being accused of "pushing out" students who make them look bad.

In New York City there continues to be much concern over the testing of underachieving students and the pressure put on schools by a mayor who wants to be known as the education mayor. Some schools are accused of giving up on students and of pressuring them to leave in order to make the system look good. These students are then pushed into underfunded alternative programs. Most of the dismissed students simply drift away from education. The New York City school system has developed code numbers that designate why students have left school. For example, at Lane High School on Jamaica Avenue in Brooklyn, where 90 percent of the students live in poverty, there are about 1,400 students who are discharged per year and the number is growing. When students are discharged under Code 89, transferred to alternative high schools, there is no follow up to see if they are actually attending. Four other codes hide what is really happening to the young who are pushed out: Code 31, 32, 36, and 38 transfer students to other programs. Code 36 provides the following reason why a student has left: "enrolled in a high school equivalency program outside the New York City school system." Students who were interviewed were unaware of their rights and spoke of being treated rudely, stating that nobody cared about them. When they were transferred to GED programs they sat around playing cards and watching videos with teachers handing out an assignment a couple of times a day; there were no classes in English or science. Age was another big issue. By law a student can enroll until the age of twenty-one. Students who were below their grade level for their age were "encouraged" to leave. While acknowledging that the practice of pushing students out has been going on in recent years, Joel Klein, the chancellor of education for New York City, has vowed to put an end to this practice. A lawsuit brought by Advocates for Children on behalf of the students at Franklin K. Lane High School has two basic goals: to get the youth back in school and to raise public awareness that all students have a legal right to remain in school until the age of twenty-one.[6]

The majority of Latinas and Latinos live in urban areas that lack the necessary funds to provide the kind of education that will allow a level playing field. For example, in New Jersey there are thirty-one districts, the Abbott Districts, that have been determined by the courts to have special needs. The name "Abbott Districts" came from the landmark case of a mother, Ms. Abbott, who in 1985 sued the State of New Jersey because the Newark School District failed to provide her child with a "thorough and efficient education" as the State Constitution promised all students. Ever since other school districts were named Abbott Districts when they met certain criteria based on need. The basic philosophy of the effort has been to close the achievement gap between suburban and urban schools. Since the funds for education come primarily from property taxes poorer districts do not have the resources to meet the needs of their students. Additional monies to remedy the inequity in funding come by matching per pupil spending of the state's most wealthy districts for those districts that are property poor. Not surprisingly the majority of poor urban school districts are where we also find the majority of our Latino students.[7] There are similar problems in forty states that are under court orders to provide more funds for school districts that are at a disadvantage when compared to suburban schools.[8]

The New Jersey State Legislature under court order to address the financial needs of the thirty districts passed a bill in 2000 that would make available $6 billion to rebuild the schools that are literally crumbling in the special needs districts. But the only way that the legislators could get the bill passed was by giving even the richest school districts funds to expand or refurbish their schools. However, in April 2006, because of the falling economy, the state declared that the funds to build new schools were gone which left school districts like Newark unable to complete their building program.

Déjà Vu All Over Again

Unlike many previous immigrant waves the current Latina/Latino immigrants are no longer going only to the large urban centers; increasingly we are experiencing the arrival of *recien llegados*, recently arrived immigrants, in small towns throughout the country. They are coming because there are jobs in agriculture, landscaping, roofing, construction, and the food industry such as the Tyson Corporation as well as the usual jobs in restaurants, hotels, and domestic service. As a result, all the battles fought over bilingual education, ESL, and the access of undocumented children to an education in the public schools have to be fought again. The influx of Latina/Latino students particularly in rural areas has left school districts across the country short of people qualified to teach the students English. School dropout rates for Latinos soared to more than 50 percent during the 1990s, especially in the South and Southwest where the schools were overwhelmed by the rapid influx of Latino students.[9] The number of students with limited English skills has doubled to five million since 1993. So great is the need that the Office of Bilingual Education, since renamed the Office of English Language Acquisition, provided $400 million to help school districts throughout the country put candidates through college or to get training in ESL or to acquire a bilingual license. Up to $665 million was to be spent to meet the needs of the schools. In Duplin County, North Carolina, Latino children are already nearly a third of the 700 students in Rose Hill–Magnolia Elementary. Their parents have come from Honduras and Mexico for jobs in turkey packing, picking tobacco, and feeding and breeding hogs. Many local residents are alarmed by the newcomers and need to be reminded that the education of children, documented or not, is a right protected by law.[10]

Throughout New Jersey there are newly established communities of Latinos who are being hired into the booming construction and landscaping industries. Many are arriving daily from Ecuador, Guatemala, and Mexico. The Latino population in New Jersey grew an amazing 51 percent between 1990 and 2000 to a total of 1,117,191 in comparison to African Americans who increased 10.1 percent for a total of 1,141,821.[11] It is estimated that there are as many as another 400,000 who are here without documents. Many cannot speak English, have little education, and few resources. Their children require ESL and bilingual instruction but many of the small school districts are slow to respond even though state law requires these programs and both state and federal funds are available. In many cases there is a hostile attitude that creates a political and psychological unwillingness to respond to their needs.

In small towns throughout New Jersey many school districts practice an unofficial policy of denial. When a school district is forced to respond because of state law, it often does so reluctantly, doing the bare minimum. As a result of their outsider status in the community and their academic problems in the schools, the danger of dropping out is very high for Latina/Latino students. In addition there is alcohol abuse, fighting, drugs, and other forms of self-wounding as ways of escaping and compensating for the brutality of capitalism and racism that they face. Conversations with Latina and Latino students reveal that they feel at risk both physically and emotionally. They were initially harassed by the African-American students and then by the white students. Some teachers see them as outsiders who are the responsibility of the ESL and bilingual teachers. Others are openly hostile and do not want them here. One of the local school boards recently cut a very successful Kinder-Plus program that did an excellent job in addressing the academic needs of Latino and other bilingual children. It was a political decision recommended by the superintendent of schools who became very uncomfortable when European-American parents protested that it was unfair to run an all-day program for students needing bilingual instruction when their children were limited to half a day. The superintendent failed to protect the Latina/Latino and other children in need of bilingual instruction. He could have defended the program by letting the public know that it was funded by the state and federal governments to prevent students from failing due to a lack of English skills. He did not want to risk his job for the sake of the most vulnerable students.

Plyler v. Doe: *The Right to Education*

In *Plyler v. Doe* the United States Supreme Court made an extraordinarily important decision that has since impacted the lives of

millions of Latina/Latino youth. In 1982 a Texas statute that with-
held state funds from local school districts for the education of undocumented children and denied the children the right to enroll
was ruled unconstitutional because it violated the Equal Protection
Clause of the Fourteenth Amendment that provides that no state
"shall deny any person within its jurisdiction the equal protection of
the laws." Justice John Brennan delivered the decision for the Court.
Justice Brennan went on to say that in his opinion, "Public education has a pivotal role in maintaining the fabric of our society and to
sustaining our political and cultural heritage; the deprivation of education takes an inestimable toll on the social, economic, intellectual, and psychological well-being of the individual, and poses an
obstacle to individual achievement."[12]

Perhaps the most serious challenge to the well-being of the *recien llegados* is the failure of school districts to enforce the law. The
New Jersey Department of Education needed to remind school districts, especially in the southern part of the state, that it is against
the law to ask students about their immigration status when they
come to register. It was disturbing to discover that many school administrators and the school board do not know the law and some
were not aware of *Plyler v. Doe*, but ignorance of the law is no ex-
cuse. The State of New Jersey is obligated to protect the right of undocumented students to a free public education. Besides this violation of federal and state law, some high schools were discouraging
students who were eighteen and older from registering. By state law
a person has the right to enroll in their local high school until the
age of twenty-one. The school district is within its rights in asking
that registering students establish residency in the school district by
requiring various documents such as a public service bill, a rent re-
ceipt, or evidence of a mortgage payment. But they are not allowed
to try to determine the immigration status of the student either directly or indirectly by asking leading questions. Various kinds of
intimidation have mobilized the Latino community that felt that
school districts were and in some areas continue to disobey the law
by not protecting the rights of the undocumented students. This
struggle in small towns in New Jersey is symptomatic of the kinds
of problems that are being confronted by the new immigrants
throughout the country.

As a result of these kinds of troubles Latina/Latino students are
at risk of dropping out. They face the difficulty of learning English,
conflict with other students, a lack of concern on the part of school
administrators and faculty, domestic problems, depression, fear of

their parents being deported, low-paying jobs, the hostility of the community, and conflict with the police. All of these issues need an immediate response. But by whom? We need deeply caring people in all communities. There are many, yet the response is often, if well meaning, fragmented with no overall strategy of how to go about building a community, a new community which includes all groups as equally valuable. As some in the community made efforts to address the concerns of the Latinos most at risk, we discovered that we cannot speak of a Latino community in these towns; we need to distinguish between the *recien llegados* and older Mexican, Puerto Rican, and Cuban communities that have been here for several generations and in the case of the Mexican community for sixteen generations.

Throughout the United States there are Chicano, Puerto Rican, Cuban, and some more recently arrived Latino groups such as Peruvians, Nicaraguans, and Colombians, who are fairly well established. These more recent communities continue to have problems but what is important to note is their response to the newest Latino groups. Throughout New Jersey there are at least three established Latino communities. The Puerto Rican community has been here for more than fifty years. Many are now successful and have professional jobs. Their children often do not speak Spanish and know little of their Puerto Rican roots. The Colombian community has been here for about fifteen years and is fairly well off economically but does not associate with the Puerto Rican community because of matters having to do with race and class. They have maintained, for the most part, a bilingual and bicultural community and their children do well in the schools. The Cubans, the majority of whom came between 1959 and 1975, are doing very well educationally, economically, and politically. Then there are the *recien llegados*. Most of these men and women and a growing number of school age children literally come every day having been attracted by the jobs and relatives who are here working. The majority are from Ecuador, Guatemala, and Mexico. The majority do not speak English, are undocumented, and have a wide range of marketable skills.

Most of the hostility against Latinas and Latinos in the towns is aimed against this newest community. So in the case of the *recien llegados* we have a classic case of discrimination based on race and class, not only by the dominant white group but also coming from some in the older Latino groups. Recently an established Colombian spoke of the Ecuadorians in racist terms, saying that he was alarmed by the arrival of so many Ecuadorians who act like animals and are mostly Indians. This comment reflects the racism and classism found in Latin America where many still want to identify only with their Spanish heritage and consider their indigenous roots to be inferior. And yet this same person responded very generously when he learned about a Latino man who was homeless. He took this man into his home and cared for him until he could get on his own feet. Hopefully there is already in this Latino man a contradiction between what he says and how he acts when faced with a real human being who ceases to be a stereotype.

Some in the Puerto Rican community who have found a degree of acceptance in the towns have mixed feelings about the *recien llegados*. Because many of them no longer speak Spanish very well they feel embarrassed because the recently arrived remind them of how they have become Americanized. Their children who speak even less Spanish and know very little if anything of their own heritage do not identify with the new Latina and Latino students in the schools and tend to shun them. The Ecuadorian, Mexican, and Guatemalan students are very much aware of this and feel resentful.

This split within the Latino communities has serious repercussions. Many of the well-established Latinas and Latinos are not as concerned about special programs for the new Latinos especially bilingual and ESL classes. The older Latino communities do not feel the need for these programs since their children are fluent in English. Also since they have settled into the wider community they do not want to open up old wounds that remind them of the hurt that they experienced when they first arrived. As a result when there was a recent controversy over bilingual and ESL issues in the schools the established Latino communities were reluctant to speak out and, as a matter of fact, knew very little about the inner workings of ESL and bilingual education and of how these programs were being implemented in the school system. Some in the Puerto Rican, Cuban, and Colombian communities are suspicious of these programs because they see them as working against the assimilation of Latino children into the mainstream of American society. Yet the primary goal of the ESL and bilingual programs is to mainstream or transition students as soon as possible into the regular curriculum.

Thus, when these programs were cut back, there was little if any resistance from the established Latino communities. The only ones who protested were caring teachers, most of whom are white, who were able to get some of the affected parents to speak out at school board meetings. But many of these parents are undocumented, do not speak English, and are single-parent working mothers or fathers who usually do not want to get involved in school politics for obvious reasons. These parents feel intimidated and together with their deference to and fear of authority as well as their problems with immigration they are very reluctant to confront school authorities. The parents feel that they have very little ability to determine or change official school policies. The way that the newly arrived Latinas and Latinos are treated by the schools is similar to the kind of reception that they receive from the other institutions in the community. Because of cultural and language issues some police are not very good at relating to the community. Some law enforcement personnel and other figures of authority assume that all Latinos are here illegally, take American jobs, and put a strain on the resources of the community. This kind of attitude places the civil rights of the newly arrived in jeopardy. They are never certain when a city ordinance is enforced if it is justified.

Recently the Latino community in Bound Brook, a town about forty-five minutes from Trenton, the state capital, accused the city fathers of carrying out inspections of their boarding homes and businesses as a form of harassment. There is evidence that Latino homes and places of commerce were singled out for special attention. Inspectors began showing up at late hours, a practice almost never used, to see if they could catch people in violation of residence codes. In addition, due to the floods that took place in the area, the Latino community found evidence that it was being denied the kind of federal and state grants that were available because some wanted to push the Latino businesses out of the town to less desirable locations.[13] Social agencies that serve a growing number of Spanish-speaking clients have few employees who speak Spanish. Health care agencies wait for the community to come to them rather than aggressively seeking out persons who need assistance. As a result this leaves the most recent arrivals at risk.

I believe that what is happening in the towns and cities in central New Jersey typifies what is taking place in small cities and towns throughout the country. In places that most of us have never heard of before such as Eybee, Tennessee, Mexicans came to work due to the demand for field workers. The migrant workers asked to have their children go to the local schools but their request was denied because the townspeople were afraid that the Mexicans might stay. In places like Rogers, Arkansas, the population of Latinos went from 400 in 1990 to 4,000 in 1998. In states which we usually do not identify with Latinas and Latinos there has been an amazing increase: 102 percent growth of la comunidad Latina in Georgia, 150 percent in Arkansas, and 110 percent in North Carolina.[14]

Currently in the U.S. fully 14 percent of all high school and grade school students are Latinas and Latinos, that is, a total of 7.1 million young people. This makes even more urgent the concern over the nationwide dropout rate for the Latino community. This danger for the future of our youth and the good of the nation as a whole will continue to grow in the years ahead. Latinas and Latinos are the youngest, fastest growing population in the nation. Almost all Latino parents want their children to learn English without losing their Spanish. The community does not equate linguistic loyalty with political loyalty. What most want is not *either/or* English or Spanish, but *both/and* Spanish and English. So why are Latinas and Latinos suffering from continuing exclusion from the dominant society? The usual studies identify three causes: poverty, language problems, and cultural barriers. These are nice terms for the harsh reality of discrimination based on racism and classism.

LA COMUNIDAD LATINA: OBSTACLES TO TRANSFORMATION

In order to go beyond mere numbers and to determine what is happening in the Latino community in their struggle to achieve excellence in education, our theoretical perspective allows us to ask what is happening on the deeper level in the lives of Latinas and Latinos. The most important question that we can ask is: "In the service of what way of life are Latinos and Latinas relating to the cultural stories of their heritage and to the issues facing them in this country?" And we also need to ask: "In the service of what ultimate way of life and sacred source are people in the dominant society relating to the Latino community?" There are four fundamentally different ways as we have seen by which people in the larger society and Latinas and Latinos are connecting to themselves, to one another, to the struggles that they face, and to the deepest source of their lives.

Latina women and Latino men were raised in the story of uncritical loyalty that caused us to be afraid of being disrespectful of our elders. We thus practice with our political faces a politics of unquestioning loyalty to others in authority. Because we exercise our historical faces out of a politics of loyalty and a personal life of self-denial we carry on the tradition as mere transmitters as we repeat the stories and way of life of our heritage. This kind of respect, obedience, deference, and loyalty is blessed by the lord of emanation who holds us within the container of ultimate truth.

Because some of us remain caught in the first act of the core drama of life there is nostalgia for what we left behind, a golden past and culture that must be preserved no matter what in this nation. This is the group that is living in the past and sees any relationship with the dominant culture as a loss. All the truth was revealed in Mexico, Puerto Rico, or in the Puerto Rican or Chicano barrios of this country, Ecuador, Cuba, El Salvador, or other Latin American nation. Parents within this way of life resist learning English or the customs and culture of the main society as a form of cultural resistance. They urge their children to be suspicious of the culture of this society that threatens to strip them of their identity. The result of this is a longing for security within the Latino culture.

Coming to this country or coming into contact with the wider society profoundly undermines the validity of truths given once for all. U.S. society allows people to question and to confront authority in order to prepare people to live a life based on competition. When Latino students experience this kind of alternative, it leads to new ideas and inspirations that cannot be repressed since they continue to raise new possibilities that can lead to an awakening of their inner self. If they take these new feelings seriously and act upon them it leads to conflict with those who want to keep them loyal and obedient.

When students accept these new insights by acting on them it leads to rebellion; they break connections with those who want to continue to embrace them and possess them as extensions of themselves. In the midst of the struggle to break away from tradition, many feel guilt because they have not yet succeeded in freeing themselves on the deeper level from the stories that are acted out in the service of emanation. All too often the "god" to whom our parents prayed and who is going to punish us is this false lord of emanation who inspires us to remain in the container of eternal security.

But we have not only come to another country or to a different town or city. We are now in a different way of life being attracted by new and competing sacred stories that are inspired by a new source, the lord of incoherence. In the wider society of the United States freedom of expression and the pursuit of one's own dreams are given preference over the demands made by others. Whereas in the traditional Latino culture one was expected to be loyal, in American culture we are expected to become powerful as individuals and to see success as the ability to command more resources and to exercise power over others. This way of life that legitimizes the pursuit of self-interest and power has no or little use for loyalty; above all what counts is my ability to get ahead, to climb the ladder, to be aggressive and individual. Professional athletes have learned to say, "It's not personal; its business," after being loyal to a team that turns around and trades them before their market value declines

Latinas and Latinos have for generations been caught in this *choque de las culturas,* the clash of cultures, living between the conflict of fundamentally different sacred sources, stories, and ways of life. On the one hand there are Latino parents who demand that their children remain loyal to the language and culture of their Latin American heritage. "En mi casa solamente se habla Español," In my house you only speak Spanish, is a command which many of us heard as we fought to make it into the dominant culture. But on the other hand, our parents realized that we needed to succeed in this society. We had to learn how to navigate between two worlds by creating a new identity. Many chose to assimilate, a choice that remains a powerful option but which entails acting out a violence against one's self and one's culture by stripping yourself of those aspects which the powerful look down upon and to take on the stories and customs of the dominant.

Parents who see their children staying out late in order to participate in school activities, demanding certain kinds of clothes, and insisting on more personal freedom to go to social events like dances where they can meet persons of the opposite sex, see their authority, their culture, their past deteriorating in front of them. As a result these Latino parents are tempted to turn to violence. Here they are in this country often having difficulty getting a job, not knowing the language, and being bossed by men and women from a different culture who often treat them with condescension. The anger at this kind of lack of respect for them and their culture undermines the stories of patriarchy and uncritical loyalty and the way of life of emanation in which they were raised. The response can be domestic violence as parents move to assert themselves or it can lead to self-wounding, drugs, heavy drinking, promiscuity, and other forms of self-destruction.

The greatest danger for the Latino community as we move into the twenty-first century is that we will not see how our lives have become fragmented. Neither the way of life of emanation nor assimilating into the story of capitalism in the service of incoherence is the answer. Why is this? People like you and me cannot be fully present nor can we express in their fullness the four faces of our being. We repressed our personal faces and experiences because we were too committed to denying our own creativity and being unquestioningly obedient. In addition we extended this kind of deference to other powerful people in the community so we had no right to question. Within this life of repression with our political face we practiced a politics of uncritical loyalty to others. Because of this denial of self, we could not enact our historical face by creating a new or different history; we were programmed to repeat the stories, culture, and way of life given to us by others. We did not believe that we had a sacred face since the truth resided in a sacred source and his agents. As a result we were not present. This lack of being a self, a person, except as the embodiment of others means that we cannot respond to fundamentally new kinds of problems. Uncritical loyalty and repression robs us of our creativity, new consciousness, forbids us to create new connections to others in the outside world, and, most serious of all, disconnects us from the deepest source of transformation, the god of transformation, who is always dismissed by the true believers in our tradition as a temptation because they have the one true sacred authority, the lord of emanation, *Dios Todopoderoso*, God Almighty, who gives ultimate justification to existing authority.

But neither is the answer for Latina/Latino students to be found by joining the powerful through assimilation. As in the service of emanation, those who assimilate and join the powerful cannot respond to fundamentally new kinds of problems. Those who join the ranks of the dominant often have no clue as to who they are and therefore cannot know what is in their best interest. People are forced to hide their personal faces because in this way of life we live in an environment in which we cannot afford to be loyal as we compete for power. Thus nobody is willing to risk their personal self since it makes them vulnerable and therefore weakens them in the race against others. In this context people practice a politics of power that reduces all of our relationships to competition against others. Our historical face becomes dedicated to seeing time as money and opportunity to acquire more fragments of power as time goes on. Our sacred face is seduced into believing that success is a blessing from the lord of incoherence to whom we pray daily to send us a few more stocks and bonds.

Latina and Latino students who join the powerful by assimilation arrest their lives in the service of incoherence. By so doing they become increasingly more removed from the community and especially those who are in need. Too often successful Latinos and Latinas consider their own *compatriotas* to be responsible for and complicit in their own failure. Stereotypes used by white European Americans are now used by persons who at one time were members of the previously excluded community. The story of capitalism takes them over so that they lose their sense of compassion and justice. They are threatened by any changes which will adversely affect their ability to better their standard of living and they will not risk their hard earned status by standing with those who are most vulnerable.

Once we are caught by stories, especially capitalism, we become permanent rebels: rebelling against the powerful so that we can have their power and against those who are below us so that they will not be able to take our power. There is no end to this kind of obsession; it is the story of every immigrant group. Everybody becomes a victim of this story and way of life especially if we remain unconscious of it. Even the poor and excluded are attracted by this story and way of life because many feel that this is the only way to make it, to be a success, to be somebody. The powerful live with the anxiety that what they have will not be sufficient to sustain themselves in a world in which the only certainty is insecurity. But the less powerful and the powerless see no other alternative; they also want to be rich.

The inherent inability of those living in the ways of life of emanation and incoherence to face new problems opens up a new and worse way of life, that of deformation, which derails us from the journey of our lives into the abyss that makes life fundamentally worse. Now our personal face is no longer repressed or hidden as it is in the ways of life of tradition and power; our face is now erased, canceled out because we dared to want to be accepted into the society. We now experience a politics of anger, violence, revenge, and exclusion by those who see us as a threat. This is the kind of response that many Latina/Latino students experience as newcomers into a strange and unwelcoming environment. Historically as time goes on life becomes worse because too many fail to intervene against the violence of exclusion. The destructive sacred source of deformation inspires the dominant to feel justified and the victims to accept their fate as less than the powerful that opens up the abyss, *el infierno*, hell for everyone.

Those who feel that their power is being undermined no longer see this as a simple competition but as a struggle for power which often leads to collusion with the way of deformation that leads to destructive death. Capitalism under severe threat will kill and maim as our foremothers and forefathers who worked the mines in the Southwest realized. In places like Clifton and Morenci, Colorado, the mine owners did not hesitate to call out vigilantes and military troops to beat, shoot, and kill Mexican miners in the early years of the twentieth century who were on strike against inhumane conditions in the mines. This example also demonstrates how capitalism has and continues to collude with racism. After all, the Anglo mine owners did not consider Mexicans worthy enough as human beings to deserve better wages, housing, or working conditions. To justify their profits made at the expense of the humanity of the Mejicanos the powerful had to assert the inferiority of the Mexicans and thus they condemned the Mexican community to an economic and political indentured servitude. Yet it was not only the Mexican people but also the Anglos who lost their humanity in the enactment of the story of racism.[15]

Our students face a dilemma. They want to be accepted by their fellow students and yet they cannot ignore their experiences that say that there is something fundamentally wrong when others do not accept them and force them to assimilate. They are questioning and entering into rebellion against ways of life and stories blessed by the lords of emanation and incoherence who deny the sacredness of their lives. But they must not rebel in order to make some changes that are merely cosmetic. Our students are daily rebelling in the schools and getting into trouble. Often neither they nor the schools know why on the deeper level of their lives they are acting out. They need to break on the deeper level so that they go beyond mere rebellion against individuals. They need to participate in a more radical rebellion by breaking with the stories and ways of life and lords who prevent them from completing their journey.

Many of us as Latinas and Latinos have remained unaware that there is a better alternative, the way of life of transformation, and so we continue to live our stories and relationships in the context of the three ways of life of emanation and incoherence that collude with deformation. Many of us were raised to believe in traditional truth legitimized by the sacred source of emanation but we have since come to see that it has not allowed us to respond to the problems of our life. Others of us joined the powerful and found that in the process we had not just climbed the ladder to power but we forgot where we came from and turned against our own community when it became an obstacle to our self-interest. Many of us began by saying that: "When I make it I will look back and bring others with me." This has proved to be naive because the stories of capitalism allied with racism are not just social constructs that we can demolish by rational analysis and effort. No, these are sacred stories inspired by underlying sacred lords who take us over and possess us so that we lose control of our lives. Likewise when we believe that we merely have to reform a patriarchal marriage in the service of emanation by making it less repressive we end by making it more of a suffocating relationship that does not allow either the men or the women to come forth as whole human beings. We cannot reform destructive stories; the only remedy is to empty them out of our lives.

As we move into the twenty-first century Latinas and Latinos need to know and teach our youth that we have not only three but *four* fundamentally different choices from within which to create and live the stories of our lives and practice the four faces of our being. Our fourth choice is the way of life of transformation. In this way of life we are inspired not by the lords who would hold us in a fragment of the core drama of life as partial men and women; now we hear from the deepest source of transformation, the god of transformation. This sacred source invites us to complete the journey to discover who we are as a self. We are now free to create fundamentally more loving and just alternatives. Only in the service of transformation are the four faces of our being fully expressed because for the first time we are fully present in our lives. Once we have freed ourselves of ways of life that demand total obedience, the search for power, and the destruction of self and other in deformation, we can now create fundamentally more loving and just responses to the issues that we need to face. Like Celie in *The Color Purple* we now enter into Act III, Scene 1, enacting the story of the transforming self, as a whole person for the first time who can say with Celie: "I have love, I have friends, I have money and you coming home soon with my children. I have never been so happy."[16] Celie had freed herself from an abusive relationship with a patriarchal male who persistently erased her face while practicing a politics of violence that made history and time take a downward turn into hell. The money she now earned provided her with economic freedom from patriarchal control; it did not come from a corporation but from her own creative labor: she made clothes that fit the personality of the person for whom she tailored them. On her journey she was guided by Shug. But it was Celie who had to take the risk to let go of a relationship to which she had become accustomed. Celie had to fight back; she needed to find the strength within herself; nobody else could do this for her.

Cleofilas in *Woman Hollering Creek* similarly needed to discover that her own life was sacred so that she could generate the strength and the courage to refuse to live her life between her two neighbors, Soledad and Dolores, loneliness and pain, the twin towers of despair for Latina women for generations. She needed to confront not only her abusive husband, Juan Pedro, but also the story of patriarchy that had disabled her. Graciela and Felice, grace and joy, became her feminine guides guiding her toward a new destiny who replaced her fate-full companions. As she crossed the arroyo, Woman Hollering Creek, on her journey to a new life without Juan Pedro, she experienced a baptism, a rebirth, as she heard her companion, Felice, yell out with triumph as she witnessed to and assisted Cleofilas as she was reborn.[17] The yell was a *grito*, a shout of protest and resistance that replaced the sobs and cries of *la llorona*, the tears of the Latina woman as victim. Both Celie and Cleofilas refused to allow their personal face to be repressed, hidden, or canceled and chose to allow their faces to emerge in all of their fullness. With the political face of their being both women refused to practice a politics of uncritical loyalty, power, and violence and chose a politics of love and compassion; neither Cleofilas nor Celie sought revenge because it would be the continuation of the same deadly story. Cleofilas and Celie demonstrated that our historical face is not frozen in a deadly past, distorted by power, nor fated to make life worse, but that our history can be radically changed when we intervene to create our destiny, an open and more loving history. The sacred faces of their being were now connected to the deepest sacred source, the god of transformation who invites us to participate as co-creators in the ongoing completion of the cosmos.

Once we have been able to experience transformation in at least one aspect of our lives we can now reach out to others with the political and historical faces of our being and guide them through the core drama of life. This means always guiding them to their own inner voice, acknowledging our own confusion, recognizing that we do not have the answers, demonstrating a willingness to put ourselves out of business in regard to this particular issue and to enter into a relationship wherein we become guides to one another in the community. Transformation is a continuous process and we need one another to participate in the struggle to achieve justice and compassion.

AFFIRMATIVE ACTION IN THE SERVICE
OF TRANSFORMATION

With the kind of analytical capacity provided by the theory of
transformation we can reevaluate and question programs to determine their intent and whether or not they are for the good of the community. For example, Affirmative Action was put in place by the
Nixon Administration largely because of the civil rebellions in the
cities that took place following the assassinations of Martin Luther
King, Jr., and Robert F. Kennedy, the shutdown of the universities
throughout the country following the invasion of Cambodia in 1970,
and the general sense of discontent with authority throughout the
nation. This program was intended by the powerful to assimilate the
best and the brightest from communities of color so that we would
join the powerful and become allies of the dominant in giving our
communities hope. By credentialing women and men of color the
message that went out was that if everybody worked hard then there
was a very good chance, almost a guarantee, of becoming a success.
In theoretical terms it meant using the federal government as a buffer on behalf of the excluded to use the relationship of subjection to
force open the doors of opportunity, that is, the realms of autonomy
and direct bargaining power that gave access to privilege. The message of white America was: "We know what you want; you want
what we have and we are going to give you a chance to get it." They
assumed that once the best and the brightest students of color made
it the logic of power would take over: they would no longer identify
with their own kind but with those who have what they desire. This
is the forceful undertow of the sacred underlying way of life of incoherence. Once we are taken over by the stories of power and capitalism in the service of incoherence we belong to this story and
way of life. But we can subvert Affirmative Action. Rather than use
it to become part of the system we can bring to this program our
own agenda, to turn Affirmative Action around from below so that
we take the opportunity to bring about new forms of compassion
and justice for ourselves and others. Affirmative Action opens doors.
When we walk through the door it is up to us to make personal, political, historical, and sacred decisions as to what we are going to do
with the possibilities.

There are those who say that Affirmative Action is unconstitutional because it is based only on race and therefore discriminates
against those who are not one of the protected groups: African Ameri-

cans, Latinas/Latinos, Asian Americans, and Native Americans. The Supreme Court recently ruled in the case of the University of Michigan's undergraduate and law school admissions policies that there could be no automatic granting of points because an applicant is a member of a community of color but that race could be considered as one of the factors toward achieving diversity in admissions. The key issue is that the Court gave its blessing to diversity as a compelling issue when assembling a student body as long as there are no quotas. This also points out that discrimination based on race and ethnicity remain as very powerful forces in our society that cannot be ignored. Affirmative Action is intended to redress grievances from the past when the only action was *confirmative action,* that is, a system that consistently confirmed almost in a sacramental manner the sacred right of white males to higher education and the professions. For people of color it is a privilege to go to law school whereas for the powerful it is their right.

Many Fortune 500 corporations and the U.S. military academies together with the leading academic institutions in the country filed friends of the court briefs in support of the University of Michigan's admissions policies. The corporations and the service academies acknowledged that they could not have diversified their executives and officer corps without the push of Affirmative Action. Justice Sandra Day O'Connor, who wrote the decision for the majority in regard to the University of Michigan School of Law, stated the benefits of diversity in the classroom: "These benefits are substantial . . ." the law school's admissions policy promotes "cross-racial understanding," helps to break down racial stereotypes, and "enables students to better understand persons of different races." These benefits are important and laudable "because classroom discussion is livelier, more spirited and simply more enlightening and interesting" when the students have "[t]he greatest possible variety of backgrounds. . . . In order to cultivate a set of leaders with legitimacy in the eyes of the citizenry, it is necessary that the path to leadership be visibly open to talented and qualified individuals from every race and ethnicity. All members of our heterogeneous society must have confidence in the openness and integrity of the educational institutions that provide this training. . . . Access to legal education (and thus the legal profession) must be inclusive of talented and qualified individuals of every race and ethnicity, so that all members of our heterogeneous society may participate in the educational institutions that provide the training and education necessary to succeed in America."[18]

Affirmative Action has already greatly helped to create a La-
tina/Latino middle class and professional elite. But we need to remove class from the process, that is, not all Latina/Latino students
and students of color need Affirmative Action. There should be a
means test connected to Affirmative Action so that people of all
backgrounds have an equal opportunity.[19] We need to avoid becoming members of the power elite. As in chapter 7 professionals in the
community need to ask: "In the service of what way of life am I
practicing law, medicine, teaching, business, or engineering?" Once
we have been given access to the power relations of U.S. society, autonomy and direct bargaining, we can make a decision to use our tal-
ents in the service of justice and compassion.

FOUR RADICALLY DIFFERENT KINDS OF EDUCATION

Education is a personal, political, historical, and sacred task.
Just as there are four kinds of love, patriotism, guides, and families
so, too, there are four fundamentally different kinds of teachers and
education. Education is a term that has its roots in the Latin word,
duco, to lead. Let us stay with this Latin root to consider the four
kinds of education. *Seduco* is the Latin root for the English word seduction; in the service of emanation the teacher as authority figure
seduces young people into believing that they have the only truth.
This kind of education prepares students to be permanent disciples
and followers who are reluctant to challenge authority. It is a deeply
repressive education that leads to self-denial and the inability of the
student to think with creative imagination since there is nothing
new. In the service of incoherence teachers train their students to
take power as their right and justify the domination of others through
competition. Thus they practice *reduco*, the reduction of all learning for the sake of power. In a liberal society it is assumed that the
competition is fair and therefore the best rise to the top. The most
destructive education, *deduco*, literally means to deduct from or to
diminish the humanity of others. Teachers who enact this kind of
education lead students to believe in fantasies based on race, class,
gender, or religion that justifies their superiority over others. The
only education that allows each of us to come forth in our wholeness is *educo*, to guide a student to their inner creativity so that
they can come forth to participate in the transformation of their society.[20]

The classroom is a political forum within which teachers can create an environment of unquestioning discipleship, competition for power, justification for treating others as less than human, or a context that encourages the creative imagination of each student. Each of us as we read of these four fundamentally different kinds of education can name on one hand those teachers who guided us to our own inner resources. Too many of our newly arrived students are feeling the pain of discrimination when they are isolated by school policies into special education, ESL, or bilingual classes where only the ESL and bilingual teachers are responsible for their success. In addition we seldom ask the question as to what kind of Latina or Latino is behind the surname, the skin color, the place of their birth, and their credentials that we are hiring to work in the schools. Only those who work for and with the community and who have an agenda which is open to all and who need each of us to be present with the fullness of our personal, political, historical, and sacred participation are guides in the service of transformation.

APPLYING THEORY TO PRACTICE: CANDIL DE LA CASA Y DE LA CALLE

I now want to provide examples of everyday life in our communities and how we can determine in the service of what way of life we are enacting the story of education by doing archetypal analysis. Archetypal analysis allows us to see the underlying meaning of the concrete reality that surrounds us. We can determine the deeper meaning, intent, ultimate value, and structure of what it is that we can and need to do together by discovering in the service of what way of life we are living the stories, the relationships, and the four faces of our being and where we are in the core drama of life.

At times we feel that we hardly know where to start because the task of transformation seems so formidable. So where do we begin? Tip O'Neill, the legendary master of Congressional politics from Massachusetts, stated that "All politics is local." We need to begin the process of transformation within the most local of politics, within our own lives and then the politics of our homes, there to face our own stories, relationships, the four faces of our being, where we are on our journey through the core drama of life, and in the service of what way of life we are practicing our life. We need to begin by practicing *jihad* within ourselves, the fight for justice in our personal lives and at home; then we are ready to practice transformation in the wider community. There is a saying in the Latino community, "Candil de la calle, oscuridad de la casa," meaning that we are the light of the world, a great guy to all around us, but at home a source of darkness, a dominant and controlling bully. In the following example I want to return to a small town in New Jersey to demonstrate that indeed all politics begins with local politics and further to illustrate the kind of struggle that goes on in daily life wherein we can be a source of light for both home and society. I have told the story of Esperanza elsewhere.[21] Let me summarize it here with an update since I last spoke with her.

Esperanza was raised in a family in which her mother and father lived the story of patriarchy that arrested her life for years in relationships and stories of dependency and frequent violence. She lived her life being faithful to others, practicing a politics of loyalty to her parents and especially her father. She was living stories and patterns which the women in her heritage had repeated for years. When Esperanza married she never left home, that is, she traded her patriarchal father for a patriarchal husband/father who was raised to accept the reality of male dominance in the story of patriarchy in the service of emanation as the only reality.

But Esperanza found the strength in herself to find a job and to begin to contribute to the family's income. This ability to learn and earn outside the home gave her a new sense of her capacity. She continued the struggle, never giving up on her marriage but also refusing to give up on her newfound sense of self. If Esperanza had remained living the stories of patriarchy and uncritical loyalty that carried with it the continuation of repression she could never have stepped forward to help the family financially at a crucial point. Emanation as a way of life and the stories of patriarchy and uncritical loyalty in its service could not respond to the new problems that the family faced. Esperanza could not go back to her life as a traditional wife and mother. Something had happened inside of Esperanza. She rediscovered the four faces of her being in a different way.

Esperanza was now ready to practice in the wider community the kind of politics of love and justice that she was enacting at home. She had become concerned about the new Latina/Latino immigrants in the community, the *recien llegados,* and the problems of discrimination their children were encountering in the school district. She learned in her struggle with patriarchal authority that it was also necessary to question the authority of a school system. Together with others Esperanza organized a successful Latina/Latino Youth Conference that was held for the first time in the history of the school district.

With this achievement Esperanza demonstrated that the political face of our being is always with us. She extended the politics of her own personal home to the wider arena of the politics of education in the community thereby practicing the politics of the family and the politics of the wider society as a continuum. The politics of male/female relationships, husband/wife and parent/children relationships are political relationships on the home front that prepare us for transforming life outside the home. In this way we become *candil de la casa y candil de la calle,* the source of light and creative action both at home and in the community.

The Ongoing Work of Transformation

Transformation is not a one-act drama. Many good things resulted from the first youth conference. The conference had become an annual tradition held on a Saturday in October. The first year was a triumph just to have it happen. The students were very happy about the event. The next three years saw some promising results. There was follow-up to the conferences that brought a series of presentations on Latina/Latino culture, history, and politics to the faculty, staff, and administrators in the school district. In addition for the first time in the history of the district there was a Latina/Latino youth organization formed at the high school, Adelante. There were frequent meetings between the superintendent and members of the community to discuss how to help the students succeed. A parent's group was being organized to monitor the progress of their children and to put an end to the isolation of parents and their children in the schools.

But the youth conference began to falter. The students were reluctant to come to school a sixth day especially because many had mixed feelings about the school that isolated them and considered them a problem. Many students could not come due to jobs and still others were not allowed to attend by protective parents. The conference was supported by the school district but it was too much like an extracurricular activity. To address these concerns one of the Latina women who worked with Esperanza came forward with a plan to make the conference an integral part of the school calendar. She argued that the conference and its attention to Latino culture, history, and politics should be shared with the entire school.

This was a brilliant political move because it brought the issue of inclusion to the heart of the school and education, the curriculum. A presentation was made to the school administration that agreed that the conference should be for the benefit of all the students and held during the school day as part of Latina/Latino heritage month and that school funds would be used to pay for it. A plan was developed to have faculty at the beginning of the school year include in their lesson plans Latino issues whether it be in literature, art, music, history, languages, science, and other subject matter. Faculty members volunteered to work with the committee in planning how to interweave aspects of la cultura Latina into their lesson plans. Together with this academic component, plans were made for a music and dance performance together with presentations highlighting the contributions of Latina women and Latino men to this country. For the past two years during Latino Heritage Month, Mariachis came to the high school. They literally electrified the school; they played the traditional Mexican music as they walked through the hallways; both teachers and students poured out of their classrooms to see and hear them. The Latino students began to feel included as an integral part of the school and their peers from other backgrounds related to them with a new kind of openness.

These efforts have been led by Latina and Latino professionals who have put into play the relationships of autonomy and the direct bargaining power that they achieved in the wider society. They chose not to enact these relationships in the service of incoherence for their own self-interest but to use them in the service of justice and compassion for the *recien llegados,* most of who are caught in powerless relationships of isolation and subjection in a society that is based on power. This is the kind of intervention that we need throughout the society in order to prevent deformation and bring about new opportunities for transforming life. This is a challenge that involves the four faces of our being. Latina women and Latino men looked at their own personal brown faces and remembered with their historical faces how they were hurt as youths because of their racial/ethnic identity and so they moved with the political faces of their being to open up a new history inspired by the deepest source of mercy and compassion to practice a politics of justice, inclusion, and love so that no child would ever be hurt this way again. This is an ongoing story of what Latina women and Latino men are capable of doing once the four faces of our being are free from the stories of capitalism and racism that disable us.

This story of struggle to obtain an education is an example of the fulfillment of the story of democracy. America at its best is not about capitalism and power that is in collusion with deformation; at its best America is about the story of democracy, a story in which each of us is sacred of the very nature of our being human. Let us look inside the story of democracy. The characteristics of this story by which we can identify its presence in our communities are as follows:

- Each person is valuable.
- Each of us needs to participate.
- We are free to break unbearable relationships.
- We can enact the four faces of our being in their wholeness.
- The power of the people rests upon conscious, critical, and creative responses to problems together with the deepest source of our being.
- Democracy recognizes an equality of needs and opportunities.
- It makes possible the formation of communities that act with justice and compassion.
- The story of democracy substitutes community for the state and self-interested power for full human capacity for each member of the community.
- The power of the people consists of entering into full dialogue with their own selves, others, and with the deepest sacred in order to confront problems.
- No person is complete until each of us is free to participate with the deepest source of transformation so that we can co-create responses to injustice.
- Both the sacred and we are transformed by practicing the story of democracy.
- Democracy creates an environment that enables each person to travel through the core drama of life again and again so that he or she is free to help others overcome poverty, injustice, and exploitation.

The story of democracy is so important today especially as a response to the twin stories of capitalism and tribalism that threatens to turn our youth into invisible and inferior objects who are accepted only if they assimilate and thereby agree that being white is preferable, who are in danger of being exiled or rejected if they are disloyal to the powerful, and who live with the possibility of being slowly exterminated by hostility, fear, and exclusion. A classic confrontation between the story of democracy and the racism of tribalism that can serve as a prototype of what is happening around the country took place in the town of Farmingville on Long Island. Two Mexican immigrant men, Israel Pérez Arvizu and Magdaleno Estrada Escamilla, were lured to a remote area by two men, Ryan D. Wagner and Christopher Slavin, thinking that they were being hired as day laborers; they were beaten almost to death. Wagner and Slavin were found guilty and sentenced to twenty-five years in prison. For a time it seemed as if things had gotten quiet but not necessarily better. Then the home of an immigrant family from Mexico was firebombed. They lived next door to the men who had been attacked.[22] Four white men were arrested for the firebombing. The response of the community demonstrates the choices that we have as citizens as we confront the changing face of America; one group, Sachem Quality of Life, a local hate group, through one of its leaders, Ray Wysolmierski, referred to illegal immigrants as terrorists: "We're trying to save this neighborhood, and they're saying we have to treat our invaders and occupiers with respect." Others enacted the story of democracy in response to this racism. Advocates for immigrants consisting of twenty-four advocacy groups spoke out and acted on behalf of the *recien llegados*. Patrick Young, chairperson of the alliance, made the very insightful statement that it was not just four young men who are at fault: "These young men grew up in an atmosphere where adults claiming to be speaking for the community depicted Latinos as criminals and terrorists."[23] This is the kind of atmosphere in which some of our students are attending local schools.

STRATEGIES OF TRANSFORMATION

In conclusion, I would like to offer some suggestions for strategies that people like you and I can realistically use to confront the challenge of education, the most important civil rights issue that la comunidad Latina faces in this new century.

We begin with our self, determined to live our stories, our relationship, and the four faces of our being in the service of the deepest source of transformation so that we can discover how we can participate in creating fundamentally better and more just schools in the communities in which we live.

We can organize and unite around the issue of education which is the most important challenge facing la comunidad Latina.

We must insist on systemic change which means recognizing that we need to participate in changing the whole community so that all of the institutions of the city, town, village are involved in responding to the needs of all the members of the community,

As we organize in the Latino community we need to simultaneously build coalitions with people of good will from all backgrounds; there will be no justice if we cannot achieve it for all groups in our community.

As we confront the challenge of education as the single most important civil rights challenge for the Latino community we need strategies for action. In order to avoid being summer soldiers and one-issue citizens, we need to avoid doing piecemeal reform. For example, if we have a conference for Latina/Latino students we cannot see this as a success because many came and heard good talks, shared Latino food, and a dance. We cannot say to the students, "We will see you next year at the next conference." Our students are in school daily facing academic problems, an undertow of hostility, the temptation to drop out, some uncaring teachers, peer groups that exclude them, fear of deportation, home situations that may be part of the problem, anger that might lead to drugs, drinking, and fighting that leads to brushes with the law and many other issues.

We as a community need to sustain our support which means the following: meet and speak with the students, make recommendations for the school curriculum, participate in the schools as a volunteer, offer to do in-service workshops or full-length courses on la cultura Latina and organize the parents in a Spanish-speaking PTA. We need to meet regularly with the superintendent regarding concerns of the community for our children, ask to use the schools in after school hours for functions sponsored by the community, go to school board meetings, and, above all, run members of the Latino community for the school board. As members of the community it is crucial for us to support day care centers and volunteer our services and if there are none, assist in putting one or several in place. Some of us can help to set up a mentoring program, arrange trips for Latina/Latino students to local colleges where Latina/Latino student organizations will be glad to host them and encourage them to go to college. Those of us who have the expertise can evaluate the ESL and bilingual programs, aggressively look for and help to hire bilingual teachers, administrators, counselors, and secretaries. Through our involvement in the schools we can find out who is dropping out and why so that preventive measures can be put in place. Ask to see the budget which is a public document, find allies among the teachers and administrators in the schools, organize Latina/Latino student organizations in the schools to have discussions about their history and culture, take students on educational trips to theatres, museums, libraries, build community pride and share our heritage with others.

We can set up scholarship funds for college, write articles for the school paper in Spanish and English and for the local town paper to share our culture. Steps need to be taken to communicate with the community to provide information in Spanish on local radio and television in regard to school closings, the school calendar for the year, essential documents for enrollment of children such as required inoculations and other necessary information. Mentoring and internship programs can open up access to the local library, police and fire departments, law firms, and other such agencies for Latina and Latino students. By establishing a tutoring program the older Latina/Latino students can take responsibility to work with younger students. In addition they can serve as volunteers to help clean littered town lots and participate in other civic work. To demonstrate their presence in the community Latina/Latino students and their parents can walk in the annual Memorial Day and July 4th parades wherein the different Latino groups can carry the American flag and the flag of their native country. We need to run our own candidates and support candidates for local office who will address the concerns of the community and help to build coalitions with other communities of color and all people of good will in the community. Finally, the local churches can be approached to provide space and resources to sponsor cultural events and educational workshops on health, drugs, liquor, gangs, male/female relationships, immigration, and other such concerns.

As I write these strategies I feel a sense of urgency because of the needs of the *recien llegados,* the most recent arrivals. Those of us who are middle-class professionals have a moral obligation to step forward to intervene before the newly arriving men and women experience the deformation of the story of racism often connected to capitalism. At a Summit Conference on Education in La Comunidad Latina held at Rutgers University I presented the following plan of action in Spanish; an English translation follows.

EL MAS IMPORTANTE DERECHO CIVIL EN EL SIGLO VEINTIUNO
ES LA EDUCACIÓN

Muy buenos días y bienvenidos a esta conferencia. Especialmente quiero reconocer a los padres y familiares de nuestros estudiantes Latinas/Latinos. Acerca del año 2050, 25% de la población de los EUA será Latina. Esto es algo estupendo. Pero a la vez que este dato nos da orgullo, nuestra comunidad Latina esta sufriendo un fracaso en la área de la educación. Por ejemplo, en Camden, New Jersey hasta 50% de los estudiantes dejan la escuela antes de graduar de la secundaria. Por toda la nación desde 32% hasta 50% de nuestros estudiantes dejan la escuela antes de acabar. Esta tragedia sucede al mismo tiempo que pasan grandes cambios en la economía del país:

- Las uniones no tienen el poder de antes para proteger a los trabajadores.
- Muchos trabajos en el sector de maniobra salieron del país.
- Los trabajos que quedan están en el sector hi-tech o el sector de servicios que no pagan bien y no ofrecen beneficios.
- Para conseguir los mejores trabajos se necesita una educación universitaria.

Aquí en el Estado Jardín de Nuevo Jersey la Legislatura pasó unas leyes dándoles mas fondos a los distritos educacionales mas necesitados, los Abbott Districts. Pero con la caída de la economía la mayoría de los fondos ya no existen. Esto daña a nuestros jóvenes. Especialmente porque a este momento llegan cada día Latinos de varios países Latino Americanos en nuestro estado. Buscan y encuentran trabajo en: construcción, agricultura, los casinos, restaurantes y trabajo doméstico. Desde 1990 hasta 2000 la población Latina del Estado aumento 34% hasta un millón tres cientos miles de personas. Y hay otros 400 cientos miles indocumentados en el estado. La comunidad Latina es la más joven y la más fértil de todo el país. Estos jóvenes requieren una educación que los prepare para el futuro. Pero muchos de ellos no hablan el idioma inglés y necesitan instrucción en Inglés como Segunda Lengua o Educación Bilingüe. Desgraciadamente cuando llegan, las escuelas no están preparadas para recibirlos y ayudarlos especialmente en las ciudades y pueblos chicos. A veces no hay maestros, secretarias, consejeros, ni administradores bilingües para ayudarlos. A veces ni hay un programa ESL. En ves de ayudar hay mucha discriminación. Nuestros jóvenes sin documentos encuentran en los salones de clase, en la cafetería, en la oficina principal, en los autobuses hostilidad, insultos y pleitos. ¿Que es lo que podemos hacer?

Estrategias de Transformación

- Es necesario enfrentar a esta situación unidos.
- Tenemos que formar Círculos Mutualistas.
- Las comunidades Latinas establecidas tienen que dar la mano a nuestras hermanas y hermanos, los recien llegados.
- Ya unidos tenemos que conocer nuestros derechos.
- La ley del estado y federal dicta que las escuelas no pueden investigar ni averiguar si uno es ciudadano o sin documentos.
- Cuando hay un grupo de 25 estudiantes que hablan un idioma extranjera como su única idioma se requiere un programa bilingüe.
- También por ley del estado cada programa bilingüe tiene que tener un grupo de padres como consejeros.
- Nosotros tenemos el derecho de enfrentar la discriminación y reportarla a los oficiales del distrito y del estado.
- Tenemos el derecho de organizar un grupo de la comunidad y demandar una cita con los varios oficiales del distrito hasta el supervisor o de la junta ejecutiva que le dicen, *school board,* para oír y responder a nuestras quejas *y no salir de la junta hasta que haya un plan de acuerdo para implementar los cambios necesarios.*
- Tenemos que organizar conferencias como ésta para educar a los maestros de nuestros hijos en los detalles de nuestras culturas e historias.
- Juntos tenemos la capacidad de enfrentar el racismo en el currículo.
- Tenemos que asistir a la junta ejecutiva del distrito.
- Tenemos que insistir que el distrito de empleo a maestros, secretarias, consejeros y administradores de nuestra raza o por lo menos personas que tengan buena voluntad.

Finalmente en estos días de tanta necesidad y peligro por nuestra comunidad Latina buscamos mujeres y hombres fuertes para enfrentar la injusticia. Quiero repartir con ustedes los requisitos para ser una mujer Latina y un hombre Latino en el servicio de la transformación:

- regresar y reconectarse con las venas abiertas de nuestro antepasado para aliviar a nuestros mismos y ayudar a nuestra comunidad aliviarse;
- redescubrir que su mismo es sagrado;
- crear relaciones de igualdad y mutualidad entre mujeres y hombres;
- rechazar la mentira que no hay nada que nosotros podemos hacer para mejorar nuestra vida;
- regresar dentro de nuestros mismos para descubrir nuestra identidad;
- voltear nuestro coraje hasta la fuerza para crear una vida mas justa y amplia;
- redescubrir nuestro cuerpo, la naturaleza, emociones, sentimientos, el femenino y la fiesta como búsqueda de comunidad;
- de educarnos y rechazar las mentiras sobre nuestra cultura y reeducarnos para reconocer que nosotros juntos con la fuente mas honda de nuestra vida, el dios de la transformación, podemos recrear nuestra sociedad con justicia y compasión.

Y ya estamos listos el hombre Latino junto con la mujer Latina para enfrentar la injusticia en la sociedad. Juntos tenemos que combatir el racismo y la discriminación contra la raza. Estos días en el área de la educación hay una necesidad bastante grande para que nosotros entremos a las oficinas de los jefes para declamar que las escuelas no están educando nuestros jóvenes. Y entonces levantar un plan de acción para mejorar la situación.

Si nosotros participamos en estas estrategias concentrando en la educación de nuestros hijos esto sería tocar todos los aspectos del bienestar de nuestra comunidad. La política de la transformación nos requiere siempre luchar para la justicia. La política de la transformación nos dirige al próximo paso en nuestra jornada siempre preguntando qué es lo que tenemos que hacer para llevar a cabo una sociedad dedicada a la justicia y la compasión?

Muchísimas gracias.

¡Y que viva la Raza![24]

The Greatest Civil Rights Challenge for the Twenty-first Century Is Education

Good morning and welcome to this conference. I want to especially recognize the parents of our Latino students. Around the year 2050, 25 percent of the population of the United Status will be Latino. This is quite extraordinary. At the same time that this gives us reason for pride our community is suffering from a disaster in the area of education. For example, in Camden, New Jersey, over 50 percent of the students leave school before they graduate from high school. Throughout the country from 32 percent to 50 percent of our youth leave school before graduation. This tragedy is taking place at the same time that the American economy is undergoing radical change:

- Unions don't have the power they once had to protect the rights of workers.
- Many maufacturing jobs have left the country.
- The jobs that remain are in the hi-tech realm or in the service sector that do not pay a living wage and have no or poor benefits.
- In order to get the best jobs a university education is required

Here in the State of New Jersey the legislature passed a law to provide more funding for those school districts most in need, the Abbott Districts. But because of a faltering economy the majority of the funding is no longer available. This places our children at risk. Currently the situation is even more dire because Latino youth are daily arriving from various Latin American countries. Their parents look for and find jobs in the following areas: construction, landscaping, the casinos, restaurants, and domestic work. From 1999–2000 the Latino population in the state grew by 34 percent. Currently there are 1,300,000 with another estimated 400,000 undocumented Latinos living in New Jersey. The Latino community is the youngest and the fastest growing ethnic group in the nation. These young people need an education that is going to prepare them for the future. But many of them do not speak English and need instruction in English as a Second Language or Bilingual Education. Unfortunately when they arrive many schools are not prepared to accept them and help them, especially in the small towns of the state. At times there are no bilingual teachers, counselors, secretaries, or administrators to help them and there isn't even a bilingual program. Instead of getting help they often face discrimination. Our undocumented youth encounter hostility, insults, and violence in the classrooms, the cafeteria, in the main office, and on the school buses. What is it that we need to do?

Strategies of Transformation

It is necessary for us to confront our current situation as a community united.

- We need to create Mutual Aid Societies.
- Established Latino communities have to reach out to our newly arrived sisters and brothers.

Now united we need to know our rights:

- State and federal laws state that schools cannot investigate or question if a student is a citizen or someone without legal documents.
- When there are twenty-five students who speak a foreign language as their only language a bilingual program is required.
- By state law every bilingual program must have a parents' advisory group.
- We have the right to confront discrimination and to report it to the local and state authorities.
- We have a right to organize a community group and to insist on a meeting with the officials of the school district including the superintendent of schools and the school board so that they can hear and respond to our complaints; *we must not leave the meeting until there is a plan put in place to implement the necessary changes.*
- We need to organize conferences like this one to educate the teachers of our children so that they become knowledgeable of our cultures and histories.
- Together we have the capacity to confront the racism in the curriculum.
- Attend school board meetings.
- We must insist that the school district hire teachers, guidance counselors, secretaries, and adminstrators from our community and/or persons who show good will toward our community.

Finally during these times of such need and hostility faced by the community our people are looking for strong women and men to confront injustice. I now want to share with you the requirements to be a Latina woman and a Latino man in the service of transformation:

- Go back and to reconnect to the open veins of our past in order to heal our souls and thereby help our community to heal itself.
- Rediscover that our self is sacred.
- Create relationships of equality and mutuality between men and women.
- Reject the lie, the sickness that there is nothing that we can do to change our lives for the better.
- Go home within ourselves to rediscover our identity.
- Turn our anger into the necessary energy to create a more just and compassionate life.
- Rediscover our bodies, nature, emotions, feelings, the feminine, and the festival as a search for community.
- Deeducate ourselves and empty ourselves of the lies about our culture and then reeducate ourselves to recognize that together with the deepest source of our being, the god of transformation, we can recreate our society with love and justice.

And now we are ready as Latina women together with Latino men to confront injustice in our society. Once again we as Latino men and Latina women need to transform our energy and anger in order to fight racism and discrimination against the community. Today the greatest need is in the realm of education that demands that we be prepared to go into the offices of the superintendents of schools to declare that the schools are not educating our children and then to develop a plan of action to better the situation.

If we participate in making the above kind of involvement a reality we can readily see that concentrating on the schools and education will touch all aspects of the lives of the Latino community and of the wider society. Once we have organized ourselves for this kind of work in regard to the issue of education, we are now experienced and capable of turning our newly won skills in being political to all other problems that face the community regarding our civil rights whether it be housing, employment, profiling by the police, legal services, immigration, health services, or any other issue. The politics of transformation means always taking the next step and asking what it is that we can and need to do together to bring about a society grounded in love and justice.

Long Live the People!

Notes

Chapter 1. A Theory of Transformation

1. Sheldon Wolin, "Political Theory as a Vocation," *American Political Science Review* 63 (December 1969).

2. Manfred Halpern first taught me the theory of transformation that he discovered and developed when I was a graduate student of his at Princeton. At the time of his death he was writing his own book, *Transforming the Personal, Political, Historical and Sacred Faces of Our Being in Theory and Practice.* Prof. Halpern asked me to finish his book which has now been completed and sent out for review. I have gained greatly from having read the chapters of his manuscript in the writing of this book. For other applications of the theory of transformation, see David T. Abalos, *The Latino Male: A Radical Redefinition* (Boulder, CO: Lynne Rienner Press, 2002), *La Comunidad Latina in the United States: Personal and Political Strategies for Transforming Culture* (Westport, CT: Praeger Press, 1998), *Strategies of Transformation toward a Multicultural Society: Fulfilling the Story of Democracy* (Westport, CT: Praeger Press, 1996), and *The Latino Family and the Politics of Transformation* (Westport, CT: Praeger, 1993).

3. Theories that only describe reality and that turn people into abstractions as numbers provide us with a fragment of the lives they lead and ignore the deeper meaning of their lives. In this regard, see Halpern, *Transforming,* ch. 14, "What Kind of a Theory Is This?"

4. D. H. Lawrence, *The Plumed Serpent* (New York: Vintage Books, 1972).

5. See Halpern, *Transforming,* Introduction, "Invitation to an Unfamiliar Journey," and ch. 14. The issue of theory and its place in the social sciences as well as our daily lives was discussed by a group of scholars brought together at the University of Chicago by the editors of *Critical Inquiry,* academe's most prestigious journal dealing with theory. The era of big theory is over seemed to be the conclusion of the participants. Psychoanalysis, structuralism, Marxism, deconstructionism, post-colonialism have all been abandoned. Based on the reporting of the event the session led to a surreal, strained, and convoluted discussion. The only good comment came in a question from a graduate student who asked "So is theory simply just a nice, simple intellectual exercise or something that should be transformative?" To which Henry Louis Gates, Jr., from Harvard responded that as far as he could tell theory had never directly liberated anybody. See Emily Eakins, "The Latest Theory Is That Theory Doesn't Matter," *New York Times,*

April 19, 2003, D9. In regard to theory as a personal and political journey of discovery, see Sheldon Wolin, *Tocqueville between Two Worlds: The Making of a Political and Theoretical Life* (Princeton, NJ: Princeton University Press, 2001).

6. In this regard, see C. G. Jung, *Man and His Symbols* (New York: Dell, 1970) and *The Collected Works of C. G. Jung*, especially, *The Archetypes and the Collective Unconscious*, ed. Michael Fordham, trans. R. F. Hull (Princeton, NJ: Princeton University Press, 1980).

7. Halpern, *Transforming*, ch. 15, "Justice," 63.

8. Ibid., ch. 9, "Transforming Love and Romantic Love."

9. Ibid., ch. 15, 62–63.

10. Ibid., 63.

11. Manfred Halpern, "How Can We Re-Discover Wisdom and Compassionate Love?" talk given to the Princeton Faculty Forum, March 1998 and to the Graduate School Colloquium, April 1999 (revised January 2000), 3.

12. Halpern, *Transforming*, ch. 1, "The Drama of Transformation: The Core Drama of Life."

13. Manfred Halpern, "Why Are Most of Us Partial Selves? Why Do Partial Selves Enter the Road into Deformation?" paper delivered at the 1991 Annual Meeting of the American Political Science Association, Washington, D.C.

14. Ibid.

15. Manfred Halpern, "Beyond Present Theory and Practice: Transformation and the Nation State," in *Transformational Politics: Theory, Study and Practice*, ed. Ed Schwerin, Christa Slaton, and Stephen Woolpert (Albany: SUNY Press, 1998).

16. Halpern, *Transforming*, ch. 1.

17. Halpern, "Why Are Most of Us Partial Selves?"

18. Halpern, *Transforming*, ch. 15, 64–65.

19. Ibid., ch. 3, "Enclosing Ourselves in Emanation as a Way of Life."

20. For a fuller discussion of the story of patriarchy in la comunidad Latina, see Abalos, *The Latino Male*, 15–16, 20–25, 52–54, 104–5, 116–24, 160–62, 172–74.

21. Halpern, *Transforming*, ch. 15, 65.

22. Manfred Halpern, "Notes on the Theory and Practice of Transformation," unpublished manuscript (1980), 1.

23. Abalos, *The Latino Family*, ch. 4. To demonstrate that the theory of transformation is not culture bound, see the article on violence in Bukharan Jewish families from the former Soviet Union as they adjust to life in the United States. Wives become independent and take jobs at times making more money than their husbands which leads to anger and violence by the men (Joseph Berger, "Old Ways Bring Tears in a New World: Immigrants Face Family Violence," *New York Times*, March 7, 2003, B1 and B4). See also Abalos, *The Latino Male*, ch. 3, "The Latino Male at Risk."

24. Marshall Berman, *The Politics of Authenticity, Radical Individualism and the Rise of Modern Society* (New York: Atheneum Press, 1972), 113–44.

25. Manfred Halpern, "The Archetype of Capitalism: A Critical Analysis in the Light of a Theory of Transformation," paper presented at the 1996 Annual Meeting of the American Political Science Association in San Francisco, 18–19. This is the best analysis of capitalism that I have seen. It is truly an original and brilliant piece of scholarship that shows us the devastating cost of this drama in the service of the partial and wounded way of life of incoherence that is always in danger of moving us into the abyss in the service of deformation as workers are turned into objects to be exploited for the benefit of the powerful. See also Halpern, *Transforming*, ch. 4, "In the Service of Incoherence: The Archetypal Drama of Capitalism," 258–315.

26. See Abalos, *The Latino Male*, 146–47.

27. Halpern, *Transforming*, ch. 15, 66.

28. Ibid., ch 5, "The Way of Life of Deformation."

29. The Baptists at their annual convention in Salt Lake City declared that women were to honor the commandment that they were to be the handmaidens of men (Katherine Biele, "Baptist Meeting in Mormon Utah Leads to Battle of the Bibles," *Christian Science Monitor*, June 11, 1998).

30. Tina Rosenberg, "Machismo Gives Good New Laws a Black Eye," *New York Times*, June 20, 1998.

31. Douglas Jehl, "Arab Honor's Price: A Woman's Blood," *New York Times*, June 30, 1999, 1, 8.

32. Halpern, *Transforming*, ch. 15, 67.

33. Ibid., 66.

34. Ibid., 67.

35. Ibid., ch. 6, "Freeing Ourselves to Participate with Our Neighbors in Transformation as a Way of Life."

36. Ibid., ch. 15, 69.

37. Ibid., ch. 8, "The Archetypal Drama of Being Competent."

38. Abalos, *The Latino Male*, 62–63, and Halpern, *Transforming*, ch. 7, "Introducing Archetypal Relationships and Dramas," 57.

39. Abalos, *The Latino Male*, 63.

40. Much of the summary above and the quotes from Halpern's theory are taken from *Transforming*, ch. 7, and from his "Four Contrasting Repertories of Human Relations in Islam: Two Pre-Modern and Two Modern Ways of Dealing with Continuity and Change, Collaboration and Conflict and Achieving Justice," in *Psychological Dimensions of Near Eastern Studies*, ed. L. Carl Brown and Norman Itzkowitz (Princeton, NJ: Darwin Press, 1977), 62.

41. Halpern, *Transforming*, ch. 7, 13–14.

42. Ibid., 16–19.

43. Ibid., 14–16.

44. Ibid., 19–22.

45. Ibid., 23–30.
46. Harry J. Brill, *Why Organizers Fail* (Berkeley: University of California Press, 1971).
47. Halpern, *Transforming*, ch. 7, 30–41.
48. Ibid., 42–44.
49. Ibid., 44–51.
50. Ibid., ch. 2, 139.
51. Ibid., 142–43.
52. Ibid., 155–56.
53. Ibid.
54. Ibid., ch. 7, 44–58.

Chapter 2. The Search for Latina/Latino Identity

1. Amy Chu, "Power to the Privileged," *New York Times*, January 7, 2003, op-ed page.
2. Juan Forero and Larry Rohter, "Native Latins Are Astir and Thirsty for Power," *New York Times*, March 22, 2003, A3.
3. For more information on Rigoberta Menchú Tum and her Nobel Lecture, see the Nobel Prize Internet Archive (www.nobelprize.org/nobel_prizes/peace/laureates/1992/).
4. For a first-rate piece of scholarship on the treatment of the indigenous people of Latin America and the struggles of Bartlomé de las Casas, the bishop of Chiapas, Mexico, to win their human rights, see Luis N. Rivera-Pagán, "A Prophetic Challenge to the Church: The Last Word of Bartolomé de las Casas," *The Princeton Seminary Bulletin* 24, no. 2, New Series (2003): 216–40.
5. The best book regarding the culture, history, and identity of the Spaniard is a brilliant scholarly volume by Américo Castro, translated by Willard F. King and Selma Margaretten, *The Spaniards, An Introduction to Their History* (Berkeley: University of California Press, 1971). His ideas opened up a whole new way for us in la comunidad Latina to understand our Spanish heritage and helped to explain why the Spanish behaved the way they did throughout Latin America. He was especially helpful in enabling me to recognize the mixed heritage of the Spaniard as a Jew, Christian, and Muslim that completely undermines the attempt to make the Spanish people pure-bred Catholics with ties to the ancient Romans and here and there a Visigoth or a Gaul.
6. A literary work, a novel by Rosa Martha Villareal, *Doctor Magdalena* (Berkeley: TQS Publications, 1995) has been excellent in helping me to see that we need to transcend our antagonism to the Spanish contribution of our culture, history, and identity. At the height of the Chicano movement and nationalism there was a strong wave of anti-Spanish sentiment. This anger remains because to this day the European Spanish together with other

European communities in Latin America continue to practice a devastating racism against the indigenous peoples. Yet it is part of who we are; our *mestizaje* is European and Spanish. So we need to deal with the anger as Villareal writes by "conquering the Conquest" or the resentment will end by turning us against our very selves. I have learned a great deal about the personal, political, historical, and sacred struggle for our identity and am deeply indebted to Chicana/Latina feminist writers and scholars who suffer from discrimination based on race, class, gender, and often because of their sexual preference. See the following works: *This Bridge Called My Back: Writings by Radical Women of Color*, ed. Cherríe Moraga and Gloria Anzaldúa (Watertown, MA: Persephone Press, 1981); Gloria Anzaldúa, *Borderlands, La Frontera: The New Mestiza* (San Francisco: Aunt Lute Books, 1987); Teresa Córdova, ed., *Chicana Voices: The Intersections of Class, Race, and Gender* (Austin: University of Texas Press, 1990); Adela de la Torre and Beatríz Pesquera, eds., *Building with Our Hands: New Directions in Chicana Studies* (Berkeley and Los Angeles: University of California Press, 1984); Alma M. García and Mario T. García, *Chicana Feminist Thought: The Basic Writings* (New York: Routledge, 1997); Elizabeth Martínez, *De Colores Means All of Us: Latina Views for a Multi-Colored Century* (Cambridge, MA: South End Press, 1998); Carla Trujillo, ed., *Living Chicana Theory* (Berkeley: Third Woman Press, 1998); Carla Trujillo, ed., *Chicana Lesbians: The Girls Our Mothers Warned Us About* (Berkeley: Third Woman Press, 1991); *Breaking Boundaries: Latina Writings and Critical Readings*, ed. Asunción Horno-Delgado, Eleana Ortega, Nina Scott, and Nancy Saporta Sternbach (Amherst: University of Massachusetts Press, 1988) as well as literary works by Sandra Cisneros, *Woman Hollering Creek* (New York: Vintage Books, 1991), *The House on Mango Street* (New York: Vintage Books, 1991), and *Caramelo* (New York: Knopf, 2003); and Demetria Martínez, *Mother Tongue* (New York: Ballantine Books, 1994) and *The Devil's Workshop* (Tucson: University of Arizona Press, 2002).

7. Octavio Paz, *El Laberinto de la Soledad* (Mexico City: Fondo de Cultura Económica, 1959), 21.

8. Gabriel García Márquez, *One Hundred Years of Solitude* (New York: Harper and Row, 1970).

9. Rolstan Adams, "The Search for the Indigenous," in *The Analysis of Hispanic Texts*, ed. Beck et al. (Jamaica, NY: Bilingual Press, 1976), 76.

10. For a discussion of conscientización in education, a radical commitment to transformation of the individual and society, see David T. Abalos, "The Church in Latin America: Excerpts from and Commentary on the Documents of the Medellín Conference," in *Cross Currents* 19, no. 2 (Spring 1969); see also the works of Paulo Freire who led the revolutionary movement of conscientización in education in Brazil and throughout Latin America, especially his classic, *The Pedagogy of the Oppressed*, trans. Myra Bergman Ramos (New York: Herder and Herder, 1970).

11. Adams, "Search for the Indigenous," 85.

12. Max Weber, *The Protestant Ethic and the Spirit of Capitalism*, trans. Talcott Parsons (New York: Prentice Hall, 1977); R. H. Tawney, *Religion and the Rise of Capitalism* (New York: Mentor Books, 1950).

13. Octavio Paz, "Reflections: Mexico and the United States," *The New Yorker*, September 17, 1979, 140.

14. Rivera-Pagán, "Prophetic Challenge to the Church."

15. Paz, "Reflections."

16. Octavio Paz, "Twilight of Revolution," *Dissent* 21, no. 1 (Winter 1974).

17. Philip Slater, *Earthwalk* (New York: Bantam Books, 1975).

18. Octavio Paz, *The Other Mexico: Critique of the Pyramid*, trans. Lysander Kemp (New York: Grove Press, 1972), 105.

19. For a description of creative isolation in the service of transformation, see Abalos, *The Latino Male*, 135–39.

20. Ralph Ellison, *Invisible Man* (New York: Vintage Books, 1972), 567–68.

21. See the study by Joan V. Bondurant, *The Conquest of Violence* (Berkeley: University of California Press, 1965).

22. See William I. Thompson's essay "Of Physics and Tantra Yoga," in *Passages about Earth: An Exploration of the New Planetary Culture* (New York: Harper and Row, 1974). In this essay Thompson brilliantly states the case that the consciousness of the scientist is crucial (91).

23. David C. Gordon, *Women of Algeria: An Essay on Change* (Cambridge, MA: Harvard University Press, 1968).

24. I learned much about this ability to affirm one's own ethnic and racial origins in order to move to a more inclusive sense of humanity from Gandhi's struggle with his identity. See Erik Erikson, *Gandhi's Truth: On the Origins of Militant Non-Violence* (New York: W. W. Norton, 1968).

25. See *The Autobiography of Malcolm X*, with the assistance of Alex Haley (New York: Grove Press, 1966), 286 and 376.

26. Mireya Navarro, "In New York's Cultural Mix, Black Latinos Carve Out a Niche," *New York Times*, April 28, 2003, B1 and B4.

27. As reported in *The Star Ledger*, August 26, 2003, in an article by Darryl Fears of the *Washington Post*, "What's in a Name? Ask a Hispanic. Or Latino; For This Ethnic Group, the Debate Is about Identity," 26.

28. Castro, *The Spaniards*, 1–48.

29. Fears, "What's in a Name?" 26.

30. Shlomo Avineri's analysis of Marx's understanding of human relationships is superb; see *The Social and Political Thought of Karl Marx* (Cambridge: Cambridge University Press, 1968).

31. In la comunidad Latina this has been the work of people like Dolores Huerta, Susan Casillas, José Adames, Frank Morales, Celia Dorantes, Luz Horta, Padre Miguel Valle, Wilt Wilenga, Alma Cantú, and José González.

32. Manfred Halpern, "Transformation and the Source of the Fundamentally New." A paper prepared for a Caucus for a New Political Science

Panel on Archetypal Epistemology in the section on Epistemological Alternatives to Behavioralism, Annual Meeting of the American Political Science Association, Chicago, September 1, 1974, 42.

33. Manfred Halpern, "Applying a New Theory of Human Relations to the Comparative Study of Racism," a paper presented for publication by the Graduate School of International Studies, University of Denver, June 1969, 34.

Chapter 3. The Politics of the Latino Family

1. Gordon, *Women of Algeria.*

2. Gregory J. Massell, "Law as an Instrument of Revolutionary Change in a Traditional Milieu, The Case of Soviet Central Asia," *Law and Society Review* 2, no. 2, (February 1968).

3. For a superb accounting of the struggle of women for over a hundred years in Cuba, including the Cuban Revolution, see Humberto Solas, *Lucía* (Havana, 1968).

4. See C. G. Jung, *Collected Works,* Bollingen Series 8 (Princeton, NJ: Princeton University Press, 1969).

5. See Christopher Lasch, *Haven in a Heartless World* (New York: Basic Books, 1979).

6. On this point of the family as bastion of the *status quo,* see the conversations between Daniel Berrigan and Charles Coles, *Geography of Faith* (New York: Bantam Books, 1971).

7. See Jung, *Man and His Symbols.*

8. In this regard, see Ann Belford Ulanov, *The Feminine in Christian Theology and Jungian Psychology* (Evanston, IL: Northwestern University Press, 1971), and Mary Daly, *Beyond God the Father: Toward a Philosophy of Women's Liberation* (Boston: Beacon Press, 1973).

9. Oscar Lewis, *Five Families* (New York: New American Library, 1959), *The Children of Sanchez* (New York: Random House, 1979), *La Vida: A Puerto Rican Family in the Culture of Poverty in San Juan and New York* (New York: Random House, 1966), and *A Death in the Sanchez Family* (New York: Random House, 1969).

10. By Latina/Latino here is meant a person from the Caribbean, Central, and South America and their descendants now living in the United States. However, there are groups in Latin America such as some of the various white ethnics in Costa Rica, and Italians and Germans in Argentina, who would not be described by the analysis given here. The main concern here is the Spanish and indigenous mestizo in Latin America. Given these individual differences it is still important and necessary to be able to generalize as long as it is recognized that there will be exceptions even among the Spanish, Indian, Mestizo communities.

11. See Berger, "Old Ways Bring Tears in a New World."

12. Based on a conversation with a Mexican father.

13. In fundamentalist Islam protecting the honor of the family is taken to an extreme that leads to deformation. The dishonoring of the family can only be restored by so-called honor killings. Members of the family, usually the men, are encouraged to kill a wayward sister or daughter. In Sindh Province in 1997, 300 women were killed for reasons of honor. The men are almost never punished. See Suzanne Goldberg, "A Question of Honor," *The Guardian*, May 27, 1999.

14. For excellent discussions of the Mother archetype, see Erich Neumann's two books: *The Origins and History of Consciousness*, Bollingen Series (Princeton, NJ: Princeton University Press, 1971) and *The Great Mother*, Bollingen Series (Princeton, NJ: Princeton University Press, 1974).

15. In this regard, see Joseph E. Kerns, *The Theology of Marriage: Historical Development of Christian Attitudes towards Sex and Sanctity in Marriage* (New York: Sheed & Ward, 1964).

16. For an excellent example of matriarchy and of transformation restricted to the kitchen, see Laura Esquivel, *Like Water for Chocolate* (New York: Doubleday, 1992) and an analysis of this novel from the perspective of the theory of transformation, Abalos, *La Comunidad Latina in the United States*, 93–120, "Latinas Overcoming Personal and Political Inequality, Matriarchy in *Like Water for Chocolate.*"

17. In this regard, see Abalos, *The Latino Family*, especially chs. 4 and 5, and *The Latino Male*, especially ch. 5.

18. Heath Dillard, *Daughters of the Reconquest: Women in Castilian Town Society 1100–1300* (Cambridge: Cambridge University Press, 1984).

19. Antonia I. Castañeda, "History and the Politics of Violence against Women," in *Living Chicana Theory*, ed. Carla Trujillo (Berkeley: Third Woman Press, 1998).

20. Sandra Messinger Cypess, *La Malinche in Mexican Literature: From History to Myth* (Austin: University of Texas Press, 1991). See also a superb article by Aída Hurtado, "The Politics of Sexuality in the Gender Subordination of Chicanas," in *Living Chicana Theory*, ed. Carla Trujillo (Berkeley: Third Woman Press, 1998), 383–428.

21. For a further description of these sacred stories, see Alfonso Caso, *The Aztecs, People of the Sun*, trans. Lowell Dunham (Norman: University of Oklahoma Press, 1959) and Irene Nicholson, *Mexican and Central American Mythology* (New York: Paul Harnlyn, 1967).

22. Nicholson, *Mexican and Central American Mythology*, 28.

23. Betty and Theodore Roszak, eds., *Masculine/Feminine* (New York: Harper and Row, 1969), foreword, 8.

24. See, for example, Marilyn French, *The Women's Room* (New York: Harcourt Brace Jovanovich, 1978).

25. Ulanov, *The Feminine*, 277–85.

26. Jolande Jacobi, "Symbols in an Individual Analysis," in *Man and His Symbols*, ed. C. G. Jung (New York: Dell, 1973), 327.

27. James Olney, *Metaphors of Self* (Princeton, NJ: Princeton University Press, 1972), 17.

28. An archetype is the necessary form in which concrete relationships manifest themselves. We can experience the archetype directly through symbols in dreams and the stories of our lives. Although universal, it is imperative that individuals constellate the archetype in a personal concrete manner. Every archetype has a negative and positive aspect. For this reason we can rebel against our mother or father without rejecting them; what we need to do is to free ourselves of the archetype of the father or mother in the service of partial ways of life so that we can rediscover them in the service of transformation. In this way we transform the possessive relationship into one of mutual liberation. Thus, a young man's mother and a young woman's father can become their friends and guides in the process of their individuation.

29. For a very powerful example of a woman who is wracked with guilt and goes through an elaborate plan just to be alone for a few hours, see the story of Laura Brown in Michael Cunningham, *The Hours* (New York: Farrar, Straus and Giroux, 1998), 142–52.

30. Leo Tolstoy, *Anna Karenina*, trans. David Magarshack (New York: New American Library, 1961), 154–55.

31. Ulanov, *The Feminine*, 284–85.

32. Ibid.

33. Latino families are facing a crisis. The growth of single parent families is cause for deep concern. In addition, the pregnancy rate for unmarried teenage women is high. Therefore, the family politics described in this chapter are even more important. The inability or refusal of Latino men and Latina women to create new and better relationships together with the stories of racism in collusion with capitalism is responsible for the breakdown of many families. The strong family unit is what empowered us to survive the racism that affected our well-being in this society. We have to struggle with each other as men and women, husband and wife, father and mother, in order to protect and nourish the next generation. For an excellent insight into la familia Latina and its problems, see Adrian Nicole LeBlanc, *Random Family: Love, Drugs, Trouble, and Coming of Age in the Bronx* (New York: Scribner, 2003).

34. As quoted in Armando B. Rendón, *Chicano Manifesto* (New York: Collier, 1971), 189.

35. June K. Singer, *The Unholy Bible* (New York: G. P. Putnam and Sons, 1970).

36. In this regard, see Alan W. Watts, *Myth and Ritual in Christianity* (Boston: Beacon Press, 1968).

37. John Neihardt, *Black Elk Speaks* (Lincoln: University of Nebraska Press, 1961).

38. For an excellent novel that portrays the struggle of the human/divine man, Jesus, see Nikos Kazantzakis, *The Last Temptation of Christ* (New York: Bantam, 1971).

39. Tomás Amalguer, "Chicano Men: A Cartography of Homosexual Identity and Behavior," *Differences* 3, no. 2 (1991): 75–100; *This Bridge*

Called My Back; Joseph Carrier, *De Los Otros Intimacy and Homosexuality among Mexican Men* (New York: Columbia University Press, 1995); David William Foster, *Sexual Textualities: Essays on Queer/ing Latin American Writing* (Austin: University of Texas Press, 1997).

40. Abalos, *The Latino Male,* 140–143.

41. Ray González, ed., *Muy Macho: Latino Men Confront Their Manhood* (New York: Doubleday, 1996); Philip Kayal, *Bearing Witness: Gay Men's Health Crisis and the Politics of AIDS* (Boulder, CO: Westview Press, 1993); Carlos A. Rodríguez Matos, ed., *Poesída: An Anthology of AIDS Poetry from the United States, Latin America, and Spain* (Jackson Heights, NY: Ollantay Press, 1995); and Rick Najera, *The Pain of the Macho and Other Plays* (Houston: Arte Público Press, 1997).

Chapter 4. The Politics of Transformation in the Latino Community

1. Manfred Halpern, "A Redefinition of the Revolutionary Situation," *Journal of International Affairs* 23, no.1 (1969): 58–59.

2. For an excellent insight into the similarities between all traditional family units regardless of race or country, see Mao's account of this struggle with his traditional Confucian father and family in Edgar Snow, *Red Star Over China* (New York: Grove Press, 1961), 132–33.

3. Especially see Lewis, *Five Families.*

4. See in this regard the very fine work on culture by Juan Gómez-Quiñones, *On Culture* (Los Angeles: UCLA, Chicano Studies Center Publications, 1986).

5. For a penetrating insight into this dilemma, see Piri Thomas, *Down These Mean Streets* (New York: Alfred A. Knopf, 1970).

6. Strategies for taking the best of both cultures are discussed in Abalos, *Strategies,* esp. ch. 5, and *La Comunidad Latina in the United States,* esp. chs. 2 and 5. One of the better critiques of American culture still many years after its publication is Philip Slater, *Earthwalk* (New York: Bantam Books, 1975).

7. For a brilliant and devastating analysis of the story of capitalism, see Halpern, *Transforming,* ch. 4.

8. See Robert McAfee Brown, *Religion and Violence* (Philadelphia: Westminster Press, 1973).

9. Ken Kesey, *One Flew Over the Cuckoo's Nest* (New York: Signet Books, 1962).

10. For an excellent discussion of male, white privilege, see "White Privilege and Male Privilege: A Personal Account of Coming to See Correspondences through Work in Women's Studies," Working Paper No. 189, Center for Research on Women, Wellesley College, Wellesley, Massachusetts, 1988.

11. Alan Paton, *Too Late the Phalarope* (New York: Charles Scribner and Sons, 1953).

12. For an explanation of this relationship, see James Hillman, *Re-visioning Psychology* (New York: Harper and Row, 1975), and Adolf Guggenbuhl-Craig, *Power in the Helping Professions* (Zurich: Spring Publications, 1976).

13. I owe this example to Jim Rebhan, one of the finest students whom I have taught, who participated in the conference at New York University during the spring semester, 1977.

14. For an excellent analysis of the empowerment of Latinos, see John Shockley, *Chicano Revolt in a Texas Town* (Notre Dame, IN: University of Notre Dame Press, 1974) and the following works: Rodolfo Acuña, *Occupied America: The Chicano's Struggle for Liberation* (San Francisco: Canfield Press, 1972); Rina Benmayor and William Flores, eds., *Latino Cultural Citizenship: Claiming Identity, Space, and Rights* (Boston: Beacon Press, 1997); Herbert Biberman, *The Salt of the Earth* produced by Independent Productions Corporation and the International Union of Mine, Mill and Smelter Workers, 1953; Juan Gómez-Quiñones, *Chicano Politics: Reality and Promise, 1940–1990* (Albuquerque: University of New Mexico Press, 1991); Alberto Sandoval-Sánchez, *José Can You See? Latinos On and Off Broadway* (Madison: University of Wisconsin Press, 1999); Juan González, *Harvest of Empire, A History of Latinos in America* (New York: Penguin Books, 2000); Peter Matthiessen, *Sal Si Puedes, César Chávez and the New American Revolution* (New York: Random House, 1969); Gloria Anzaldúa, ed., *Making Face, Making Soul, Haciendo Caras: Creative and Critical Perspectives by Women of Color* (San Francisco: Aunt Lute Books, 1990); and *Borderlands, La Frontera.*

15. See Alan Pifer, *Bilingual Education and the Hispanic Challenge: The Annual Report of the President* (New York: Carnegie Corporation, 1979), 16.

16. As quoted in Ronald Takaki, *A Different Mirror* (Boston: Little, Brown, 1993), 328.

17. See Richard Griswold del Castillo, *The Treaty of Guadalupe Hidalgo* (Norman: University of Oklahoma Press, 1990) that tells the story of the aftermath of the war and the harsh consequences for Mexicans to this day.

18. See the pioneering work by William Carrigan of Rowan University, New Jersey, "The Causes and Characteristics of Mexican American Lynchings, 1848–1928," British Association for American Studies, *Individual Conference Paper Reports,* 84 (Spring/Summer 2001). See also the film, *The Ballad of Gregorio Cortez,* directed by Robert Young, PBS, American Playhouse, 1992, that tells the story of the Texas Rangers and their pursuit of one man, Gregorio Cortez, by hundreds of white men to save face and gain revenge.

19. See the excellent books by Stephen J. Pitti, *The Devil in Silicon Valley* (Princeton, NJ: Princeton University Press, 2004) and Benjamin Heber Johnson, *Revolution in Texas* (New Haven, CT: Yale University Press, 2003) and a wonderfully researched article by William Carrigan and Clive

Webb, "Mob Violence against Persons of Mexican Origin and Descent," *Journal of Social History* 37, no. 2 (Winter 2003): 411–38. Pitti in his book specifically refers to the racism in California as the devil; because he also describes the brutality of capitalism alongside the devil of racism, I took the liberty of calling this combination of violent stories the double devil of capitalism and tribalism.

20. Eric Schlosser, "A Side Order of Human Rights," *New York Times*, April 6, 2005, A23.

21. For an excellent article that traces the politics of bilingual education, see Carlos J. Ovando, "Politics and Pedagogy: The Case of Bilingual Education," *Harvard Educational Review* 60, no. 3 (August 1990): 341–56.

22. Mario Barrera, *Race and Class in the Southwest* (Notre Dame, IN: University of Notre Dame Press, 1979), 54–57.

23. U.S. Bureau of the Census, "Sex by Educational Attainment for the Population 25 Years and Over (Hispanic or Latino 17), 2000." For the poverty figures for 2004, see The National Poverty Center, University of Michigan (www.npc.umich.edu).

24. Pifer, *Bilingual Education*, 9–10, and for more data based on the Census 2000, see Sandra Gardner, "ACE Minorities in Higher Education 2001–2002 Report Generate Enlightened Comments," *The Hispanic Outlook* 13, no. 16 (May 19, 2003): 10. For the data on poverty and income levels, see www.factfinder.census.gov.

25. "Fighting School Resegregation," editorial, *New York Times*, January 27, 2003, A24.

26. See Juan Andrade and Andrew Hernández with the assistance of Jacqueline Campbell, *The Almanac of Latino Politics 2000* (Chicago: United States Hispanic Leadership Institute, 1999), 1–3; Dean E. Murphy, "New Californian Identity Predicted by Researchers," *New York Times*, February 17, 2003, A14.

27. Murphy "New Californian Identity," discusses the findings of Harry Pachón, the president of the Tomás Rivera Policy Insitute at Claremont College, who found that the assimilationist process is very strong in the California- and American-born Latino in comparison to foreign-born.

28. Neumann, *Origins and History of Consciousness*, 165.

29. Carl Gustave Jung, *Memories, Dreams, Reflections* (New York: Vintage, 1973), 252–53.

30. *The Blood of the Condor*, a film by Oscar Soriano and Jorge Sanjines, 1969.

31. Gerald McDermott, *Arrow to the Sun* (New York: Viking Press, 1974).

32. Jung, *Memories*, 256.

33. Joseph G. Jorgensen, *The Sun Dance Religion: Power for the Powerless* (Chicago: University of Chicago Press, 1972), 1.

34. J. E. Brown, *The Sacred Pipe* (Baltimore: Penguin Books, 1971), 95.

35. Jorgensen, *The Sun Dance Religion*, 226–27.

36. Jung, *Man and His Symbols*, 230.

37. Herbert Silberer, *Hidden Symbolism of Alchemy and the Occult Arts* (New York: Dover, 1971), 319.

38. *Historia Cultural de Puerto Rico 1493–1969* (San Juan: Editorial Universitario, Universidad de Puerto Rico, 1975), 48.

Chapter 5. Latinas/Latinos and the Sacred

1. Halpern, *Transforming*, ch. 13, "Choosing between Four Fundamentally Different Sacred Sources of Our Being within the Core Drama of Life."

2. *Hispanic Ministry: Three Major Documents* (Washington, DC: United States Conference of Catholic Bishops, 2002), 29–48.

3. Ibid., 49.

4. Ibid., 79.

5. *"Latino Case Studies" A Study of Hispanics in the Archdiocese of New York*, vol. 1, edited by Ruth Doyle and Olga Scarpetta, The Office of Pastoral Research, Archdiocese of New York, 1982.

6. *Strangers No More: Together on the Journey of Hope* (Washington, DC: United States Conference of Catholic Bishops, 2004), 30–31.

7. *Encuentro and Mission: A Renewed Pastoral Framework for Hispanic Ministry* (Washington, DC: United States Conference of Catholic Bishops, 2002), 4.

8. Padre Miguel Valle, an outstanding young priest from Colombia, a minister of the Gospel in the service of transformation, made this comment in a sermon given at the Latino Mass at St. Anthony of Padua Church in Hightstown, New Jersey, on Sunday, September 18, 2005. The congregation consisted primarily of undocumented parishioners.

9. Halpern, *Transforming*, ch. 13, 605–20.

10. This is the position taken by Bishop Spong in his latest book, *The Sins of Scripture: Beyond Texts of Hate to the God of Love* (San Francisco: Harper Collins, 2005). See the review by A. Regina Schulte in *Corpus Reports* 32, no. 1.

11. Ibid., 23.

12. Emile Durkheim, *The Elementary Forms of the Religious Life*, trans. Joseph W. Swain (New York: The Free Press, 1969). Max Weber, *The Religion of China: Confucianism and Taoism*, trans. and ed. Hans Gerth (Glencoe, IL: The Free Press, 1951); *The Religion of India: The Sociology of Hinduism and Buddhism*, trans. Hans H. Gerth (Glencoe, IL: The Free Press, 1958); *The Protestant Ethic and the Spirit of Capitalism; The Sociology of Religion*, trans. Ephraim Fischoff, introduced by Talcott Parsons (Boston: Beacon Press, 1963); *The Methodology of the Social Sciences*, trans. and ed. Edward A. Shils and Henry A. Finch, with a foreword by Edward A. Shils (Glencoe, IL: The Free Press, 1949). Karl Marx and Friedrich Engels, *On Religion*, introduced by Reinhold Neibuhr (New York: Schocken, 1964).

13. Sigmund Freud, *The Future of an Illusion*, trans. W. O. Robson-Scott, revised and ed. James Strachey (Garden City, NY: Anchor, 1964).

14. Ernest Troeltsch, *The Social Teaching of the Christian Churches*, trans. Olive Wyon (New York: Macmillan, 1931).

15. Wilfred Cantwell Smith, *The Meaning and End of Religion: A New Approach to the Religious Traditions of Mankind* (New York: New American Library, 1964).

16. Halpern, *Transforming*, ch. 13, 4–5.

17. Bernard Lonergan, S.J., "Theology in Its New Context," in *Theology of Renewal*, vol. 1, ed. L. K. Shook, C.S.B (Montreal: Palm Publishers, 1968).

18. For another study that takes the religious seriously, see Ninian Smart, *The Science of Religion and the Sociology of Knowledge* (Princeton, NJ: Princeton University Press, 1973).

19. See W. I. Thompson, *Passages about Earth: An Exploration of the New Planetary Culture* (New York: Harper & Row, 1974) for an excellent application of this threefold process.

20. For a discussion of alchemy as a sacred process of transformation symbolized by work with metals, see Titus Burckhardt, *Alchemy* (Baltimore: Penguin, 1971).

21. For the significance of the moon as a symbol of woman's mysteries as well as a symbol of transformation, see M. Esther Harding, *Woman's Mysteries Ancient and Modern* (New York: Bantam, 1973).

22. See Brown, *The Sacred Pipe*, 23 n. 10; 80–83.

23. This is also Bernard Lonergan's conclusion in his own epistemological studies. See his article "Cognitional Structures," in *Studies in Honor of Bernard Lonergan, S.J.*, ed. Frederick E. Crowe, S.J., *Continuum* 2, no. 3 (Fall 1964).

24. Alex Altmann, "The Delphic Maxim in Medieval Islam and Judaism," in *Studies in Religious Philosophy and Mysticism* (London: Routledge and Kegan Paul, 1969), 1–40.

25. Werner Heisenberg, *Physics and Beyond* (New York: Harper & Row, 1971), and Thomas S. Kuhn, *The Structure of Scientific Revolutions*, 2nd ed. (Chicago: Chicago University Press, 1970), 89.

26. Thompson, *Passages About Earth*, 91.

27. Halpern, "Transformation and the Source of the Fundamentally New," 24.

28. Dennis Overby, "How Islamic Scholars Won, and Lost, the World Lead in Science," *New York Times*, October 30, 2001, F1, quoting Muslim scholar, Dr. Pervez Hoodbhoy, a Pakistani physicist and professor at Quaide-Azam University in Islamabad, from his book, *Islam and Science, Religious Orthodoxy and the Battle for Rationality*.

29. Ibid., F5.

30. Halpern, *Transforming*, ch. 15, 712.

31. Halpern, "Transformation and the Source of the Fundamentally New," 20.

32. An old Muslim proverb attributed to Al Ghazzali (d. 1111) as quoted in ibid., 10.

33. Arthur O. Lovejoy, *The Great Chain of Being: A Study of the History of an Idea*, William James Lectures delivered at Harvard University, 1933 (Cambridge, MA: Harvard University Press, 1950).

34. Halpern, "Transformation and the Source of the Fundamentally New," 25.

35. Lonergan, "Theology in Its New Context," 41.

36. Halpern, "Transformation and the Source of the Fundamentally New," 24.

37. Ibid., 22.

38. Halpern, *Transforming*, ch 13, 622–23.

39. The author wrote his doctoral dissertation ("The Breakdown of Authority in the Roman Catholic Church in the United States," Princeton Theological Seminary, November 1971) as a personal, political, historical, and sacred statement describing the process of transformation as discussed here, that is, uprooting, creating, and nourishing the fundamentally new and more just in his own life and as shared by other Catholics.

40. Ibid., 6.

41. I served as a guest editor together with Alberto Pulido for a special issue, *The Latino Community and the Sacred* of *Latino Studies Journal* 5, no. 1 (September 1994). See especially Luis D. G. Leon, "Somos Un Cuerpo en Cristo: Notes on Power and the Body in an East Los Angeles Chicano/Mexicano Pentecostal Community," 60–86. This special issue represents a variety of perspectives and understanding of the sacred and how it impacts on our personal, political, and historical participation as Latinas and Latinos in the society around us.

42. U.S. Census Bureau, Table 14.1 Poverty Status of the Population in 2006 by Sex, Age, Hispanic Origin and Race: 2004.

43. Richard Scaine, "The Religious Right," one of a series of white papers for *Corpus Reports* 32, no. 1 (January–February 2006): 8–9. This is a brilliant article that gives us a historical perspective of the roots of fundamentalism in the U.S. as well as a penetrating insight into this way of thinking and living. See also Jim Wallis, *God's Politics: Why the Right Gets It Wrong and the Left Doesn't Get It* (San Francisco: Harper, 2005); David Brock, *Blinded by the Right* (New York: Crown, 2002); and Halpern, *Transforming*, ch. 5.

44. Paul Henggler, "Perils in Letting Faith Dictate Policy," *The Star Ledger*, March 17, 2003.

45. As quoted in Jackson Lears, "How War Became a Crusade," *New York Times*, March 11, 2003, A25.

46. As quoted by Jennifer Loren of the AP, "The President's Public Sermons," *The Star Ledger*, March 19, 2003, 9.

47. A quote from David Gergen as reported by Laurie Goodstein, "A President Puts His Faith in Providence," *New York Times*, February 9, 2003, 4.

48. Ibid. This is the perspective given by Elaine Pagels when asked about Mr. Bush's use of religion to justify his crusade.

49. See A. P. Thornton, *The Imperial Idea and Its Enemies* (London: Macmillan, 1959), Introduction, ix–x.

50. Nicholas B. Kristoff, "God, State and the Media," *New York Times*, March 4, 2003, A25.

51. *Newsweek*, September 5, 2005, 51–65.

52. See the article by David Firestone, "DeLay is to Carry Dissenting Message on a Mid East Tour," *New York Times*, July 25, 2003, A1 and A8.

53. See Robert Wright's review of Jon Krakauer, *Under the Banner of Heaven, New York Times Book Review* August 3, 2003, 7.

54. Tamar Lewis, "A Catholic College, A Billionaire's Idea Will Rise in Florida," *New York Times*, March 10, 2003, A1 and A18.

55. Carl Hulse, "Democrats Design Agenda in Bid to Hold Hispanic Support," *New York Times*, July 9, 2003, A20.

56. Rachel L. Swarns, "Republicans Put Immigration Laws Back on the Political Agenda," *New York Times*, August 4, 2003, A9.

57. "The Rigged Trade Game," *New York Times* editorial, July 20, 2003, A10.

58. Amadou Toumani Toure and Blaise Compaore, the presidents respectively of Mali and Burkina Faso, "Your Farm Subsidies Are Strangling Us," *New York Times*, July 11, 2003, A17.

59. *New York Times*, editorial, August 8, 2005.

60. Rick Lazio, "Some Trade Barriers Won't Fall, Subsidizing U.S. Farmers Hurts Us in the End," *New York Times*, August 9, 2003, A11.

61. Elizabeth Becker, "U.S. Corn Subsidies Said to Damage Mexico," *New York Times*, August 27, 2003, p. C4.

62. "The Rigged Trade Game," July 20, A10; "The Great Catfish War," July 22, A18; "The Long Reach of King Cotton," August 5, A14; "Napoleon's Bittersweet Legacy," August 11, A14; and "A French Roadblock to Free Trade," August 31, 2003, A8.

63. "The Long Reach of King Cotton."

64. As reported by Warren Bass in his review of Stephen Kinzer, *All The Shah's Men, New York Times Book Review*, August 10, 2003, 13.

65. See Halpern, *Transforming*, chs. 1 and 13.

66. Neumann, *The Origins and History of Consciousness*.

67. Halpern, *Transforming*, ch. 13, 627.

68. From an earlier version of Halpern, *Transforming*, ch. 5 "The Human Being in the Image of God: A Cosmos of Creative Participation," 62.

69. Jonathan Mahler, "With Jesus as Our Connector," *New York Times Magazine*, March 27, 2005, 33.

70. Michael Luo, "Preaching a Gospel of Wealth in a Glittery Market, New York," *New York Times*, January 15, 2006, 1 and 28.

71. Henry Corbin, *Creative Imagination in the Sufism of Ib'n Arabi*, trans. Ralph Manheim, Bollingen Series 91 (Princeton, NJ: Princeton University Press, 1969), 277–81.

72. Ebrahim Moosa, "Pilgrims at Heart," *New York Times*, January 10, 2006, A25.

73. See Erikson, *Gandhi's Truth*, 253, 395, 423.

74. From an earlier version of Halpern, *Transforming*, ch. 5, 35.

75. Ibid., 35.

76. Virgilio Elizondo, *Galilean Journey: The Mexican American Promise* (Maryknoll, NY: Orbis Press, 1983).

77. See Burckhardt, *Alchemy*, 133–38.

78. Erich Neumann, *The Great Mother*, trans. Ralph Manheim, Bollingen Series 47 (Princeton, NJ: Princeton University Press, 1974), 203–4.

79. Neihardt, *Black Elk Speaks*, 48–49.

80. Miguel Ángel Asturias, *El Señor Presidente*, trans. Frances Partridge, Nobel Prize Library, vol. 2 (New York: Alex Gregory; Del Mar, CA: CRM Publishing, 1972), 9–168.

81. Fyodor Dostoevsky, *The Brothers Karamazov* (New York: New American Library, 1958), 222–44.

82. Gustavo Gutiérrez, *A Theology of Liberation*, trans. and ed. Sister Caridad Inda and John Eagleson (Maryknoll, NY: Orbis Press, 1973); Juan Luis Segundo, S.J., *A Theology for Artisans of a New Humanity*, in collaboration with the staff of the Peter Faber Center in Montevideo, Uruguay, trans. John Drury (Maryknoll, NY: Orbis Press, 1974). In this latest series Segundo makes it clear that the methodology that he has employed, namely, dialectical and archetypal analysis, demands a reformulation of all the basic theological issues: God, Church, sacraments, history, person, grace, and the world.

83. Rivera-Pagán , "A Prophetic Challenge to the Church: The Last Word of Bartolomé de Las Casas," 236.

84. In this regard, see Elaine Pagels, *Beyond Belief* (New York: Random House, 2003).

85. *The Spiritual Exercises of Saint Ignatius Loyola*, trans. with a commentary and a translation of the *Directorium in Exercitia* by W. H. Longridge (London and Oxford: A. R. Mowbray, 1950). For a good explanation of the *Exercises*, see Karl Rahner, S.J., *Spiritual Exercises*, trans. Kenneth Baker, S.J. (New York: Herder and Herder, 1965).

86. Made for and distributed by the Maryknoll Fathers, Maryknoll, NY, 1973, directed and produced by Thomas Cohen.

87. From an earlier version of Halpern, *Transforming*, ch. 20, "The Counter Tradition," 48.

88. Conversations with Maryknoll missionaries in Chaclacayo and Lima, Peru, between June 28 and July 3, 1975.

89. From an earlier version of Halpern, *Transforming*, ch. 20, 28–29.

90. R. M. Brown, *Religion and Violence* (Philadelphia: Westminster Press, 1974).

91. From an earlier version of Halpern, *Transforming*, ch. 20, 93–94.

92. See Jung, ed., *Man and His Symbols*, 266–85.

93. Brown, *The Sacred Pipe*, "The Sun Dance," 67–100.

94. Hermann Hesse, *Demian* (New York: Bantam, 1966), 94, and Jung, *Collected Works*, vol. 9.

95. D. H. Lawrence, *Phoenix II, Uncollected, Unpublished and Other Prose Works*, collected and ed. Warren Roberts and Harry T. Moore (New York: Viking Press, 1970). See especially his short story "Reflections on the Death of a Porcupine," 460–74, where he has an excellent discussion of the Holy Spirit as the restless wind that transforms chaos into incarnation.

96. From an earlier version of Halpern, *Transforming*, ch. 20, 34.

97. Ulanov, *The Feminine*. See also Daly, *Beyond God The Father*.

Chapter 6. The Politics of Liberation versus the Politics of Assimilation

1. For an excellent reinterpretation of middle-class and salaried professionals see Manfred Halpern, "Toward a Transforming Analysis of Social Class," in *Commoners, Climbers, and Notables*, ed. C. A. O. Van Nieuwenhuijza (Leiden: E. J. Brill, 1977).

2. For a provocative study of repression, see Norman O. Brown, *Life Against Death* (New York: Vintage, 1959). Also Herbert Marcuse, *Eros and Civilization* (New York: Vintage, 1955).

3. George Orwell's *1984*, following Rousseau's insight, illustrates how modern society reduces all passion to loyalty for the state.

4. For a discussion of the story of tribalism, see Abalos, *La Comunidad Latina in the United States*, 73–75.

5. Richard Rodríguez never realizes or at least does not acknowledge this sadness but rushes to be like the others. See his *Hunger of Memory: The Education of Richard Rodríguez* (New York: Bantam, 1983).

6. This is the theme of one of the best American political novels, Ken Kesey's *One Flew Over the Cuckoo's Nest*.

7. Rendón, *Chicano Manifesto*, 181–82.

8. The systematic nurturing of the anti-self in both traditional and modern society is brilliantly outlined by Marshall Berman in *The Politics of Authenticity* .

9. Tom Robbins, *Even Cowgirls Get the Blues* (New York: Bantam, 1976), 114–15.

10. Brown, *Life Against Death*, 23–67.

11. Richard Wagner, *Parsifal*, libretto English version by Stewart Robb (New York, London: G. Schirmer), 22.

12. Marguerite Yourcenar, *The Abyss*, trans. Grace Frick (New York: Farrar, Straus and Giroux, 1976), 221–22.

13. Freire, *Pedagogy of the Oppressed*.

14. This insight into Plato's view of education as political I owe to Paul Friedlander, *Plato*, trans. Hans Meyerhoff, Bollingen Series 59 (Princeton, NJ: Princeton University Press, 1973), especially chs. 1, 2, and 4.

15. Ellison, *Invisible Man*, epilogue, 559–68.

Chapter 7. Latina/Latino Professionals: A Transforming Middle Class

1. Berman, *The Politics of Authenticity*, 217–18.

2. *New York Times*, June 24, 2003, 1, and the op-ed piece by Orlando Patterson, "Affirmative Action Is Not about Diversity as Much as Fairness," *New York Times*, June 22, 2003, 11.

3. For much of my analysis regarding the professionalization of the professions I am indebted to Magali Sarfatti Larson's excellent study *The Rise of Professionalism: A Sociological Analysis* (Berkeley: University of California Press, 1977).

4. To see this process of professionalization in medicine, nursing, and hospital care, see David T. Abalos, "Strategies of Transformation in the Health Delivery System" in *The Nursing Forum* 17, no. 3 (1978). For a more recent article on professionalism in the delivery of health care, see David T. Abalos, "The Personal, Political, Historical, and Sacred Drama of Transformation: Cultural Implications for Latinos, Latinas with Disabilities and Those Who Provide Care and Support," *Journal of Religion, Disability, and Health* 9, no. 4 (2005): 29–54.

5. Larson, *The Rise of Professionalism*, xii.

6. Halpern, "A Redefinition of the Revolutionary Situation," 64.

7. Abalos, "Strategies of Transformation in the Health Delivery System."

8. See the series of articles by David Barstow and Lowell Bergman in *New York Times*, January 8 and 10, 2003: "At a Texas Foundry an Indifference to Life," A1 and A18; "Deaths on the Job, Slaps on the Wrist," A1, A16–17. See also *Frontline*, "A Dangerous Business," a PBS presentation produced by WGBH Boston, a co-production with the *New York Times* and the CBC shown on January 9, 2003, Neil Docherty and David Rummel producers.

9. Robert Merton, "The Machine, the Worker, and the Engineer," as quoted in Larson, *The Rise of Professionalism*, 237.

10. Larson, *The Rise of Professionalism*, 201.

11. J. A. Jackson, ed., *Professions and Professionalizalization* (Cambridge: Cambridge University Press, 1970), 4–5.

12. Larson, *The Rise of Professionalism*, 237.

13. Berman, *The Politics of Authenticity*, quoting Rousseau, 101.

14. Halpern, "Toward a Transfoming Analysis of Social Class."

15. For an excellent explanation of Plato's political vision, see Friedlander, *Plato*, esp. 85–107.

16. Halpern, "Toward a Transforming Analysis of Social Class," 74.

17. Larson, *The Rise of Professionalism*, 243–44.

18. Halpern, "Toward a Transforming Analysis of Social Class," 72.

19. Paz, "Reflections: Mexico and the United States," 140.

20. Rousseau's letter to d'Alembert, section 126, as quoted in Berman, *The Politics of Authenticity*, 215.

21. I am greatly indebted for my understanding of *daimon* in Plato and Socrates to Friedlander's *Plato*, 32–58.

22. See Shlomo Avineri, "Marx's Vision of Future Society," *Dissent* 20 (Summer 1973): 323–31.

23. As reported on *Sixty Minutes*, CBS, "Pillar of the Community," Sunday, November 27, 1983 and again April 29, 1984.

24. Maureen Dowd, "Could Thomas Be Right?" op-ed, *New York Times*, June 25, 2003, A25.

Chapter 8. Choices for La Comunidad Latina: Creating the Present and the Future Now

1. Lewis, *La Vida* and *Five Families*.

2. René Marqués, *La Carreta* (Rio Piedras, Puerto Rico: Editorial Cultural, 1971).

3. Susan Sheehan, *A Welfare Mother* (Boston: Houghton Mifflin, 1976); Cisneros, *Caramelo*; LeBlanc, *Random Family*.

4. Simon Romero, "Scene of Horror and Despair in Trailer," *New York Times*, May 16, 2003, A20; Kate Zernik and Ginger Thompson, "Deaths of Immigrants Uncover Makeshift World of Smuggling," *New York Times*, Sunday, June 29, 2003, 1 and 25.

5. *El Norte*, a film directed by Gregory Nava, Independent Films, 1983.

6. George James, "On the Street, Looking for Work," *New York Times*, February 2, 2003, section 14, 1 and 10.

7. Steven Greenhouse, "Suit Claims Discrimination against Hispanics on the Job; Bias Rising with Immigration, Experts Say," *New York Times*, March 9, 2003, A20.

8. Charlie LeDuff, "Los Angeles County Weighs Cost of Illegal Immigration," *New York Times*, May 21, 2003, A25.

9. James, "On the Street, Looking for Work."

10. Andrés Martínez, "Policing a Fine, Porous Line across the Perilous West Desert Corridor," *New York Times*, October 14, 2002, A18.

11. "Called by God to Help," op-ed, *New York Times*, March 22, 2006.

12. *The Almanac of Latino Politics 2004*, ed. Juan Andrade, foreword by Henry Cisneros (Chicago: The United States Hispanic Leadership Institute, 2004), 11.

13. "Border Illusions," editorial, *New York Times*, May 16, 2006.

14. Editorial, *New York Times*, May 21, 2006, 13.

15. Ginger Thompson, "Behind Roses' Beauty, Poor and Ill Workers," *New York Times*, February 13, 2003, A1, A3.

16. Ibid.

17. Juan Forero, "As Bolivian Miners Die, Boys Are Left to Toil," *New York Times*, March 24, 2003, A3.

18. As quoted in Juan Forero, "Bolivia Indians Hail the Swearing In of One of Their Own as President," *New York Times*, January 23, 2006, A10.

19. Elena Padilla, *Up From Puerto Rico* (New York and London: Columbia University Press, 1969), 28–29.

20. Marqués, *La Carreta*, 99.

21. Tato Laviera, *La Carreta Made a U-Turn* (Houston: Arte Público Press, University of Houston, 1981).

22. Lewis, *Five Families*.

23. Sheehan, *A Welfare Mother*.

24. LeBlanc, *Random Family*, 405–6.

25. Ibid.

26. See the insightful review by Margaret Talbot in *New York Times Book Review*, February 9, 2003, 12–13.

27. See Abalos, *The Latino Family*, esp. 87–113, "The Latino Family at Risk."

28. Ibid., 115–151, "Creating New Archetypal Dramas in the Latino Family."

29. For an application of the theory of transformation before I knew about ways of life, see Abalos, "Strategies of Transformation in the Health Delivery System."

30. See Elaine Pagels, *The Gnostic Gospels* (New York: Random House, 1979), Introduction, xv, and her more recent work, *Beyond Belief*.

31. Leslie Marmon Silko, *Ceremony* (New York: Penguin Books, 1977), 254.

32. Sandoval-Sánchez, *José, Can You See?* 170–97.

33. Dolores Prida, *Beautiful Señoritas and Other Plays*, ed. Judith Weiss (Houston: Arte Publico Press, 1991). *Coser y Cantar* and *Botánica* are included in this collection.

34. Roy Conboy, *When el Cucui Walks* (San Francisco: Z Plays, 1993).

35. Villareal, *Doctor Magdalena*.

36. Sandoval-Sánchez, *José, Can You See?* 196–97.

37. Ibid., 197.

38. Anzaldúa, *Borderlands, La Frontera*; see also *Borderless Borders*, ed. Frank Bonilla et al. (Philadelphia: Temple University Press, 1998), especially the essay by María de los Angeles Torres, "Transnational Political and Cultural Identities: Crossing Theoretical Borders," 169–182. See also Bonmayor and Flores, *Latino Cultural Citizenship*; and *Breaking Boundaries*, ed. Asunción Horno-Delgado et al. (Amherst: University of Massachusetts Press, 1989).

39. Robert Courtney Smith in a very fine book, *Mexican New York: Transnational Lives of New Immigrants* (Berkeley: University of California Press, 2006), 25, cites scholars as speaking of only three possible paths for second generation immigrants: they can assimilate such that they lose their own cultural heritage, they can assimilate into an inner-city culture of violence, or they can use their ethnicity to circumvent racism and define themselves in a unique way. In this chapter we have seen that there are four fundamentally different choices for Latinos: remaining in an emanational embrace in the past, assimilating into the power structures and rejecting our heritage in the service of incoherence, descending into violence against one's self and others in deformation, or choosing to create the fundamentally more loving and just in all aspects of our lives.

40. Dr. Juan Andrade and Andrew Hernández with the assistance of Jacqueline Cambell, *The Almanac of Latino Politics 2000* (Chicago: The United States Hispanic Leadership Institute, 1999), Introduction, v.

41. Adam Nagourney and Janet Elder "Hispanics Back Big Government and Bush, Too," *New York Times,* August 3, 2003, A1 and A22.

42. Paul Krugman, "Stimulus for Lawyers," *New York Times,* January 14, 2003, A27, and Bob Herbert, "Leave No Child Behind," *New York Times,* July 11, 2002, A23.

Chapter 9. The Politics of Education: The Most Important Civil Rights Issue Facing La Comunidad Latina

1. See Jodi Wilgoren, "New Governors Discover the Ink Is Turning Redder," *New York Times,* January 14, 2003, A24, and Robert Pear, "Most States Cutting Back on Medicaid, Survey Finds," *New York Times,* January 14, 2003, A24.

2. U.S. Census Bureau, "Poverty: 2004 Highlights."

3. U.S. Census Bureau, "Educational Attainment by Race and Hispanic Origin: 1960–2004," Tables 214 and 215.

4. Sandra Gardner, "ACE Minorities in Higher Education 2001–2002 Report," *Hispanic Outlook in Higher Education* 13, no. 16 (May 19, 2003): 11–13. See also Adalyn Hixson, "Latinos by the Numbers: A Statistical Sampler," *Hispanic Outlook in Higher Education* 12, no. 16 (May 2, 2003): 18–20.

5. U.S. Census, "Sex by Educational Attainment for the Population 25 Years and Over," Census 2000 Summary File 3, "Hispanic or Latino Population 25 Years and Over."

6. Jennifer Medina, "To Cut Failure Rate, Schools Shed Students," *New York Times,* July 31, 2003, A1 and B8; Tamar Lewin. "High School under Scrutiny for Giving Up on Its Students," *New York Times,* August 1, 2003, A1 and B6.

7. See the Education Law Center web site: hhtp://www.edlawcenter. org.

8. Editorial, *New York Times*, April 30, 2002.

9. Genaro Armas, "School Dropout Rate Soared for Hispanics in the 1990s," *The Star Ledger*, October 11, 2002, 17.

10. Yilu Zhao, "Wave of Pupils Lacking English Strains Schools," *New York Times*, August 5, 2002, A1 and A9.

11. Brian Donohue, "Finding a Political Voice," *The Star Ledger*, June 29, 2003, Section 10, 1 and 6.

12. U.S. Supreme Court *Plyler v. Doe*, 457 U.S. 202 (1982); see the Touro Law Center, Huntington, NY, web site: http://www.tourolaw.edu/patch/Plyler.

13. *The Star Ledger*, April 2002.

14. Peter Jennings, *ABC National News*, Special on the Latino Community in the U.S., January 21, 2000.

15. For an excellent account of the struggle of Mexican miners in Clifton and Morenci, Arizona, see *Los Mineros*, telescript by Hector Galán and Paul Espinosa, narrated by Luis Valdéz and introduced by David McCullough, *The American Experience*, PBS, 1990.

16. Alice Walker, *The Color Purple* (New York: Harcourt, 2003), 215.

17. Cisneros, "Woman Hollering Creek," in *Woman Hollering Creek*, 55–56. See the excellent article by Veronica A. Guerra, "The Silence of the Obejas: Evolution of Voice in Alma Villanueva's 'Mother, May I' and Sandra Cisneros's 'Woman Hollering Creek,'" in *Living Chicana Theory*, ed. Carla Trujillo (Berkeley: Third Woman Press, 1998), 320–51.

18. "Excerpts from Justices' Opinions on Michigan Affirmative Action Cases," *New York Times*, June 24, 2003, A24–25.

19. Orlando Patterson, "Affirmative Action: The Sequel," *New York Times*, June 22, 2003.

20. For a further development of education in the service of four fundamentally different ways of life, see Abalos, *Strategies*, 118–20.

21. See Abalos, *The Latino Male*, 113–15.

22. Elissa Gootman, "Old Tensions over Immigrants after Firebombing," *New York Times*, July 14, 2003, B1–2, and "Suffolk Teenagers Charged in Fire at Home of Mexicans," *New York Times*, August 1, 2003, B5.

23. Bruce Lambert, "Advocates for Immigrants Say Suffolk Officials Foster Bias," *New York Times*, August 2, 2003, B5.

24. David T. Abalos, presentation made at Rutgers University to Latino students, parents, community activists, and teachers, March 29, 2003.

Index

Abbott Districts, 259, 285, 288
affirmative action, 7, 42, 164, 203, 220
  in the service of transformation,
    274–76, 309n2, 313nn18, 19
  See also confirmative action
alchemist, 145, 148, 174
Algeria, 69, 79–80
alienation, 56, 65, 71, 138, 200, 219
Allah, 151
American Council on Education,
    257–58
Anglo-Saxon, 52, 61, 63, 96, 106, 133
archetypal
  analysis, 48–50, 152–53, 191, 277,
    307
  mandala as symbol, 34, 100, 134–35,
    183, 207, 244–45
  relationships, xvi, 33, 33–35, 40,
    45–46, 97, 100, 110, 117, 153,
    222, 246, 293
  stories of, 224
  ways of life, xvii, 2, 5, 11, 14–16, 33,
    46–48
archetype, xiv–xviii, 13–16, 19, 27, 49,
    59–60, 91, 152–53, 183
  of capitalism, 293
  collective unconscious, 292
  definition, 299
  of journey, 9, 91, 167–70
  of justice and compassion, 213
  of self, 183
Asociación de Trabajadores Agrícolares
    (A.T.A.), 112
assimilation, x, 3, 5, 10, 61, 67, 121,
    140, 250, 252, 264, 268
  bilingual education and, 128
  definition, 185
  as form of self hatred, 5–6, 22,
    200
  politics of, 61, 185–97
  way of life of incoherence, 22–23,
    248

assimilationist, 222–23
  model, 236–38
Asturias, Miguel Ángel, 59, 61, 85,
    175–76
authority
  definition, 218
  emanational, 37
  and Latino parents, 22–23, 55, 79–84
  legitimate, 99–100
  and lord of emanation, 223–25
  and Maryknoll missionaries, 179
  masculine, 26, 38, 80, 90
  teachers and education, 108, 276–78
  transformative and pseudo, 218
  and values, 27, 37
autonomous zones
  of jurisdiction, 40
  of power, 41, 123
autonomy, 55, 65, 68–69, 77, 97–100
  in Anglo world, 22
  definition, 40–42
  and direct bargaining, 214–17,
    274–76
  —as subdominant relationship, 109
  as dominant relationship in U.S.,
    67–68, 109–10, 113–19
  inherited relationship of, 215
  relationship of, 204–8, 211
  in the service of deformation, 113
  in the service of incoherence,
    113–14, 206–7, 246
  in the service of transformation,
    41,116, 121, 246, 249
Ave Maria University. *See* Monaghan,
    Tom
Aztecs, 9, 52, 55, 130, 135, 145–46,
    298n21
  domesticating the sacred, 137
  god as lord of emanation, 168
  gods, 145
  indigenous vision, 58
  lord of war and deformation, 135

315

Index

DAVID T. ABALOS

is professor of religious studies and sociology at Seton Hall University. He is the author of a number of books including *The Latino Family and the Politics of Transformation.*

3144